ENGENDERING AMERICA

A Documentary History, 1865 to the Present

by

Sonya Michel

*University of Illinois
at Urbana–Champaign*

and

Robyn Muncy

University of Maryland–College Park

His manner reminds me of Bobby Kennedy.

with

Ruth Fairbanks

and

Elisa Miller

McGraw-Hill College

Boston   Burr Ridge, IL   Dubuque, IA   Madison, WI   New York   San Francisco   St. Louis
Bangkok   Bogotá   Caracas   Lisbon   London   Madrid
Mexico City   Milan   New Delhi   Seoul   Singapore   Sydney   Taipei   Toronto

McGraw-Hill College

A Division of The **McGraw·Hill** Companies

ENGENDERING AMERICA: A DOCUMENTARY HISTORY, 1865 TO THE PRESENT

This book is printed on acid-free paper.

1 2 3 4 5 6 7 8 9 0 DOC/DOC 9 3 2 1 0 9 8

ISBN 0–07–044361–0

Editorial director: *Jane E. Vaicunas*
Senior sponsoring editor: *Lyn Uhl*
Developmental editor: *Monica Freedman*
Senior marketing manager: *Suzanne Daghlian*
Project manager: *Jill R. Peter*
Production supervisor: *Sandy Ludovissy*
Design manager: *Stuart D. Paterson*
Senior photo research coordinator: *Lori Hancock*
Compositor: *Carlisle Communications, Ltd.*
Typeface: *10/12 Times Roman*
Printer: *R. R. Donnelley & Sons Company/Crawfordsville, IN*

Cover designer: *Lisa Gravunder*

Library of Congress Cataloging-in-Publication Data

Engendering America : a documentary history, 1865 to the present /
   [edited by] Sonya Michel, Robyn Muncy. — 1st ed.
     p.   cm.
   ISBN 0–07–044361–0
    1. Women—United States—History—19th century—Sources.
2. Women—United States—History—20th century—Sources. 3. Men—
United States—History—19th century—Sources. 4. Men—United
States—History—20th century—Sources. 5. United States—Social
conditions—19th century—Sources. 6. United States—Social
conditions—20th century—Sources. I. Michel, Sonya, 1942– .
II. Muncy, Robyn.
HQ1410.E54   1999
305.3'0973—dc21   98–29229
                                          CIP

www.mhhe.com

For
Tess (RM)
and
Sydney and Caleb (SM)

ACKNOWLEDGMENTS

Many people have generously assisted us with this project. First and foremost, we thank all the scholars who have made gender their subject of study. They have created the rich field from which we harvested so many of the ideas for both documents and commentary.

Second, we thank Ruth Fairbanks and Elisa Miller, whose work extended so far beyond the usual tasks of research assistants that we decided to include them as "junior" co-authors. In collecting documents used in at least half of the chapters, they contributed significantly to shaping them.

We are also grateful to the staff of Campus Publishing Services at the University of Illinois at Urbana-Champaign, whose persistent efforts to track down copyrights and obtain permissions must be counted as a form of historical research in its own right.

Finally, we would like to acknowledge the people we worked with at McGraw Hill—Lyn Uhl, Monica Freedman, Jill Peter, and Rachael Morgan, as well as their staffs—for their professional guidance and most of all for their faith in this project from the very outset and unflagging enthusiasm all along.

S. M. and R. M.

Much of the fun of doing this volume has come from pursuing new avenues of research and following up suggestions. I had several excellent guides: Leslie Rowland graciously shared her encyclopedic knowledge of the Freedman's Bureau records, Darryl Scott and Kenneth Goings provided other references for documents in African American history, and Linda Clemmons suggested sources on Native Americans.

I also had a great deal of practical help from Elisa Miller, who, in addition to finding documents, made countless follow-up trips to the UIUC libraries and fearlessly surfed the Internet for obscure references, publishers, and endless minutiae; and from Anne Berggren, who skillfully deciphered and typed dozens of documents. Regina Felix and Sammi King also provided crucial last-minute editorial assistance.

It has been a pleasure to work with Robyn Muncy, who has been a font of endless creativity and steady encouragement, and who has somehow figured out a way to communicate her warmth and distinctive laugh by e-mail. Collaboration at its best is a mix of endorsement and challenge; Robyn always struck the proper balance.

My family, nuclear and extended, has shared the joys and frustrations of this project, as they have so many others. My dedication goes to my grandchildren, Sydney and Caleb, who are poised to shape the gender history of the twenty-first century.

S. M.

For suggesting specific documents, I wish to thank Meg Alessi, Clark Davis, Robert Frame, Margaret Rose, Stephen Meyer, Angela Darlene LeBlanc, and Tony Speranza. For locating much necessary information, I thank the amazing research assistant, Christy Regenhardt, whose own work on Marilyn Monroe and American manhood cannot appear in print soon enough. For ideas about World War I posters, I gratefully acknowledge Meg Alessi, Joseph Harris, and the entire posters group from the University of Maryland's History 433 in Spring 1997. Stephen Meyer and Clark Davis shared extremely interesting and helpful unpublished papers. Angela LeBlanc, head of Stanford's project on the Black Panther Party, Lucia Diamond, archivist at the University of California's School of Law, and Yelena Luckert, colleague and librarian extraordinaire at the University of Maryland's McKeldin Library—all participated in one of the most exhilarating research adventures I have ever had: we located a fascinating document that ultimately proved unusable. The thrill of the hunt was worth every minute; thank you all.

Sonya Michel suggested this project several years ago, before either of us could have known what a huge undertaking it would be. I thank her for that originating inspiration, as well as the intellectual challenge, the experience of collaboration, and the broadening of my education that her great idea has provided.

For riding with me on the roller coaster of anxiety and joy built by the quest for that one perfect document or one final illustration, I want to thank Tony and Tess Speranza. Tess, this one's for you.

R. M.

CONTENTS

PART B   **Gender Anarchy, 1890–1930**

THE COMING GAME
Yale versus Vassar

FIGURE 1.1
This image, drawn by magazine illustrator Charles Dana Gibson in 1895, depicted the battle between the sexes. It captured one theme of twentieth-century gender history by suggesting that women and men were becoming more alike and that sometimes they would be battling over the same turf. (*Source:* Life *26 [Nov. 21, 1895], pp. 330–31.*)

CHAPTER 1

Introduction: What Is Gender?

Over the past few years, the history of gender has emerged as a distinct field. It has grown out of women's history as that vital intellectual enterprise expanded through research in several related fields, particularly men and masculinity, sexuality and homosexuality. Research on masculinity arose from women's historians' recognition that definitions of femininity have changed over time and that different cultures and subcultures have attached different meanings to bodies of the same biological sex. The history of sexuality took up women's historians' understanding that not all of history occurs in public spaces or as public events; private life must be studied as well (indeed, the very definitions of "public" and "private" must be reconsidered). Investigations of homosexualities took this insight one step further, demonstrating the importance of sexual orientation not only in the creation of modern personal identities but also in the mobilization of social movements.

The emergence of these new fields means that history must be "rewritten" once again. Just as women's historians once chided colleagues in mainstream history for using the formula "add women and stir," so we now realize that this new scholarship cannot simply be tacked on to the existing historiography of women. Parallel histories of women and men, or gays and straights, or of public and private life, are not sufficient; instead we now seek to reorganize historical syntheses around the category of gender.

In this volume, we use the word "gender" to refer to the meanings attached to sexual differences between men and women. Although women and men may be biologically different from each other—that is, they have different reproductive systems—we show that the significance of that difference has changed over time and varied according to class, race, ethnicity, and region at any one time. Thus, we assume that most differences between women and men are not *natural* but have been created by human beings themselves. To put it another way, the meanings of sexual (biological) difference are and have been culturally and socially constructed.

1

Examples may help to illustrate what we mean by gender. When Europeans emigrated from England, France, and Germany to North America in the seventeenth century, they commonly saw women as sexually insatiable, easily tempted by the devil, and thus unreliable in their religious faith. The same set of beliefs held that men more easily exerted self-control over their sexual appetites, resisted the devil, and thus stood firm in the faith. During the early nineteenth century, descendants of those same Europeans in the United States developed a new set of beliefs about women and men: that women had little or no sexual need, were naturally spiritual, and thus more stalwart in their religious commitments than men and that men suffered nearly uncontrollable sexual lust, naturally attended to things material (not spiritual) and so were distracted from the faith by their competitive pursuit of material advantage. The term gender, then, refers precisely to these ever-changing traits associated with womanhood and manhood, the differences between women and men.

Examples from our own era may further our understanding of the term "gender." Many people in the late twentieth century believe that women are inherently more nurturing than men and that men are naturally more aggressive than women. These qualities, they claim, are immutable, emerging as they do from biological differences, especially differences in hormone production. We want to argue instead that aggressiveness in men and nurturing in women may not be natural, but instead may be created by particular human societies and are thus part of the *gender* identities of women and men in some cultures. It seems likely to us that our society has socialized women and men to display these traits and that moreover our assumptions that women are nurturing and men are aggressive mold our interpretations of women's and men's behavior. For example, when male and female professors behave in precisely the same helpful way to students, we may see the female professors as nurturing and motherly and the male professors as consummate professionals. It is the gender lens of our particular culture in this case that leads us to see difference.

A final example: Our students have sometimes argued that surely biology at least makes men taller than women and thus explains why men are better basketball players than women. Skill in basketball would then be a natural difference stemming from biology, not a culturally constructed gender difference. We want to entertain the possibility that even differences in height and concomitant skill in basketball are not biological but are created by specific cultures. After all, some women are taller than some men even now. So, it is not universally true that men are taller than women even in the late twentieth century. We want to keep open the possibility that if we as a society *expected* women to be as tall as men, fed girls and boys the same all through childhood and adolescence, exercised them without regard to sexual difference, offered them athletic scholarships of equal value and in equal abundance, opened athletic careers without regard to sexual difference, dressed them similarly, gave them the same medical attention and advice, that maybe the average height of women and men would eventually be the same and they would compete equally on America's basketball courts.

While we do not claim that we are sure this would be the outcome or that such an outcome is actually desirable, we offer this example as a way of showing how far gender may extend. We hope it frees your imagination to see gender where you may once have seen natural (i.e., biological) differences.

Just as the meanings of manhood and womanhood have changed over time, so have the categories of sexual identity. Before the late nineteenth century, for instance, most European-descended Americans assumed that everyone was heterosexual. In fact, that assumption was so universal that they did not even need the concepts of heterosexuality and homosexuality. Most were aware that some people occasionally engaged in homosexual *behavior,* but these instances of same-sex relations were believed to constitute individual crimes, not to suggest a permanent sexual orientation toward people of the same sex. They were sins to be repented, not expressions of a fixed identity. During the late nineteenth century, however, ideas about sexuality began to change, and, by the 1920s, the predominant belief in the United States was that homosexuality and heterosexuality were distinct and enduring identities. Over the course of the twentieth century, people assuming homosexual identities built subcultures and political movements all their own. Sexual identities as well as gender are thus historical.

Moreover, the relationships between gender and sexuality have changed over time and varied from place to place. For example, masculinity is usually presumed to include an exclusively heterosexual orientation, but at times some men have been "permitted" to engage in homosexual behaviors without losing their claim to manhood. Those who "acted the manly part" (i.e., penetrated) in the sex act continued to be seen as real men while those who "took the woman's part" (i.e., were penetrated) became "fairies" or considered themselves a third sex rather than being either men or women. (See especially Chapter 6.) At other times, particular *sexual* orientations have generated distinctive *gender* identities. For instance, "fairy" constituted a particular gender identity among homosexual men in the early twentieth century, and "butch" and "femme" were gender identities that structured many working-class lesbian communities between the 1940s and 1970s.

All of these complexities remind us that we cannot speak of "women" and "men" as though their nature remains stable over time. Rather, we must analyze the meanings and characteristics of these and other terms related to gender and sexuality in specific historical contexts. We should, moreover, be suspicious of claims that specific gender characteristics are "natural," "instinctive," or "inherent" for members of either sex.

Throughout this volume, we draw attention to intersections between race and ethnicity, on the one hand, and gender and sexuality on the other. Since 1865, certainly, these different aspects of identity have continuously shaped each other. That is, race and ethnicity (often along with class) have worked together with gender to define one another; race or ethnicity has always been embodied in a sexed being. So, for instance, when one person speaks to another of "women," each imagines women of a particular race, perhaps white, Asian American or African American. Rarely, when we hear the word "woman," do we picture women of all races and ethnicities. Moreover, when we speak of Asian American women, we may picture women very different from European American or African American women. In these ways, race and gender have been inseparable categories.

Furthermore, throughout American history, putative gender characteristics have contributed to the formation of racial and ethnic hierarchies that almost invariably place white European American men at the apex. For example, from the mid-nineteenth century on, the alleged sexual rapacity of African American men was used to justify their violent persecution, while the perceived effeminacy of East European Jewish men and the failure of East European Jewish women to behave in a "ladylike" fashion rationalized pervasive anti-Semitism. In almost every instance of racial and ethnic discrimination, white European American heterosexual men have been set up as the norm from which others are said to deviate.

The creation of genders and sexualities has occurred and continues to occur on multiple levels and in many different areas of society and culture. Socialization within particular families helps to create specific sorts of women and men, but family dynamics alone cannot explain how particular forms of women and men are produced. (Just ask those parents who, in the 1970s, tried on their own to raise gender-neutral children!) The ways that families function, the roles that men and women play within families, the ideas that families have about proper male and female behavior—all these come from the larger arenas of society, politics, and culture. Thus, historians must look to popular and mass cultures, public policies, education, the shape of institutions, and the labor market to discover how specific kinds of women and men have been produced at any given time in American history. Gender and sexual identities are created as much by public institutions and discussions as by private family relationships.

At different times, specific arenas have assumed more importance in creating gender categories. For example, throughout much of the nineteenth century, family and religion were especially significant sites for producing particular versions of manhood and womanhood. From the turn of the century onward, schools and public places of amusement became more important. At the same time, local forms of popular culture such as hometown newspapers and county fairs yielded to the more homogenizing influence of the mass culture disseminated in movies and on the radio. Urbanization, mobility, and population growth allowed for greater anonymity and social-sexual experimentation. These changes allowed heterosexual women to begin expressing sexual desire more openly and also permitted homosexual communities to coalesce, the latter forming a half-hidden, often ironic parallel society in the early twentieth century.

Significantly, at certain moments, different aspects of American life pushed gender in contradictory directions. For example, in the 1950s, mass culture in the form of movies and television programs and much federal legislation reemphasized the differences between women and men, while the labor market, some union activism, and rates of educational attainment tended to make men and women more alike.

To comprehend these shifting terrains of gender history, this volume offers material from a wide range of sources. We have included documents from personal papers, popular and mass culture, the literature of the social, psychological, and behavioral sciences, governmental, religious, educational, and civic organizations, social movements, and the built environment. We have made an effort to include the voices of both well-known figures and ordinary people. In order to uncover gender in communities that have left few conventional historical sources, we have turned to evidence such as blues lyrics, political songs, government posters, oral interviews, and soap opera scripts. We have included visual evidence such as photographs and drawings that we expect readers to use just as they do written documents to understand the history of gender.

Interpreting documents can be a very tricky business, and we want to say a word especially about analyzing sources from popular and mass culture. We do not believe that these sources—fiction, advertisements, posters, movies, and the like— always precisely reflected ideas about or practices of manhood and womanhood in a particular community. What they do represent are some of the resources from which Americans might have cobbled together gender identities; they reveal ideas on which some may have drawn to mold their behavior as women and men.

From this broad spectrum of sources, we hope that readers will gain an understanding of how gender and sexuality have been defined and constructed over time; how individuals lived in and responded to their material, social, and cultural surroundings; and how they looked and sounded—how they performed their identities and presented themselves as women and men, as gays and straights in everyday life.

Taking the broad view, these documents tell a story of expanding possibilities. While the nineteenth-century United States certainly produced a variety of gender and sexual identities, the late twentieth century created an even richer spectrum. This expansion of identities and roles has taken place at the same time that men and women have become more alike in many ways: in their labor market participation, levels and kinds of political participation, legal privileges and obligations, opportunities for education, and, to some extent, familial roles. This does not suggest that women and men have achieved equality by any means—indeed, one of the great disappointments of the twentieth century is that women remain subordinate to men. By the same token, homosexuals remain marginalized and at risk in many segments of American society. Nevertheless, in the twentieth century the trend has been toward greater acknowledgement of the similarities between women and men while at the same time creating an increasingly varied assortment of gender and sexual roles and identities.

This process of expansion has not, of course, occurred in an uninterrupted, linear fashion. The wars, youth cultures, and social movements that brought about dramatic changes in codes of gender often created in their wake periods of retrenchment and backlash. As gender and sexual identities proliferated, so too did new forms of social policing. Sometimes this took the form of laws that incarcerated or fined those engaged in particular kinds of gender or sexual behavior. At other times, new gender and sexual possibilities were discouraged through protective legislation or therapeutic and social services that portrayed specific behaviors or orientations as "abnormal" or "pathological." The 1930s and 1980s, for example, saw particularly harsh measures against homosexual expressions but at the same time new possibilities for women.

In order to bring into relief these changing contours of sexuality and gender since 1865, we have developed our own periodization. Sometimes it coincides with that of more conventional historiography, but at others it goes its own way. The four periods are: The Beginning of the End of Victorianism (1865–1900); Gender Anarchy (1890–1930); Gender and Inter-National Crises (1930–1963); and Gender in Revolution (1963–present). Each period brought change in gender systems, but the eras dating from 1890–1930 and from 1963 to the present were periods of the most profound gender transformation, so we have devoted special attention to these pivotal epochs. We have divided the book into parts, each part documenting one of these periods. Because human history does not fall neatly into eras, our parts occasionally overlap. For instance, some of the trends discussed in the first part originated in the nineteenth century but extended into the twentieth; thus the documents come from the first period as well as the second. This cannot be avoided in a book that unfolds topically rather than strictly chronologically. By showing some cases when our periods overlap, we are able to do justice to the ways that one historical era actually shades into another.

As readers study the documents included in this volume, we hope that they will come to understand that gender has pervaded American history. In fact, shifts in gender and sexual identities must be included among the major events of U.S. history. Similarly, the gender dimensions of other sorts of events or trends, whether social, economic, or political, must be acknowledged and explained. The documents demonstrate that gender has infiltrated even seemingly "neutral" discourses (i.e., discussions that would seem not to be about manhood or womanhood at all) and that gendered metaphors have positioned Americans in the domains of politics and labor as well as in households and everyday life. That is, gender has in some way structured nearly every institution of American life.

We provide section and chapter introductions as well as headnotes for each document, but we do not offer definitive interpretations. Instead, we hope that each reader will actively engage with the documents and develop her or his own interpretation. Sometimes, beginning historians want to argue against the opinions expressed by authors in the past; they care most about whether the writers were right or wrong. This approach can be very interesting, but it can also get in the way of doing history. Instead of debating with authors from the 1880s, historians read documents to learn something about the era that produced them. So, for instance, when reading a medical treatise on homosexuality from 1923, historians ask, What does this treatise tell me about medical views of homosexuality in 1923? Our first concern is not so much whether the author was accurate or inaccurate, but rather, what can we learn about gender and sexuality in 1923? Similarly, we go to a document from 1993 and ask: What does this document tell me about the way some group of Americans saw the issue of homosexuality in 1993? How had ideas changed since 1923?

Further to guide this process of interpretation, readers might ask themselves the following questions: What is the relationship between collective gender identities and personal self-definitions? How have conceptions and performances of sexual identities shaped public events and cultural trends? How have changes in the built environment affected the gendered bodily experience of space, time, and the material world? Responses to these kinds of questions, resulting in knowledge of the history of gender, will help students better understand their own lives and experience as well as the American past.

Before presenting the documents, we need to issue two disclaimers. First, although we have shortened many documents, we have left spelling errors, punctuation mistakes and awkward phraseology just as the authors wrote them. Second, we have not been able by any stretch of the imagination to provide in this one volume comprehensive coverage of gender and sexual identities among Americans since 1865. We have supplied instead a sampling of documents, illustrating a portion of America's rich history of gender and sexuality. Our intent is to stimulate interest in further research among our readers so that we ourselves might learn more from their efforts.

RECOMMENDED READINGS

Amott, Teresa, and Julie Matthaei. *Race, Gender, and Work: A Multi-Cultural Economic History of Women in the United States.* Rev. ed. Boston, 1996.

Baum, Charlotte, Paula Hyman, and Sonya Michel. *The Jewish Woman in America.* New York, 1976.

Butler, Judith. *Gender Trouble: Feminism and the Subversion of Identity.* New York, 1990.

Carnes, Mark C., and Clyde Griffen, eds. *Meanings for Manhood: Constructions of Masculinity in Victorian America.* Chicago, 1990.

Costigliola, Frank. "The Nuclear Family: Tropes of Gender and Pathology in the Western Alliance." *Diplomatic History* 21 (1997):163–85.

D'Emilio, John, and Estelle Freedman. *Intimate Matters: A History of Sexuality in America.* New York, 1988.

Duberman, Martin Baml, Martha Vicinus, and George Chauncey, eds. *Hidden From History: Reclaiming the Gay and Lesbian Past.* New York, 1989.

Filene, Peter G. *Him/Her/Self: Sex Roles in Modern America.* Baltimore, 1986.

Griswold, Robert L. *Fatherhood in America: A History.* New York, 1993.

Higginbotham, Evelyn Brooks. "African-American Women's History and the Metalanguage of Race." *Signs* 17 (Winter 1992):251–74.

Katz, Jonathan, ed. *Gay American History: Lesbians and Gay Men in the U.S.A.: A Documentary History.* New York, 1992.

Kessler-Harris, Alice. *Out to Work: A History of Wage-Earning Women in the United States.* New York, 1982.

Kimmel, Michael S. *Manhood in America: A Cultural History.* New York, 1996.

Melosh, Barbara, ed. *Gender and American History Since 1890.* New York, 1993.

Rotundo, E. Anthony. *American Manhood: Transformations of Masculinity from the Revolution to the Modern Era.* New York, 1993.

Scott, Joan. *Gender and the Politics of History.* New York, 1988.

Sedgwick, Eve Kosofsky. *The Epistemology of the Closet.* Berkeley, 1990.

The Beginning of the End of Victorianism, 1865–1900

The latter third of the nineteenth century was a time of outward unification and progress but also one of inner conflicts and uneven development in the United States. The signs of apparent cohesiveness were everywhere. With the ending of the Civil War, the Union was restored, and African Americans were granted the rights of citizenship. As westward expansion increased the size of the nation, the completion of the transcontinental railroad and the advent of modern communications seemed to reduce the distance between the two coasts. The rapid growth of industrial productivity, fostered by the formation of more efficient business structures and national markets, spread the fruits of technological advancement.

But deepening inequalities prevented all Americans from enjoying the material, social, and political benefits of prosperity and progress in equal measure. Under Reconstruction, the federal program established to safeguard the political and economic rights of newly freed African Americans, the South produced a new hierarchy of race and gender that continued to disadvantage blacks severely. Euro-American appropriation of the Trans-Mississippi West and Southwest subjugated indigenous Indian and Mexican populations, radically transforming their way of life. Construction of the railroads, as well as the miles of streets and sewers required by the growth of cities, depended on the exploitation of immigrant workers, first Chinese and later Southern and Eastern Europeans. And industrialization came at the expense of fledgling labor organizations, whose strikes and demonstrations were firmly and often violently suppressed by employers working in concert with state and federal governments.

Victorianism, the reigning gender ideology of the mid- to late nineteenth century, at once expressed the optimism of industrial capitalism and masked its inequalities and internal conflicts. According to its dictates, society was ideally divided into two spheres, public and private, male and female. The centerpiece was the private middle-class home, a "haven in a heartless world" that was intended to offer a counterbalance to the amoral realm of commerce and politics, a showplace

for the goods that manufacturing now made available, and a model for proper behavior and social standards. At the heart of that home was the devoted housewife
and mother, whose chief duties were tending to her family and presiding over the
elaborate rituals of everyday life. She was to create a respite for her breadwinner-
husband and vigilantly guard the propriety and morals not only of her family but of
society as a whole.

But the Victorian home was inherently unstable, for its smooth operation depended upon strict gender and class roles which individual women and men were
not always able—or willing—to fulfill. Middle-class men were expected to support
their households fully, but their earnings were vulnerable not only to personal whim
and misfortune but also to the unpredictable vicissitudes of the economy. Many men
of this class, feeling constrained by the symbiotic world of family and business,
sought refuge in all-male settings such as clubs and lodges.

Though popular culture enshrined the Victorian mother as "the angel in the
house," women began to rebel against what they saw as a restricting and stifling
role. After earning degrees at newly opened women's colleges and coeducational
land grant universities, many middle-class daughters rejected their lifetime assignment to home and family. Between 1870 and 1920, female college graduates were
four to six times less likely to marry than their nongraduate sisters. Instead, they
committed themselves to careers in public activism, demanded admission to male
professional bastions such as law and medicine, and created new professions for
themselves in fields like social work and nursing. They also pressed for civil and political rights, including suffrage, liberalized divorce laws, child custody, and property rights.

Victorians were, implicitly, heterosexual, though few troubled to identify
themselves as such, for they could not imagine an alternative. Their complacency,
however, belied the sexual ferment that was brewing beneath late nineteenth-
century society. Since male and female appetites were presumed to be incommen-
surate (men were regarded as sexually rapacious while women were seen as
"passionless," consenting to sex only for purposes of procreation), the sexual balance was far from harmonious. As urban spaces gave rise to the anonymity and excitement of sexual "demi-mondes," respectable *paters familias* as well as
adventurous youths sought sexual satisfaction outside the confines of proper
courtship and marriage. The relative sexual innocence of the period allowed men
to consort freely with either female prostitutes or "fairies"—flagrant male
homosexuals—without fear of compromising their masculinity. It also permitted
women, under the protective guise of "passionlessness," to engage in "smashing"
or "passionate friendships" with other women, or live in lifelong same-sex "Boston
marriages," which, for many, were preferable to heterosexual marriage.

The images of Victoriana that dominated popular culture—the complicated
clothing, highly decorated parlors, lavish meals, and elaborate social gatherings—
concealed the labor power of the millions of Americans who made it all possible.
Whether or not they aspired to such comforts, the women and men who worked as
domestic servants, factory operatives, laborers and fieldhands—the majority of
American society—had no access to a middle-class way of life. Since few men
earned a "family wage," all family members, including children, were expected to

contribute to the household coffers, thus defying middle-class gender ideals. With the consolidation of capital into fewer and fewer hands, class, racial, and ethnic divisions hardened. Despite traditional American rhetoric about the rewards of individual effort and hard work, prospects for upward mobility for the African Americans and newly-arrived immigrants who made up the bulk of the working class were dim. All of these cleavages—social, economic, and sexual—undermined Victorian ideology at the moment it reached its peak in American culture.

FIGURE 2.1
According to a rumor that spread at the end of the Civil War, Jefferson
Davis, President of the Confederacy, escaped capture by the Union Army
by disguising himself in female clothing. Dozens of cartoons and
drawings repeated the tale. This one appeared on an 1865 sheet music
cover. (*Source: Mark B. Neely et al.,* The Confederate Image. *Copyright
© 1987 by the University of North Carolina Press. Used by permission of the
publisher. Image courtesy of The Lincoln Museum, Fort Wayne, IN [# 3544].*)

CHAPTER 2

Reconstructing Gender

Reconstruction refers to the years between 1865 and 1877 when the federal government committed resources—both military and economic—to ensuring the integration of ex-slaves into the politics, economy, and society of the South. Some historians consider this a revolutionary period (and the years after 1877 a counter-revolution), so remarkable were the changes and possibilities created and then abandoned.

The immediate postwar years were a time of economic and social chaos in the South. Farms and plantations lay in ruins, with the bulk of the former work force— slaves—having fled. Freed women and men roamed the region, seeking homes, jobs, land, and, most important, kin. "In their eyes, the work of emancipation was incomplete until the families which had been dispersed by slavery were reunited," reported one agent of the Freedmen's Bureau, the federal agency that had been established in 1865 to provide relief and assistance to the former slaves.

Though charged with protecting blacks in labor negotiations, the Freedmen's Bureau could not prevent widespread exploitation. (Indeed, any measure of racial justice in the South required armed intervention by the federal government.) Whites had regarded slaves as a major source of wealth as well as labor power; now they attempted to mold their former "property" into a cheap, docile work force. Blacks, however, wanted to work their own land. The system of sharecropping emerged as a kind of compromise, permitting blacks to control their own agricultural labor while still allowing whites to profit from it.

Many African Americans migrated to Southern cities, but here they faced fresh economic difficulties. Blacks were routinely relegated to the least skilled jobs in the tobacco industry and barred altogether from newly opened textile plants. A few skilled men found work in the building trades, while the majority of women settled for domestic service, where they struggled with white housewives over the conditions of their work.

African Americans quickly understood that if they were to make social and economic progress, they would need political power. With passage of the Fourteenth and Fifteenth Amendments, all African Americans were formally granted the protections of citizenship and African American men gained the right to vote, sit on juries, and hold office. Most Southern whites, however, were not prepared to allow blacks to exercise their new rights. Led by the Ku Klux Klan, whites mounted a systematic campaign of psychological and physical intimidation that for decades kept Southern blacks under the shadow of random violence and lynching.

The ideology and practice of racism that emerged in the postbellum South were everywhere bound up with gender. While black men sought to define their manhood in terms of economic self-sufficiency, political rights, and the ability to protect black women, whites portrayed them as a sexual threat to white women. At the same time whites expected black women to work for wages, denying them the option of caring for their families, as white women did.

HE DROPPED HIS PANTALOONS
George Cooper and Henry Tucker

Gender is often used as a metaphor for political, social, or economic relations that do not, at first glance, appear to have anything to do with womanhood or manhood. Take, for example, the depiction of Jefferson Davis, president of the Confederacy, in the 1865 song, "Jeff in Petticoats" (see fig. 2.1). According to the legend repeated in this song and in dozens of prints, lithographs, and poems from the period (the Library of Congress has an entire collection devoted to such materials), as he sought to elude capture by Union troops after the surrender of General Robert E. Lee at Appomattox, Davis disguised himself by wearing some of his wife's clothing. Though *The New York Times* reported on an Army dispatch purportedly attesting to this event, the story was later proven to be untrue. Yet it was widely circulated throughout the immediate postwar years.

Why would Northerners choose this particular image as a way to denigrate their former enemy? And why would Southerners perceive it as such a deep insult? What does it say about the gender system that prevailed throughout both North and South during this period? And what does it say about the political situation during the early years of Reconstruction? (*Note:* the words crinoline, pantaloons, and stays refer to undergarments commonly worn by women in the nineteenth century.)

1. Jefferson Davis was a hero bold,
    You've heard of him, I know,
    He tried to make himself a King
    Where southern breezes blow;
    But "Uncle Sam," he laid the youth
    Across his mighty knee,
    And spanked him well, and that's the end
    Of brave old Jeffy D.

Source: "Jeff in Petticoats: A Song for the Times," words by George Cooper, music by Henry Tucker (New York: Wm. A. Pond & Co., 1865).

Chorus

> Oh! Jeffy D!
> You "flow'r of chivalry,"
> Oh royal Jeffy D!
> Your empire's but a tin-clad skirt,
> Oh charming Jeffy D.

2. This Davis, he was always full
   Of bluster and of brag.
   He swore, on all our Northern walls,
   He'd plant his Rebel rag;
   But when to battle he did go,
   He said, "I'm not so green,
   To dodge the bullets I will wear
   My tin-clad crinoline." (Chorus)

3. Now when he saw the game was up,
   He started for the woods,
   His bandbox hung upon his arm
   Quite full of fancy goods.
   Said Jeff, "They'll never take me now,
   I'm sure I'll not be seen.
   They'd never think to look for me
   Beneath my crinoline." (Chorus)

4. Jeff took with him, the people say,
   A mine of golden coin,
   Which he, from banks and other places,
   Managed to purloin;
   But while he ran, like every thief,
   He had to drop the spoons,
   And maybe that's the reason why
   He dropped his pantaloons. (Chorus)

5. Our union boys were on his track
   For many nights and days,
   His palpitating heart it beat,
   Enough to burst his stays;
   Oh! what a dash he must have cut
   With form so tall and lean;
   Just fancy now the "What is it?"
   Dressed up in crinoline! (Chorus)

6. The ditch that Jeff was hunting for,
   He found was very near,
   He tried to "shift" his base again,
   His neck felt rather queer;
   Just on the out-"skirts" of a wood
   His dainty shape was seen,
   His boots stuck out, and now they'll hang
   Old Jeff in crinoline. (Chorus)

THEY THEN SEIZED ME
Roda Ann Childs

In the antebellum South, whites frequently referred to African American women as "Jezebels"—lascivious women (unlike white women, who were portrayed as pure) who supposedly had insatiable sexual appetites. By blaming female slaves for being seductive, white masters could avoid taking moral responsibility for preying sexually upon black women. Slave women could do little to defend themselves or their reputations, and male slaves, even husbands, were forced to stand by helplessly.

As freedwomen, African Americans made every effort to put a stop to such assaults, while freedmen saw it as a primary duty to protect "their women." This was so important that many African American men refused to allow their wives to work in situations where they might once again become vulnerable to white men's sexual advances. However, as the following document indicates, white men continued to prey upon black women whenever they got the chance. Why did these white men attack Roda Ann Childs? Why did the attack take the specific form that it did? What message were they trying to send her and her husband?

[Freedmen's Bureau, Griffin, Georgia] Sept. 25, 1866
Rhoda Ann Childs came into this office and made the following statement:
"Myself and husband were under contract with Mrs. Amelia Childs of Henry County and worked from Jan. 1, 1866, until the crops were laid by, or in other words until the main work of the year was done, without difficulty. Then, (the fashion being prevalent among the planters) we were called upon one night, and my husband was demanded; I Said he was not there. They then asked me where he was. I Said he was gone to the water mellon patch. They then Seized me and took me Some distance from the house, where they 'bucked' me down across a log, Stripped my clothes over my head, one of the men Standing astride my neck, and beat me across my posterior, two men holding my legs. In this manner I was beaten until they were tired. Then they turned me parallel with the log, laying my neck on a limb which projected from the log, and one man placing his foot upon my neck, beat me again on my hip and thigh. Then I was thrown upon the ground on my back, one of the men Stood upon my breast, while two others took hold of my feet and stretched My limbs as far apart as they could, while the man Standing upon my breast applied the Strap to my private parts until fatigued into stopping, and I was more dead than alive. Then a man, Supposed to be an ex-confederate Soldier, as he was on crutches, fell upon me and ravished me. During the whipping one of the man ran his pistol into me, and Said he had a hell of a mind to pull the trigger, and Swore they ought to Shoot me, as my husband had been in the 'God damned Yankee Army,' and Swore they meant to kill every black Son-of-a-bitch they could find that had ever fought against them. They then went back to the house, Seized my two daughters and beat them, demanding their father's pistol, and upon failure to get that, they en-

Source: Affidavit of Roda Ann Childs, Griffin, Georgia, September 25, 1866, in *Freedom: A Documentary History of Emancipation, 1861–1867*. Series 2, *The Black Military Experience*, ed. Ira Berlin, Joseph P. Reidy, and Leslie S. Rowland (New York: Cambridge University Press, 1982), p. 807; reprinted by permission.

tered the house and took Such articles of clothing as Suited their fancy, and de-camped. There were concerned in this affair eight men, none of which could be recognized for certain.

her

Roda Ann X Childs

mark

THEY WERE ACCUSED OF COHABITING TOGETHER
Joint Select Committee, U.S. Congress

The more African American men pressed for their political and economic rights, the more violent became the Ku Klux Klan's campaign of repression. Their acts were so numerous and so reprehensible that in 1871 Congress formed a joint select committee to investigate. The resulting report, broken down by state, was published in twenty volumes.

As the following document illustrates, many of the Klan's acts were specifically sexual in nature. Do you see any continuities between this testimony and Roda Ann Child's statement? Stallings' testimony is extremely shocking. Does it seem credible to you? Why or why not?

Atlanta, Georgia, November 6, 1871

WILLIAM H. STALLINGS sworn and examined.

By the CHAIRMAN:

Question. State your age, where you were born, where you now live, and what is your present occupation?

Answer. I am thirty-eight years old; I was born in the city of Augusta, in this State, and now live there; I am a carpenter by trade—a mechanic.

Question. We are inquiring into the manner in which the civil laws for the protection of person and property are executed in this State, how far the rights of persons and property are respected and secured. I would like you to give us any information you have that will illustrate the matter of our inquiry.

Answer: Well, sir, I know very little, of my own knowledge, in comparison with what I have heard. . . . I have heard Doctor M. E. Swinney, of Augusta, relate a case of a colored man and a white woman in Jackson County.

Question. What was that case as he related it to you?

Answer: Well, they were accused of cohabiting together. He said that the colored man was taken out into the woods, a hole dug in the ground and a block buried in it, and his *penis* taken out, and a nail driven through it into the block; that a large butcher or cheese knife, as they call it, very sharp was laid down by him, and light-wood piled around him and set on fire; the knife was put there so that he could cut it off and get away, or stay there and burn up. Doctor Swinney said that he cut it off and jumped out. Doctor Swinney did not tell me that he saw this himself, but he said he knew the parties concerned in it. I have heard him say often that he knew all the parties who did it. After the colored man did this, they took the woman, laid her

Source: *Report of the Joint Select Committee to Inquire into the Condition of Affairs in the Late Insurrectionary States (1872),* 42nd Congress, 2nd Session, pt. 7; pp. 1119–21.

down on the ground, then cut a slit on each side of her orifice, put a large padlock in it, locked it up, and threw away the key, and then turned her loose. She went so for two or three days, and then sent for Doctor Swinney to cut it out. I do not know whether he said he cut it out or got there just as the other physician had done it; but he saw the place.

Question. Did he prescribe for the woman?

Answer. I do not know; I do not recollect whether he said he did or not.

Question. He stated that he knew the parties who were concerned in it?

Answer. Yes, sir; he stated that he knew the parties. And there was another case I have heard him speak of, of the Creech family, father and son [whites], and a negro woman in the same county. I have sat down and listened to him state all this at several different times.

Question. What was the case of the Creech family?

Answer. I do not recollect what they were accused of; but they had a grocery and sold liquor; that was one thing, for he said he had often stopped there and taken a drink himself, as he was going to his place from the railroad station. He spoke of several letters that were written to Creech ordering him to leave there. Creech advised with him what to do, and he advised him to leave just as quickly as possible, or they would kill him. A few days after that the body of the young man was found in the creek about two hundred yards from the house, and his father and the body of the colored woman were found in a mill-pond. I do not recollect how far off they said the mill-pond was from there; it was right in the neighborhood.

Question. You do not recollect what they had against Creech?

Answer. One thing, I think, was about selling liquor.

Question. Where was the doctor living at the time you heard him make these statements?

Answer. He was staying in Johnson County.

Question. At the time you heard these statements from him?

Answer. That was in Augusta; and at one time I heard him relate the cases in the capitol building here.

Question. Do you know whether he left Johnson County?

Answer. I have heard him say often that he would have to leave there; that the Ku-Klux had been to his house and treated him pretty rough, and that he would not live there; that no [white] person could live down there in any peace and work colored hands on his farm. . . .

AM I A MAN?
Henry MacNeal Turner

Under the Reconstruction Acts of 1867, each of the former Confederate states was to hold a constitutional convention and elect a new legislature for which black men, for the first time, would be eligible to vote and to run. Henry MacNeal Turner (1834–1915), a self-educated African American minister, was elected to the Georgia legislature in 1868. By that time he had already amassed considerable political experience. In 1866, as a representative of Georgia's statewide black convention, he had gone to Washington, D.C. to consult with the Radical Republicans (supporters of abolition and emancipation who pressed forcefully for the rights of African Americans after the Civil War); he had also been a member of Georgia's constitutional convention. In the legislature, Turner displayed his balanced views and political astuteness by supporting measures to help white economic recovery as well as gain higher wages for black workers. His moderation could not, however, prevent his white colleagues, who held a majority, from voting to expel him and all other black representatives from the legislature in September, 1868.

In the following statement, Turner protested against this blatant act of racism. How does he defend black men's right to hold office? How does he link political rights to manhood?

Before proceeding to argue this question upon its intrinsic merits, I wish the members of this House to understand the position that I take. I hold that I am a member of this body. Therefore, sir, I shall neither fawn or cringe before any party, nor stoop to beg them for my rights. Some of my colored fellow members, in the course of their remarks, took occasion to appeal to the sympathies of members on the opposite side, and to eulogize their character for magnanimity. It reminds me very much, sir, of slaves begging under the lash. I am here to demand my rights. . . .

The scene presented in this House, to-day, is one unparalleled in the history of the world. . . . Never has a man been arraigned before a body clothed with legislative, judicial or executive functions, charged with the offense of being of a darker hue than his fellowmen . . . charged with an offense committed by the God of Heaven Himself. Cases may be found where men have been deprived of their rights for crimes and misdemeanors; but it has remained for the State of Georgia, in the very heart of the nineteenth century, to call a man before the bar, and there charge him with an act for which he is no more responsible than for the head which he carries upon his shoulders. . . .

Whose Legislature is this? Is it a white man's Legislature, or is it a black man's Legislature? Who voted for a Constitutional Convention, in obedience to the mandate of the Congress of the United States? Who first rallied around the standard of Reconstruction? Who set the ball of loyalty rolling in the State of Georgia? And whose voice was heard on the hills and in the valleys of his State? It was the voice of the brawny-armed Negro, with the few humanitarian-hearted white men who came to our assistance. I claim the honor, sir, of having been the instrument of convincing hundreds—yea, thousands—of white men, that to reconstruct under the measures of the United States Congress was the safest and the best course for the interest of the State.

Let us look at some facts in connection with this matter. Did half the white men of Georgia vote for this Legislature? Did not the great bulk of them fight, with all their strength, the Constitution under which we are acting? And did they not fight against the organization of this Legislature? And further, sir, did they not vote against it? Yes, sir! And there are persons in this Legislature today, who are ready to spit their poison in my face, while they themselves opposed, with all their power, the ratification of this Constitution. They question my right to a seat in this body, to represent the people whose legal votes elected me. . . . We are told that if black men want to speak, they must speak through white trumpets; if black men want their sentiments expressed, they must be adulterated and sent through white messengers, who will quibble, and equivocate, and evade, as rapidly as the pendulum of a clock.

Source: Quoted in Ethel M. Christler, "Participation of Negroes in the Government: 1867–1870," M.A. thesis, Atlanta University, 1932.

If this be not done, then the black men have committed an outrage, and their Representatives must be denied the right to represent their constituents.

The great question, sir, is this: Am I a man? If I am such, I claim the rights of a man. Am I not a man because I happen to be of a darker hue than honorable gentlemen around me?

We have pioneered civilization here; we have built up your country; we have worked in your fields, and garnered your harvests, for two hundred and fifty years! And what do we ask of you in return? Do we ask you for compensation for the sweat our fathers bore for you—for the tears you have caused, and the hearts you have broken, and the lives you have curtailed, and the blood you have spilled? Do we ask retaliation? We ask it not. We are willing to let the dead past bury its dead; but we ask you now for our rights.

You have all the elements of superiority upon your side; you have our money and your own; you have our education and your own; and you have your land and our own, too. We, who number hundreds of thousands in Georgia, including our wives and families, with not a foot of land to call our own—strangers in the land of our birth; without money, without education, without aid, without a roof to cover us while we live, nor sufficient clay to cover us when we die! . . .

You may expel us, gentlemen, but I firmly believe that you will someday repent it. The black man cannot protect a country, if the country doesn't protect him; and if, tomorrow, a war should arise, I would not raise a musket to defend a country where my manhood is denied. The fashionable way in Georgia when hard work is to be done, is, for the white man to sit at his ease, while the black man does the work; but, sir, I will say this much to the colored men of Georgia, as if I should be killed in this campaign, I may have no opportunity of telling them at any other time: Never lift a finger nor raise a hand in defense of Georgia, unless Georgia acknowledges that you are men, and invests you with the rights pertaining to manhood. . . .

AN OPEN, DELIBERATE INSULT TO THE WOMEN OF THE NATION
Elizabeth Cady Stanton

In the years before the Civil War, whites as well as blacks waged a concerted campaign to end slavery. It was no coincidence that the women who played a leading role in the abolitionist movement also became the pioneers of American feminism. Determined individuals like Sarah Grimké (1792–1873), Angelina Grimké (1805–1879), Lucretia Mott (1793–1880), Lucy Stone (1818–1893) and Elizabeth Cady Stanton (1815–1902) extended to women as well as slaves the philosophy of natural rights, which held that since all human beings were born equal, they should all enjoy equal political rights.

Stanton belonged to the branch of the abolitionist movement that called for political action rather than "moral suasion," a principle that she also applied to women's rights. Stanton organized the first women's rights convention at Seneca Falls, New York in 1848 and, with her longtime colleague Susan B. Anthony (1820–1906), worked to improve women's status through married women's property rights, divorce reform, and suffrage.

Before Reconstruction, this first generation of feminists had come to depend on male abolitionists like Frederick Douglass, Wendell Phillips, and Gerrit Smith to support women's rights as adamantly as they did those of African Americans. Together in 1866 they formed the American Equal Rights Association with the goal of campaigning for universal adult suffrage (that is, enfranchisement for both African Americans and women). Reconstruction, however, drove a wedge between the two causes and their advocates. Some male abolitionists, arguing that women's suffrage was a divisive issue that would jeopardize the already precarious struggle for black rights, advised the women to wait until black rights had been secured. Stone, along with Douglass and other activists who supported this position, formed the American Woman's Suffrage Association. Stanton and Anthony, however, felt deeply betrayed by this move and vowed to continue struggling for women's suffrage under the banner of another new organization, the National Woman's Suffrage Association.

In numerous speeches around the country as well as in the pages of *The Revolution,* a radical feminist newspaper they founded in 1868, Stanton and Anthony expounded on a range of issues concerning women, including suffrage. At first they took the position that women's right to vote was equal to that of African American men; later they claimed that the rights of native-born white women should actually take precedence because they were better educated and morally superior to men of the "lower orders."

The more radical they became, the further Stanton and Anthony moved from their former alliance with the abolitionists, even to the point of repeating some of the racist slurs about black men's sexual aggression usually found coming from white supremacists. In the following selection, how does Stanton try to establish women's superiority? Can you trace the movement of the argument from a natural rights position to one of radical feminism?

We object to the proposed amendment of the Constitution of the United States securing "Manhood Suffrage," for several reasons.

1st, Because a government based on the caste and class principle, on the inequality of its citizens, cannot stand. This experiment has been often and fully tried. It matters not whether under a despotism, a monarchy, or a republic, whether based on family, nobility, wealth, education, color or sex, it must prove a failure in the future as it has uniformly in the past. There is only one safe, sure way to build a government, and that is on the equality of all its citizens, male and female, black and white. The aristocratic idea in any form is opposed to the genius of our institutions and the civilization of the age. Of all kinds of aristocracy, that of sex is the most odious and unnatural, invading as it does our homes, desecrating our family altars, dividing those whom God has joined together, exalting the son above the mother who bore him, and subjugating everywhere moral power to brute force. A government like this would not be worth all the blood and treasure this nation so freely poured out in the last Revolution.

2nd, We object to a "man's government," because the male element, already too much in the ascendant, is a destructive force; stern, selfish, aggrandizing; loving war, violence, conquest, acquisition; breeding discord, disorder, disease and death.

See what a record of blood and cruelty the pages of history reveal, through what slavery, slaughter and sacrifice, through what inquisitions and imprisonments,

Source: Elizabeth Cady Stanton, "Manhood Suffrage," *The Revolution,* vol. 2, no. 25 (December 24, 1868): 392–93.

pains and persecutions, black codes and gloomy creeds, the soul of humanity has struggled for the centuries, while mercy has veiled her face, and all hearts have been dead alike to love and hope. Thus has the masculine element overpowered the feminine, crushing out all the diviner elements of human nature. . . .

What can we gain as a nation by "Manhood Suffrage," having too much of the man power in government already? If the civilization of the age calls for an extension of the suffrage, a government of the most virtuous, educated men and women would better represent the whole humanitarian idea, and more perfectly protect the interests of all, than could a representation of either sex alone. But to ignore the influence of woman in the legislation of the country, and blindly insist upon the recognition of every type of brutalized, degraded manhood, must prove suicidal to any government on the footstool, hence we protest against the extension of suffrage to another man, until enough women are first admitted to the polls to outweigh the dangerous excess of the male element already there.

So long as there is a disfranchised class, and that class the women of the nation, "a man's government" is worse than a "white man's government," because in proportion as you multiply the tyrants, you make the condition of the subjects more hopeless and degraded. John Stuart Mill, in his work on Liberty, shows clearly that the condition of one disfranchised man in a nation is worse than that of a whole nation under one man, because in the latter case, if the one man is despotic, the nation can easily throw him off, but what can the one man do with a nation of tyrants over him?

Just so if a woman finds it hard to bear the oppressive laws of a few Saxon Fathers, of the best orders of manhood, what may she not be called to endure when all the lower orders, natives and foreigners, Dutch, Irish, Chinese and African, legislate for her and her daughters?

This "Manhood Suffrage" is an appalling question, and it would be well for thinking women, who seem to consider it so magnanimous to hold their own claims in abeyance until all men are crowned with citizenship, to remember, that the lowest classes of men are invariably the most hostile to the elevation of woman as they have known her only in ignorance and degradation and ever regarded her in the light of a slave.

3d, We object to the proposed amendment because it is an open, deliberate insult to the women of the nation. Now, when the attention of the whole world is turned to this question, when the women of France, England, Switzerland and even Russia are holding their conventions, and demanding enfranchisement, and their rulers everywhere giving them a respectful hearing, shall the women of "the freest government on the earth" be set aside in this way without notice or apology! While poets and philosophers, statesmen and men of science are all alike pointing to woman as the new hope for the redemption of the world, shall American Senators, claiming to be liberal, laugh at and suppress our petitions, and boast in our conventions of their courage to vote Woman's Suffrage down in the Capitol, and thus degrade their own mothers, wives and daughters, in their political status, below unwashed and unlettered ditch-diggers, boot-blacks, hostlers, butchers, and barbers.

Think of Patrick and Sambo and Hans and Yung Tung who do not know the difference between a Monarchy and a Republic, who never read the Declaration of Independence or Webster's spelling book, making laws for Lydia Maria Child, Lucretia Mott, or Fanny Kemble.[1] Think of jurors drawn from these ranks to try young girls for the crime of infanticide.

---

[1]Child and Kemble, along with Mott, were prominent white female reformers of the day.

Would these gentlemen who, on all sides, are telling us "to wait until the negro is safe" be willing to stand aside and trust all *their* interests in hands like these? . . .

6th, We object to the proposed amendment, because it raises a more deadly opposition to the negro than any he has yet encountered. It creates an antagonism between him and woman, the very element most needed to be propitiated in his behalf. Suffrage for all could easily be carried in every state; but when you propose to lift the negro above the woman, and make him her Ruler, Legislator, Judge and Juror, if even northern women rebel, what can you expect at the south? The "negro element" at the south, of which we hear so much, may make voters for the republican party, but it does not give us what we need in government. The people are concerned about deeper principles than such as serve the shifting purposes of politicians.

We hear much high-sounding talk about "saving the country," but what is a country to the women who have no voice in the laws that govern them? What is a country to the suffering masses; the denizens of garrets, and cellars, and mud cabins, on the lonely prairies, so long as all the fruit of their industry is stolen by their rulers?

THESE WOMEN HAVE ALWAYS BEEN USED TO WORKING OUT
M. C. Fulton

Victorian family ideals rested on the assumption that mothers were not to work but to remain at home caring for their children, and that children should spend their early years as "little learners," not "little earners." Southern whites, however, did not believe that such values should be extended to freedpeople. As slaves, African American women and all but the youngest children had always worked, whether as fieldhands or domestic servants, and many whites fully expected that they would continue to do so.

Freedwomen, for their part, attempted to stay out of the labor force—not because they subscribed to white, middle-class Victorian notions, but because they wanted, for the first time, to establish comfortable households and attend to their children. They especially sought to avoid situations where they would be directly controlled by white employers and subjected to arbitrary orders and sexual harassment. Because wages for African American men were so low, however, few could afford to support a family on their earnings alone. By the end of Reconstruction, half of all African American women over age sixteen, most of them married, had become wage-earners.

Whites did not rely entirely on the market to drive black women into the labor force; they also turned to local authorities and, when that did not work, to intimidation. The following documents illustrate different methods used by whites to achieve their ends. In the first, a white planter tries to convince the Georgia Freedmen's Bureau that freedwomen should be channeled into fieldwork (presumably for himself or other white planters). What reasons did this man offer for why these women should be made to work? What does this letter tell us about the preferences of African Americans regarding women and work? How might they have explained the conditions deplored by M. C. Fulton?

Snow Hill near Thomson Georgia April 17th 1866

Dear Sir— Allow me to call your attention to the fact that most of the Freedwomen who have husbands are not at work—never having made any contract at all— Their husbands are at work, while they are as nearly idle as it is possible for them to be, pretending to spin—knit or something that really amounts to nothing for their husbands have to buy them clothing I find from my own hands wishing to buy of me—

Now these women have always been used to working out & it would be far better for them to go to work for reasonable wages & their rations—both in regard to health & in furtherance of their family wellbeing—Say their husbands get 10 to 12—or 13$ per month and out of that feed their wives and from 1 to 3 or 4 children—& clothe the family— It is impossible for one man to do this & maintain his wife in idleness without stealing more or less of their support, whereas if their wives (where they are able) were at work for rations & fair wages—which they can all get; the family could live in some comfort & more happily— besides their labor is a very important percent of the entire labor of the South—& if not made avaible, must affect to some extent the present crop— Now is a very important time in the crop—& the weather being good & to continue so for the remainder of the year, I think it would be a good thing to put the women to work and all that is necessary to do this in most cases is an order from you directing the agents to require the women to make contracts for the balance of the year— I have several that are working well—while others and generally younger ones who have husbands & from 1 to 3 or 4 children are idle—indeed refuse to work & say their husbands must support them. Now & then there is a woman who is not able to work in the field—or who has 3 or 4 children at work & can afford to live on her childrens labobor—with that of her husband— Even in such a case it would be better she should be at work— Generally however most of them should be in the field—

Could not this matter be referred to your agents They are generally very clever men and would do right. I would suggest that you give this matter your favorable consideration & if you can do so to use your influence to make these idle women go to work. You would do them & the country a service besides gaining favor & the good opinion of the people generally.

I beg you will not consider this matter lightly for it is a very great evil & one that the Bureau ought to correct—if they wish the Freedmen & women to do well— I have 4 or 5 good women hands now idle that ought to be at work because their families cannot really be supported honestly without it. This should not be so—& you will readily see how important it is to change it at once— I am very respectfully Your obt servant

M. C. Fulton

Source: M. C. Fulton to General Davis Tillson (Assistant Commissioner of the Freedmen's Bureau), 17 April 1866, in *Families and Freedom: A Documentary History of African-American Kinship in the Civil War Era* ed. Ira Berlin and Leslie S. Rowland (New York: The New Press, 1997), pp. 185–87; reprinted by permission.

FIGURE 2.2

In this 1865 engraving entitled "Emancipation," Thomas Nast, the famous nineteenth-century political cartoonist and graphic artist, depicted African American life before emancipation (on the left) and after (on the right). How does the image of the family at the center compare with that of the "ideal" Victorian family? How closely did African American family life during this period come to resemble the image depicted here? (*Source: Philadelphia: S. Bott, 1865; courtesy of the Library of Congress.*)

IDLE MEN, WOMEN OR CHILDREN SHALL SUFFER THE PENALTY
I AM Committee

The following is the text of a broadside or leaflet that was posted on the doors of freedpeople in several rural Tennessee counties early in 1867. Such notices were written by groups of whites who called themselves "regulators" and, claiming "I am everywhere," engaged in the kind of intimidation and violence that was soon to become the trademark of the Ku Klux Klan. In the eyes of the "I AM" Committee, what kinds of employment for blacks were acceptable? not acceptable? Why? How did the committee attempt to "regulate" blacks' behavior? (*Note:* "look up a saplin" is a term meaning lynching or hanging.)

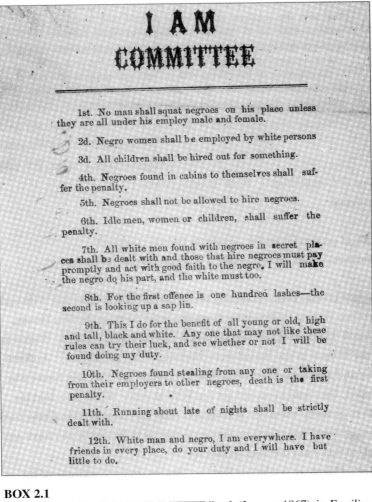

I AM COMMITTEE

1st. No man shall squat negroes on his place unless they are all under his employ male and female.

2d. Negro women shall be employed by white persons

3d. All children shall be hired out for something.

4th. Negroes found in cabins to themselves shall suffer the penalty.

5th. Negroes shall not be allowed to hire negroes.

6th. Idle men, women or children, shall suffer the penalty.

7th. All white men found with negroes in secret places shall be dealt with and those that hire negroes must pay promptly and act with good faith to the negro. I will make the negro do his part, and the white must too.

8th. For the first offence is one hundred lashes—the second is looking up a sap lin.

9th. This I do for the benefit of all young or old, high and tall, black and white. Any one that may not like these rules can try their luck, and see whether or not I will be found doing my duty.

10th. Negroes found stealing from any one or taking from their employers to other negroes, death is the first penalty.

11th. Running about late of nights shall be strictly dealt with.

12th. White man and negro, I am everywhere. I have friends in every place, do your duty and I will have but little to do.

BOX 2.1
Source: Broadside, "I AM COMMITTEE," n.d. (January 1867), in *Families and Freedom: A Documentary History of African-American Kinship in the Civil War Era,* ed. Ira Berlin and Leslie S. Rowland (New York: The New Press, 1997), p. 189; reprinted by permission.

WE DESIRE TO LIVE COMFORTABLY
Washerwomen of the South

In both the North and the South, domestic service was one of the few occupations in which African American women could be assured of finding work. Freedwomen found themselves negotiating wages, hours, and working conditions with white employers who preferred to give peremptory orders as they had always done under slavery. To protect their autonomy, freedwomen avoided live-in jobs and, when possible, worked out of their own homes; many became washerwomen.

As they began to perceive that they were performing an essential service to urban, middle-class families, these black workers organized to improve their lot. There is evidence of at least three protests on the part of Southern washerwomen between 1866 and 1881. The 1881 strike was mounted in Atlanta on the eve of the International Cotton Exposition, the first such event to be held in the South. Though the strike apparently ended in failure for the washerwomen, it was particularly embarrassing to leaders of the "New South."

How did the washerwomen's methods of organizing and rhetoric change over time? Were white employers their only targets? What accounts for their increasing militancy? In what ways did the white press imply that the washerwomen's behavior defied gender norms?

Jackson, Mississippi, June 20, 1866

Dear Mayor:

At a meeting of the colored Washerwomen of this city, on the evening of the 18th of June, the subject of raising the wages was considered, and the following preamble and resolution were unanimously adopted:

Whereas, under the influence of the present high prices of all the necessaries of life, and the attendant high rates of rent, we, the washerwomen of the city of Jackson, State of Mississippi, thinking it impossible to live uprightly and honestly in laboring for the present daily and monthly recompense, and hoping to meet with the support of all good citizens, join in adopting unanimously the following resolution:

Be it resolved by the washerwomen of this city and county, That on and after the foregoing date, we join in charging a uniform rate for our labor, and any one belonging to the class of washerwomen, violating this, shall be liable to a fine regulated by the class. We do not wish in the least to charge exorbitant prices, but desire to be able to live comfortably if possible from the fruits of our labor. We present the matter to your Honor, and hope you will not reject it. The prices charged are:

$1.50 per day for washing
$15.00 per month for family washing
$10.00 per month for single individuals

We ask you to consider the matter in our behalf, and should you deem it just and right, your sanction of the movement will be gratefully received.

Yours, very truly,
THE WASHERWOMEN OF JACKSON

Source: *Daily Clarion,* Jackson, Mississippi, June 24, 1866; rpt. in *The Black Worker,* ed. Philip Foner and Ronald Lewis (Philadelphia: Temple University Press, 1978), vol. 1:345.

SO-CALLED WASHERWOMEN, ALL COLORED, GO FOR EACH OTHER AND THE HEATHEN CHINESE

Monday night colored women, emboldened by the liberties allowed their fathers, husbands and brothers, decided to have a public hurrah of their own, and as the men had demanded two dollars for a day's labor they would ask $1.50 or $9 per week. As women are generally considered cleansers of dirty linen, their first move was against the steam laundry, corner of Avenue A and Tenth Street, owned by J. N. Harding.

About 6:30 A.M. colored women began collecting around his house, until they numbered about twenty-five. The laundry women were soon seen coming to work. When met and told that they should not work for less than $1.50 per day, four turned back; but, one, a Miss Murphy went into the house and began working. Seeing this, the women rushed in, caught her and carried her into the street, and by threats forced her to leave. . . .

This success . . . emboldened the women to further demonstrations. The cry was raised, "Let's lock them out for good; here's nails I brought especially." An axe lying in the wood pile was grabbed, and the laundry house doors and windows secured. Then off they started for the heathen Chinese, who "washes Mellican man clothes so cheapee." Down Market street they went, led by a portly colored lady, whose avoir-dupois is not less than 250.

On the way many expressions as to their intentions were heard, such as "We will starve no longer," "Chinese got no business coming here taking our work from us." Each California laundry was visited in turn, beginning at Slam Sing's and ending at Wau Loong's corner of Bath Avenue and Postoffice Street.

At these laundries all the women talked at once, telling [the Chinese men] that "they must close up and leave this city within fifteen days or they would be driven away," each Chinaman responding, "Yees, yees," "Alice rightee," "Me go, yees," and closed their shops. The women . . . scattered after avowing they would . . . visit each place where women are hired, and if they receive less than $1.50 per day or $9 per week they would force them to quit.

Source: *Galveston* [Texas] *News,* August 1, 1877; rpt. in *The Black Worker,* vol. 2:167–68.

July 24, 1881

TO THE CITIZENS OF ATLANTA

It is well known, and has been for years, that the washerwomen of Atlanta receive less compensation for their labors than was paid for similar labor anywhere else, and far less than was paid here for other similar services.

More than twelve months since, at the suggestion of Mrs. Askew, from Rome [Georgia], the Washerwomen's association was organized and now numbers over eight hundred members.

Much care and attention has been devoted to ascertaining the prices and rules that prevail for washing in other localities, and the association has finally agreed

Source: *The Atlanta Constitution,* July 24, 26, 29, 30 and August 3, 1881.

upon a schedule of prices for service, which will average from ten to twenty per cent less than is charged for the same services in other localities. We are not unmindful of the fact that even this change from the practice so long in vogue, will to some extent change the domestic service of the city.

But the citizens of Atlanta may rest assured that while the Association intends to protect their rights, they do not intend in any single instance to demand more, and earnestly request the citizens to examine our schedule of prices herewith, and consider the labor to be performed before condemning our action.

PRICE LIST

Washerwomen's Association of Atlanta.

Family washing, including fancy dresses, etc, per doz, $1; family washing, excluding fancy fluted dresses for ladies and children; plain clothes per dozen, 50 cts; starched clothes per dozen, $1; for rough dried clothes per dozen, 15 to 25 cts. . . .

SAVANNAH CARTER, President
MRS ASKEW, Vice-President

THE NEW STEAM LAUNDRY

"It is an Ill Wind That Blows no Good."

The washerwomen of Atlanta having "struck" for very unreasonably high prices, a number of our most substantial citizens have quietly gone to work to make up a large cash capital, and will at an early day (as the stock is nearly all subscribed already) start an extensive Steam Laundry. The capacity of the new Laundry will be equal to the wants of the whole city, and everything will be done on the latest and most approved methods. Clothes sent to the laundry in the morning will be returned to the owners in the evening of the same day. From fifty to one hundred smart Yankee girls, experienced in the business, will be employed in running it, and the calculation of those having the enterprise in hand, is that at a very moderate charge, say an average of twenty to thirty cents per dozen, the profits will be sufficient to give all the stockholders fair dividends and their washing besides. We are glad to chronicle this movement. It will be a great boon to housekeepers in more ways than one.

July 26, 1881

THE DOUGHTY WASHWOMEN
Holding Out for an Advance in Wages

The washerwomen's strike is assuming vast proportions and despite the apparent independence of the white people, is causing quite an inconvenience among our citizens.

In one instance the demand for one dollar per dozen was acceded to. Those who decline to give this price are still wanting washers. Several families who decline to pay the price demanded, have determined to send their clothes to Marietta [Georgia] where they have secured laundry service. The strikers hold daily meetings and are exhorted by the leaders, who are confident that the demands will be granted. The committees still visit the women and induce them to join the strike and when a refusal is met with threats of personal violence are freely indulged in to such an extent as to cause a compromise with their demands. There are some families in Atlanta who have been unable to have any washing done for more than two weeks.

Not only the washerwomen, but the cooks, house servants and nurses are asking an increase. The combinations [organizations] are being managed by the laundry ladies.

July 29, 1881

THE WET CLOTHES
THE WASHERWOMEN BRING HOME.
The Story of the Organization Fully Told by Captain

Starnes, Who Says a White Man and $300 Back the Strikers

—The Way the Ranks are Increased

Police court was well attended yesterday morning, and Recorder Glenn added $186 to the city treasury by fines imposed.

Among other cases disposed of were those against Matilda Crawford, Sallie Bell, Carrie Jones, Dora Jones, Ophelia Turner and Sarah A. Collier. This sixtette of ebony hued damsels was charged with disorderly conduct and quarreling, and in each case, except the last, a fine of five dollars was imposed, and subsequently paid. In the case of Sarah A. Collier, twenty dollars was assessed, and the money not being paid, the defendant's name was transcribed to the chain gang, where it will remain for forty days.

Each of these cases resulted from the washerwomen's strike. As members of that organization they have visited women who are taking no part in the strike and have threatened personal violence unless their demands were acceded to and their example followed. During their rounds they met with persons who opposed the strike and who declined to submit to their proposition to become members. This opposition caused an excessive use of abusive and threatening language and the charge of disorderly conduct and quarreling as the result. . . .

[According to Police Captain William Starnes,] ". . . this society was first organized about one year ago. The first meeting was held in the church on Summer Hill, but only a few women attended. They tried hard to get up a strike but could not succeed and the thing soon broke because no one would join. This year however they have been successful and to-day nearly 3,000 negro women are asking their white friends who supported them during the cold, hard winter to pay them a dollar a dozen for washing.

. . . The society that now exists is about two weeks old. . . . Twenty negro women and a few negro men met in Summer Hill church and discussed the matter. The next night the negro preachers in all the churches announced a mass meeting of the washerwomen the following night. . . . The meeting was a big one and the result was an organization. . . . Since then there has been meetings every night or two, and now there is a society in every ward of the city and the strikers have increased from about 20 to 3,000 in less than three weeks. . . .

[The women] make speeches and pray. They swear they will never wash another piece for less than one dollar a dozen, but they will never get it and will soon give in. In fact, they would have caved before this but for the white man who is backing this strike.

. . . They have a fund of $300 and feel confident of getting what they ask. . . .

The committee first goes to those who have no connection with the organization and try to persuade them to join. Failing in this they notify them they must not take any more washing at less than one dollar a dozen, and threaten them with cowhides, fire and death if they disobey. . . . The result is their ranks are daily swelling. Why last night there was a big meeting . . . and fifty additions were made to the list. They passed resolutions informing all women not members of their society to quit work, or stand the consequences. . . . I am going to arrest every one who threatens any woman, and I am going to try to get the chain gang full, then they will stop. . . ."

July 30, 1881

THE WASHERWOMEN

Dora Shorter and Annie King, two more of the belligerent washerwomen, were yesterday before Recorder Glenn for trial. The charge against the duet was disorderly conduct and quarrelling and the evidence sustained the charge. Recorder Glenn imposed a fine of twenty dollars against each, and in disposing of the cases said, "In these cases I will impose a fine of twenty dollars upon each of the defendants, but hereafter, when the evidence is as conclusive as it is here, I will punish the offenders by sending them to the chain gang."

August 3, 1881

THE WASHING AMAZONS

Among other resolutions passed by the city council Monday night was one imposing a license of $5 per annum upon all washerwomen who belong to any organization having for its object an excessive pay for work.[2]

This action of the council has fallen like a bombshell in the camps of the strikers, and has induced quite a number to withdraw from the organization. There are many, however, who laugh at the resolution and say emphatically that they will neither give in nor pay the license. . . . That they are willing for the world to know just how they stand is evidenced by the following letter received by Mayor English yesterday:

WASHING SOCIETY, Atlanta, Ga., August 1—Mr. Jim English, Mayor of Atlanta—Dear Sir: We, the members of our society, are determined to stand to our pledge and make extra charges for washing, and we have agreed, and are willing to pay $25 or $50 for license as a protection, so we can control the washing for the city. We can afford to pay these license, and will do it before we will be defeated, and then we will have full control of the city's washing at our own prices, as the city has control of our husband's work at their prices. Don't forget this. . . . We mean business this week of no washing.

Yours respectfully,
From 5 Societies, 486 Members

[2]Historian Tera Hunter has found that this report was inaccurate; the city council did not pass the resolution that evening, and in fact defeated it when it was brought up for a vote several weeks later.

Last evening there was a big meeting of the organization on Wheat street, it is estimated that fully 500 women and men were present, and the action of the council was made the feature of the evening. It was discussed by the men and women, and many of the speeches were of the most "expressive" character. They openly denounced the council for imposing the tax, and defied an attempt to collect the same. But this spirit of bravado was not entertained or manifested by all. Quite a number advocated a compromise measure and intimated an intention to seek work at any price.

The strike, thanks to Recorder Glenn [and] Bill Starnes . . . , has about reached its finale, and in a week at the furthest the washerwomen will be bending over their tubs, singing songs as loudly as if they had succeeded.

With Atlanta's people the question is a leading . . . topic of discussion. Our business men are astonished at the colored people's stupidity in not seeing that they are working their own ruin. In a short time winter will again be upon them, and then they will once more be calling for aid. Many gentlemen say that when this time comes, and it will surely come, they will refuse to give anything toward sustaining those who now decline to work for a fair remuneration.

One gentleman, whose washerwoman is his tenant, was told by her that she could not wash any more for less than a dollar a dozen. "All right," said the gentleman, and the woman started off, happy in the thought that she had succeeded, but just as she reached the door with the clothing the gentleman said, "Mary, I have decided to raise my rent. Hereafter you must pay me $20 per month rent. "Why?" asked the woman. "Because," said the merchant, "you have gone up on washing, I will go up on house rent." The woman agreed to take the washing at the usual price.

And here is another feature for the strikers. If they persist in their exorbitant demands, they will find house rent going up so rapidly that they will have to vacate.

THE VIRGIN WHITENESS OF OUR GEORGIA
Elizabeth Elliott Lumpkin

For more than a decade, Southern whites steadfastly resisted federal efforts to bring at least a semblance of racial equality into the region. In 1877, over the vociferous objections of the Radical Republicans, Congress finally put an official end to Reconstruction, leaving Southern blacks without any federal support or protection in their continuing political and economic struggles. The most adamant whites continued to cling to the hope of eventually restoring the South to its antebellum glory, a vision that was embodied in a form of civil religion known as "The Lost Cause."

To keep the Cause alive, white Southerners organized along gender lines, with men forming Confederate veterans' groups in each state and women setting up chapters of the Daughters of the Confederacy. As the following document from 1903 indicates, the spirit of the Confederacy remained viable well into the twentieth century. Using this speech as an example, consider the ways in which race, masculinity, and chivalry became linked in the rhetoric of The Lost Cause.

Source: "Miss Lumpkin to Georgia Veterans," address by Elizabeth Elliott Lumpkin to State Reunion, Augusta, 1903, rpt. in *Confederate Veteran* 1, 2 (February 1904):69–70.

FIGURE 2.3
In 1915, D. W. Griffith released his famous epic film, *The Birth of a Nation.* Based on the bestselling 1905 novel *The Clansman* by Thomas Dixon, the film presents an idiosyncratic account of the Civil War and its aftermath that glorifies the Ku Klux Klan as the defender of white Southern womanhood from predatory African American men. This scene depicts the innocent white Elsie Stoneman (Lillian Gish) with her hooded rescuers. (*Still courtesy of the Museum of Modern Art.*)

Most Honored Veterans, Ladies and Gentlemen: They have asked me to speak to you; I who am a Georgia woman, a woman whose baby eyes looked first into the mother eyes of Georgia and, meeting their splendid tenderness and beauty, smiled back and lay content, a woman whose childish feet stayed on the red old hills of Georgia, whose young woman's heart became a harp, whose tense strings vibrated to the deeds of the men and women of Georgia, whose lips shall meet those mothers lips in the last lingering kiss of life.

"Aunt Minervy Ann" says: "'Tain't big houses, 'tain't land, 'tain't fine clothes, what makes quality; hit's des a long line er graveyards stretching way back to Virgin'y er fudder wid a whole heap er graves in 'em whar' dar's a heap er folks what knowed how to treat t'other folks." You know how to treat "other folks," for am I not a Georgian and know what you do?

You have greeted me, but how can I find words to give you greeting when every pulsing heart beat says: "I love you"—you grand old men who guarded with your lives the virgin whiteness of our Georgia. . . .

As a daughter who has felt the sunshine of your skies, I bow to the majesty of your glory, and to your spirit I would pour out the fondest affection and strew flowers upon your pathway. . . .

I would rather be a woman than a man. What woman would not, if she could be a Southern woman and be loved by Southern men—in this land where a man may with honor love a thousand, and yet love *only one,* and that one for eternity?

What woman would not, if she might, give up her love to those Southern men? . . .

My father was a Confederate soldier, and, though I love him and honor his dear name above all other men, with that glory to crown his head, he must needs be to me a thousand-fold greater. But there is one honor we may not have, we daughters of Georgia. I have said it before and repeat it—an honor our lovely mothers gloried in. We can work with tireless fingers, we can run with tireless feet for these men, "but *they* could love and marry Confederate soldiers!" . . .

Once there was a gallant old Confederate soldier, who was starving in prison. He had not seen his beloved for two years, and they told him if he could reach home he might go. In sight of the old home she came out to meet him, and their two boys were at her side.

"O, I am home and well again, well again, beloved!" he cried. Then he held out his arms, smiled, and died. And that smile never left him. . . .

I do want to say one word about the books used in our schools. The man or woman who would place in the schools of the South a text-book that does not do full and complete justice to the Confederate soldier would, with unholy hands, tear afresh the scars he bears; they would pluck out his dim old eyes and turn him out into a pitiless world, friendless, homeless, nameless, and nationless. They shall not leave you unhonored!

All these things we shall teach your children in our schools, by our firesides, in our songs and stories. And do you teach them also. Let the children hear the old stories of storm and war and battle, let them sing with you the dear old songs of Dixie. Let them come to your reunions, and they will bear you in their arms when you are weary with the years. Aye, they will do more than that. They will build monuments of memories in their heart of hearts, and on the summit will be the image of a Confederate sire, and at the base will be wrapped a Confederate flag. . . .

We do not believe your sons will fail; but should they seem to forget, your daughters never will. As the women of the South in the past were steadfast, true, and loyal, so the women of the South in the future will be loyal and true forever. . . .

OF A YOUTH WHO LOVES ME
Walt Whitman

Though Walt Whitman (1819–1892) did not figure directly in the politics of Reconstruction, his work was widely discussed during this era, revealing that advocates of racial equality were not the only ones to challenge the mid-nineteenth-century social order. Though Whitman has now become firmly ensconced in the canon of American literature, his sexual candor shocked many of his contemporaries. In Victorian society, it was simply not acceptable to mention parts of the anatomy or sexual intercourse, even metaphorically—and Whitman was often far more direct. Because homosexuality was not generally part of their sexual lexicon, Whitman's critics occupied themselves with his references to heterosexual acts. It was not until the advent of gay and lesbian studies in the 1970s that historians like Jonathan Ned Katz began to notice that his poetry was full of homosexual allusions. Katz also discovered correspondence between Whitman and other men that confirmed this interpretation.

Whitman's most famous collection of poems, *Leaves of Grass,* first published in 1855, went through several different editions. In 1860 he added two new sections, "Enfans d'Adam" (The Children of Adam) and "Calamus,"[3] which included some of his most scandalous poems. "Enfans d'Adam" suggested encounters between the speaker (presumably Whitman) and both women and men, but in "Calamus," the poet refers almost exclusively to other men. How does Whitman's style reinforce what he wants to convey about the pleasures of the body? What evidence do these poems provide about how relationships between men were viewed in the mid-nineteenth century?

Enfans d'Adam.
3.

1. O MY children! O mates!
   O the bodies of you, and of all men and women, engirth me, and I engirth them,
   O they will not let me off, nor I them, till I go with them, respond to them,
   And respond to the contact of them, and discorrupt them, and charge them with the charge of the Soul.

   ....

3. The love of the body of man or woman balks account—the body itself balks account,
   That of the male is perfect, and that of the female is perfect.

4.

1. A WOMAN waits for me—she contains all, nothing is lacking,
   Yet all were lacking, if sex were lacking, or if the moisture of the right man were lacking.

   ....

7. It is I, you women—I make my way,
   I am stern, acrid, large, undissuadable—but I love you,
   I do not hurt you any more than is necessary for you,
   I pour the stuff to start sons and daughters fit for These States—I press with slow rude muscle,
   I brace myself effectually—I listen to no entreaties,
   I dare not withdraw till I deposit what has so long accumulated within me.

   ....

Calamus.
26.

WE two boys together clinging,
One the other never leaving,
Up and down the roads going—North and South excursions making,
Power enjoying—elbows stretching—fingers clutching,
Armed and fearless—eating, drinking, sleeping, loving,
No law less than ourselves owning—sailing, soldiering, thieving, threatening,
Misers, menials, priests alarming—air breathing, water drinking, on the turf or the sea-beach dancing,

---

[3]Calamus is the name of a fragrant root or grass often used medicinally.
Source: Walt Whitman, *Leaves of Grass* (Boston: Thayer and Eldridge, 1860), pp. 291; 302–5; 369; 371–3.

With birds singing—With fishes swimming—With trees branching and leafing,
Cities wrenching, ease scorning, statutes mocking, feebleness chasing,
Fulfilling our foray.

29.

ONE fitting glimpse, caught through an interstice,
Of a crowd of workmen and drivers in a bar-room, around the stove, late of a winter
    night—And I unremarked, seated in a corner;
Of a youth who loves me, and whom I love, silently approaching, and seating himself
    near, that he may hold me by the hand;
A long while, amid the noises of coming and going—of drinking and oath and smutty
    jest,
There we two, content, happy in being together, speaking little, perhaps not a word.

32.

WHAT think you I take my pen in hand to record?
The battle-ship, perfect-model'd, majestic, that I saw pass the offing to-day under full
    sail?
The splendors of the past day? Or the splendor of the night that envelops me?
Or the vaunted glory and growth of the great city spread around me?—No;
But I record of two simple men I saw to-day, on the pier, in the midst of the crowd,
    parting the parting of dear friends,
The one to remain hung on the other's neck, and passionately kissed him,
While the one to depart, tightly prest the one to remain in his arms.

RECOMMENDED READINGS

Clinton, Catherine, and Nina Silber, eds. *Divided Houses: Gender and the Civil War.* New York, 1992.

Du Bois, Ellen. *Feminism and Suffrage: The Emergence of an Independent Women's Movement in America, 1848–1969.* Ithaca, 1978.

Edwards, Laura. *Gendered Strife and Confusion: The Political Culture of Reconstruction.* Urbana, 1997.

Faust, Drew. *Mothers of Invention: Women of the Slaveholding South in the American Civil War.* Chapel Hill, 1996.

Foner, Eric. *Reconstruction: America's Unfinished Revolution.* New York, 1988.

Goings, Kenneth W., and Raymond A. Mohl, eds. *The New African American Urban History.* Thousand Oaks, CA, 1996.

Hodes, Martha. *White Women, Black Men: Illicit Sex in the Nineteenth–Century South.* New Haven, 1997.

Hunter, Tera W. *To 'Joy My Freedom: Southern Black Women's Lives and Labors after the Civil War.* Cambridge, MA, 1997.

Michel, Sonya. "The Reconstruction of White Southern Manhood." In *Different Restorations: Reconstruction and "Wiederaufbau" in Germany and the United States: 1865, 1945, and 1989,* ed. Norbert Finzsch. Providence, RI, 1996.

Sterling, Dorothy, ed. *We Are Your Sisters: Black Women in the Nineteenth Century.* New York, 1984.

Desiring to give the admirers of Ivory Soap an opportunity to contribute to its literature the manufacturers offered prizes for the best twelve verses suitable for use as advertisements 27,388 contributions were received. To the following was awarded the

FIRST PRIZE.

Our grandmothers, dressed in their linsey,
    Would kindle a fire in a hole,
And over it swing a big kettle
    On two forked sticks and a pole.
With lye they had strained through the ashes,
    And scraps that were lying around,
They made for our fathers and mothers,
    A soft saponaceous compound.
But now in great buildings that cover
    More ground than a fortress of old,
In caldrons of brass and of copper,
    That glisten like silver and gold;
With oils from the far-away tropics,
    And alkali made from the dew,
Are mingled the essence of roses
    And lilies and jassamine too.
The result of this rare combination,
    Is the Ivory Soap of to-day,
To-morrow, next week, and thereafter,
    Forever and ever and aye.
                    JOHN A. CONWELL, Aurora, Ind.

FIGURE 3.1

Progress, according to America's captains of industry, made life easier for everyone. This advertisement for Ivory Soap appeared in *Ladies' Home Journal* in 1893. Why do you think the judges awarded first prize to this particular poem? (*Source:* Ladies Home Journal, *vol. 10 [January, 1893], p. 28.*)

CHAPTER 3

Gender Industrialized

The United States began the nineteenth century as an industrial laggard, but by 1890 its economy was the most productive in the world. Technological innovations such as the telegraph and telephone modernized communications, cash registers and typewriters sped business transactions, electricity gradually displaced other forms of power, and huge factories run on the principles of "scientific management" turned out an ever-growing array of products more cheaply and plentifully than ever before.

Industrialization had profound social as well as economic implications. As the scale of business grew, manufacturing began to outstrip agriculture, and machines replaced handwork. Artisans, farmers, and small-scale merchants lost control over production and distribution. The assembly line broke down manufacturing into a series of discrete operations, "de-skilling" individual employees and yielding oversight to a middle stratum of managers and supervisors. Men whose gender identity had once depended on being independent producers were now forced to base their manhood on earning a "family wage."

Both employers and male workers upheld the notion of the family wage as a white male prerogative, to the detriment of minority men and wage-earning women of all races. Trade unions largely excluded women on the grounds that they undercut men's earnings and opportunities for work. It was true that employers often tried to hire women at lower wages, but, women labor activists argued, if unions fought on their behalf they could ensure higher wages for workers of both sexes. However, in addition to outright discrimination, gender stereotypes and masculinized work cultures kept women out of the most lucrative jobs.

In similar ways, white male workers and employers also limited employment opportunities for Latinos, Asians, and African Americans. Despite these impediments, however, the prospect of industrial employment attracted waves of immigrants from Asia and Southern and Eastern Europe as well as native-born Americans to urban areas and milltowns, where they crowded into hastily built tenements and company housing.

Industrialization also gave rise to a large new middle class whose men filled the growing ranks of managers, salesmen and clerks, and whose women concerned themselves with the living conditions of the working classes, the poor, Indians, and other marginalized groups. Civic-minded housewives and their single, college-educated daughters identified as problems child labor, child neglect, high rates of infant and maternal mortality, poor sanitation, occupational health and safety, alcoholism, and desertion. They formed a network of local and national organizations that historian Sara Evans calls the "maternal commonwealth." Convinced that their special understanding of the needs of women and children imbued them with a duty to assist, these women achieved a number of noteworthy reforms, but their work was also marked by a certain condescension (for example, the belief that immigrants should be "Americanized") that put off the very people they sought to help.

THE CHILDREN AND WOMEN WILL NOT BE SENT OUT
TO EARN THEIR LIVING
John Stafford

According to the ideology of free labor, which dominated Northern thinking in the antebellum era, every American had the right to work himself up from being a wage-earner to becoming an independent producer, whether craftsman, merchant, or farmer. It was the perception that slavery threatened this right by undercutting the wages of the free laborer, as much as (or perhaps even more than) a commitment to freeing African Americans, that inspired many Northerners to take up arms against the South.

Free labor ideology implicitly posited the independent producer as a white man who was the head of his household and its sole or primary source of support. This linkage provided the economic underpinnings for Victorianism, with its prescriptions for white female domesticity and devotion to motherhood. As industrialization made it increasingly difficult for the majority of men to achieve the status of independent producer, that goal was replaced by one that was more realistic but still preserved men's place as heads of households: earning a family wage.

White male workers' right to earn a family wage became one of the chief rallying cries of the American Federation of Labor, a coalition of craft unions that formed under the leadership of Samuel Gompers (1850–1924) in 1886. The AFL felt justified in opposing any group of workers who might lower the wage scale or interfere with what it saw as fair competition among equals. Thus the organization routinely sought to exclude women and members of racial and ethnic minorities from the labor force, as the following two documents illustrate.

The first is an article from the *American Federationist* which places adequate wages for men at the center of social well-being. Classify the different kinds of arguments the author is making. How do they support each other? What sort of "ideal family" is the author envisioning?

Source: John Stafford, "The Good that Trade Unions Do," *American Federationist,* vol. 9, no. 7 (July 1902), pp. 353–58.

Wages are raised through the efforts of the trade unions. It is interesting to consider what specific benefits are derived from advanced wages: . . .

More and better food, clothing and shelter.

Wives saved from becoming wage-earners.

Children, and especially young girls, prevented from becoming wage-earners.

More education for workers, and for children.

Diminution of poverty, crime, pauperism, and prostitution.

Increase of marriages and decrease of divorces.

Lessening of discontent.

Diminution of imposition by chattel mortgage sharks.

Carefulness and skill induced, and workmanship improved.

Increased mobility of the laboring classes.

Wealth distributed more equally.

Labor unions strengthened. . . .

As wages advance, the family of the workingman is provided with more and better food. In Europe the majority of the workingmen eat meat only once a week, usually on Sunday, as a luxury; and even then the meat is too often of a poor grade. In America, especially in those occupations that have no strong unions, meat or other strengthening food, although eaten oftener than in Europe, is still all too rarely eaten, and there is lack of sufficient food of nourishing qualities. Insufficient food brings on diseases of the stomach which in turn cause death. During hard times deaths from these diseases are very numerous at our hospitals and charitable institutions. . . .

Hunger undermines the health. A sufficient quantity of good food will, therefore, in all cases where it is now lacking, produce better health.

Ill health robs the sufferer of time for labor, hence, if his health improves he will get more time for work and his earnings will be increased. This will give him more purchasing power, and add to the comfort of himself and family and indirectly contributes to the benefit of society as a whole. . . .

Better health also means better offspring, for some diseased conditions are transmitted to offspring. . . .

Healthier parents producing healthier children are thereby improving the human race. . . .

When a laborer gets higher wages he naturally tries to get a better house in a better neighborhood. When laborers are badly fed, clothed and housed, it is an indication of social disease, just as sores on the body are an evidence of disease within.

The dwellings of the poor are usually small and stuffy. Any attempt at ventilation lets in a quantity of air which is large in proportion to the rooms, cooling them too rapidly. They are often badly constructed and admit drafts of cold air, in and out of season. These things make home uncomfortable and undesirable, causing the inmates to resort to the streets, to saloons and other questionable places. Better houses cause less exposure to untimely drafts. The air is better because it takes longer to pollute a larger quantity of air than a smaller quantity. The homes are more comfortable. They are factors in promoting morality. . . .

More home comforts lead to less intemperance. The latter leads to greater health and longer life.

Young people who frequent the street because their homes are uncomfortable, easily get into bad company, and often, becoming familiar with vice, are more easily led into crime.

When a workingman prospers so that he can have a house in a better location, he has the advantages of purer air, better associates. . . .

FIGURE 3.2
Advertisements like this one suggested that certain material goods were necessary components of comfortable family life. Mass production lowered the cost of major items like organs and pianos, and installment purchase made it possible for lower-income families to buy them, but for the majority of working-class families, such items were unheard-of luxuries. (*Source:* Ladies' Home Journal, *vol. 9 [January, 1892], back cover.*)

While our times may not furnish so revolting and so brutal a spectacle as that of the employment of children in the mines of England some fifty years ago, yet we have conditions as detrimental to the health, though perhaps somewhat less revolting to the senses. There is not so much child labor in the dark, damp mines, but it has not disappeared. . . .

[According to one labor expert,] "The average life of the factory girl is only thirty years. The children who work in the factory look like little old men and women, and they are more vicious than old men and women, ruined before they are ripe. The child who enters the factory as an operative leaves hope behind. . . ."

Higher wages prevent children's becoming wage-earners, for if the father can earn enough to support his family and make them comfortable he will not send his children out to work.

When children become wage-earners they take the places of grown persons and thus increase competition between laborers. This competition lowers wages, and hence, if this competition is diminished wages will tend to rise again, especially if the trade is unionized.

When children and their mothers are not obliged to earn a living they get a better training. This embraces a better home, school education, better morals, more refinement, and leads to better citizenship. The child can not have a better friend than its mother, and none whose influence for good is so wise. Rev. Wm. Banks says, in "White Slaves":

"Before the church or the state, there must be the home. Destroy that, and the whole fabric of our civilization will come crashing to the ground in one common ruin. But the reduction of wages below the comfort point means inevitably, the deterioration of the home. The father and mother and children must know each other, if the home is to be welded together with mutual love. Acquaintance of that character, however, requires that they shall be together under such conditions that they may come to enjoy the gifts and talents that each possess. But wages are being reduced to the point where the home is only a sleeping barrack and a lunch counter for supper and breakfast. Remember that poor wages mean long hours; and long hours that exhaust all the energy of the laborer mean ignorance; ignorance, when it is finished, means immorality.

"There is only about so much force in the average human being. If all this force is put into one's daily toil, there is none left for helpful conversation, for sympathetic communion at home, for uplifting reading, or for worship. Persevere in that course, and you reach barbarism; the road leads that way."

Better education gives rise to less inequality between the child of the rich and that of the poor. . . . A better education leads also to better citizenship and to more brain development. . . .

Better mental development is also a result of preventing child labor, for the factory child becomes mentally dwarfed by the continuous monotony of his task. . . .

When the wages of the head of the family are high enough to support the family, the children and women will not be sent out to earn their living. It appears from statistics of New England that only fifty-six per cent of skilled laborers and only nine per cent of unskilled laborers receive wages enough to support their families. They send out their wives and children to make up the deficit. And this is in a country where population is not yet dense, and where the bird of freedom is supposed to scream daily. If, however, wages rise, the number of young girls who are wage-earners will diminish. . . .

When girl wage-earners decrease, competition between wage-earners decreases also, because there are just so many less persons seeking work. This leads to higher wages [for men].

Fewer girl wage-earners means less prostitution. The low wages received in stores and factories often drives them to other methods of earning living wages. The obscene conversation and forced evil associations in factories and shops, with girls or men who have become depraved, is apt to cause their ruin. When vice becomes familiar it is no longer feared or abhorred.

Less prostitution means better health; for the "business" as it is called, is an unhealthy one. The exposure by reason of scant clothing, the irregular hours, the excesses and the accompanying indulgence in liquors, the accompanying diseases, lower the vitality at an alarming rate, if they do not absolutely destroy life.

A person who has a very low vitality, or who has the seeds of sexual disease implanted in the system, does not produce healthy offspring, and that portion of the race which is so propagated deteriorates, resulting in a race of paupers or criminals, or it dies out.

Less wage-earning by girls leads to better mental development, for there cannot be much development when the mind is continually chained to one certain simple operation of a large machine, for ten, twelve or fourteen hours per day.

Girls who are wage-earners in mills or stores have little opportunity to learn housework, for the few hours they may have at home are needed for rest. . . .

Girls who do not go to the factory secure better household training. This improved training makes them more competent to teach their own children, and they, therefore, become better mothers. They also are better cooks, have a better education, better morals, more refinement, and their children become better citizens. Bad cooking is productive of bad health, much domestic wrangling, and of great waste. Good cooking is the reverse.

Where girls and women work in public places the percentage of female criminals increases, as is shown by statistics. Less wage-earning by girls, therefore, leads to less criminality of women.

MANHOOD GIVES TITLE TO RIGHTS
Samuel Gompers and Herman Gutstadt

The following pamphlet, also published by the AFL and coauthored by Samuel Gompers, encapsulates the kinds of racist arguments commonly used by labor's "aristocracy" to justify discrimination against racial and ethnic minorities, particularly immigrants. One can detect the influence of social Darwinism, a nineteenth-century ideology that justified social inequality on the basis of a biologically based hierarchy which ranked racial groups according to the level of "civilization" they had supposedly attained.

In this instance, the perceived threat to white labor came from the Chinese. Immigration by male Chinese workers (or "coolies," as they were derogatorily known) had been encouraged around midcentury, when the transcontinental railroad was being built. Once it was completed, however, the demand for Chinese labor dropped off abruptly and in 1882 the first Chinese Exclusion Law was passed, prohibiting further immigration. It was renewed in 1892 and made permanent in 1902. Chinese men had difficulty finding work and also forming households and families because American law as well as Chinese custom had restricted immigration for Chinese women and prohibited intermarriage.

This document is a rich one for scholars of gender and race. What qualities are said to distinguish the Chinese from native-born Americans? Why do the Chinese pose a threat to American workers? How do the authors justify slavery? How do they reinforce the notion that the "ideal" worker is a white male? What is the link between adequate wage-earning and citizenship?

. . . The ladies' furnishing and undergarment trade is almost entirely under the control of the Chinese. Their stores are scattered everywhere throughout San

Source: Samuel Gompers and Herman Gutstadt, "Some Reasons for Exclusion; Meat vs. Rice. American Manhood against Asiatic Coolieism; Which Shall Survive?" (Washington, D.C.: American Federation of Labor, 1901).

Francisco, and the American manufacturers have been gradually driven out. One or two who may still remain employ [native-born white] girls at most scanty wages.

The cigar, boot and shoe, broom-making, and pork industries were for many years entirely in the hands of the Chinese, depriving many thousands of Americans of their means of livelihood. As their power grew they became independent, and in the pork industry they had secured so strong a hold that no white butcher dared kill a hog for fear of incurring the displeasure of the Chinese. This state of affairs became so obnoxious and unbearable that the retail butchers could no longer submit, and with the assistance of the wholesale butchers and the citizens generally finally succeeded in wresting the monopoly from the hands of their Chinese oppressors.

In factories owned by white employers the Chinese employees refused to work together with white men, and upon one occasion at least positively struck against them, refusing to work unless the white help was discharged. This instance so aroused the State of California that an anti-Chinese convention was called and held at the city of Sacramento March 10, 1886, in which the most representative citizens of California took part. . . . [The memorial drafted by this convention and sent to the President, the Senate, and the House of Representatives read in part:]

"That there is more mere money profit in dollars in a homogeneous population than in one of the mixed races, while the moral and political objections are unanswerable.

"That, while the Chinaman works industriously enough, he consumes very little, either of his own production or of ours.

"That he imports from China much that he eats and much that he wears, while a vast catalogue of articles consumed by our own people, the production and sale of which makes our commerce and our life what it is, the Chinaman does not use at all.

"That he underbids all white labor and ruthlessly takes its place and will go on doing so until the white laborer comes down to the scanty food and half-civilized habits of the Chinaman, while the net results of his earning are sent regularly out of the country and lost to the community where it was created.

"And while this depleting process is going on the laboring white man to whom the nation must in the long run look for the reproduction of the race and the bringing up and educating of citizens to take the place of the present generation as it passes away, and, above all, to defend the country in time of war, is injured in his comfort, reduced in his scale and standard of life, necessarily carrying down with it his moral and physical stamina.

"But what is even more immediately damaging to the State is the fact that he is kept in a perpetual state of anger, exasperation, and discontent, always bordering on sedition, thus jeopardizing the general peace and creating a state of chronic uneasiness, distrust, and apprehension throughout the entire community. . . ."

For many years it was impossible to get white persons to do the menial labor usually performed by Chinese. . . . Absolute servility was expected from those who took the place of the Chinaman, and it will take years to obliterate these traces of inferiority and re-establish the proper relations of employer and employee.

[According to the report of the Special Committee on Chinese Immigration to the California State Senate, 1878,] "A serious objection to slavery, as it existed in the Southern States, was that it tended to degrade white labor. The very same objection exists against Chinese labor in this State.

"The recent troubles in San Francisco are attributable to a class commonly known as 'hoodlums,' young [white] men who have grown up in idleness, without occupation of any kind and who in various ways prey upon society. This class is peculiar to San Francisco. Many of our thinkers argue that it owes its existence to the presence of a large Chinese population. For several years after the settlement of this State by Americans the population was an adult population. There were no boys. As boys grew up they found the places filled by Chinese, and very naturally looked upon any labor they performed as servile and degrading. Their pride, whether true or false is immaterial, kept them from entering the lists by the side of an abhorred race. If this view of the subject is correct, a fearful responsibility rests at the door of the advocates of Chinese labor.

"The employment of Chinese as agricultural laborers is most generally in droves, held in some sort of dependence by a head man or agent of the Chinese companies. The workmen live in sheds or in straw stacks, do their own cooking, have no homes, and are without interest in their work or the country. The white laborer who would compete with them must not only pursue the same kind of life, but must, like them, abdicate his individuality. The consequence would be lamentable, even if the white laborer should succeed by such means in driving the Asiatic from the field. We would in that event have a laboring class without homes, without families, and without any of the restraining influences of society.

"The slave owner at the South had an interest in his laborers, and even if the voice of humanity was silenced, yet that interest made him care for them. He gave them houses to live in, took care of them in sickness, and supported them when old age rendered them incapable. The owner of the Chinese laborers in this State has no such interest. His interest is co-extensive with and limited by the ability of his slave to earn money. In sickness he turns him over to the charity of the public. When disabled by age he leaves him to fate. It takes no prophet to foretell that if white labor is brought down to the level of Asiatic labor the white laborer will meet like treatment.

"The slaves of the South were, as a race, kind and faithful. The Chinese, as a race, are cruel and treacherous. In this by contrast all the advantage was with Southern slavery.

"On the whole, it is our judgment that unrestricted Chinese immigration tends more strongly to the degradation of labor, and to the subversion of our institutions, than did slavery at the South. It has all of the disadvantages of the African slavery, and none of its compensations."

. . . [According to an 1885 report by the San Francisco Board of Supervisors,] "In a sanitary point of view Chinatown presents a singular anomaly. With the habits, manners, customs, and whole economy of life violating every accepted rule of hygiene; with open cesspools, exhalations from waterclosets, sinks, urinals, and sewers tainting the atmosphere with noxious vapors and stifling odors; with people herded and packed in damp cellars, living literally the life of vermin, badly fed and clothed, addicted to the daily use of opium to the extent that many hours of each day or night are passed in the delirious stupefaction of its influence, it is not to be denied that, as a whole the general health of this locality compares more than favorably with other sections of the city which are surrounded by far more favorable conditions. . . ."

"It is from such pestholes as these that the Chinese cooks and servants who are employed in our houses come. Cleanly though they may be in appearance while acting in the capacity of domestic servants, they are nevertheless born and reared in these habits of life. The facility with which they put on habits of decency when they become cooks and servants simply adds other testimony to their ability to adapt themselves to circumstances when it is in their best interest to do so. But the instinct of the race remains unchanged; and when the Chinese servant leaves employment in an American household he joyfully hastens back to his slum and his burrow, to the grateful luxury of his normal surroundings, vice, filth, and an atmosphere of horror." . . .

As to their morality, they have no standard by which a Caucasian might judge them. . . . "It is a less difficult problem to ascertain the number of women and children in Chinatown than it is to give with accuracy the male population. First, because they are at present comparatively few in numbers; and, second, because they can nearly always be found in the localities which they inhabit. This investigation has shown, however, that whatever may be the domestic family relations of the Chinese Empire, here the relations of the sexes are chiefly so ordered as to provide for the gratification of the animal proclivities alone, with whatever result may chance to follow in the outcome of procreation."

There are apparently in Chinatown but few families living as such, with legitimate children. In most instances the wives are kept in a state of seclusion, carefully guarded and watched, as though "eternal vigilance" on the part of their husband "is the price of their virtue." Wherever there are families belonging to the better class of the Chinese, the women are guarded and secluded in the most careful manner. . . . With some few exceptions, the rule seems to be that they are here in a state of concubinage merely to minister to the animal passions of the other sex, with such perpetuation of the race as may be a resultant consequence, or else to follow the admitted calling of the prostitute, generally of the lowest possible grade, with all the wretchedness of life and consequence which the name implies. . . .

The most revolting feature of all, however, is found in the fact that there are so large a number of children growing up as the associates, and perhaps protegés, of the professional prostitutes. In one house alone, in Sullivan's alley, your committee found the inmates to be nineteen prostitutes and sixteen children. In the localities habited largely by prostitutes, women and children, who apparently occupy this intermediate family relationship already alluded to, live in adjoining apartments and intermingle freely, leading to the conclusion that prostitution is a recognized and not immoral calling with the race, and that it is impossible to tell by a survey of their domestic customs where the family relationship leaves off and prostitution begins. . . .

[A minister who had lived in China testified:]

> "The women as a general thing are slaves. They are bought or stolen in China and brought here. They have a sort of agreement to cover up the slavery business, but it is all a sham. . . ."

The Chinese are only capable of working under the present unsatisfactory system. All progress, then, to an improved organization of capital and labor would be arrested. We might have greater growth, but never greater development. It was estimated . . . that there were a million idle men in the United States in 1886. Certainly the 76,000 Chinese in California at that time stood for 76,000 white men waiting for employment. . . . If it be our only aim to increase our wealth so as to hold our own in the markets of the world, are we not, without the aid of Chinese coolies, capable of doing it, and at the same time preserve the character of our population and insure the perpetuity of our institutions? It is not wealth at any cost that sound public policy requires, but that the country be developed with equal pace and with a desirable population, which stands not only for industry, but for citizenship. . . .

The experience of the South with slave labor warned us against unlimited Chinese immigration considered both as a race question and as an economic problem. The Chinese, if permitted freely to enter this country, would create race antagonisms which would ultimately result in great public disturbance. . . .

If we were to return to the ante-bellum ideas of the South, now happily dis-carded, the Chinese would satisfy every requirement of a slave or servile class. They work well, they are docile, and they would not be concerned about their po-litical conditions; but such suggestions are repulsive to American civilization. America has dignified work and made it honorable. Manhood gives title to rights, and the Government being ruled by majorities, is largely controlled by the very class which servile labor would supersede, namely, the free and independent work-ingmen of America. The political power invested in men by this Government shows the absolute necessity of keeping up the standard of population and not permitting it to deteriorate by contact with inferior and nonassimilative races.

WE HAVE IT IN OUR POWER
Clare de Graffenreid

Though wage-earning women were largely excluded from men's labor organiza-tions in the latter half of the nineteenth century, they did mobilize on their own be-half. Among the most active women were those who worked in all-female occupations such as sewing and laundering, but factory operatives and typographers in "mixed" industries also formed associations. In the late 1870s the Knights of Labor, a more militant and democratic organization than the AFL, began to admit women, eventually recruiting over half a million.

Middle-class women also sought to improve conditions for wage-earning women, though their aims and attitudes often conflicted with those of the wage-earners themselves, for they regarded employment for women as a temporary mis-fortune, not a permanent feature of their lives. According to these reformers, work outside the home prevented married women from fulfilling their domestic responsi-bilities and was likely to corrupt single women. Nevertheless, recognizing that for some women, work was a necessity, middle-class reformers established organiza-tions such as the Working Women's Protective Union, chartered in 1863, to defend female wage-earners from unscrupulous employers and also to "protect women's purity and honor"—that is, keep them out of prostitution.

The Working Girls' Society, which specifically sought to recruit young single working women, had similar aims. The first chapter was founded in 1885 in New York City by Grace Hoadley Dodge, a wealthy New Yorker who came from a fam-ily renowned for its philanthropic activities. Dodge's idea was to provide an attrac-tive retreat for young women after their days' work, where, in addition to relaxation and socializing, they would be exposed to morally and culturally uplifting influ-ences that would eventually lead them to embrace a domestic role.

Dodge's idea did not, however, work out exactly as she had intended. Young working women flocked to the societies (between 1885 and 1897, eighteen centers were running in New York City alone, with a weekly attendance of 9,000), but in-stead of listening passively to talks about manners and fashion, they began to dis-

Source: Clare de Graffenreid, "What Do Working Girls Owe One Another?" in Association of Working Girls' Societies, *Discussions of the Convention Held in New York City, April 15th, 16th, and 17th, 1890* (New York), 1890, pp. 74–79.

cuss ways in which they could join together to improve their lot as wage-earners, transforming the society into an incipient union for women.

The following document, taken from the records of an 1890 convention that brought together representatives of a number of Working Girls' Societies in the New York area, captures the organization in the process of making this transition. In analyzing the speech and the discussion that followed, try to sort out statements that reflect the influence of the Victorian reformers who started the societies and those that indicate growing collective conscience on the part of the young women. As they discuss their interests as workers, do you see any parallels with the kinds of points stressed in "Meat vs. Rice"? Do you think their positions would lead these young women to side with the AFL or against it?

All great social and political causes, a recent critic observed, have first made their way among the working classes. The inspiring ideas came perhaps from a dreamer, but they waxed strong because the masses welcomed what the wealthy and cultivated have frowned upon or persecuted. We workers of today are pledged to the noblest of causes. A great idea, a lofty purpose must by our conduct and preaching be made to prevail in modern society and mould the industries of the future. It is the idea that the advancement of women depends as largely upon those women who earn their bread by the sweat of their brow, as upon the education or training of idlers or students or even home-keepers and care-takers. Women in business life are the entering wedge which will cleave custom or prejudice and make a wider range possible for female effort. Alone, singly, our powers and reach are feeble. But standing by each other, we can show the value of union. Backing this great crusade for every worthy post must be the purpose, the firm resolve, never to fall back upon our womanhood as excuse for deficiency or failure. As [labor reformer] Helen Campbell says, it must be a question of character and efficiency, not a question of sex. We have it in our power to make the employment of women in nearly all pursuits a recognized necessity, not as now a favor accompanied with lower pay and other odious discriminations. To render woman's work indispensable her services must be thorough and unassailable at each point. . . . Wage-earning women owe it to one another to uphold the dignity of labor and the character of workers as if we alone represented the whole industrial army and the eyes of the world were on us as its flag-bearer. Every toiler must do her duty as though there were no other worker living on whom she might depend to take up dropped threads or repair neglect. . . .

Next to thoroughness and integrity in our service, ranks our obligation of faithfulness and loyalty to each other. The sisterhood of the clubs should include also the workroom, where—is it not sadly true?—girls are sometimes far from loyal to each other. Severe is the temptation, when living is hard at best and want is imminent, to take unfair advantages to secure more work or a better job. Even without such awful goad of poverty it happens sometimes that great opportunities are lost to women workers through petty faults, or temper, or spite. Girls often abuse their forewomen, quarrel among themselves, or stand up foolishly for their rights when trifling concessions would accomplish more. . . . As a result, an employer, harassed with unnecessary bickerings, turns off [fires] all his girls; or a deserved promotion causes such wrath that he resolves no more to reward merit, but to keep everybody at the same low wages. . . .

Men, with good reason, charge that it is difficult to operate plans of any sort which require unselfish action among large bodies of women. "Girls have more grit than men," said the leader of a strike, "when you get them on their high horse in a meeting. But if one wants a spring frock, or another's young man is out of work and money, why, she'll slip back to her loom, and before you know it there's an end of the fight and you're dead whipped."

Women also, who have tried to conduct righteous strikes in behalf of the suffering and abused, declare that they cannot depend even on the girls whose injuries are greatest, one and another falling away from the cause, as her private interests seem to clash with the general good. Not only is the leader who has risked all this left shamefully in the lurch, but the downfall is wrought of a great reform, which would have helped all women. When some brave girl consents, if others will speak out, to put a grievance before the employer, often at the decisive moment the supporters weaken and withdraw, leaving the spokeswoman in the attitude of a faultfinder with whom none sympathize. The history of woman's advancement is the history of just such failures in concerted action, hence we have moved but by inches instead of by miles.

Until self is subordinated to the common welfare, until we strengthen instead of undermining each other, the day will never dawn of equal wage and equal opportunity for women with men.

One influence that pulls down instead of lifting our whole sisterhood, is the class difference that marks off the factory girl from the saleswoman, the tobacco worker from the dressmaker, and so through the whole social scale. . . . By class distinction is not meant that self-respect which rightly holds one aloof from vulgar or imprudent companions, for we all need to be careful of our associations and good name. What is blameworthy, what we owe it to each other to suppress, is the air of superiority or condescension. The only superiority on which we toilers and standard-bearers for our sex may pride ourselves, is the capacity for conscientious work. . . . If we are better educated than they, does not this good fortune lay upon us the sacred obligation to help them retrieve lacking advantages? Our social standing is higher, perhaps. Is it not a duty thus marked out for us, to lift others to our level, not push them back into obscurity? Have we personal gifts above our companions? Then wit, tact, grace, or accomplishment should be used to brighten sadder lives. . . .

To promote woman's advancement, we must strive for her economic independence in society and before the law, protecting her from degrading industries or conditions. As wage-earners, it behooves us to open new trades and lines of work, claiming wherever possible equal pay for equal service and responsibility. Free competition with men is not desirable. Under our present social system, who would not be hammer must be anvil, who would not trample others must be trampled. Woman can be equal with man, without being like man. Special vocations for the sexes, suitable occupations for each must be our aim, lest we become second-rate men.

At present most women are dependent for a livelihood on some man, or want to be. The power to earn her own living in proper channels would assure her economic equality, nor need she then form her whole character and model her career alone with a view of attracting men. As an independent wage-earner, she would be better able to develop her special gifts of womanhood; and whether married or single, the ability to maintain herself honorably whenever she chooses, is essential to her dignity and freedom. To gain these ends women must stand shoulder to shoulder. There must be no falling back on comfortable homes as a reason for taking less than our services are worth; no working for mere pocket-money, thus underbidding the self-supporting girl without a home; no lowering of already small wages by forcing in child-rivals; no desertion of useful organizations from the pinch of personal want, or motives of personal resentment. The essential fact of organization is that when one member suffers all members suffer with it.

This is better than competition, which means warfare. Organization means united effort, and women must test its power, less for aggression than for resistance and progress. All the best work of the world is done by organization. One weak wage-earner is a cipher, but backed by a hundred brave, steady, loyal, and keen-witted working girls, bound by common zeal for the general good, this one feeble toiler becomes a tremendous object. Did we know how to get our rights, fewer wrongs would cry for remedy. What our sex lacks is clear thinking, prompt doing. We scatter, where we should combine our energies. Each denounces wrong, and all agree to denounce wrong together. . . . A better era of recognition and justice to women will be ushered in when five thousand girl-workers, representing fifty thousand alert self-educating and self-denying toilers, will rally and, abreast and trumpet-tongued, voice a common woe or a common want.

DISCUSSION
From the Industrial Society, Hoboken.

1. A working girl is doing other working girls an injury when she consents to work for less than "living wages." A girl who is supported by her parents and only works for pocket-money or to buy her clothes, or a young married woman who works for the same objects, can afford to take lower wages than a girl who has to pay her own board, etc.

2. Foreigners should not be brought over to compete with American girls. They will work for less than "living wages," because they are accustomed to go without what an American girl would consider the common decencies of life.

3. Older hands in a store or factory should do what they can to help new-comers. We believe in this as a general principle, but the new-comers sometimes show themselves ungrateful. For instance, in the silk mill in which many of our members are employed, new hands, or "learners" as they are called, work for one and a half cents less a yard than the old hands. They in some cases remain "learners" for four years, and the price of labor is thus lowered.

4. We do not approve of the principle of strikes. We should prefer to see all matters referring to labor and capital, regulated by law. For this purpose representatives should be sent to Congress who would really represent the wage-earners and their interests.

5. . . . Strikes, in rare instances and in the present state of the laws, are justified, when the employer attempts to bring the wages paid down to starvation rates. They will only succeed if the girls all go out together and if they all remain firm.

6. If one girl sees another doing her work badly, she should not report her, but rather try to show her how to do the work. If a girl sees any dishonesty, she should warn the offender and if it continues she should then tell the employer.

7. It ought to make no difference in the quality of a girl's work whether she has a good or a bad employer. It is always to a girl's interest to do the work well, for she then feels that she is independent and can always get another place.

8. One good and pure-minded girl often elevates the tone of those working with her. Any girl with common sense will be disgusted with the conversation of a "tough" girl.

Girls soon divide into groups according to their tastes and characters. If the good girls predominate, the "toughs" are afraid to talk out. One good girl has more influence than one "tough." We have noticed the superiority of girls belonging to our societies. Their good thoughts are strengthened here. They are helped by the Practical Talks [offered by the socieities].

HE ALLOWS HIMSELF TO "HAVE FUN" WITH THE WORKING GIRLS
A Shopgirl

Women labor activists were especially concerned about the plight of women who worked in sweatshops, the small, labor-intensive workshops that predominated in certain industries such as the needle trades. With few alternatives, newly-arrived immigrants were often compelled to put up with highly exploitative conditions. In this case, however, one young woman chose to speak out by writing to *The Jewish Daily Forward,* a highly influential socialist newspaper that was published in Yiddish and reached millions of garment workers in New York City. What made this shopgirl so vulnerable? How might a union have helped her?

Dear Editor,

I am one of those unfortunate girls thrown by fate into a dark and dismal shop, and I need your counsel.

Along with my parents, sisters and brothers, I came from Russian Poland where I had been well educated. But because of the terrible things going on in Russia we were forced to emigrate to America. I am now seventeen years old, but I look younger and they say I am attractive.

A relative talked us into moving to Vineland, New Jersey, and here in this small town I went to work in a shop. In this shop there is a foreman who is an exploiter, and he sets prices on the work. He figures it out so that the wages are very low, he insults and reviles the workers, he fires them and then takes them back. And worse than all of this, in spite of the fact that he has a wife and several children, he often allows himself to "have fun" with some of the working girls. It was my bad luck to be one of the girls that he tried to make advances to. And woe to any girl who doesn't willingly accept them.

Though my few hard-earned dollars mean a lot to my family of eight souls, I didn't want to accept the foreman's vulgar advances. He started to pick on me, said my work was no good, and when I proved to him he was wrong, he started to shout at me in the vilest language. He insulted me in Yiddish and then in English, so the American workers could understand too. Then, as if the Devil were after me, I ran home.

I am left without a job. Can you imagine my circumstances and that of my parents who depend on my earnings? The girls in the shop were very upset over the foreman's vulgarity but they don't want him to throw them out, so they are afraid to be witnesses against him. What can be done about this? I beg you to answer me.

Respectfully,
A Shopgirl

Source: Letter from "A Shopgirl" to "Bintel Brief," *The Jewish Daily Forward,* 1907; in *A Bintel Brief,* comp. Isaac Metzker, (Garden City, NY: Doubleday, 1971), p. 72.

SIMPLE, PRACTICAL KNOWLEDGE
Hampton Institute

One of the main goals of African Americans in the post–Civil War South was to acquire the education that had been systematically denied to them under slavery. Southern states did not, however, have public schools, so African Americans were faced with the dual task of building institutions for themselves while simultaneously campaigning for universal education. Due to persistent white opposition to black education, the outcome was not equal education for all but the highly stratified segregated school system that became one of the hallmarks of the Jim Crow South.

In their quest for education, Southern blacks had assistance from the Freedmen's Bureau, Republican politicians, and white Northern benevolent organizations and missionary societies. The motives of these reformers were mixed. While some believed that African Americans could benefit from—and deserved—the same kind of education available to whites, others contended that because blacks were not fit for full social and political participation in society, their education should prepare them for only the lowest occupations such as domestic service and manual labor.

One advocate of this latter position was Samuel Chapman Armstrong (1839–1893), a white retired Union general who, with the aid of the American Missionary Society, founded the Hampton Institute in Virginia in 1868. Armstrong believed that economic efficiency would attract Northern capital to the South; accordingly, black elementary schools should teach black children to become "productive" members of the labor force. The goal of the Hampton Institute was to train black teachers who would then inculcate in black students the principle of the "dignity of labor" and serve as role models. Future female teachers, for example, were urged to avoid fancy clothing and instead wear "thick-soled shoes and simple dresses."

Tuskegee Institute in Alabama, founded in 1881 by Armstrong's prize student, Booker T. Washington (1856–1915), was designed along similar lines. In both schools, the curriculum emphasized Christian morality and consisted of both general subjects and practical courses in manual training. Students were also required to work in one of the maintenance or service departments, such as the laundry, housekeeping, print shop, or dairy.

The excerpts below are taken from the Hampton Institute catalogue for 1898–99. How did notions of gender determine the types of occupations for which male and female teachers (and, ultimately, their students) were being trained?

MIDDLE YEAR

Manual Training *For Boys. Course in Wood-turning requiring about 120 hours.* Turning between centers: centering, roughing with gouge, turning to size, testing with calipers, smoothing with skew chisel, measuring and cutting to length, turning straight tapers, outer curve, inner curve, combination of curves in making chisel

Source: *Catalogue of the Hampton Normal and Agricultural Institute, Hampton, Virginia, for the Academic Year 1898–99* (Hampton: Institute Press, 1899), pp. 22–23, 26–27.

FIGURE 3.3

Practical training at Hampton Institute was strictly gendered; men were taught trades such as blacksmithing, carpentry, woodturning, printing, and shoemaking, while women were restricted to courses in sewing, dressmaking, cooking, and practical nursing. (*Sources: Wheelwright Shop,* Catalogue of the Hampton Normal and Agricultural Institute for 1897–98 *(Hampton: Institute Press, 1898), p. 71; Class in Cooking,* Catalogue for 1899–1900, *p. 36.*

handle, testing by the eye, cutting shoulders, cutting beads, cutting flutes, turning section on square piece, sand-papering, polishing with shellac.

Face Plate Work:—knob, corner block, match box, barrel, vase, and napkin ring.

In connection with the above exercises there are taught the following:— Reading drawings, lessons on materials used, care of lathes with names of parts.

Course in Tin-Smithing, requiring about 100 hours:—Laying out and developing patterns for cylinders, cones, pyramids and other geometric forms. Cutting to straight and curved lines, joining edges by seaming, riveting and soldering. Making up useful articles, such as a tin cup, square pan or box, covered pail, dust-pan, etc., two and three piece elbows in stove pipe, making T joints, Y joints, sheet-iron dripping-pan and chimney top. Use of fluxes, on tin, galvanized iron, copper, lead and zinc. Use of all the common tinner's tools and machines.

Manual Training   *For Girls. Sewing*;—Continuation of the work of the Junior year. Each student cuts and makes for herself a full set of underclothes.

Cooking, three and a half months, four hours a week. The aim of the course is to teach the principles underlying good cooking, and to give the simple, practical knowledge needed in the home life of the South.

The course of instruction includes making and care of fires, dish washing and care of kitchen, talks on fuels and foods. Baking apples, potatoes, etc., boiling vegetables and eggs, steaming. Lessons in buying meat. Cooking of meats, warmed-over dishes, soups, broiling and stewing. Simple and invalid cooking. Biscuits and cookies, bread, plain cake, plain pastry. Cooking of poultry, fish, and eggs. Tea, coffee, cocoa. Setting table.

These lessons are accompanied by instruction in the chemistry of cooking so far as it applies in the practical work.

SENIOR YEAR

Special Lessons in Nursing and Hygiene (*for girls.*) Instruction in the care of a sick-room and the small attentions necessary to the comfort of an invalid; different ways of ventilating a room; bathing; the functions of the skin, preparation of the different local applications, including poultices, mustard plasters, etc., and the methods of applying the roller bandage, the triangle and cravat. . . .

Manual Training   *For boys. Course in Forging requiring about 120 hours.* The building and care of fires, heating the iron. Drawing square iron to a point, to flat, to bevel, and to round. Drawing from round to square, from square to octagon, from octagon to round. Bending rings of round and flat iron. Pointing and bending a staple. Drawing, bending and twisting in making a hook. . . . Punching and cutting square and hexagon nuts. . . .

For girls. Sewing. Students are given talks on colors and material used, and taught to draft and cut from patterns, and each girl makes herself a dress.

NOW THEY BUILD HOUSES
Carl Schurz

A number of the students at Hampton Institute were Native Americans who had been sent there by the Bureau of Indian Affairs; others attended the Carlisle Indian

Industrial School in western Pennsylvania, which adhered to a similar philosophy. By the 1880s, most of the Native American population had been confined on reservations. The East Coast tribes had been driven West, and indigenous Western tribes had been subjugated by a series of bloody wars with federal troops. Initially based on tribal ownership of land, the reservations were broken up into smaller parcels after passage of the Dawes Severalty Act in 1887, which allowed individual ownership of plots. All of this was part of the federal plan to "civilize" the Indians, that is, compel them to live according to Euro-American standards.

Not surprisingly, Victorian gender roles were an essential component of the government's plan. In 1881, Carl Schurz (1829–1906), then Secretary of the Interior, described this plan in detail. How does Schurz characterize the Indians' former way of life? What has induced them to change? How will their new gender roles differ from their old ones?

> . . . To fit Indians for their ultimate absorption in the great body of American citizenship, three things are suggested by common sense as well as philanthropy.
>
> That they be taught to work by making work profitable and attractive to them.
>
> That they be educated, especially the youth of both sexes.
>
> That they be individualized in the possession of property by settlement in severalty with a fee simple title, after which the lands they do not use may be disposed of for general settlement and enterprise without danger and with profit to the Indians.
>
> This may seem a large programme, strangely in contrast with the old wildlife of the Indians, but they are now more disposed than ever before to accept it. Even those of them who have so far been in a great measure living upon the chase, are becoming aware that the game is fast disappearing, and will no longer be sufficient to furnish them a sustenance. In a few years the buffalo will be exterminated, and smaller game is gradually growing scarce except in the more inaccessible mountain regions. The necessity of procuring food in some other ways is thus before their eyes. The requests of Indians addressed to the government for instruction in agriculture, for agricultural implements, and for stock cattle, are in consequence now more frequent and pressing then ever before. A more general desire for the education of their children springs from the same source, and many express a wish for the allotment of farm tracts among them, with "the white man's paper," meaning a good, strong title like that held by white men. . . . The general state of feeling among the redmen is therefore now exceedingly favorable to the civilizing process. That Indians can be successfully employed at various kinds of mechanical work, has already been tested. A respectable number of their young men serve as apprentices in the saddler, blacksmith, shoe-maker, tinsmith and carpenter shops at the agencies in the West, as well as the Indian schools, and their proficiency is much commended. . . . Many Indians who, but a few years ago, did nothing but hunting and fighting, are now engaged in building houses for their families, and, with some instruction and aid on the part of the Government, they are doing reasonably well. . . . The significant point is that, recognizing the change in their situation, Indian men now almost generally accept work as a necessity, while formerly all the drudgery was done by their women. The civilized tribes in the Indian Territory and elsewhere have already proved their capacity for advancement in a greater measure.

Source: Carl Schurz, "Present Aspects of the Indian Problem," *North American Review,* vol. 133, n. 296, (1881), pp. 13–17.

One of the most important agencies in the civilizing process is, of course, education in schools. The first step was the establishment of day-schools on the reservations for Indian children. . . . With the exception of a few hours spent in school, the children remained exposed to the influence of their more or less savage home surroundings, and the indulgence of their parents greatly interfered with the regularity of their attendance and with the necessary discipline. Boarding schools at the agencies were then tried, as far as the appropriations made by Congress would permit, adding to the usual elementary education some practical instruction in housework and domestic industries. The results thus obtained were perceptibly better, but even the best boarding-school located on Indian reservations, in contact with no phase of human life except that of the Indian camp or village, still remains without those conditions of which the work of civilizing the growing Indian generation stands most in need.

The Indian, in order to be civilized, must not only learn how to read and write, but how to live. . . .

The results gained at these [boarding] institutions are very striking. The native squalor of the Indian boys and girls rapidly gives way to neat appearance. A new intelligence, lighting up their faces, transforms their expression. Many of them show an astonishing eagerness to learn, quickness of perception, pride of accomplishment, and love for their teachers. . . .

Especial attention is given in the Indian schools to the education of Indian girls. . . . This is of particular importance. The Indian woman has only so far been a beast of burden. The girl, when arrived at maturity, was disposed of like an article of trade. The Indian wife was treated by her husband alternately with animal fondness, and with the cruel brutality of the slave-driver. Nothing will be more apt to raise the Indians in the scale of civilization than to stimulate their attachment to permanent homes, and it is woman that must make the atmosphere and form the attraction of the home. She must be recognized, with affection and respect, as the center of domestic life. If we want the Indians to respect their women, we must lift up the Indian women to respect themselves. This is the purpose and work of education. If we educate the girls of to-day, we educate the mothers of to-morrow, and in educating those mothers we prepare the ground for the education of generations to come. Every effort made in that direction is, therefore, entitled to especial sympathy and encouragement. . . .

THE NATURAL ENEMY OF THE SALOONS
Frances E. Willard

One of the mainstays of the "maternal commonwealth" was the Woman's Christian Temperance Union, founded in 1874 by Frances Willard (1839–1898). An all-female organization, the WCTU did not reject the idea of gender difference but in fact claimed political power on the grounds that women were "naturally" superior to men. Acting on the belief that drinking destroyed American homes by diverting men from their assigned roles as breadwinners, the WCTU raided saloons, smashed liquor barrels and prevailed upon men to "take the pledge" of temperance. In addition to their work on temperance and suffrage, members followed a "Do-Everything" program which included a range of social services to the poor and single mothers.

The "Home Protection Ballot" was the centerpiece of the WCTU's struggle for woman suffrage. In an 1879 manual, Willard explained in detail how to mount a local campaign and included as a sample the suffrage petition used by the Illinois chapter. The back of the petition contained a supporting article women were to have printed in their hometown newspapers. How do the petition and article link temperance and suffrage? What image of women is presented? Why do you think the petition calls for only a limited franchise for women?

FOR GOD AND HOME AND NATIVE LAND

HOME PROTECTION PETITION . . .

TO THE SENATE AND HOUSE OF REPRESENTATIVES OF THE STATE OF ILLINOIS:

Whereas, In these years of temperance work the argument of defeat in our contest with the saloons has taught us that our efforts are merely palliative of a disease in the body politic, which can never be cured until law and moral suasion go hand in hand in our beloved state; and

Whereas, The instincts of self-protection and of apprehension for the safety of her children, her tempted loved ones, and her home render women the natural enemy of the saloons; *Therefore,* your petitioners, men, and women of the State of Illinois, having at heart the protection of our homes from their worst enemy, the legalized traffic in strong drink, do hereby most earnestly pray your honorable body that, by suitable legislation, it may be provided that in the State of Illinois the question of licensing at any time, in any locality, the sale of any and all intoxicating drinks shall be submitted to and determined by ballot, in which women of lawful age shall be privileged to take part, in the same manner as men, when voting on the question of license.

BACK OF THE PETITION
[Please have this Printed in Local Papers.]

. . . In a recent "Monday Lecture," REV. JOSEPH COOK, of Boston, spoke thus:

"There stands a noble statehouse in the cornfields near Springfield, Illinois, and Lincoln's grave lies under its shadow. Above his grave a legislature will be petitioned this winter by ladies of Illinois to give women of legal age the right to vote in cases of local option under temperance laws. . . . In New Hampshire the line has already been broken as to the exclusion of women from participation in the settlement of questions closely touching the home. Let it be noticed that New Hampshire, a conservative New England state, has just given to women the right to vote on all questions concerning the school laws. I am not a woman suffragist. Do not applaud this platform under the mistaken idea that I am a defender of extreme positions as to woman's rights. I am meditating on that theme. But this I dare say, that one of the fragments of self-protection for women—namely, a

Source: Frances E. Willard, *Home Protection Manual* (New York: The Independent, 1879), 27–28.

right to vote, concerning temperance laws, when the question of local option is up—I am willing to defend, and intend to defend, to the end of the chapter. Great natural justice is on the side of such a demand. Woman's interests are among the chief ones concerned; and as to family divisions, why, they come largely from temperance laxness. Woman surely has political intelligence enough to understand the difference between license and no license, especially when she has suffered under a lax execution of temperance laws. The difference is so plain between local freedom and no local freedom to sell liquor that woman without any great participation in the turmoil of politics might be expected to have an intelligent vote on this subject. I know that many cultivated and refined women say they do not want women to vote, because they do not want to increase the amount of ignorant suffrage. Well, I respect the intelligence and the refinement of the ladies who make such remarks; but I believe that on most moral questions woman is likely to be more intelligent and certainly more disinterested than man. I am told by many of the best authorities that women who are opposed to female suffrage at large are usually in favor of this modified measure. I am assured that a majority of the thoughtful, cultivated women of the United States, or certainly of the Northern states, can be expected to favor this demand for a vote to be given to women in questions of local option, concerning temperance laws. If a majority of women want such a vote, Heaven grant their desire! Women would be united on this topic. Woman's vote would be to city vices depending on intemperance what the lightning is to the oak. God send us that lightning!" [Applause.]

NOT SO LONG AS WOMEN ARE CHEAP LABOR
Mary Kenney O'Sullivan

While the WCTU and the other women's suffrage organizations were made up largely of middle-class women, working-class women, led by the Women's Trade Union League, also struggled for the vote. The league was founded in 1903 by Mary Kenney O'Sullivan, a bookbinder from Chicago, and William English Walling, a wealthy New England reformer. Bringing together women of all classes, the coalition aimed at improving the conditions of women workers. Because of O'Sullivan's central role, the WTUL (unlike the Working Women's Protective Union or the Working Girls' Society discussed earlier in this chapter) gave working-class women a voice in the organization from the outset. O'Sullivan, frustrated by her years working as an organizer for the AFL, understood that the male-dominated trade unions were unwilling to struggle on women's behalf. The WTUL exerted pressure by recruiting female members into unions and then demanding that they be protected.

How does O'Sullivan think having the vote will specifically help women workers? How do her arguments differ from those of the WCTU, or of Elizabeth Cady Stanton (presented in Chapter 2)? How does O'Sullivan's view of women's employment compare with that of the AFL officials presented earlier in this chapter?

Source: Mary Kenney O'Sullivan, "Why the Working Woman Needs the Vote," pamphlet (New York: National American Woman Suffrage Association, n.d. [1910]).

Every year more and more women are going into industry. Why is that?

1. COST OF LIVING is rising, and in many families the woman's wages are needed to eke out the family income.
2. THE STANDARD OF LIVING is rising, and workingmen's families demand better conditions, and MUST have a larger income to meet them.
3. Women living in cities can no longer help sustain the family by farm work, dairy work, or by spinning and weaving; therefore their only ways of helping to provide for the family are

EITHER to take work home, which in most cases produces the evil results of sweat-shop work with poor conditions of work and poorer pay;

OR to go out to work in factory or shop.

Now, IS the woman's work a help to the family in the long run?

NOT SO LONG AS WOMEN ARE CHEAP LABOR.

Every union man knows how dangerous and harmful is the competition of child labor; it is dangerous BECAUSE IT IS CHEAP, and cuts down the man's wages.

Women's labor, AS LONG AS IT IS CHEAP, is just as dangerous, and for just the same reason. When women organize and vote they will get EQUAL PAY for EQUAL WORK, and they will no longer compete unfairly with men. Then men's wages will improve, and, though fewer women will be employed at the higher wages, this will not be a hardship because the increase in the man's wages will give the family the large income needed without its being necessary for so many women to work outside the home.

Woman suffrage has been endorsed not only by the American Federation of Labor, but also by the State Federations of Labor of California, Connecticut, Colorado, Illinois, Indiana, Kansas, Maine, Maryland, Massachusetts, Michigan, Minnesota, New Hampshire, New York, Ohio, Oklahoma, Oregon, Pennsylvania, Tennessee, Washington, West Virginia and others.

Workingwomen, protect your own interests and demand VOTES FOR WORKING WOMEN.

SHE CALLED ME "HER BOY"
M. Carey Thomas

Until the late nineteenth century, the notion of passionlessness dominated European American middle-class ideas about women's sexual feelings toward men. To be sure, many individual women experienced powerful sexual awakenings during courtship or marriage, but they tended to confide their feelings only to their diaries or to close friends, leaving women's public image pristine. This denial of women's sexuality also extended to same-sex relationships, opening up a vast social space in which women could express intense feelings toward one another both verbally and physically without arousing suspicion that they shared anything more than a passionate—but sexually innocent—friendship. As we shall see in Chapter 6, the notion of passionlessness began to break down during the 1890s, with the publication of British sexologist Havelock Ellis' articles about "mannish lesbians," women whose feelings toward other women were as strong and sexual as any man's. From then on, women's same-sex relationships tended to come under suspicion.

A daughter of the Victorian age, M. Carey Thomas (1857–1935), the founding dean and second president of Bryn Mawr College, grew up in a family of strong women who valued their friendships with other women, both relatives and friends, and inspired Carey, as she called herself, to do the same. Encouraged by her Quaker parents to pursue both education and a career, Thomas took advantage of the new opportunities opening up for women. To prepare for college she attended the Howland School in upstate New York and in 1875 joined the first class of women admitted to Cornell University.

Thomas' journal entries from these years indicate that school and college engaged her emotions as well as her intellect. The following excerpts reveal Thomas' feelings about her female classmates, but it should be noted that while at Cornell she also became involved with a young man named Francis Gummere, whom she eventually threw over out of fear that marriage would prevent her from pursuing a career. After college and throughout her adult life, Thomas sustained several enduring relationships with women, including one with Mary Garrett, a fellow educator who lived openly with her in the Deanery at Bryn Mawr.

At several points in her journal, Thomas describes herself as having "smashed" on another young woman. Historians have conducted lively debates about the substance and meaning of this term and the passionate friendships between women it seemed to connote. Some have argued that while not necessarily sexual (in the sense of involving genital contact), these relationships were nonetheless fully committed and emotionally satisfying. What do the following excerpts tell us about Thomas' feelings toward other women during this period in her life? In what way does the idea of passionlessness permit her to express herself freely?

Spring 1873 [undated]

. . . I took up my journal today though with the intention of writing about a friendship of last term in case it should never be renewed that at least I may have *some* remembrance. It was with Libbie Conkey—we got acquainted, how I hardly know. The girls said we "smashed" on each other or "made love" I don't know—I only know it was elegant. She called me "her boy" her "liebe knabe" and she was my "Elsie." We used to see each other oftenest in Professor Satterthaite's room in the gallery of the gymnasium hall and there after supper we would sit and talk in the twilight. Then after all the classes I would wait for her and we would walk over together— we studied Latin—she was reading the Fifth book of Virgil and I read it with her for fun (I think we learnt something else except Latin, at least I learned to care for her more than I knew). Always in fact *every* Sunday evening last term, after tea, we would talk and at last I cared so much about her that my lessons were a secondary matter. Well, the end of the term came—I wrote her a piece of poetry—we said "Goodbye"—she went to Rochester, I home—that is all about the very pleasantest friendship that I have ever had. Of course she may come back next year and we have letters, but her "boy" is very lonely here. There is nobody I care about that *way*

Source: *The Making of A Feminist: Early Journals and Letters of M. Carey Thomas,* ed. Marjorie Housepian Dobkin (Kent, Ohio: Kent State University Press, 1979), pp. 90, 116–19; reprinted with permission.

now—Oh Journal why is it that when you get to care so much about people life is nothing but Goodbyes, some longer, some shorter—But now my own "sweetheart" goodbye once more on paper, and if we should never meet again this page of my journal will always call up "Memories and Remembrance sweet" of my darling Elsie.

June 12, 1877

Sage College, Cornell University. . . . At first I rather looked down on the girls in our hall. Miss Hicks, Miss Putnam, Miss Mills, Miss Head and Miss Mitchell—they seemed more interested in fun than anything else. And not one of them was smart except Miss Hicks; the other girls in the Sage were good enough students but not ladies, and the gentlemen, except Prof. Boyesen, were second rate, "half cut" Bessie would say.

Well, I began to see more and more of Miss Hicks. She got in the habit of coming and reading me her mother's letters and of bidding me good night. We used to go and study some time in Casquadilla woods and when it would get dark we would sit under her blue shawl and talk. Then we came across Swinburne's "Atalanta in Calydon"[1] and Miss Hicks would come in her wrapper after I was in bed and we would read it out loud and we learned several of the choruses. One night we had stopped reading later than usual and obeying a sudden impulse I turned to her and asked, "Do you love me?" She threw her arms around me and whispered, "I love you passionately." She did not go home that night and we talked and talked. She told me she had been praying that I might care for her.

That was the beginning and from that time, it was the fall of '75, till June '77 we have been inseparable. I put this all down because I cannot understand it. I am sure it is not best for people to care about each other so much. In the first place it wasted my time—it was a pleasure to be with Miss Hicks and as I cared to be with no one else, I would have spent all that time in reading. It was different with her—as she likes a great many people and liked the other girls and would have wasted her time anyway. In the second place it was almost more pain than pleasure because we quarreled so. All our ideas were opposite. Miss Hicks' mother I think is rising in society and there is not the least bit of fastidiousness in Miss Hicks' nature. She likes everyone. She cares for everyone's opinion. She would do a great many things I did not think suitable. I would object and say more than I ought to and Miss Hicks would fling herself on the lounge in a passion of tears and sometimes we would both cry—altogether it was dreadful—yet all the time we cared about each other so much that we could not give up our friendship. Again and again we gave up in despair and then we would care and have such lovely times that we began again and the whole thing was over again. Often I prayed that I might stop loving her.

This high tragedy seems ridiculous written but I know I shall forget the possibility of such things unless I do. It seems rather too bad when one goes to college to study to be distracted by such things. It was not Miss Hicks' fault but I know I did not study as well because of her, but I could not help it. I was mastered by it—one

---

[1]Extravagantly emotional, the writings of Swinburne, a British Romantic poet, were as scandalous to his contemporaries as Walt Whitman's were to Victorian Americans. According to Thomas's biographer Helen Horowitz, however, Swinburne's poetry provided Thomas and her friends with a language for their own feelings.

thing that made our friendship as unpleasant as it sometimes was was my feeling that I ought not to give way to it. Miss Hicks has no generous abandon in study—her companionship did not help me, I think, in an intellectual way. I tell her she ought to be obliged to me. I taught her to love passionately and to be passionately angry. Neither of which she had experienced before.

She is lovely in many ways. She has a sweet simplicity and straightforwardness about her, an utter faithfulness—I would trust her absolutely with any secret—she is naturally very smart but I think, at least until she came to Cornell, she studies because she had nothing else to do and because of her love of approbation. She wants to be an architect and seems very fond of it but I do not feel as if she would make a success. She seems to me to be easily turned aside by people. It is hard to talk to her—I never feel except when she is angry as if she were really saying what she feels with all her heart. In her manners she wants a certain quiet self assurance. I think she will probably get married. These are almost all unfavorable things but I leave out all her prettiness and her traits of character that attract me—in fact I just fell in love with her and I did it gradually too (not that adoring worship I had for Libbie [Conkey], nor the equal fun and earnest loving devoted friendship Carrie and I have) but, that Atalanta night I knew I did not care as much as she did and so it went on, I getting fonder and fonder of her until it was as I say—all the time against my better judgment and yet I cannot tell why it was. She is lovely, in many many ways much better than I am.

RECOMMENDED READINGS

Aron, Cindy Sondik. *Ladies and Gentlemen of the Civil Service: Middle-Class Workers in Victorian America.* New York, 1987.

Baron, Ava, ed. *Work Engendered: Toward a New History of American Labor.* Ithaca, 1991.

Blewett, Mary. *Men, Women, and Work: A Study of Class, Gender and Protest in the Nineteenth-Century New England Shoe Industry.* Urbana, 1988.

Gabler, Edwin. *The American Telegrapher: A Social History, 1860–1900.* New Brunswick, 1988.

Horowitz, Helen Lefkowitz. *The Power and Passion of M. Carey Thomas.* New York, 1994.

Ignatiev, Noel. *How the Irish Became White.* New York, 1995.

Janiewski, Dolores. *Sisterhood Denied: Race, Gender, and Class in a New South Community.* Philadelphia, 1985.

Kwolek-Folland, Angel. *Engendering Business: Men and Women in the Corporate Office, 1870–1930.* Baltimore, 1994.

Levine, Susan. *Labor's True Women: Carpet Weavers, Industrialization, and Labor Reform in the Gilded Age.* Philadelphia, 1984.

Lystra, Karen. *Searching the Heart: Women, Men and Romantic Love in Nineteenth-Century America.* New York, 1992.

Roediger, David. *The Wages of Whiteness: Race and the Making of the American Working Class.* New York, 1991.

Smith-Rosenberg, Carroll. *Disorderly Conduct: Visions of Gender in Victorian America.* New York, 1985.

Yung, Judy. *Unbound Feet: A Social History of Chinese Women in San Francisco.* Berkeley, 1995.

Gender Anarchy, 1890–1930

Between the 1890s and 1930, the Victorian gender system crumbled. Dominant gender ideals were transformed, and with them the ways that women and men actually lived. Because there was no consensus even on the ideals within a single class during these years, we have identified the period as an era of gender anarchy.

At the base of this upheaval lay the expansion and reorganization of production that industrialization had set in motion. By 1900, the United States outproduced every other country in the world and actually manufactured more each year than its three closest competitors combined. Financial and industrial enterprises increasingly aggregated smaller enterprises into huge corporations, promoting the specialization of both manufacturing and office work. Economic expansion drew unprecedented numbers of immigrants to the United States, created new types of jobs that transformed the work lives and expectations of both women and men, encouraged the migration of rural dwellers to urban areas, and pushed the United States onto the world stage.

Gender was implicated in every one of these trends. Each immigrant ship steaming to New York or San Francisco, for instance, disgorged with its passengers their unique gender systems. Between 1880 and 1930, both the pace and origins of immigration changed. Over twenty-five million newcomers arrived in the United States during this period; more than eight million between 1901 and 1910 alone. While China and northern and western Europe had supplied most previous immigrants, southern and eastern Europe provided the bulk of this "new immigration." Over three million Italians, at least three million Slavs, and two million eastern European Jews counted among the new arrivals. After 1900, immigration from Mexico and the Philippines increased as well, with over one million Mexicans resettled before the Great Depression.

Varying economic roles embodied the conflicting gender ideals of America's increasingly diverse population. Married African American women, for example, were much more likely to work for pay than any other group of married women. In the face of impossibly low wages for male breadwinners, some immigrant groups—and most native-born whites—chose to keep wives home and to send children into the labor market, but African Americans often preferred to keep children in school as long as possible and to rely instead on mothers' wage-earning. Likewise, Jewish immigrants from eastern Europe had fewer qualms about women's economic activity than many other immigrant groups, and Chinese immigrant men, vastly outnumbering Chinese women, formed bachelor communities in western cities where men did work traditionally associated with women as well as men.

While economic dilemmas carried over from earlier decades, the late nineteenth century brought new difficulties for black Americans. In the 1890s, with Reconstruction only a memory, southern states began to take the vote away from black men—and many poor whites—through poll taxes, unfairly enforced literacy tests, and lynchings. As the testimony of Henry MacNeal Turner would suggest, this challenged black manhood. Many of those states also passed laws that required racial segregation in public places and even in private relationships (some states forbade interracial marriages). By the 1910s, these assaults combined with the promise of employment in the North to open a decades long migration of African Americans from the rural South to the urban North and West, an exodus called the Great Migration. Relocation to urban areas as well as white offensives against black freedoms reformulated gender identities among many African Americans.

In fact, urbanization, the emergence of mass culture (especially in the forms of movies, radio, and phonograph records), and the general commercialization of entertainment upset gender expectations among all newcomers to America's growing cities at the turn of the century. Wage-earning gave young people access to these new diversions and helped them to establish a youth culture that set them apart from their elders. Among their peers, America's youth experimented with sex to a degree that their parents had not and created new sexual expectations, especially among women. The same conditions allowed gay men and lesbians to form communities protected by urban anonymity and distance from familial supervision.

Problems generated by the vast movement of peoples into urban areas helped to produce a period of such vital reform activity that the years between 1890 and 1920 are often designated the Progressive era. Working mostly in gender-segregated organizations with gender-specific tactics, male and female reformers demanded governmental social services for those dislocated and exploited by the reorganization of production. They also tried to protect government from corruption by both unscrupulous corporate interests and what they considered the inexperience of newcomers to American cities. Progressives won a broad array of changes which, taken together, strengthened the state, politicized womanhood—especially by winning women the vote—and diminished the perceived "independence" of white men.

The American government increased its power in foreign as well as domestic policy in this period. Through participation in the Spanish-American-Cuban-Filipino War (1898) and repeated military interventions in Central America and the Caribbean, the United States came to dominate many of its southern neighbors. Distant and delayed participation in World War I not only inserted U.S. diplomats into European politics but more importantly lifted the United States to the position of a creditor rather than a debtor nation.

While the war temporarily opened new employment possibilities for women and narrowed the acceptable options for manly identification, it ultimately encouraged the continuation of trends that led in the 1920s to the shadowy emergence of a new, dominant gender system. This modern gender ideal held that in politics, education, employment, and sexuality, women and men were more alike than Victorian women and men were expected to be. But the modern gender system continued to subordinate women to men and to promote great variations among classes, races, and ethnicities.

This section is organized topically. Consequently, documents in each chapter span the entire period from 1890 to 1930. In some cases, you may wish to read all the documents from the 1910s or 1920s in an effort to devise a portrait of gender/sexual systems within a particular decade.

FIGURE 4.1
"One of the Disadvantages of Being in Love with an Athletic Girl." Artists drew the New Woman as physically adventurous, a far cry from the frailty and timidity of the Victorian ideal. (*Source:* Life *39 [May 22, 1902], pp. 446–47.*)

CHAPTER 4

Varieties of New Women

One of the most important manifestations of gender anarchy between 1890 and 1930 was "the new woman." The new woman emerged into popular consciousness with her greatest power in the final decade of the nineteenth century. As the documents in this and subsequent chapters (particularly Chapters 6 and 7) will show, her characteristics ranged across a broad spectrum, but popular representations often pictured the new woman as a robust young woman, athletic and adventurous. She exuded self-confidence and independence.

In the minds of some Americans, the newness of the new woman derived from her access to higher education. Whereas in 1870, only 21 percent of undergraduates were women; by 1920, women accounted for nearly half (47 percent) of undergrads. (Still, less than 5 percent of Americans attended college at all.) As they graduated, these women swelled the ranks of elementary school teachers and pioneered new women's professions like social work, librarianship, and public health nursing.

Indeed, many believed that economic independence defined the new woman, whether she enjoyed it only briefly before marriage or throughout her life. Women's participation in gainful employment increased from under 15 percent of American women in 1870 to over 24 percent in 1910. By then, 51 percent of single women worked for wages. As important, women began to move into occupations previously reserved for men. The percentage of employed women in clerical service, retail sales, and professional occupations increased markedly. As secretaries, telephone operators, and school teachers, however, women rarely achieved authority over men; the new occupational hierarchy maintained women's subordination.

Black women did not enjoy these new opportunities to the same degree as whites. Black women remained employed overwhelmingly in agriculture and domestic service. Retail sales and clerical positions in white-owned businesses went almost exclusively to white women; only in black-owned businesses—a smaller and more precarious sector of the economy—could African American women find such employment. Factory jobs remained an option mostly for European immigrants or

European Americans. Like white women, black women gained access to higher ed-ucation and from there to some professions, especially school teaching. But, again, opportunities were less lucrative and plentiful than for white women.

Political activism marked black and white women equally as new women. Building on earlier efforts, millions of American women agitated for suffrage, lobbied for public social services, and organized anti-racist campaigns between 1890 and 1930. Expressing political opinions, stepping into the polling booth (many states granted women suffrage before the federal amendment was ratified in 1920), and organizing lobbies drew the energies of many activist women. Sometimes these women justified their political participation by arguing that, as potential or actual mothers, they brought to government values and agendas unique to them as women. Moreover, women activists were particularly success-ful when they pushed for legislation that might improve the lives of women and children. Because of this, some historians refer to female politicos of the early twentieth century as "maternalists."

By the 1920s, however, a second generation of new women emerged. This younger group seemed to care less about increasing the public power of women as a group than providing greater possibilities for individual self-expression and achievement. This "flapper," with her bobbed hair, short skirts, and dancing feet, represented a final version of the New Woman. Documents in this chapter illus-trate, among other things, this generational divide between New Women.

TO BE A WOMAN THEN IS SUBLIME
Anna Julia Cooper

The 1890s represented a paradoxical period in African American women's history. On the one hand, black women faced the steady spread of legal segregation, racial violence, and the disenfranchisement of black men in southern states. On the other hand, middle-class black women burst into public life determined not only to better the position of women within black communities but also to battle white supremacy on behalf of all African Americans.

Anna Julia Cooper (1858–1964) embodied the highest hopes of many middle-class black women. Born in Raleigh, North Carolina to an enslaved man and a free woman, Cooper spent much of her life in Washington, D.C., where for decades she served as a devoted, rigorous, and often controversial teacher and school adminis-trator. Her own education came first from Oberlin College, where she earned a B.A. in 1884 and an M.A. in 1887. After years of teaching mathematics and languages, she completed her Ph.D. at the University of Paris in 1925.

In 1892, Cooper published her first autobiography, *A Voice from the South*. In the excerpts that follow, she presented her vision of the new woman. According to

Source: Anna Julia Cooper, *A Voice from the South, By a Black Woman of the South* (Xenia, Ohio: The Aldine Printing House, 1892), pp. 50–51, 131–36, 142–45.

Cooper, what were the characteristics and possibilities of the new woman? How, in her mind, did race affect women's positions and responsibilities?

To-day there are one hundred and ninety-eight colleges for women, and two hundred and seven coeducational colleges and universities in the United States alone offering the degree of B.A. to women, and sending out yearly into the arteries of this nation a warm, rich flood of strong, brave, active, energetic, well-equipped, thoughtful women . . . who have given a deeper, richer, nobler and grander meaning to the word "womanly" than any one-sided masculine definition could ever have suggested. . . .

To-day America counts her millionaires by the thousand; questions of tariff and questions of currency are the most vital ones agitating the public mind. In this period, when material prosperity and well earned ease and luxury are assured facts from a national standpoint, woman's work and woman's influence are needed as never before; needed to bring a heart power into this money getting, dollar-worshipping civilization; needed to bring a moral force into the utilitarian motives and interests of the time; needed to stand for God and Home and Native Land *versus gain and greed and grasping selfishness.* . . .

Now the periods of discovery [of America], of settlement, of developing resources and accumulating wealth have passed in rapid succession. Wealth in the nation as in the individual brings leisure, repose, reflection. The struggle with nature is over, the struggle with ideas begins. We stand then, it seems to me, in this last decade of the nineteenth century, just in the portals of a new and untried movement on a higher plain and in a grander strain than any the past has called forth. . . .

In the era about to dawn, her [woman's] sentiments must strike the keynote and give the dominant tone. And this because of the nature of her contribution to the world.

Her kingdom is not over physical forces. Not by might, nor by power can she prevail. Her position must ever be inferior where strength of muscle creates leadership. If she follows the instincts of her nature, however, she must always stand for the conservation of those deeper moral forces which make for the happiness of homes and the righteousness of the country. In a reign of moral ideas she is easily queen. . . .

The colored woman of to-day occupies, one may say, a unique position in this country. In a period of itself transitional and unsettled, her status seems one of the least ascertainable and definitive of all the forces which make for our civilization. She is confronted by both a woman question and a race problem, and is as yet an unknown or an unacknowledged factor in both. While the women of the white race can with calm assurance enter upon the work they feel by nature appointed to do, while their men give loyal support and appreciative countenance to their efforts [to improve society], recognizing in most avenues of usefulness the propriety and the need of woman's distinctive co-operation, the colored woman too often finds herself hampered and shamed by a less liberal sentiment and a more conservative attitude on the part of those for whose opinion she cares most. That this is not universally true I am glad to admit. There are to be found both intensely conservative white men and exceedingly liberal colored men. But as far as my experience goes the average man of our race is less frequently ready to admit the actual need among the sturdier forces of the world for women's help or influence. The great social and economic questions await her interference, that she could throw any light on problems of national import, that her intermeddling could improve the management of school systems, or elevate the tone of public institutions, or humanize and sanctify the far reaching influence of prisons and reformatories and improve the treatment of lunatics and imbeciles,—that she has a word worth hearing on mooted questions in political economy, that she could contribute a suggestion on the relations of labor and capital, or offer a thought on honest money and honorable trade, I fear the majority of "Americans of the colored variety" are not yet prepared to concede. It may be that they do not yet see these questions in their right perspective, being absorbed in the immediate needs of their own political complications. . . .

Fifty years ago woman's activity according to orthodox definitions was on a pretty clearly cut "sphere," including primarily the kitchen and the nursery, and rescued from the barrenness of prison bars by the womanly mania for adorning every discoverable bit of china or canvass with forlorn looking cranes balanced idiotically on one foot. The woman of to-day finds herself in the presence of responsibilities which ramify through the profoundest and varied interests of her country and race. Not one of the issues of this plodding, toiling, sinning, repenting, failing, aspiring humanity can afford to shut her out, or can deny the reality of her influence. No plan for renovating society, no scheme for purifying politics, no reform in church or in state, no moral, social, or economic question, no movement upward or downward in the human plane is lost on her. . . . No woman can possibly put herself or her sex outside any of the interests that affect humanity. All departments in the new era are to be hers, in the sense that her interests are in all and through all; and it is incumbent on her to keep intelligently and sympathetically *en rapport* with all the great movements of her time, that she may know on which side to throw the weight of her influence. She stands now at the gateway of this new era of American civilization. In her hands must be moulded the strength, the wit, the statesmanship, the morality, all the psychic force, the social and economic intercourse of that era. To be alive at such an epoch is a privilege, to be a woman then is sublime.

In this last decade of our century, changes of such moment are in progress, such new and alluring vistas are opening out before us, such original and radical suggestions for the adjustment of labor and capital, of government and the governed, of the family, the church and the state, that to be a possible factor though an infinitesimal in such a movement is pregnant with hope and weighty with responsibility. To be a woman in such an age carries with it a privilege and an opportunity never implied before. But to be a woman of the Negro race in America, and to be able to grasp the deep significance of the possibilities of the crisis, is to have a heritage, it seems to me, unique in the ages. In the first place, the race is young and full of the elasticity and hopefulness of youth. All its achievements are before it. It does not look on the masterly triumphs of nineteenth century civilization with that *blasé* world-weary look which characterizes the old washed out and worn out races which have already, so to speak, seen their best days. . . .

Everything to this race is new and strange and inspiring. There is a quickening of its pulses and a glowing of its self-consciousness. Aha, I can rival that! I can aspire to that! I can honor my name and vindicate my race! Something like this, it strikes me, is the enthusiasm which stirs the genius of young Africa in America; and the memory of past oppression and the fact of present attempted repression only serve to gather momentum for its irrepressible powers. Then again, a race in such a stage of growth is peculiarly sensitive to impressions. Not the photographer's sensitized plate is more delicately impressionable to outer influences than is this high strung people here on the threshold of a career.

What a responsibility then to have the sole management of the primal lights and shadows! Such is the colored woman's office. She must stamp weal or woe on the coming history of this people. May she see her opportunity and vindicate her high prerogative.

THE INDIVIDUALIZATION OF WOMEN
Charlotte Perkins Stetson Gilman

Surely one of the most innovative thinkers on the subject of new women was Charlotte Perkins Gilman (1860–1935). Like Anna J. Cooper, this New England-born writer, lecturer, and activist based her optimism about women's future on the opening of higher education to women, the flow of women into every sector of the economy, and contemporary theories of evolution. Gilman believed that the human race had reached a stage in its development that would inevitably equalize the public power of women and men—despite real differences between the two.

Perhaps best known for her short story, "The Yellow Wall-paper" (1892), Gilman established herself as one of the leading theorists of women's advancement with the publication of *Women and Economics* (1898), excerpted here. In this piece, she expressed her concern that women win economic independence from men; for, economic dependence, she thought, stunted women's growth toward full humanity. To make it possible for married women with children to remain gainfully employed, Gilman imagined kitchenless homes. Food, she hoped, would be prepared by professionals outside of homes just as professionals would care for children during the day. Most women would then be able to maintain paid employment and family life rather than suffering in isolated, undervalued domestic labor.

According to Gilman, what were the characteristics of the new woman? How did she differ from the ideal Victorian woman? Compare this new woman with Cooper's.

> The period of women's economic dependence is growing to a close. . . .
>
> Have we not all observed the change even in size of the modern woman, with its accompanying strength and agility? The Gibson Girl and the Duchess of Towers,[1]—these are the new women; and they represent a noble type, indeed. The heroines of romance and drama to-day are of a different sort from the Evelinas and Arabellas of the last century. Not only do they look differently, they behave differently. The false sentimentality, the false delicacy, the false modesty, the utter falseness of elaborate compliment and servile gallantry which went with the other falsehoods,—all these are disappearing. Women are growing honester, braver, stronger, more healthful and skilful and able and free, more human in all ways. . . .

---

[1]Charles Dana Gibson was an illustrator famed for drawing independent women, young, tall, athletic, and forceful. The Duchess of Towers, just such a character, appeared in George du Maurier's novel, *Peter Ibbetson.*

Source: Charlotte Perkins Stetson (Gilman), *Women and Economics: A Study of the Economic Relation Between Men and Women as a Factor in Social Evolution* (Boston: Small, Maynard, & Company, 1898), pp. 137–38, 148–54; 157–58; 159–60, 265–69.

In the fiction of to-day women are continually taking larger place in the action of the story. They are given personal characteristics beyond those of physical beauty. And they are no longer content simply to *be:* they *do.* They are showing qualities of bravery, endurance, strength, foresight, and power for the swift execution of well-conceived plans. They have ideas and purposes of their own; and even when, as in many cases described by the more reactionary novelists, the efforts of the heroine are shown to be entirely futile, and she comes back with a rush to the self-effacement of marriage with economic dependence, still the efforts were there. Disapprove as he may, use his art to oppose and contemn as he may, the true novelist is forced to chronicle the distinctive features of his time; and no feature is more distinctive of this time than the increasing individualization of women. . . .

A truer spirit is the increasing desire of young girls to be independent, to have a career of their own, at least for a while, and the growing objection of countless wives to the pitiful asking for money, to the beggary of their position. More and more do fathers give their daughters, and husbands their wives, a definite allowance,—a separate bank account,—something which they can play is all their own. The spirit of personal independence in the women of to-day is sure proof that a change has come.

For a while the introduction of machinery which took away from the home so many industries deprived woman of any importance as an economic factor; but presently she arose, and followed her lost wheel and loom to their new place, the mill. To-day there is hardly an industry in the land in which some women are not found. Everywhere throughout America are women workers outside the unpaid labor of the home, the last census giving three million of them. . . . Without here going into its immediate advantages or disadvantages from an industrial point of view, it is merely instanced as an undeniable proof of the radical change in the economic position of women that is advancing upon us. . . .

One of the most noticeable features is the demand in women not only for their own money, but for their own work for the sake of personal expression. Those who object to women's working on the ground that they should not compete with men or be forced to struggle for existence look only at work as a means of earning money. They should remember that human labor is an exercise of faculty, without which we should cease to be human; that to do and to make not only gives deep pleasure, but is indispensable to healthy growth. Few girls today fail to manifest some signs of this desire for individual expression. It is not only in the classes who are forced to it: even among the rich we find this same stirring of normal race-energy. To carve in wood, to hammer brass, to do "art-dressmaking," to raise mushrooms in the cellar,—our girls are all wanting to do something individually. . . .

In body and brain, wherever she touches life, woman is changing gloriously from the mere creature of sex, all her race-functions[2] held in abeyance, to the fully developed human being, none the less true woman for being more truly human. What alarms and displeases us in seeing these things is our funny misconception that race-functions are masculine. . . . Much effort is wasted in showing that women will become "unsexed" and "masculine" by assuming these human duties. . . . we are assured that the endeavor of women to perform these masculine economic functions marks a decadent civilization, and is greatly to be deprecated. There would be some reason in this objection if the common racial activities of humanity,

---

[2]Gilman defines "race-functions" as economic activities.

into which women are now so eagerly entering, were masculine functions. But they are not. . . . "Masculine" and "feminine" are only to be predicated of reproductive functions,—processes of race-preservation. The processes of self-preservation are racial, peculiar to the species, but common to either sex. . . .

So the "new woman" will be no less female than the "old" woman, though she has more functions, can do more things, is a more highly specialized organism, has more intelligence. She will be, with it all, more feminine, in that she will develope far more efficient processes of caring for the young of the human race than our present wasteful and grievous method, by which we lose fifty per cent. of them [the young]. . . .

The rapid extension of function in the modern woman has nothing to do with any exchange of masculine and feminine traits: It is simply an advance in human development of traits common to both sexes, and is wholly good in its results. . . .

To man, so far the only fully human being of his age, the bachelor apartment of some sort has been a temporary home for that part of his life wherein he had escaped from one family and not yet entered another. To woman this possibility is opening to-day. More and more we see women presuming to live and have a home, even though they have not a family. . . .

The primitive home, based on the economic dependence of woman, with its unorganized industries, its servile labors, its smothering drag on individual development, is becoming increasingly unsuitable to the men and women of to-day. . . .

There is no cause for alarm. We are not going to lose our homes or our families, nor any of the sweetness and happiness that go with them. But we are going to lose our kitchens [from the home], as we have lost our laundries and bakeries. The cook-stove will follow the loom and wheel, the wool-carder and shears. We shall have homes that are places to live in and love in, to rest in and play in, to be alone in and to be together in; and they will not be confused and declassed by admixture with any industry whatever.

In homes like these the family life will have all its finer, truer spirit well maintained; and the cares and labors that now mar its beauty will have passed out into fields of higher fulfilment. The relation of wife to husband and mother to child is changing for the better with this outward alteration. All the personal relations of the family will be open to a far purer and fuller growth. . . .

A mother economically free, a world-servant instead of a house-servant; a mother knowing the world and living in it,—can be to her children far more than has ever been possible before. Motherhood in the world will make that world a different place for her child.

SHE LONGS FOR THE FREEDOM
Alice C. Fletcher

Ironically, at the same time that middle-class black and white women were expanding their horizons in the economic and political world, possibilities for many American Indian women were shrinking. As the following document points out, generalization about native women in the late nineteenth century is always suspect because different groups of indigenous people had different gender systems. Nevertheless, in many groups women traditionally enjoyed a broader field of activity and a higher status than European American women. The enforcement of U.S. laws and customs on American Indians thus meant decreased power and privilege for many native women.

One commentator on this trend was Alice Cunningham Fletcher (1838–1923), an ethnologist who devoted her life to the study and management of American Indians. Although Fletcher was herself an early new woman—a founder in 1873 of the Association for the Advancement of Women, an independent professional, and an effective lobbyist—her activities on behalf of native groups sometimes contributed to the losses suffered by native women. Most significantly, Fletcher advocated dividing common tribal lands into individual allotments for each Indian family. Under the Dawes Act of 1887, this practice became a federal policy and Fletcher a director of allotment for the federal government. Where land division was successfully enforced, it pulled land ownership—with its attending power and status—away from native women.

According to Fletcher, what was the gender division of labor among native peoples before European contact? How were the laws of whites forcing that gender system to change? How did Fletcher's life suggest that some new women opened their own vistas by unintentionally closing those of others?

In order to appreciate the problems that confront the Indian woman to-day, it may be well to glance at her position, work and influence under aboriginal conditions. While her former status is broken and fragmentary at the present time, it is still a potent factor in her struggle with the new social forces which are already upon her.

If the notion still lingers that the Indian tribes are all one people, using the same or similar languages, preserving the same social forms, and subject to the same conditions of environment, a glance at the Linguistic Map, prepared by Major Powell, Director of the Bureau of Ethnology, will at once dispel this illusion.

The map shows 58 linguistic stocks. Now, within each stock there are many languages, and these again are divided into varying dialects, so that, with these facts before us, we cannot think of the Indians as one people; their diversity of language implies a diversity of customs and habits. . . .

If we look from the map representing the undisturbed territory occupied by Indians three centuries ago to that which shows the tracts held by him to-day, we behold a startling transformation. The wide areas controlled by the different linguistic stocks have shriveled to the limits of reservations, and these become less and less in extent each year as the lands cease to be a tribal possession and are allotted into individual holdings. . . .

. . . It would be impossible to take one tribe as typical of all, but there were certain features in common, and of these only those which affected woman's position and work will be at this time considered.

Every tribe was composed of a number of kinship groups or clans, each of which was organized within itself and was represented in the central government of the tribe whatever its form. . . .

In most tribes of this country, descent was traced through the mother, that is, the child belonged to the clan of its mother, and not to that of its father. The father was a dweller in the domicile of his wife. In the tribes where descent was by the father, where the child belonged to the gens of the father and not to that of the mother, the woman did not . . . lose her place in her gens and become absorbed in that of

Source: Alice C. Fletcher, "The Indian Woman and Her Problems," *Southern Workman* 28 (May 1899):172–76.

her husband. The Indian woman when she married neither changed her name nor relinquished any of her gentile or clan rights. In the tribe, the kinship group, rather than the family, as we understand it, was the political unit. . . .

[In earlier periods], [m]an was the hunter and the warrior, the provider of the raw material, the sole defender of the family. Woman was the conserver of his labor, the industrial factor, the property maker and owner, and the caretaker.

In one of the sacred Indian legends it is said: "In the time that went before, the men carried clubs for weapons." This brief mention points out man's earliest duty. It was he who met the enemy, who battled with the animals to obtain food and pelts, he made clear and safer the inner space wherein woman's skill turned the trophies of his strength into things of use, and gave them a new value. She tanned the pelts and made them into garments; she tilled the soil; she fashioned the utensils of wood and of pottery; she wove the fibre into cloth; and it was she that gave expression to beauty in decoration upon articles that ministered to the daily comfort of the family. All this work of woman's brain and hands, which has since developed into industries that are now controlling forces in civilization, required for its birth and infancy conditions of safety and peace. Such conditions could only be secured and preserved by the training of men to the skillful use of weapons, to alertness and readiness to defend the family in daytime or night against danger that lurked on every hand. . . . These customs emphasized the distinctive employments of the sexes, and because of this, because the line of demarkation in avocation was a sex line, the readjustment of labor upon a different basis has been attended with difficulties that require time and favoring circumstances for their solution.

Under the old tribal regime woman's industries were essential to the very life of the people, and their value was publicly recognized. While she suffered many hardships and labored early and late, her work was exalted ceremonially and she had a part in tribal functions. Her influence in the growth and development of tribal government, tribal ceremonies, and tribal power shows that her position had always been one of honor rather than one of slavery and degradation.

[Now that Indians live under peaceful circumstances], [w]oman's work has been taken from her by man, and with each appropriation she has been bereft of importance in the community. . . .

At this point the Indian woman is confronted with problems hard for her to solve. In the old time she was an outdoor worker, she cultivated the fields, she was in the free fresh air from morning until night. Now her work is within doors; if she toils in the fields her husband or father is disgraced; she is taught to regard indoor employment, to cook, to wash and iron, to sew, to scrub, as the sole avocation of women. She longs for the freedom of the outside air, and her health and spirits suffer from confinement. There is now no possible reward for her work; there are now no tribal ceremonies at the time of planting, when the priest invoked the blessing of the mysterious power upon the seed and the fields,—no picturesque rites praying for the vivifying showers, and, when the corn stands green and its leaves rustle in the breeze, the woman cannot now look upon the fields as the fruit of her labor blessed by the powers above, bringing food for her family. . . .

There are also new laws to distress her. Formerly she owned all the home property, the lodge and all its belongings; other property was hers to do with as she pleased. Today if she be married, she find herself under a domination that did not exist in the olden times, and from which she cannot escape. She is irked and disheartened by these strange enforcements that have come she knows not how, nor does she apprehend what they mean for her and for society.

Permit me to mention another weight put upon this woman already loaded with strange burdens. It comes from the crude teaching that evil and sin came to the race solely through woman, who is thereby accursed. I have heard this bald statement preached to the Indians by well meaning men, who thought they were speaking God's truth; and I have heard it echoed by Indian men to Indian women to the hurt of the latter. To such an assertion the Indian woman has no answer, save the God-given answer of her own unselfish love for those dependent upon her, but what is that, in the face of the white man's authority backed by the unseen hand of the law.

A WORKER AT THE AGE OF FOURTEEN
Hilda Satt Polacheck

The waves of immigrants who flooded U.S. shores between 1880 and 1920 further complicated the gender scene. They brought with them unique gender systems that were partially transformed under pressure from their new situation. Families of eastern European Jews, for instance, often relied partially on income from wives while in Europe, but in the United States the wages of Jewish daughters proved more vital to family survival. One study concluded in fact that immigrant Jewish daughters brought home approximately 40 percent of their families' incomes.

Hilda Satt (1882–1967) was one of these daughters. In 1892, she left Poland and settled with her family in Chicago, not far from Jane Addams' Hull House.[3] Leaving school for paid employment at age fourteen, Satt embodied a working-class new woman, who spent at least a portion of her adolescence pursuing paid employment and experiencing a world outside the household. Later in her life, Hilda Satt Polacheck wrote a memoir, excerpts from which follow. In what ways did Satt fit the description of new women outlined by Charlotte Perkins Gilman; in what ways did she differ from it?

I went to school and told Mrs. Torrance that I was not coming back to school. I shall never forget that leave-taking. I looked at the beloved—yes, beloved—blackboard where I had learned to write my first English words. . . . My desk, at which I had spent the first happy years in America. I had finished the fifth grade at the time. I was fourteen years old. It looked as if this would be the end of my schooling.

Mother shed many tears when I told her that I was going to work. But she realized that there was nothing else to do and she agreed to the plan. It was God's will, she said, and we had to accept it.

The first day that I left the house with my small bundle of lunch under my arm was a day of inner struggle for a little girl. I had mixed emotions in my heart. I was glad that I could help feed the family, but I could not forget that I would not go to school again. I did not realize at the time that it was possible to study away from school and that there were classes at Hull-House.

---

[3]Hull House, the most renowned social settlement in the United States, housed middle-class women and men who offered classes and a variety of services to their immigrant neighbors on Chicago's southwest side.

Source: Hilda Satt Polacheck, *I Came A Stranger: The Story of a Hull-House Girl*, ed. Dena J. Polacheck Epstein (Urbana, Ill.: University of Illinois Press, 1989), 56–58, 63, 75.

Of that eventful day, when I went to work for the first time, many memories keep coming to me. It was dark when we left the house. We walked down what was then Twelfth Street, now known as Roosevelt Road, over many viaducts and a bridge that spanned the Chicago River and the railroad tracks. It was beginning to get light as we approached the river and I could not help comparing the dirty, slimy water with the clear sparkling water of my dear Vistula.

We arrived at State Street and walked down a flight of stairs to the street below. The factory looked very large and imposing to me. It was a six-story brick building. We got into the elevator, my first elevator ride, and were taken to the fourth floor, I believe. There my name was taken and I presented my working permit. I had become an adult and a worker at the age of fourteen.

I was assigned to a knitting machine and a girl was stationed at my side to teach me the complicated rudiments of knitting. There were about four hundred machines in the room, which covered an entire floor of the building. In front of each machine sat a girl or woman on a high stool. I had no difficulty learning the trade and I was soon able to earn four dollars a week. The work was piecework, and the harder one worked, the more one made. But the pay was so regulated that even the fastest worker could not make over five dollars a week. At that time, however, five dollars would buy food for a family of six. So, between my sister's and my pay the family could exist.

We worked from seven thirty in the morning till six in the evening, six days a week. We had a half hour for lunch, which we ate sitting in front of the machine. . . .

I had been working there about two weeks when, during the morning, I heard the most agonizing shriek I had ever heard. Soon the power stopped and it became so quiet that our hearts almost stopped beating. Quiet except for the piercing shriek that kept coming from across the room. My sister came up to me and put her arms around me and told me not to be afraid. A girl had caught her hand in the machine. The machine had to be taken apart before the poor girl could be freed. . . .

Several months after I started working in the knitting factory, the doors of the toilets were removed so that there was no privacy while performing natural functions. The reason given for this utter lack of consideration was that girls were spending too much time in the toilet. This could not be true, as the girls were eager to make as much money as possible and no one could earn money sitting in the toilet.

Very often a machine would break down, and we had to wait till the repairman came to fix it. . . . That meant less money in the weekly pay envelope. Each machine had about eighty needles, and while running at full speed a needle would jump out of place and break. This was no fault of the worker, but in addition to losing time to change the needle, we had to pay a penny for it. . . .

One evening, as my sister and I were leaving the factory, we saw a man at the entrance with his arms full of leaflets. As each girl came out of the building she was handed a leaflet. We read it in front of a lamppost. We were being asked to come to a meeting to help organize a union. My sister and I talked about it all the way home. She was reluctant about going. She was always more cautious than I was. I, however, decided to go to the meeting.

This was my introduction to trade unionism. About one hundred girls and a few men were gathered in a small smoky room. A man called the meeting to order and told us of the advantages of an organized union. He urged us to organize a union. When he had finished his formal talk, he asked if anyone had anything to say. There was a dead silence. And then, impulsively, I rose and said that I had a lot to say. The words came tumbling out of my mouth as if they had been stored within me. I asked the girls why we had to pay for broken needles that were broken accidentally. Why was there only one mechanic to keep all those machines in repair? Why did we not object to having the doors removed from the toilets? Were we not entitled to some privacy and a little decency? That was all the meeting needed; a reminder of real grievances. The union was organized that night.

The next morning when I came to work I was called into the forelady's office and given whatever pay I had coming and was told that I was a troublemaker and that I was to get out and never come back.

The bookkeeper had been sent to the meeting and she had reported the part I had played in helping to organize the union. And so ended my four-year career as a knitter. . . .

One day the girl working next to me [in the shirtwaist factory where I found subsequent employment] brought a paperbound book with her, which she read while eating her lunch. I made it my business to find out what she was reading. I do not remember the name of the book, but it was written by Bertha M. Clay. . . . It was all about an elegant lady, dressed in silks and satins and laces, who was having an awful time with her lovers. It seems that many men were in love with her and she had to decide who was worthy of her love. She finally decided and married and "lived happily ever after."

I must confess that the first Bertha M. Clay book brought a sort of glow. For a little while I could forget cuffs. But when I read the second book by the then-popular author, I had the feeling that I had already read it. . . .

One evening in 1900, after a particularly boring day at the factory, I decided to walk over to Hull-House three blocks from where I lived. . . .

For ten years [thereafter] I spent most of my evenings at Hull-House [taking classes and working in the Labor Museum.]

My sister and I were now earning enough money so that we could allow ourselves an occasional visit to the theater. The only one we knew of was the Bijou on Halsted Street near Jackson. This theater was within walking distance of our home, so that we did not have to pay carfare. Every penny counted in those days. As I look back on those hair-raising melodramas, I am comforted by the thought that they cost only ten cents. But they did introduce us to the theater.

Some of the plays were called *The White Slave, East Lynne, Ten Nights in a Barroom, Bertha the Sewing Machine Girl, Two Orphans,* and many others. In these plays the villain was always punished and the hero always married the beautiful golden-haired girl.

I HAD TO DANCE WITH ANYONE
Elisa Silva to Manuel Gamio

In the late 1920s, social scientist Manuel Gamio conducted interviews with dozens of Mexican immigrants to the United States. He analyzed those interviews in *Mexican Immigration to the United States* (1930). The next year, anthropologist Robert Redfield published English translations of many of Gamio's interviews. One of those interviews follows.

Source: Robert Redfield, trans., *The Mexican Immigrant: His Life Story; Autobiographic Documents Collected by Manuel Gamio*, pp. 159–62. Copyright ©1931 by University of Chicago Press.

Although Gamio's work suggested a tremendous variety of experience among Mexican immigrants, some trends emerged. Most of the one and a half million Mexicans who migrated north between 1900 and 1930 did so because they needed work. Moreover, political upheaval in Mexico after the revolution of 1910 disrupted life in many villages and threatened young men with involuntary military service. Building railroads and mining ore drew many of those young men into the southwest United States, and California's need for agricultural labor drew men, women, and children. Women rarely migrated alone, but men often did, and many originally intended not to remain too long in the United States.

Elisa Silva was one of those who migrated with her family. At the time of the following interview, she had lived in the United States for three years. Were Silva and her sisters new women? How did their immigrant experience differ from that of Hilda Satt's?

I am twenty-three years old. I was married in Mazatlan when I was seventeen. My husband was an employee of a business house in the port but he treated me very badly and even my own mother advised me to get a divorce. A short time after I was divorced my father died. Then, my mother, my two sisters and I decided to come to the United States. As we had been told that there were good opportunities for earning money in Los Angeles, working as extras in the movies and in other ways, we sold our belongings and with the little which our father had left us we came to this place, entering first at Nogales, Arizona. From the time we entered I noticed a change in everything, in customs, and so forth, but I believed that I would soon become acclimated and be able to adjust myself to these customs. When we got to Los Angeles we rented a furnished apartment and there my mother took charge of fixing everything up for us. My sisters and I decided to look for work at once. One of my sisters, the oldest who knew how to sew well, found work at once in the house of a Mexican woman doing sewing. My mother then decided that my youngest sister had better go to school and that I should also work in order to help out with the household expenses and with the education of my sister. As I didn't know how to sew or anything and as I don't know English I found it hard to find work, much as I looked. As we had to earn something, a girl friend of mine, also a Mexican, from Sonora, advised me to go to a dance-hall. After consulting with my mother and my sisters I decided to come and work here every night dancing. My work consists of dancing as much as I can with everyone who comes. At the beginning I didn't like this work because I had to dance with anyone, but I have finally gotten used to it and now I don't care, because I do it in order to earn my living. Generally I manage to make from $20.00 to $30.00 a week, for we get half of what is charged for each dance.[4] Each dance is worth ten cents so that if I dance, for example, fifty dances in a night I earn $2.50. Since the dances are short, ten cents being charged for just going around the ball-room, one can dance as many as a hundred. It all depends on how many men come who want to dance. Besides there are some who will give you a present of a dollar or two. This work is what suits me best for I don't need to know any English here. It is true that at times

---

[4]In the mid-1920s, the California Industrial Welfare Commission set the minimum wage for women workers in most industries at $16.00 per week. In 1923, only 9 percent of women in the mercantile industry earned more than $30.00 per week.

I get a desire to look for another job, because I get very tired. One has to come at 7:30 in the evening and one goes at 12:30, and sometimes at 1 in the morning. One leaves almost dead on Saturdays because many Mexican people come from the nearby towns and they dance and dance with one all night. In Mexico this work might perhaps not be considered respectable, but I don't lose anything here by doing it.[5] It is true that some men at times make propositions to me which are insulting, but everything is fixed by just telling them no. If they insist one can have them taken out of the hall by the police. One man whom I liked a lot here in the hall deceived me once. He was a Mexican. But since that time it hasn't happened to me again. My mother takes a lot of care of me so that I won't make any bad steps. My sisters do the same.

Of the customs of this country I only like the ones about work. The others aren't anything compared to those of Mexico. There the people are kinder than they are here, less ambitious about money. I shall never really like living this way, besides since I don't know English and believe that it won't be so easy for me to learn it, I don't believe I will ever be able to adjust myself to this country. I don't have time to study English, nor do I like it.

Life, to be sure, is easier here because one can buy so many things on credit and cheaper than in Mexico. But I don't know what it is that I don't like. My youngest sister, who is in a business college learning English, says that she likes this city a lot and the United States as a whole and that if we go to Mazatlan she will stay here working. She is thinking of learning typewriting and stenography, both in English and in Spanish, so as to work in some American business, which will pay her well.

I don't suffer in the matter of food, for my mother cooks at home as if we were in Mexico. There are some dishes which are different but we generally eat Mexican style and rice and beans are almost never lacking from our table.

I am a Catholic, but I almost never go to church. Sometimes before coming to the dance hall I go to church, even if it only be to pray a little. I think that I have only confessed myself some four times in my life. My mother is very Catholic. She, and my younger sister also, go to mass every Sunday. At home we have a large image of the heart of Jesus and my sisters pray to it at night.

I don't think of remarrying because I am disillusioned about men, but perhaps if some day I should find one who would really care for me I would love him a lot. If I do marry some day it would be with a Mexican. The Americans are very dull and very stupid. They let the women boss them. I would rather marry an American than a *pocho*, however.

FEMINIST—NEW STYLE
Dorothy Dunbar Bromley

While Elisa Silva was earning five cents a dance, journalist Dorothy Dunbar Bromley was insisting that modern women were free to chose their life's work and effortlessly combine it with marriage and children. Given that, according to the census, only 11 percent of married women worked for pay at this time and the vast ma-

---

[5]Compare with *The Social Evil in Chicago* in Chapter 6.

FIGURE 4.2
New women of the 1920s participated fully in consumer culture. They often expressed their rebellion against gender traditions by purchasing forbidden products—cigarettes or alcohol—and frequenting commerical entertainments—movies and dance halls—instead of through political activism or athletic accomplishment. (*Source: National Photo Company Collection, 1924, Negative Number LC-USZ6242070, Prints and Photographs Division, Library of Congress, Washington, D.C.*)

jority of those because of dire economic need, Bromley's "Feminist—New Style" was a rare woman indeed. Nevertheless, she represented an important version of the new woman who emerged in the 1920s, and her sentiments provide a significant contrast with older women like Anna J. Cooper and Charlotte P. Gilman.

Bromley's piece unfortunately confused one issue. She lumped into her understanding of "feminist—old style" thousands of women who rejected the feminist label altogether. "Feminist" came into use in the United States during the 1910s, when a small group of young radicals—most associated with socialism—identified themselves as feminists. During the 1920s, the elite, white National Woman's Party won the name for its portion of the women's movement, which emphasized women's individuality and demanded perfect legal equality with men. The much larger contingent of the women's movement, which emphasized women's difference from men and supported protective legislation for women workers (see Chapter 7), refused the name. Bromley thus used the term loosely in her nevertheless revealing article.

How did Bromley's new woman differ from Cooper's or Gilman's? How did her attitudes compare with Elisa Silva's?

> The Queen is dead. Long live the Queen!
> Is it not high time that we laid the ghost of the so-called feminist?
> "Feminism" has become a term of opprobrium to the modern young woman. For the word suggests either the old school of fighting feminists who wore flat heels and had very little feminine charm, or the current species who antagonize men with their constant clamor about maiden names, equal rights, woman's place in the

world, and many another cause . . . *ad infinitum.* Indeed, if a blundering male assumes that a young woman is a feminist simply because she happens to have a job or a profession of her own, she will be highly—and quite justifiably insulted: for the word evokes the antithesis of what she flatters herself to be. Yet she and her kind can hardly be dubbed "old-fashioned" women. What *are* they, then? . . .

Numbers of these honest, spirited young women have made themselves heard in article and story. But since men must have things pointed out to them in black and white, we beg leave to enunciate the tenets of the modern woman's credo. Let us call her "Feminist—New Style."

First Tenet. Our modern young woman freely admits that American women have so far achieved but little in the arts, science, and professions as compared with men. . . .

Second Tenet. Why, then, does the modern woman care about a career or a job if she doubts the quality and scope of women's achievement to date? There are three good reasons why she cares immensely: first, she may be of that rare and fortunate breed of persons who find a certain art, science, or profession as inevitable a part of their lives as breathing; second, she may feel the need of a satisfying outlet for her energy whether or not she possesses creative ability; third, she may have no other means of securing her economic independence. And the latter she prizes above all else, for it spells her freedom as an individual, enabling her to marry or not to marry, as she chooses—to terminate a marriage that has become unbearable, and to support and educate her children if necessary. . . .

Third Tenet. She will not, however, live for her job alone, for she considers that a woman who talks and thinks only shop has just as narrow a horizon as the housewife who talks and thinks only husband and children—perhaps more so, for the latter may have a deeper understanding of human nature. She will therefore refuse to give up all of her personal interests, year in and year out, for the sake of her work. In this respect, she no doubt will fall short of the masculine ideal of commercial success, for the simple reason that she has never felt the economic compulsion which drives men on to build up fortunes for the sake of their growing families.

Yet she is not one of the many women who look upon their jobs as tolerable meal-tickets or as interesting pastimes to be dropped whenever they may wish. On the contrary, she takes great pride in becoming a vital factor in whatever enterprise she has chosen, and she therefore expects to work long hours when the occasion demands.

But rather than make the mistake that some women do of domesticating their jobs, i.e. burying all of their affections and interests in them, or the mistake that many men make of milking their youth dry for the sake of building up a fortune to be spent in a fatigued middle age, she will proceed on the principle that a person of intelligence and energy can attain a fair amount of success—perhaps even a high degree of success—by the very virtue of living a well-balanced life, as well as by working with concentration.

Fourth Tenet. Nor has she become hostile to the other sex in the course of the struggle to orient herself. On the contrary, she frankly likes men and is grateful to more than a few for the encouragement and help they have given her.

In the business and professional worlds, for instance, Feminist—New Style has observed that more and more men are coming to accord women as much responsibility as they show themselves able to carry. She and her generation have never found it necessary to bludgeon their way, and she is inclined to think that certain of the pioneers would have got farther if they had relied on their ability rather than on their militant methods. To tell the truth, she enjoys working with men, more than with women, for their methods are more direct and their view larger, and she finds that she can deal with them on a basis of frank comradeship. . . .

Fifth Tenet. By the same corollary, Feminist—New Style professes no loyalty to women *en masse,* although she staunchly believes in individual women. Surveying her sex as a whole, she finds their actions petty, their range of interests narrow, their talk trivial and repetitious. . . .

Ninth Tenet. She readily concedes that a husband and children are necessary to the average woman's fullest development, although she knows well enough that women are endowed with varying degrees of passion and of maternal instinct. Some women, for instance, feel the need of a man very intensely, while others want children more than they want a husband, want them so much, in fact, that they vow they would have one or two out of wedlock if it were not for the penalty that society would exact from the child, and if it were not for the fact that a child needs a father as much as a mother.

But no matter how much she may desire the sanction of marriage for the sake of having children, she will not take any man who offers. First of all a man must satisfy her as a lover and a companion. And second, he must have the mental and physical traits which she would like her children to inherit. . . .

If Feminist—New Style finds it practicable to have children she will resolve from the start not to sacrifice everything to them—for their sake as well as her own. During the years of their babyhood she may find it necessary to give up her work, either partially or wholly; but as soon as possible she will organize the family life so as to resume her own interests. . . .

But whether or no the nursery-school is the solution, the fact remains that the mother who has managed in one way or another to retain her own special interests will have a growing fund of wisdom and experience to share with her children. And, furthermore, she will avoid the sin of struggling to possess them body and soul and of expecting them to make great sacrifices for her later in life because she once gave up everything for them. . . .

Tenth Tenet. But even while she admits that a home and children may be necessary to her complete happiness, she will insist upon more *freedom and honesty within the marriage relation.*

She considers that the ordinary middle-class marriage is stifling in that it allows the wife little chance to know other men, and the husband little chance to know other women except surreptitiously. It seems vital to her that both should have a certain amount of leisure to use exactly as they see fit, without feeling that they have neglected the other. . . .

Finally. Feminist—New Style proclaims that men and children shall no longer circumscribe her world, although they may constitute a large part of it. She is intensely self-conscious whereas the feminists were intensely sex-conscious. . . . She knows that it is her American, her twentieth-century birthright to emerge from a creature of instinct into a full-fledged individual who is capable of molding her own life. And in this respect she holds that she is becoming man's equal.

RECOMMENDED READINGS

Anderson, Karen. *Changing Woman: A History of Racial Ethnic Women in Modern America*. New York, 1996.

Banta, Martha. *Imaging American Women: Idea and Ideals in Cultural History*. New York, 1987.

Cott, Nancy F. *Grounding of Modern Feminism*. New Haven, 1987.

Fass, Paula. *The Damned and the Beautiful: American Youth in the 1920s*. New York, 1977.

Glenn, Susan. *Daughters of the Shtetl: Life and Labor in the Immigrant Generation*. Ithaca, N.Y., 1990.

Gordon, Lynn D. *Gender and Higher Education in the Progressive Era*. New Haven, Conn., 1990.

Hill, Mary A. *Charlotte Perkins Gilman: The Making of a Radical Feminist, 1860–1896*. Philadelphia, 1980.

Horowitz, Helen Lefkowitz. *Alma Mater: Design and Experience in the Women's Colleges from their Nineteenth Century Beginnings to the 1930s*. New York, 1984.

Lane, Ann J. *To Herland and Beyond: The Life and Work of Charlotte Perkins Gilman*. New York, 1990.

Pascoe, Peggy. *Relations of Rescue: The Search for Female Moral Authority in the American West, 1874–1939*. New York, 1990.

Rapp, Rayna, and Ellen Ross. "The 1920s: Feminism, Consumerism, and Political Backlash." In Judith Friedlander et al., eds. *Women in Culture and Politics: A Century of Change*. Bloomington, Ind., 1986, pp. 52–61.

FIGURE 5.1
Advertisements for *The Virile Power of Superb Manhood* suggest not only interest in strenuous manhood but also beliefs about the role of sex, tobacco, and alcohol in creating ideal men. (*Source:* Physical Culture, *2, 2 [November 1899], p. 2.) Courtesy of the Rare Book Room, Main Library, University of Illinois at Urbana–Champaign.*

CHAPTER 5

Manhood and the Strenuous Life

One historian has written of the 1890s, "While women became more manly, men became more martial." This observation captures many of the nuances of gender transformation at the turn of the century. As women changed, so did men, and the changes in women's sense of themselves deeply affected male identity.

Moreover, many of the same trends that reshaped womanhood also affected manhood, but with different ramifications. For instance, while corporate capitalism opened new employment opportunities for women, it threatened the "independence" of many men. During the early nineteenth century, American manhood had rested in part on the independence presumably afforded a man by owning his own farm or business. As suggested in Chapter 3, many men, reduced to wage-earning by industrialization, had to cope with a loss of such independence. The increasing scope of corporate capitalism at the turn of the century meant that, although occupations remained divided on the basis of gender, even higher percentages of American men would never achieve the kind of economic independence on which their manhood had once seemed to rest. They would instead spend all of their working lives as employees of someone else—as workers, managers, or salesmen for large corporations. Some men, believing that this loss of independence signaled the end of American manhood, thrashed around trying to find some other foundation on which to build their manly identities.

Partisan politics had been another pillar upholding nineteenth-century American manhood. Party affiliation, handed down from one generation of men to the next, constituted a part of manly inheritance. Participation in partisan mass rallies, torchlight parades and election day rowdies was so critical to manly identity that men who in the 1870s and 1880s proclaimed themselves nonpartisan were chided as "Miss Nancys."

In the 1890s, partisan politics began losing viability as a source for manly identity. Why? First, more states granted women the vote. Second, for black men in the South—and some poor white men—the 1890s brought actual *dis*enfranchisement:

through poll taxes, literacy tests, and lynchings, white southerners gradually shoved most African American men out of electoral politics. Finally, the election of 1896 ended an era of close elections and high voter turn-outs. After that, as political power seeped out of political parties and into organized interest groups, voters more readily shed their partisan inheritance.

During the 1890s, then, the pillars of middle-class American manhood began deteriorating. If women could earn a living and fewer men could hope for the kind of economic independence their fathers had anticipated; if women appeared in practically every public space, including the polling booth; if inherited partisan affiliation and participation were no longer available to all men and were open to some women; then what did it mean to be a man? Documents in this section illustrate a few of the responses to what some historians call this "masculinity crisis," a condition that lasted well into the new century.

THE STRENUOUS LIFE
Theodore Roosevelt

The most popular proponent of a new American manhood was Theodore Roosevelt (1858–1919). President of the United States from 1901 to 1909, Roosevelt set himself among progressive reformers by pushing the federal government (perhaps erratically) toward regulation of big business in defense of workers and consumers.

Roosevelt also advocated an activist foreign policy. He served as assistant secretary of the Navy (1897–1898), and then made a name for himself by organizing a group of soldiers to fight for Cuban independence from Spain in the Spanish-American-Cuban-Filipino War (1898). Quick victory against Spain opened a fascinating national discussion about the terms of the peace, especially about what should become of Spain's former holdings in the Pacific and Caribbean. Roosevelt participated fiercely in that debate, and his famous speech, "The Strenuous Life," delivered in April 1899 to a Chicago men's club, articulated his position. Among other things, he insisted that the United States must not allow all of Spain's former colonies to govern themselves but must rule at least the Philippines and Puerto Rico as dependent states.

Roosevelt's speech reveals the ways that gender crept into national conversations that would not seem to be about manhood or womanhood at all. Even foreign policy often depended on gendering enemy nations as female, for instance, and was seen as an arena in which particular kinds of men might be produced. What was an American man, according to Roosevelt? What did foreign policy have to do with creating American manhood and vice versa? What role did race play in Roosevelt's understanding of American manhood?

In speaking to you, men of the greatest city of the West, men of the State which gave to the country Lincoln and Grant, men who preeminently and distinctly embody all that is most American in the American character, I wish to preach, not the

Source: Theodore Roosevelt, "The Strenuous Life," in *The Strenuous Life* (New York: Century Company, 1901), pp. 1–4, 6–10, 16–18.

FIGURE 5.2
In this humorous rendition of the strenuous life, fencing, shooting, wrestling, and boxing decide matters at a meeting of Theodore Roosevelt's cabinet. Roosevelt is the boxer wearing glasses. (*Source:* Life *39 [April 24, 1902], p. 353.*)

doctrine of ignoble ease, but the doctrine of the strenuous life, the life of toil and effort, of labor and strife; to preach that highest form of success which comes, not to the man who desires mere easy peace, but to the man who does not shrink from danger, from hardship, or from bitter toil, and who out of these wins the splendid ultimate triumph.

A life of slothful ease, a life of that peace which springs merely from lack either of desire or of power to strive after great things, is as little worthy of a nation as of an individual. I ask only that what every self-respecting American demands from himself and from his sons shall be demanded of the American nation as a whole. Who among you would teach your boys that ease, that peace, is to be the first consideration in their eyes—to be the ultimate goal after which they strive! You men of Chicago have made this city great, you men of Illinois have done your share, and more than your share, in making America great, because you neither preach nor practise such a doctrine. You work yourselves, and you bring up your sons to work. . . . We do not admire the man of timid peace. We admire the man who embodies victorious effort; the man who never wrongs his neighbor, who is prompt to help a friend, but who has those virile qualities necessary to win in the stern strife of actual life. It is hard to fail, but it is worse never to have tried to succeed. . . .

In the last analysis a healthy state can exist only when the men and women who make it up lead clean, vigorous, healthy lives; when the children are so trained that they shall endeavor, not to shirk difficulties, but to overcome them; not to seek ease, but to know how to wrest triumph from toil and risk. The man must be glad to do a man's work, to dare and endure and to labor; to keep himself, and to keep those dependent on him. The woman must be the housewife, the helpmeet of the homemaker, the wise and fearless mother of many healthy children. . . . When men fear work or fear righteous war, when women fear motherhood, they tremble on the brink of doom. . . .

We of this generation do not have to face a task such as that our fathers faced [in the Civil War], but we have our tasks, and woe to us if we fail to perform them! We cannot, if we would, play the part of China, and be content to rot by inches in ignoble ease within our borders, taking no interest in what goes on beyond them, sunk in scrambling commercialism; heedless of the higher life, the life of aspiration, of toil and risk, busying ourselves only with the wants of our bodies for the day, until suddenly we should find, beyond a shadow of question, what China has already found, that in this world the nation that has trained itself to a career of unwarlike and isolated ease is bound, in the end, to go down before other nations which have not lost the manly and adventurous qualities. If we are to be a really great people, we must strive in good faith to play a great part in the world. We cannot avoid meeting great issues. All that we can determine for ourselves is whether we shall meet them well or ill. In 1898 we could not help being brought face to face with the problem of war with Spain. All we could decide was whether we should shrink like cowards from the contest, or enter into it as beseemed a brave and high spirited people; and, once in, whether failure or success should crown our banners. So it is now. We cannot avoid the responsibilities that confront us in Hawaii, Cuba, Porto Rico, and the Philippines. All we can decide is whether we shall meet them in a way that will redound to the national credit, or whether we shall make of our dealings with these new problems a dark and shameful page in our history. To refuse to deal with them at all merely amounts to dealing with them badly. We have been given a problem to solve. If we undertake the solution, there is, of course, always danger that we may not solve it aright; but to refuse to undertake the solution simply renders it certain that we cannot possibly solve it aright. The timid man, the lazy man, the man who distrusts his country, the over-civilized man, who has lost the great fighting, masterful virtues, the ignorant man, and the man of dull mind, whose soul is incapable of feeling the mighty lift that thrills "stern men with empires in their brains"—all these, of course, shrink from seeing the nation undertake its new duties; shrink from seeing us build a navy and an army adequate to our needs; shrink from seeing us do our share of the world's work, by bringing order out of chaos in the great, fair tropic islands from which the valor of our soldiers and sailors has driven the Spanish flag. These are the men who fear the strenuous life, who fear the only national life which is really worth leading. . . .

. . . The guns that thundered off Manila and Santiago left us echoes of glory, but they also left us a legacy of duty. If we drove out a medieval tyranny only to make room for savage anarchy, we had better not have begun the task at all. It is worse than idle to say that we have no duty to perform, and can leave to their fates the islands we have conquered. Such a course would be the course of infamy. It would be followed at once by utter chaos in the wretched islands themselves. Some stronger, manlier power would have to step in and do the work, and we would have shown ourselves weaklings, unable to carry to successful completion the labors that great and high-spirited nations are eager to undertake. . . .

In the West Indies and the Philippines alike, we are confronted by most difficult problems. It is cowardly to shrink from solving them in the proper way; for solved they must be, if not by us then by some stronger, and more manful race. If we are too weak, too selfish, or too foolish to solve them, some bolder and abler people must undertake the solution. Personally, I am far too firm a believer in the greatness of my country and the power of my countrymen to admit for one moment that we shall ever be driven to the ignoble alternative.

The problems are different for the different islands. Porto Rico is not large enough to stand alone. We must govern it wisely and well, primarily in the interest of its own people. Cuba is, in my judgment, entitled ultimately to settle for itself whether it shall be an independent state or an integral portion of the mightiest of republics. . . . The Philippines offer a yet graver problem. Their population includes half-caste and native Christians, warlike Moslems, and wild pagans. Many of their people are utterly unfit for self-government, and show no signs of becoming fit. Others may in time become fit but at present can only take part in self-government under a wise supervision, at once firm and beneficent. We have driven Spanish tyranny from the islands. If we now let it be replaced by savage anarchy, our work has been for harm and not for good. I have scant patience with those who fear to undertake the task of governing the Philippines, and who openly avow that they do fear to undertake it, or that they shrink from it because of the expense and trouble; but I have even scanter patience with those who make a pretense of humanitarianism to hide and cover their timidity, and who cant about "liberty" and the "consent of the governed," in order to excuse themselves for their unwillingness to play the part of men. Their doctrines, if carried out, would make it incumbent upon us to leave the Apaches of Arizona to work out their own salvation, and to decline to interfere in a single Indian reservation. Their doctrines condemn your forefathers and mine for ever having settled in these United States. . . .

TO LIVE BY THE PRODUCTIONS OF OUR HANDS
Booker T. Washington

As Theodore Roosevelt urged America's white men to demonstrate manliness by ruling those he considered racially inferior, America's black men struggled to carve out manly identities for themselves. With disenfranchisement, lynchings, and Jim Crow laws spreading across the South and racial discrimination in the labor market preventing many African American men from supporting their families, black men faced special difficulties defining themselves as men. Moreover, one way that the most powerful men in America maintained their preeminence was by effeminizing minority men. White Protestants often likened Jewish or black men to women, thus rhetorically marginalizing them by setting them outside common gender expectations.

Booker T. Washington (1856–1915) offered one response to those difficulties. Born a slave, Washington spent his life in the South; he battled to obtain an education and in 1881 founded the Tuskegee Institute in Alabama. Tuskegee, which offered a full academic curriculum, won acclaim for its program of industrial education and its founder a reputation for promoting economic self-sufficiency among black people. In 1900, Washington underscored that commitment with the founding of the National Negro Business League, an organization dedicated to building black business enterprises.

Source: Booker T. Washington, *Up From Slavery: An Autobiography* (Garden City, New York: Doubleday, 1901), pp. 218–25.

Washington came to the fore as a race leader with a speech he delivered in 1895 before the Cotton States and International Exposition in Atlanta, Georgia. White organizers of the Exposition envisioned the New South as a commercial and industrial center integrated into an international economy. Despite inviting Washington to speak at the opening of the Exposition and encouraging black southerners to construct exhibits demonstrating the "progress of the Negro since freedom," they were also white supremacists. Washington's oration, sometimes called the Atlanta Compromise, spoke shrewdly to the aspirations of the Exposition's white designers. It sought on the one hand to persuade black southerners temporarily to accept the new limitations on their social freedoms and political power and on the other to convince white southerners to employ black labor instead of importing immigrant workers.

Some historians have seen this speech as evidence of Washington's capitulation to white racism, and in some measure, it was; but that evaluation is too simple. The speech subtly criticized lynching and looked forward to the end of "racial animosities." It also made clear Washington's expectation that economic success would soon break down the walls of racial discrimination in other arenas. History, of course, proved that hope unwarranted: Washington underestimated the sources and power of racism. But, given white America's glorification of economic success in the late nineteenth century, his predictions seemed reasonable to many at the time.

In this piece, he rarely referred directly to manliness, but his definition of manhood is implied throughout. Given Washington's willingness to let social and political freedoms go, what did he consider the crux of black manhood? How did his assumptions about manhood differ from those of Henry MacNeal Turner (Chapter 2)? What did those differences reveal about the changes in African American prospects since the end of Reconstruction? Keep this in mind as you read the subsequent article by W.E.B. DuBois.

Mr. President and Gentlemen of the Board of Directors and Citizens: One-third of the population of the South is of the Negro race. No enterprise seeking the material, civil, or moral welfare of this section can disregard this element of our population and reach the highest success. I but convey to you, Mr. President and Directors, the sentiment of the masses of my race when I say that in no way have the value and manhood of the American Negro been more fittingly and generously recognized than by the managers of this magnificent Exposition. . . .

Not only this, but the opportunity here afforded will awaken among us a new era of industrial progress. Ignorant and inexperienced, it is not strange that in the first years of our new life we began at the top instead of at the bottom; that a seat in Congress or the State Legislature was more sought than real estate or industrial skill; that the political convention or stump speaking had more attractions than starting a dairy farm or truck garden.

. . . To those of my race who depend on bettering their condition in a foreign land, or who underestimate the importance of cultivating friendly relations with the Southern white man, who is their next door neighbor, I would say, "Cast down your bucket where you are"—cast it down in making friends in every manly way of the people of all races by whom we are surrounded.

Cast it down in agriculture, mechanics, in commerce, in domestic service, and in the professions. And in this connection it is well to bear in mind that whatever other sins the South may be called to bear, when it comes to business, pure and simple, it is in the South that the Negro is given a man's chance in the commercial world, and in nothing is this Exposition more eloquent than in emphasizing this chance. Our greatest danger is that in the great leap from slavery to freedom we may overlook the fact that the masses of us are to live by the productions of our hands, and fail to keep in mind that we shall prosper in proportion as we learn to dignify and glorify common labour and put brains and skill into the common occupations of life; shall prosper in proportion as we learn to draw the line between the superficial and the substantial, the ornamental gewgaws of life and the useful. No race can prosper till it learns that there is as much dignity in tilling a field as in writing a poem. It is at the bottom of life we must begin, and not at the top. Nor should we permit our grievances to overshadow our opportunities.

To those of the white race who look to the incoming of those of foreign birth and strange tongue and habits for the prosperity of the South, were I permitted I would repeat what I say to my own race, "Cast down your bucket where you are." Cast it down among the eight millions of Negroes whose habits you know, whose fidelity and love you have tested in days when to have proved treacherous meant the ruin of your firesides. Cast down your bucket among these people who have, without strikes and labour wars, tilled your fields, cleared your forests, builded your railroads and cities, and brought forth treasures from the bowels of the earth, and helped make possible this magnificent representation of the progress of the South. Casting down your bucket among my people, helping and encouraging them as you are doing on these grounds, and to education of head, hand, and heart, you will find that they will buy your surplus land, make blossom the waste places in your fields, and run your factories. While doing this, you can be sure in the future, as in the past, that you and your families will be surrounded by the most patient, faithful, law-abiding, and unresentful people that the world has seen. As we have proved our loyalty to you in the past, in nursing your children, watching by the sick bed of your mothers and fathers, and often following them with tear-dimmed eyes to their graves, so in the future, in our humble way, we shall stand by you with a devotion that no foreigner can approach, ready to lay down our lives, if need be, in defense of yours, interlacing our industrial, commercial, civil, and religious life with yours in a way that shall make the interests of both races one. In all things that are purely social we can be as separate as the fingers, yet one as the hand in all things essential to mutual progress.

There is no defense or security for any of us except in the highest intelligence and development of all. If anywhere there are efforts tending to curtail the fullest growth of the Negro, let these efforts be turned into stimulating, encouraging, and making him the most useful and intelligent citizen. . . .

There is no escape through law of man or God from the inevitable:—

The law of changeless justice bind
Oppressor with oppressed;
And close as sin and suffering joined
We march to fate abreast.

Nearly sixteen millions of hands will aid you in pulling the load upward, or they will pull against you the load downward. We shall constitute one-third and more of the ignorance and crime of the South, or one-third its intelligence and progress; we shall contribute one-third to the business and industrial prosperity of the South, or we shall prove a veritable body of death, stagnating, depressing, retarding every effort to advance the body politic.

Gentlemen of the Exposition, as we present to you our humble effort at an exhibition of our progress, you must not expect overmuch. Starting thirty years ago with ownership here and there in a few quilts and pumpkins and chickens (gathered from miscellaneous sources), remember the path that has led from these to the inventions and production of agricultural implements, buggies, steam-engines, newspapers, books, statuary, carving, paintings, the management of drug-stores and banks, has not been trodden without contact with thorns and thistles. While we take pride in what we exhibit as a result of our independent efforts, we do not for a moment forget that our part in this exhibition would fall far short of your expectations but for the constant help that has come to our educational life, not only from the Southern States, but especially from Northern philanthropists, who have made their gifts a constant stream of blessing and encouragement.

The wisest among my race understand that the agitation of questions of social equality is the extremest folly, and that progress in the enjoyment of all the privileges that will come to us must be the result of severe and constant struggle rather than of artificial forcing. No race that has anything to contribute to the markets of the world is long in any degree ostracized. It is important and right that all privileges of the law be ours, but it is vastly more important that we be prepared for the exercises of these privileges. The opportunity to earn a dollar in a factory just now is worth infinitely more than the opportunity to spend a dollar in an opera-house.

In conclusion . . . let this be constantly in mind that, while from representations in these buildings of the product of field, of forest, of mine, of factory, letters, and art, much good will come, yet far above and beyond material benefit will be that higher good, that, let us pray God, will come, in a blotting out of sectional differences and racial animosities and suspicions, in a determination to administer absolute justice, in a willing obedience among all classes to the mandates of law. Thus, this, coupled with our material prosperity, will bring into our beloved South a new heaven and a new earth.

TO DEFEND AND ASSERT
W.E.B. DuBois

Although both white and black Americans initially responded warmly to Washington's position on race relations, it did not go undisputed. A different attitude was voiced eloquently by W.E.B. DuBois (1868–1963), an African American leader who, unlike Washington, was born and lived much of his life in the North.

DuBois enjoyed the finest education the United States had to offer. He earned his B.A. from Harvard University in 1890, an M.A. in 1891, and a Ph.D. in 1895, the year that Washington delivered the Atlanta Compromise. DuBois taught for several years, first at Wilberforce University and then at Atlanta University.

While in Atlanta, DuBois helped to found the Niagara Movement, an alternative to the anti-racist strategies of Washington. Leaders of the Niagara Movement

Source: W.E.B. DuBois, "I Am Resolved," 3 *The Crisis* (January 1912), p. 113.

argued that Washington's accommodation with southern racial policies was unacceptable, that black men and women must fight for complete equality with white people. In 1909, DuBois co-founded the National Association for the Advancement of Colored People (NAACP), a racially integrated organization committed to full racial equality. From 1910–1934, DuBois edited the journalistic organ of the NAACP, *The Crisis,* for which he also did much of the writing. The following excerpt from *The Crisis* encapsulates DuBois's ideas about African American manhood. How do they differ from those of Booker T. Washington? Compare and contrast them with those of Theodore Roosevelt.

I am resolved *in this New Year to play the man—to stand straight, look the world squarely in the eye, and walk to my work with no shuffle or slouch.*

I am resolved *to be satisfied with no treatment which ignores my manhood and my right to be counted as one among men.*

I am resolved *to be quiet and law abiding, but to refuse to cringe in body or in soul, to resent deliberate insult, and to assert my just rights in the face of wanton aggression.*

I am resolved *to defend and assert the absolute equality of the Negro race with any and all other human races and its divine right to equal and just treatment.*

I am resolved *to be ready at all times and in all places to bear witness with pen, voice, money and deed against the horrible crime of lynching, the shame of Jim Crow legislation, the injustice of all color discrimination, the wrong of disfranchisement for race or sex, the iniquity of war under any circumstances and the deep damnation of present methods of distributing the world's work and wealth.*

I am resolved *to defend the poor and the weak of every race and hue, and especially to guard my mother, my wife, my daughter and all my darker sisters from the insults and aggressions of white men and black, with the last strength of my body and the last suffering of my soul.*

For all these things, I am resolved unflinchingly to stand, and if this resolve cost me pain, poverty, slander and even life itself, I will remember the Word of the Prophet, how he sang:

"Though Love repine and Reason chafe,
  There came a Voice, without reply,
'Tis man's Perdition to be safe
  When for the Truth he ought to die!"

THERE ARE NO LAUNDRIES IN CHINA
Lee Chew

Immigration certainly required formidable effort from every newcomer, but it often created a different sort of strenuous life from the one prescribed by Roosevelt. Paralleling the case of women, male immigrants often brought with them expectations of manhood that simply could not be fulfilled on American soil. Adjusting those expectations constituted one of the rigors of immigrant experience.

Source: Lee Chew, "The Biography of a Chinaman," *Independent* 55 (February 19, 1903), pp. 417–23.

Compared to Europe, Asia supplied a smaller but substantial portion of the "new immigration." Between the California Gold Rush in 1848 and the Immigration Act of 1924, about one million Asians entered the United States. These numbers would surely have been even higher except for anti-Asian hostility in the United States, which produced laws specifically discouraging Asian immigration, as discussed in Chapter 3. Such exclusions prevented the growth of Chinese American communities in the United States. Moreover, all Asian immigrants were denied U.S. citizenship.

Lee Chew arrived in San Francisco before the Exclusion Act. In 1903, his brief autobiography was published by *The Independent* (originally an antislavery serial) as part of a series of life stories by "undistinguished Americans." What were the expectations of men in Lee Chew's Chinese village? How did Lee Chew, a businessman in New York in 1903, have to change his expectations of manhood once in the United States? Does "Meat vs. Rice" (Chapter 3) help us to understand Lee Chew's experiences?

> The village where I was born is situated in the province of Canton, on one of the banks of the Si-Kiang River. It is called a village, although it is really as big as a city, for there are about 5,000 men in it over eighteen years of age—women and children and even youths are not counted in our villages.
>
> All in the village belonged to the tribe of Lee. They did not intermarry with one another, but the men went to other villages for their wives and brought them home to their fathers' houses. . . .
>
> When I was a baby I was kept in our house all the time with my mother, but when I was a boy of seven I had to sleep at nights with other boys of the village— about thirty of them in one house. The girls are separated the same way—thirty or forty of them sleeping together in one house away from their parents—and the widows have houses where they work and sleep, though they [the children] go to their fathers' houses to eat. . . .
>
> All the men of the village have farms, but they don't live on them as the farmers do here; they live in the village, but go out during the day time and work their farms, coming home before dark. My father has a farm of about ten acres, on which he grows a great abundance of things—sweet potatoes, rice, beans, peas, yams, sugar cane, pineapples, bananas, lychee nuts and palms. The palm leaves are useful and can be sold. Men make fans of the lower part of each leaf near the stem, and waterproof coats and hats, and awnings for boats, of the parts that are left when the fans are cut out. . . .
>
> Our people working together make these things, the mandarin has nothing to do with it, and we pay no taxes, except a small one on the land. We have our own Government, consisting of the elders of our tribe—the honorable men. When a man gets to be sixty years of age he begins to have honor and to become a leader, and then the older he grows the more he is honored. We had some men who were nearly one hundred years, but very few of them.
>
> In spite of the fact that any man may correct them for a fault, Chinese boys have good times and plenty of play. . . .
>
> It was not all play for us boys, however. We had to go to school, where we learned to read and write and to recite the precepts of Kong-foo-tsze and the other Sages, and stories about the great Emperors of China. . . .
>
> I worked on my father's farm [from age ten] until I was about sixteen years of age, when a man of our tribe came back from America and took ground as large as four city blocks and made a paradise of it. . . .

The man had gone away from our village a poor boy. Now he returned with un-limited wealth, which he had obtained in the country of the American wizards. . . .

The wealth of this man filled my mind with the idea that I, too, would like to go to the country of the wizards and gain some of their wealth, and after a long time my father consented, and gave me his blessing, and my mother took leave of me with tears, while my grandfather laid his hand upon my head and told me to re-member to live up to the admonitions of the Sages, to avoid gambling, bad women and men of evil minds, and so to govern my conduct that when I died my ancestors might rejoice to welcome me as a guest on high. . . .

. . . When I got to San Francisco, which was before the passage of the Exclusion act, I was half starved, because I was afraid to eat the provisions of the barbarians, but a few days' living in the Chinese quarter made me happy again. A man got me work as a house servant in an American family, and my start was the same as that of almost all the Chinese in this country.

The Chinese laundryman does not learn his trade in China; there are no laun-dries in China. The women there do the washing in tubs and have no washboards or flat irons. All the Chinese laundrymen here were taught in the first place by American women just as I was taught. . . .

I did not know how to do anything, and I did not understand what the lady told me, but she showed me how to cook, wash, iron, sweep, dust, make beds, wash dishes, clean windows, paint and brass, polish the knives and forks, etc., by doing the things herself and then overseeing my efforts to imitate her. She would take my hands and show them how to do things. . . .

It was twenty years ago when I came to this country, and I worked for two years as a servant, getting at the last $35 a month. . . .

When I first opened a laundry it was in company with a partner, who had been in the business for some years. We went to a town about 500 miles inland, where a railroad was building. We got a board shanty and worked for the men employed by the railroads. Our rent cost us $10 a month and food nearly $5 a week each, for all food was dear and we wanted the best of everything—we lived principally on rice, chickens, ducks and pork, and did our own cooking. The Chinese take nat-urally to cooking. It cost us about $50 for our furniture and apparatus, and we made close upon $60 a week, which we divided between us. We had to put up with many insults and some frauds, as men would come in and claim parcels that did not belong to them, saying they had lost their tickets, and would fight if they did not get what they asked for. Sometimes we were taken before Magistrates and fined for losing shirts that we had never seen. On the other hand, we were making money, and even after sending home $3 a week I was able to save about $15. When the railroad construction gang moved on we went with them. The men were rough and prejudiced against us, but not more so than in the big Eastern cities. It is only lately in New York that the Chinese have been able to discontinue putting wire screens in front of their windows, and at the present time the street boys are still breaking the windows of Chinese laundries all over the city, while the police seem to think it a joke.

We were three years with the railroad, and then went to the mines, where we made plenty of money in gold dust, but had a hard time, for many of the miners were wild men who carried revolvers and after drinking would come in to our place to shoot and steal shirts, for which we had to pay. One of these men hit his head hard against a flat iron and all the miners came and broke up our laundry, chasing us out of town. They were going to hang us. We lost all our property and $365 in money. . . .

Luckily most of our money was in the hands of Chinese bankers in San Francisco. I drew $500 and went East to Chicago, where I had a laundry for three years, during which I increased my capital to $2,500. After that I was four years in Detroit. I went home to China in 1897, but returned in 1898, and began a laundry business in Buffalo. But Chinese laundry business now is not as good as it was ten years ago. American cheap labor in the steam laundries has hurt it. So I determined to become a general merchant, and with this idea I came to New York and opened a shop in the Chinese quarter. . . .

. . . Chinese, who are sober, or duly law abiding, clean, educated and industrious are shut out [from immigration and citizenship]. There are few Chinamen in jails and none in the poor houses. There are no Chinese tramps or drunkards. Many Chinese here have become sincere Christians, in spite of the persecution which they have to endure from their heathen countrymen. More than half the Chinese in this country would become citizens if allowed to do so, and would be patriotic Americans. But how can they make this country their home as matters are now? They are not allowed to bring wives here from China, and if they marry American women there is a great outcry. . . .

HE FELT RATHER THAN REASONED
Edgar Rice Burroughs

In 1912, Edgar Rice Burroughs (1875–1950) published the first of many best-selling novels featuring Tarzan, the son of English nobility who, through several quirks of fate, was raised by apes in an African jungle. This ape-man, combining human intelligence with the strength, ferocity, and cunning of beasts, embodied for many Americans an ideal manhood.

Like Roosevelt's strenuous manhood, Tarzan's masculinity served as a biting critique of Victorian manliness, with its emphasis on refined manners, physical ease, and responsibility to others. Unlike the more pacific hero of later jungle movies, the original Tarzan killed with exuberant triumph or in service of witty pranks. He had no loyal animal sidekicks but was instead the ultimate loner, violently dominating both animals and humans, until he met the American girl, Jane Porter. In fact, by the time that Jane was marooned in Africa (with several associates, including Tarzan's English cousin, William Cecil Clayton), Tarzan had left his "tribe" of apes to live entirely on his own. His successor as ape-king, the vicious Terkoz, appears in the following excerpt from the first Tarzan novel, *Tarzan of the Apes*.

Although his bestial upbringing was crucial to Tarzan's gender identity, Burroughs made clear that inherited racial characteristics also played a role. Drawing on Darwinist ideas, Burroughs attributed Tarzan's keen intelligence and moral code to his "superior" Anglo-Saxon genes. Tarzan's victory over Terkoz symbolized what many turn-of-the-century white Americans believed to be the inevitable triumph of their advanced race over primitive ones.

According to this brief selection, what qualities did the manly Tarzan possess? How did this "red-blooded man" treat women? What qualities did a woman need in

Source: Edgar Rice Burroughs, *Tarzan of the Apes* (New York, 1912), pp. 152–57, 162–65.

order for Tarzan's version of manhood to exist? In what ways might this kind of manhood have been a response to "over-civilized" Victorian manhood? How does his manliness compare with that of Roosevelt's?

From the time Tarzan left the tribe of great anthropoids [apes] in which he had been raised, it was torn by continual strife and discord. Terkoz proved a cruel and capricious king, so that, one by one, many of the older and weaker apes, upon whom he was particularly prone to vent his brutish nature, took their families and sought the quiet and safety of the far interior.

But at last those who remained were driven to desperation by the continued truculence of Terkoz, . . .

There were no formalities. As Terkoz reached the group, five huge, hairy beasts sprang upon him.

At heart he was an arrant coward, which is the way with bullies among apes as well as among men; so he did not remain to fight and die, but tore himself away from them as quickly as he could and fled into the sheltering boughs of the forest. . . .

For several days he wandered aimlessly, nursing his spite and looking for some weak thing on which to vent his pent anger.

It was in this state of mind that the horrible, man-like beast, swinging from tree to tree, came suddenly upon two women in the jungle.

He was right above them when he discovered them. The first intimation Jane Porter had of his presence was when the great hairy body dropped to the earth beside her, and she saw the awful face and the snarling, hideous mouth thrust within a foot of her.

One piercing scream escaped her lips as the brute hand clutched her arm. Then she was dragged toward those awful fangs which yawned at her throat. But ere they touched that fair skin another mood claimed the anthropoid.

The tribe [of apes] had kept his women. He must find others to replace them. This hairless white ape would be the first of his new household, and so he threw her roughly across his broad, hairy shoulders and leaped back into the trees, bearing Jane away. . . .

For a moment he [Tarzan] scrutinized the ground below and the trees above, [where Terkoz had captured Jane] until the ape that was in him by virtue of training and environment, combined with the intelligence that was his by right of birth, told his wondrous woodcraft the whole story as plainly as though he had seen the thing happen with his own eyes. . . .

Three miles were covered before Tarzan overtook them, and then Terkoz, seeing that further flight was futile, dropped to the ground in a small open glade, that he might turn and fight for his prize or be free to escape unhampered if he saw that the pursuer was more than a match for him.

He still grasped Jane in one great arm as Tarzan bounded like a leopard into the arena which nature had provided for this primeval-like battle.

When Terkoz saw that it was Tarzan who pursued him, he jumped to the conclusion that this was Tarzan's woman, since they were of the same kind—white and hairless—and so he rejoiced at this opportunity for double revenge upon his hated enemy.

To Jane the strange apparition of this god-like man was a wine to sick nerves.

From the description which Clayton and her father and Mr. Philander had given her, she knew that it must be the same wonderful creature who had saved them [from attack by various wild animals], and she saw in him only a protector and a friend.

But as Terkoz pushed her roughly aside to meet Tarzan's charge, and she saw the great proportions of the ape and the mighty muscles and the fierce fangs, her heart quailed. How could any vanquish such a mighty antagonist?

Like two charging bulls they came together, and like two wolves sought each other's throat. Against the long canines of the ape was pitted the thin blade of the man's knife.

Jane—her lithe, young form flattened against the trunk of a great tree, her hands tight pressed against her rising and falling bosom, and her eyes wide with mingled horror, fascination, fear, and admiration—watched the primordial ape battle with the primeval man for possession of a woman—for her.

As the great muscles of the man's back and shoulders knotted beneath the tension of his efforts, and the huge biceps and forearm held at bay those mighty tusks, the veil of centuries of civilization and culture was swept from the blurred vision of the Baltimore girl.

When the long knife drank deep a dozen times of Terkoz' heart's blood, and the great carcass rolled lifeless upon the ground, it was a primeval woman who sprang forward with outstretched arms toward the primeval man who had fought for her and won her.

And Tarzan?

He did what no red-blooded man needs lessons in doing. He took his woman in his arms and smothered her upturned panting lips with kisses.

For a moment Jane lay there with half-closed eyes. For a moment—the first in her young life—she knew the meaning of love.

But as suddenly as the veil had been withdrawn it dropped again, and an outraged conscience suffused her face with its scarlet mantle, and a mortified woman thrust Tarzan of the Apes from her and buried her face in her hands. . . .

Now he was surprised that she repulsed him.

He came close to her once more and took hold of her arm. She turned upon him like a tigress, striking his great breast with her tiny hands.

Tarzan could not understand it.

A moment ago and it had been his intention to hasten Jane back to her people, but that little moment was lost now in the dim and distant past of things which were but can never be again, and with it the good intention had gone to join the impossible.

Since then Tarzan of the Apes had felt a warm, lithe form close pressed to his. Hot, sweet breath against his cheek and mouth had fanned a new flame to life within his breast, and perfect lips had clung to his in burning kisses that had seared a deep brand into his soul—a brand which marked a new Tarzan.

Again he laid his hand upon her arm. Again she repulsed him. And then Tarzan of the Apes did just what his first ancestor would have done.

He took his woman in his arms and carried her into the jungle. . . .

When Jane realized that she was being borne away a captive by the strange forest creature who had rescued her from the clutches of the ape she struggled desperately to escape, but the strong arms that held her as easily as though she had been but a day-old babe only pressed a little more tightly.

So presently she gave up the futile effort and lay quietly, looking through half-closed lids at the face of the man who strode easily through the tangled undergrowth with her.

The face above her was one of extraordinary beauty.

A perfect type of the strongly masculine, unmarred by dissipation, or brutal or degrading passions. For, though Tarzan of the Apes was a killer of men and of beasts, he killed as the hunter kills, dispassionately, except on those rare occasions when he had killed for hate—though not the brooding, malevolent hate which marks the features of its own with hideous lines.

When Tarzan killed he more often smiled than scowled, and smiles are the foundation of beauty. . . .

Presently Tarzan took to the trees, and Jane, wondering that she felt no fear, began to realize that in many respects she had never felt more secure in her whole life than now as she lay in the arms of this strong, wild creature, being borne, God alone knew where or to what fate, deeper and deeper into the savage fastness of the untamed forest.

When, with closed eyes, she commenced to speculate upon the future, and terrifying fears were conjured by a vivid imagination, she had but to raise her lids and look upon that noble face so close to hers to dissipate the last remnant of apprehension.

No, he could never harm her; of that she was convinced when she translated the fine features and the frank, brave eyes above her into the chivalry which they proclaimed. . . .

As Tarzan moved steadily onward his mind was occupied with many strange and new thoughts. Here was a problem the like of which he had never encountered, and he felt rather than reasoned that he must meet it as a man and not as an ape.

The free movement through the middle terrace, which was the route he had followed for the most part, had helped to cool the ardor of the first fierce passion of his new found love.

Now he discovered himself speculating upon the fate which would have fallen to the girl had he not rescued her from Terkoz.

He knew why the ape had not killed her, and he commenced, to compare his intentions with those of Terkoz.

True, it was the order of the jungle for the male to take his mate by force; but could Tarzan be guided by the laws of the beasts? Was not Tarzan a Man? But what did men do? He was puzzled; for he did not know.

He wished that he might ask the girl, and then it came to him that she had already answered him in the futile struggle she had made to escape and to repulse him. . . .

A feeling of dreamy peacefulness stole over Jane as she sat down upon the grass where Tarzan had placed her, and as she looked up at his great figure towering above her, there was added a strange sense of perfect security.

As she watched him from beneath half-closed lids, Tarzan crossed the little circular clearing toward the trees upon the further side. She noted the graceful majesty of his carriage, the perfect symmetry of his magnificent figure and the poise of his well-shaped head upon his broad shoulders.

What a perfect creature! . . .

Jane reeled and would have fallen, had not Tarzan, dropping his burden, caught her in his arms. . . .

She could not analyze her feelings, nor did she wish to attempt it. She was satisfied to feel the safety of those strong arms, and to leave her future to fate; for the last few hours had taught her to trust this strange wild creature of the forest as she would have trusted but few of the men of her acquaintance.

As she thought of the strangeness of it, there commenced to dawn upon her the realization that she had, possibly, learned something else which she had never really known before—love. . . .

TO BE LOYAL EACH DAY
Pacific Electric Railway's Every Employee

Among the readers of *Tarzan* were the mushrooming numbers of white-collar workers whose disciplined lives utterly contradicted the freedom of Tarzan's jungle life. White-collar occupations constituted the fastest growing sector of the labor market in the early twentieth century: positions for salaried professionals, managers, and clerks multiplied so rapidly that by 1910, this new middle class outnumbered independent businessmen and professionals by over two million people.

Many salaried men worked for large corporations. (Over 1,800 businesses dissolved into consolidations between 1895 and 1904.) In these big firms, white-collar men enjoyed a kind of security that they probably could not have attained in their own small businesses or professional practices, but they forfeited the freedom to make their own decisions, the power to run things their own way, the independence of mind and action that nineteenth-century middle-class manhood seemed to require.

Different men responded to this dilemma in different ways. Some looked outside their work for the source of their identities as men, perhaps hunting or camping Tarzan-style during vacations or on weekends. Others, however, sought to create a definition of manliness that encompassed the qualities required by white-collar occupations. Such was the case for a group of men who in 1922 worked for the Pacific Electric Railway in Los Angeles. What did it mean to be a man, according to these white–collar employees? How did this definition compare and contrast to Roosevelt's or to DuBois's? What would Tarzan have thought of this version of manhood?

OUR NEW YEAR'S RESOLUTION
The Pledge

To be loyal each day to Our Company.
To conserve its material and protect its well-being.
To strive diligently to better its financial interests and there-by safeguard our own.
To be more courteous and considerate of all our patrons and there-by earn their increased respect and good-will.
To make the Golden Rule a fact and not merely a precept.
To be a *Man,* filling a *Man's place* in a man's game, and prove our's the best manned industry in Southern California.

Signed
Every Employee

Source: "Our New Year's Resolution," *The Pacific Electric Magazine Issued by the Employes of the Pacific Electric Railway* 6 (January 10, 1922), p. 1.

I'M A BOY RIGHT ON
William Lee Conley "Big Bill" Broonzy

Employee magazines provide one historical source on manhood in the 1920s; popular music provides another. One especially rich new genre developed at the turn of the century among African Americans in the Mississippi Delta: the blues. Black musicians playing in juke joints and barrelhouses, at picnics, and community celebrations created this unique music to express the aching for love, adventure, success, and escape. The Great Migration carried this southern, rural form into northern cities, and, in 1920, recording companies began introducing it to listeners beyond the reach of live performers.

One popular blues singer and composer was Big Bill Broonzy (1893–1958). Born in Mississippi, Broonzy first earned his living as a preacher and sharecropper while playing music on the side. He joined the army during World War I and then spent the 1920s in Chicago. He continued to play and write music, even to record a bit, but had to make his living as a cook, porter, or janitor. Despite becoming a much-recorded blues artist in the 1930s, he could not give up his day jobs until 1953.

In 1928, Broonzy composed a song that lamented and protested the failure of white Americans to recognize the manhood of black Americans. What does this document reveal about the relationship between race and gender in America during the 1920s? What did Broonzy himself believe should have earned him the designation "man"?

> When I was born in this world, this is what happened to me:
> I was never called a man and now I'm fifty-three.
> I wonder when will I be called a man
> Or do I have to wait 'till I get ninety-three?
> When Uncle Sam called me I knew I would be called the real
>   McCoy
> But when I got in the army they called me soldier boy.
> I wonder when will I be called a man
> Or do I have to wait 'till I get ninety-three?
> When I got back from overseas, that night we had a ball;
> I met the boss the next day, he told me 'Boy get you some
>   overall.'
> I wonder when will I be called a man
> Or do I have to wait 'till I get ninety-three?
> I worked on a levee camp and a chain gang too;
> A black man is a boy to a white, don't care what he can do.
> I wonder when will I be called a man
> Or do I have to wait 'till I get ninety-three?
> They said I was undereducated, my clothes was dirty and
>   torn;
> Now I got a little education, but I'm a boy right on.
> I wonder when will I be called a man
> Or do I have to wait 'till I get ninety-three?

Source: Big Bill Broonzy, "When Will I Get To Be Called A Man?" in Yannick Bruynoghe, *Big Bill Blues: William Broonzy's Story* (London: Cassell and Company, 1955), pp. 44–45.

THE BLUES CAME 'LONG
James Eddie "Son" House, Jr.

Blues lyrics expressed many aspects of manly and womanly identity, sometimes even the competition of one sort of manhood or womanhood with another. The blues communicated those conflicts so clearly, especially because many blues artists participated directly in many different communities, where expectations of manhood and womanhood varied dramatically.

Son House (1902–1988) lived this complicated life. Like Big Bill Broonzy, he began his musical and professional life in churches, singing in a choir as a child and preaching at age fifteen. During the 1920s, he began to play guitar and to dabble in the blues, which took him into spaces frowned on by the respectable classes. The qualities required of men in church and those expected of men in juke joints simply did not jibe, and so many a musician had to practice multiple versions of manhood or choose between them. House, another Mississippian, captured that conflict in "Preachin' the Blues," penned sometime after the mid-1920s. What versions of manhood appeared in these lyrics? How did they conflict? Were they at all reconcilable?

Oh, I'm gonna get me a religion
I'm gonna join the Baptist Church,
Oh, I'm gonna get me a religion
I'm gonna join the Baptist Church:
I'm gonna be a Baptist Preacher
And I sure won't have to work.

Oh, I'm gonna preach these blues and
I want everybody to shout,
Mmmmmmmmmmm
And I want everybody to shout:
I'm gonna do like a prisoner—
I'm gonna roll my time on out.

Oh, in my room
I bowed down to pray,
Oh—I was in my room
I bowed down to pray:
Then the blues came 'long and they
Blowed my spirit away.

Oh, I have religion
On this very day,
Oh, I have religion
On this very day:
But the women's and whiskey, well they
Would not let me pray.

Source: Son House, "Preachin' the Blues," in Eric Sackheim, comp., *The Blues Line: A Collection of Blues Lyrics* (Hopewell, N.J.: Grossman Publishers, 1993), pp. 212–213.

Oh—I wish I had me
A heaven of my own,

(Great God amighty)
Yeahhh
A heaven of my own:
Well, I'd give all my women
A long long happy home.

Well, I love my baby
Just like I love myself:
Well, I love my baby
Just like I love myself.

Ohhhhhhhh
Just like I love myself:
Well, if she don't have me
She won't have nobody else.

Well, I'm gonna fold my arms
I'm gonna kneel down in prayer,
Oh, I'm gonna fold my arms
Gonna kneel down in prayer:
When I get up I'm gonna
See if my preaching suit a man's ear
Well, I met the blues this morning
Walking just like a man,
Ohhhh-oh-ohhhhhh
Walking just like a man:
I said, Good morning blues
Now give me your right hand.

Now there's nothing now baby
Lord, that's gonna worry my mind,
Ohhhhh
Nothing that's gonna worry my mind:
Oh, to satisfy
I got the longest *line.*

Oh, I got to stay on the job
I ain't got no time to lose,
Yeahh
I ain't got no time to lose:
I swear to God
I've got to preach these gospel blues.

(Great God amighty)
Oh—I'm gonna preach these blues
And choose my seat and set down:
When the spirit comes, sisters,
I want you to jump straight up and down.

RECOMMENDED READINGS

Bederman, Gail. *Manliness and Civilization: A Cultural History of Gender and Race in the United States, 1880–1917*. Chicago, 1995.

Dubbert, Joe L. "Progressivism and the Masculinity Crisis." *The Psychoanalytic Review* 61 (Fall 1974). Reprinted in Elizabeth H. and Joseph H. Pleck, eds. *The American Man*. Englewood Cliffs, N.J., 1980, 303–320.

Griffen, Clyde. "Reconstructing Masculinity from the Evangelical Revival to the Waning of Progressivism: A Speculative Synthesis." In *Meanings for Manhood: Constructions of Masculinity in Victorian America,* ed. Mark C. Carnes, and Clyde Griffen. Chicago, 1990, 183–204.

Higham, John. "Reorientation of American Culture in the 1890s." In *Writing American History*. Bloomington, Ind. 1970, 73–102.

Lomax, Alan. *Land Where the Blues Began*. New York, 1993.

McMillen, Neil. *Dark Journey: Black Mississippians in the Age of Jim Crow*. Chicago, 1990.

Takaki, Ronald. *Strangers From A Different Shore: A History of Asian Americans*. New York, 1989.

Torgovnick, Marianna. *Gone Primitive: Savage Intellects, Modern Lives*. Chicago, 1990.

FIGURE 6.1
A turn-of-the-century cigarette manufacturer marketed
Egyptian Kings to men who favored same-sex
relationships. What does this image have in common
with Walt Whitman's depiction of same-sex relationships
in Chapter 2? Compare these men with those pictured in
"Enlist in the Navy," a recruitment poster from World
War I, located in Chapter 7. (*Source: Warshaw Collection
of Business Americana, Negative Number 88-12368,
National Museum of American History, Smithsonian
Institution, Washington, D.C.*)

CHAPTER 6

Sexuality in the Making of New Women and New Men

Between 1890 and 1930, Americans' sexual practices and identities changed dramatically. The changes were most obvious in urban areas, where first working-class and then younger middle-class women displayed increasing sexual assertiveness and gay men and lesbians created communities of their own. Reformers strove to suppress this sexual activity, but by the 1920s were generally defeated. By that time, most cultural authorities imputed sexual desire to all women and sanctioned sex as necessary to a healthy human life. Moreover, despite police surveillance, gay and lesbian communities thrived in the 1920s.

These changes produced profound results. The assumption that both women and men needed sex to lead sound lives made frank discussion of sexual issues a hallmark of modernity. It also encouraged the reformulation of marriage. Defined explicitly in the 1920s, companionate marriage required that marital partners be buddies and that both husband and wife achieve sexual satisfaction. The belief that women and men needed to have sex for reasons other than procreation legitimized the birth control movement.

This new sexual system, radically breaking with Victorian gender ideals, had some disadvantages for American women. For instance, it cast suspicion on women who chose to live their lives with other women. As mentioned earlier, a greater percentage of American women born between 1860 and 1880 remained unmarried than in any other age cohort in American history. Many of these women lived in households with other individual women or in female communities like settlement houses or women's colleges. Indeed, such female communities proved to be one source of women's political and professional power in the early twentieth century. As the life of M. Carey Thomas previously suggested, many women in relationships like these did not think of themselves as sexually involved with other women. Instead, they experienced their love for one another as an intense emotional bond, which they interpreted as passionate friendship. With the growing belief in women's sexual need, however, women without men, once presumed innocently asexual, now risked being stigmatized as either lesbian or sexually repressed. This risk, vastly increasing in the 1920s, chipped away at many women's friendships, communities, and public power.

Still, as sex moved toward a central place in ideas about human motivation and satisfaction, homosexuality emerged as a sexual identity, which helped to liberate many women and men from the assumption of heterosexuality and to stimulate the creation of gay and lesbian communities. To argue that homosexuality emerged as an identity does not mean that homosexual acts occurred for the first time. After all, Walt Whitman's poetry publicized ardent relationships among men in the 1860s. It means instead that homosexuality began to be regarded as a permanent aspect of identity. Instead of believing, as many had previously, that each homosexual act was an individual, sinful choice—like stealing—many Americans came to believe that homosexuality was caused either by a biological anomaly or experiences early in childhood. In either case, homosexuals were not so much making a choice about their sexuality as they were fulfilling a biological or psychological imperative. (Homo)sexuality was thus seen as an integral aspect of who a person was.

One peculiarity of the early twentieth-century understanding of homosexuality was that many commentators considered it to involve a reversal of gender identities. That is, for example, they judged men whose dress, deportment, and role in the sex act were conventionally manly as "normal" men even when they had sex with other men. Only those men who affected "womanly" manners, speech, and dress (like those pictured in the first illustration of this chapter) were believed to be fully homosexual. As the following documents demonstrate, sexual identities of all kinds, ideas about sex, and the actual practice of sex have varied over time and from place to place.

TRUE CHIVALRY RESPECTS ALL WOMANHOOD
Ida B. Wells

Lynching may seem a strange subject for a chapter on sex, but during the 1890s southern whites consistently pulled sex into their justification for the annual torture and murder of scores of black people, mostly men. Lynching was not new to the South in the 1890s, but it vastly increased in that decade, and, according to some observers, the rationale more consistently involved sex. Lynchers claimed that their black victims were guilty of raping white women. Sexual relations between black men and white women were so taboo at the time that potential critics of extra-legal violence fell silent in the face of this charge.

This justification for lynching reminds us that sex—both its practice and ideas about it—was implicated in maintaining gender and race hierarchies. In Chapter 2, for instance, we saw white southerners use the rape of Roda Ann Childs to enforce the subordination of black people. While the rape of black women by white men

Source: Ida B. Wells, *A Red Record Tabulated Statistics and Alleged Causes of Lynching in the United States* (Chicago, 1895), Chapter 1.

FIGURE 6.2
Jesse Washington, eighteen years old, was burned alive before an estimated 15,000 people in Waco, Texas on May 15, 1916. In a sham trial, only seven days after the crime, he had been found guilty of assault and murder. (*Source: Visual Materials from the Records of the National Association for the Advancement of Colored People, Negative Number LC-USZ62-35740, Prints and Photographs Division, Library of Congress, Washington, D.C.*)

routinely went unprosecuted, however, even consensual sex between white women and black men often met with violence. The testimony of William Stallings in Chapter 2 narrated such a case. Moreover, the myth of the black rapist, attributing brutish sexuality to black men and sexual vulnerability to white women, was used to justify domination by white men, who claimed responsibility for controlling black men and protecting white women.

One of the earliest critics of this myth was Ida B. Wells (1862–1931). Born a slave in Holly Springs, Mississippi, Wells became a journalist and world-renowned antiracist activist. In the 1890s, Wells penned several editorials and pamphlets exposing the recent increase in lynchings (over 800 in the period between 1889 and 1893). In *A Red Record,* excerpted here, she showed that the majority of black men lynched were not even accused, much less found guilty, of rape. In view of that fact, Wells made a brilliant rhetorical move: she reformulated the gender identities of the characters in the myth of the black rapist. How did she reassign the roles of victim, chivalrous hero, sexual brute, and sexual aggressor? How, in other words, did she redefine relationships between gender and race?

... In slave times the Negro was kept subservient and submissive by the frequency and severity of the scourging, but, with freedom, a new system of intimidation came into vogue; the Negro was not only whipped and scourged; he was killed.

Not all nor nearly all of the murders done by white men, during the past thirty years in the South, have come to light, but the statistics as gathered and preserved by white men, and which have not been questioned, show that during these years more than ten thousand Negroes have been killed in cold blood, without the formality of judicial trial and legal execution. . . .

Naturally enough the commission of these crimes began to tell upon the public conscience, and the Southern white man, as a tribute to the nineteenth century civilization, was in a manner compelled to give excuses for his barbarism. His excuses have adapted themselves to the emergency, and are aptly outlined by that greatest of all Negroes, Frederick Douglass, in an article of recent date, in which he shows that there have been three distinct eras of Southern barbarism, to account for which three distinct excuses have been made.

The first excuse given to the civilized world for the murder of unoffending Negroes was the necessity of the white man to repress and stamp out alleged "race riots." . . .

Then came the second excuse, which had its birth during the turbulent times of reconstruction. By an amendment to the Constitution the Negro was given the right of franchise, and, theoretically at least, his ballot became his invaluable emblem of citizenship. . . . The southern white man would not consider that the Negro had any right which a white man was bound to respect. . . . "No Negro domination" became the new legend on the sanguinary banner of the sunny South, and under it rode the Ku Klux Klan, the Regulators, and the lawless mobs, which for any cause chose to murder one man or a dozen as suited their purpose best. . . .

. . . The government which had made the Negro a citizen found itself unable to protect him. It gave him the right to vote, but denied him the protection which should have maintained that right. Scourged from his home; hunted through the swamps; hung by midnight raiders, and openly murdered in the light of day, the Negro clung to his right of franchise with a heroism which would have wrung admiration from the hearts of savages. He believed that in that small white ballot there was a subtle something which stood for manhood as well as citizenship, and thousands of brave black men went to their graves, exemplifying the one by dying for the other. . . .

Brutality still continued; Negroes were whipped, scourged, exiled, shot and hung whenever and wherever it pleased the white man so to treat them, and as the civilized world with increasing persistency held the white people of the South to account for its outlawry, the murderers invented the third excuse—that Negroes had to be killed to avenge their assaults upon women. There could be framed no possible excuse more harmful to the Negro and more unanswerable if true in its sufficiency for the white man.

. . . the Negro feels to-day that after all the work he has done, all the sacrifices he has made, and all the suffering he has endured, if he did not, now, defend his name and manhood from this vile accusation, he would be unworthy even of the contempt of mankind. It is to this charge he now feels he must make answer.

If the Southern people in defense of their lawlessness, would tell the truth and admit that colored men and women are lynched for almost any offense, from murder to a misdemeanor, there would not now be the necessity for this defense. But when they intentionally, maliciously and constantly belie the record and bolster up these falsehoods by the words of legislators, preachers, governors and bishops, then the Negro must give to the world his side of the awful story.

A word as to the charge itself. In considering the third reason assigned by the Southern white people for the butchery of blacks, the question must be asked, what the white man means when he charges the black man with rape. Does he mean the crime which the statutes of the civilized states describe as such? Not by any means. With the Southern white man, any mesalliance existing between a white woman and a colored man is a sufficient foundation for the charge of rape. The Southern white man says that it is impossible for a voluntary alliance to exist between a white woman and a colored man, and therefore, the fact of an alliance is a proof of force. In numerous instances where colored men have been lynched on the charge of rape, it was positively known at the time of the lynching, and indisputably proven after the victim's death, that the relationship sustained between the man and woman was voluntary and clandestine, and that in no court of law could even the charge of assault have been successfully maintained.

It was for the assertion of this fact, in the defense of her own race, that the writer hereof became an exile; her property destroyed and her return to her home forbidden under penalty of death, for writing the following editorial which was printed in her paper, the Free Speech, in Memphis, Tenn., May 21, 1892:

". . . Nobody in this section of the country believes the old threadbare lie that Negro men rape white women. If Southern white men are not careful, they will overreach themselves and public sentiment will have a reaction; a conclusion will then be reached which will be very damaging to the moral reputation of their women." . . .

In his remarkable apology for lynching, Bishop Haygood, of Georgia, says: "No race, not the most savage, tolerates the rape of woman, but it may be said without reflection upon any other people that the Southern people are now and always have been most sensitive concerning the honor of their women—their mothers, wives, sisters and daughters." It is not the purpose of this defense to say one word against the white women of the South. Such need not be said, but it is their misfortune that the chivalrous white men of that section, in order to escape the deserved execration of the civilized world, should shield themselves by their cowardly and infamously false excuse, and call into question that very honor about which their distinguished priestly apologist claims they are most sensitive. To justify their own barbarism they assume a chivalry which they do not possess. True chivalry respects all womanhood, and no one who reads the record, as it is written in the faces of the million mulattoes in the South, will for a minute conceive that the southern white man had a very chivalrous regard for the honor due the women of his own race or respect for the womanhood which circumstances placed in his power. That chivalry which is "most sensitive concerning the honor of women" can hope for but little respect from the civilized world, when it confines itself entirely to the women who happen to be white. Virtue knows no color line, and chivalry which depends upon complexion of skin and texture of hair can command no honest respect. . . .

The Negro may not have known what chivalry was, but he knew enough to preserve inviolate the womanhood of the South which was entrusted to his hands during the [Civil] war. The finer sensibilities of his soul may have been crushed out by years of slavery, but his heart was full of gratitude to the white women of the North [who came as teachers after emancipation], who blessed his home and inspired his soul in all these years of freedom. Faithful to his trust in both of these instances, he should now have the impartial ear of the civilized world, when he dares to speak for himself as against the infamy wherewith he stands charged.

It is his regret, that, in his own defense, he must disclose to the world that degree of dehumanizing brutality which fixes upon America the blot of a national crime. Whatever faults and failings other nations may have in their dealings with their own subjects or with other people, no other civilized nation stands condemned before the world with a series of crimes so peculiarly national. It becomes a painful duty of the Negro to reproduce a record which shows that a large portion of the American people avow anarchy, condone murder and defy the contempt of civilization.

THE GHASTLY LIFE OF FALLEN WOMEN
Chicago Vice Commission

Early in the twentieth century, many American cities formed vice commissions to study the problem of prostitution. To pursue their charge, middle-class and elite commissioners infiltrated their cities' new commercial entertainments (dance halls, theaters, amusement parks) to gather information on the exchange of sex for money. Here they found, in addition to professional prostitution, working-class youth enjoying themselves and devising very different ideas about sexual propriety from those the commissioners held.

In 1910, Chicago joined this trend. The mayor appointed a committee of upstanding citizens to visit the city's seedier districts in an effort to understand the scope and causes of prostitution and other sexual misbehavior. He hoped for recommendations of public policies that might help to eradicate these blights on the midwest's greatest city. The report of this vice commission revealed sexual practices among a spectrum of Chicago's working classes as well as the gender ideals of the investigators themselves, who were especially concerned about the lives of working girls living away from their families. At the time, these girls were called "women adrift," and they constituted about 20 percent of urban wage-earning women.

As you read selections from the report of the Chicago Vice Commission, contrast the views of sex offered by the commissioners and the subjects of their study. What was the place of sexuality in the identities of the new women studied by the report? Compare these working-class new women with Elisa Silva and Hilda Satt in Chapter 4.

The Economic Side of the Question [of prostitution]. The life of an unprotected girl who tries to make a living in a great city is full of torturing temptations. First, she faces the problem of living on an inadequate wage: Six dollars a week is the average in mercantile establishments. . . .

Hundreds, if not thousands, of girls from country towns, and those born in the city but who have been thrown on their own resources, are compelled to live in cheap boarding or rooming houses on the average wage of six dollars. How do they exist on this sum? . . . there is no doubt that many girls *do* live on even six dollars and do it *honestly,* but we can affirm that they *do not* have nourishing food, or comfortable shelter, or warm clothes, or any amusement, except perhaps free public dances, without outside help, either from charity in the shape of girls' clubs, or friends in the country home. How can she possibly exist to say nothing of live?

Is it any wonder that a tempted girl who receives only six dollars per week working with her hands sells her body for twenty-five dollars per week when she learns there is a demand for it and men are willing to pay the price? On the one hand her employer demands honesty, faithfulness and a "clean and neat appearance," and for all this he contributes from his profits an average of six dollars for every week. Her honesty alone is worth this inadequate wage disregarding the consideration of her efficiency. In the sad life of prostitution, on the other hand, we find here the employer demanding the surrender of her virtue, pays her an average of twenty-five dollars per week. Which employer wins the half starved *child* to his side in

Source: Vice Commission of Chicago, *The Social Evil in Chicago* (Chicago: Gunthorp-Warren Printing Company, 1911), pp. 42–44, 47, 210–13.

this unequal battle? It would be unjust, however, to cast any reflection upon those girls who are brave and pure, by intimating that because they earn so small a wage they must necessarily be in the same class with those other girls who, unable to survive longer the heroic battle against poverty and self-sacrifice, have succumbed and gone down. . . .

The Man's Part. The end of the battle is not yet for those girls who struggle on alone and unprotected with their more pressing financial problems. The greatest menace is before her—the Man. See her as he meets her at the door of her place of employment! See her as she returns to her cheap boarding house! Huddled away among coarse and vulgar male companions, lonely, underfed and hungry—hungry not only for food, but for a decent shelter, for a home, for friends, for a sympathetic touch or word; tired from a hard day's toil even to the point of recklessness— starving for honest pleasures and amusements—and with what does she meet? The advance of men without either a spark of bravery or honor, who hunt as their unlawful prey this impoverished girl, this defenseless *child* of poverty, unprotected, unloved and uncared for as she is plunged into the swirling, seething stream of humanity; the advances of men who are so low that they have lost even a sense of sportsmanship, and who seek as their game an underfed, a tired, and a lonely girl.

She suffers, but what of him? She goes down, and is finally sacrificed to a life of shame, but what of him? He escapes as a "romancer." It is not just! . . .

To one who hears the ghastly life story of fallen women it is ever the same— the story of treachery, seduction and downfall—the flagrant act of man—the ruin of a soul by man.

It is a man and not a woman problem which we face today—commercialized by man—supported by man—the supply of fresh victims furnished by men—men who have lost that fine instinct of chivalry and that splendid honor for womanhood where the destruction of a woman's soul is abhorrent, and where the defense of a woman's purity is truly the occasion for a valiant fight.

Typical Cases. . . . September 21st. Mag was seen at the dance hall on North Clark street. She works in one of the large department stores at a salary of $5.00 per week. She has a furnished room on North Clark street. At one time she had a baby which died. She was "hustling" certain nights in the week, and claims she does it to help support herself.

September 24th. There were about 200 girls in a dance hall at (X994) avenue.[1] One of these, Lillie, about 19 years of age, works in a department store and receives a salary of $5.00 per week. She will take presents from her men friends, but refuses the actual money. One of these friends gave her a bracelet the week previous. He is a clerk in the same store.

Violet, another girl at this dance, is about 18 years of age, and works in a department store at $6.00 per week. She has two steady friends, who take her out each week, and give her $2.00 a week. This brings up her salary to $10.00 per week. They take her to a room downtown, but she would not give the name of the place. She lives at home with her parents, and when she goes out tells them she is going to a show with a girl friend.

Bell, another one of the girls at this dance, works in a millinery store and receives $4.00 per week. One day when she was nearly broke a fellow proposed to take her out, and she agreed to the proposition. Bell is about 20 years of age and very good looking.

---

[1]Investigators coded places and people so as to protect those involved.

Bessie solicits every night in (X995), a notorious cafe at (X996) State street. Until recently she worked in a department store at $6.00 per week, but concluded this was not enough, and as she had no other way of increasing her salary, started to solicit in this place. She goes home in the morning at either 2:00 or 2:30 A.M. and often takes with her from $5.00 to $30.00; she charges $5.00.

October 8th. Dora was attending a dance at the (X997). At present she works in one of the large department stores and receives $11.00 per week. Recently a friend gave her a pair of gloves, and has promised her an old gold bracelet. He is an insurance agent. She makes dates with anyone who asks her. Her sister, Tantine, works in another department store as a clerk and receives $7.00 per week. . . .

October 3rd. . . . One of the most notorious dance halls in Chicago is at (X1014) North Clark street. On Saturday nights many girls who come to this dance are semi-professional or professional prostitutes. On Saturday and Sunday nights, the attendance is about 300, and many of these girls are waitresses, house maids and clerks in department stores. The ones who do not charge for their services are all called "charity." . . .

During the time given to this part of the work three amusement parks were investigated by two investigators whose reports corroborate each other. These parks were (X1026a), (X1026b) and (X1026c).

According to common report the conditions in these parks, especially (X1026a), had been unfavorable earlier in the summer. In September, the time of the investigation, these conditions had improved. In general it was found that there were many young girls who were unaccompanied, flirting with young boys and men and suggesting participation in different forms of amusement.

Usually there are saloons near the entrances of these parks, and young girls were seen in the rear rooms of these places. Couples also came into these saloons from the park.

September 13th. Investigator met Rose (X1027), a girl about 21 years old, from (X1028), Illinois. She stood near the Scenic Railway, and remarked that it was tiresome not to have some one to take her around, and she had never been on a Scenic Railway. She works in a butter factory and has a private room and a few steady friends who came to see her. She receives $1.00 per day in the butter factory and pays $2.00 for her room and has to eat two meals per day in a restaurant. She lives at (X1028a) and would go out for $2.00. . . .

WE MUST SET MOTHERHOOD FREE
Margaret Sanger

At the same time that Chicago's vice commissioners wrung their hands over the sexual escapades of young women adrift, Margaret Higgins Sanger (1883–1966) raised the banner of birth control. She argued that control of reproduction was the most important prerequisite of women's liberation. For providing contraceptive information and devices, she was constantly under threat of arrest because the dissemination of such knowledge through the U.S. mails remained illegal until the 1930s.

Source: Margaret Sanger, *Woman and the New Race* (New York: Truth Publishing Company, 1920), pp. 5, 7, 25, 29, 44–46, 57–58, 94–95, 116–17.

Controversy around Sanger's work diminished somewhat during the 1920s. Before she founded the American Birth Control League (1921), her work for sex education and contraceptive availability associated her with radical, especially working-class causes. After that, she pushed for middle-class respectability, urging that doctors serve as the conduits for contraceptive information. Given that many women could not afford professional medical care, contraceptive knowledge under this arrangement became more exclusively the property of privileged women.

Birth control made possible an openly sexual middle-class womanhood. Sanger believed that women ought to be able to enjoy sex without fear of pregnancy, and she offered a method for making that possible. In this way, she participated in creating the modern, sexualized woman, a new gender identity altogether, and one that made women seem more like men than before.

Around 1920, Sanger took up the eugenics standard. She argued that by choosing to have children only with fine and fit men, women had it in their power to create a better human race. The goal of producing a better race of human beings through selective breeding had in the United States and elsewhere horrendous consequences for those believed "unfit" by those in power.

In the following selections from Sanger's *Woman and the New Race,* how did Sanger define the new woman? How did her definition compare with those of Gilman, Cooper, or Bromley (Chapter 4)? How would Sanger have responded to Chicago's vice commissioners; to the working-class subjects of their study?

To-day, . . . woman is rising in fundamental revolt. . . . Millions of women are asserting their right to voluntary motherhood. They are determined to decide for themselves whether they shall become mothers, under what conditions and when. . . .

Even as birth control is the means by which woman attains basic freedom, so it is the means by which she must and will uproot the evil she has wrought through her submission. . . .

War, famine, poverty and oppression of the workers will continue while woman makes life cheap. They will cease only when she limits her reproductivity and human life is no longer a thing to be wasted. . . .

We must . . . not permit an increase in population that we are not prepared to care for to the best advantage—that we are not prepared to do justice to, educationally and economically. We must popularize birth control thinking. We must not leave it haphazardly to be the privilege of the already privileged. We must put this means of freedom and growth into the hands of the masses.

We must set motherhood free. We must give the foreign and submerged mother knowledge that will enable her to prevent bringing to birth children she does not want. We know that in each of these submerged and semisubmerged elements of the population there are rich factors of racial culture. Motherhood is the channel through which these cultures flow. Motherhood, when free to choose the father, free to choose the time and the number of children who shall result from the union, automatically works in wondrous ways. It refuses to bring forth weaklings; refuses to bring forth slaves; refuses to bear children who must live under the conditions described [previously: poverty and want]. It withholds the unfit, brings forth the fit; brings few children into homes where there is not sufficient [income?] to provide for them. Instinctively it avoids all those things which multiply racial handicaps. Under such circumstances we can hope that the 'melting pot' will refine. We shall see that it will save the precious metals of racial culture, fused into an amalgam of physical perfection, mental strength and spiritual progress. Such an American race, containing the best of all racial elements, could give to the world a vision and a leadership beyond our present imagination. . . .

The immorality of large families lies not only in their injury to the members of those families but in their injury to society. If one were asked offhand to name the greatest evil of the day one might, in light of one's education by the newspapers. . . . say prostitution, the oppression of labor, child labor, or war. Yet the poverty and neglect which drives a girl into prostitution usually has its source in a family too large to be properly cared for by the mother. . . . Labor is oppressed because it is too plentiful; wages go up and conditions improve when labor is scarce. Large families make plentiful labor and they also provide the workers for the child-labor factories as well as the armies of the unemployed. That population, swelled by overbreeding, is a basic cause of war, we shall see in a later chapter. . . .

The basic freedom of the world is woman's freedom. A free race cannot be born of slave mothers. A woman enchained cannot choose but give a measure of that bondage to her sons and daughters. No woman can call herself free who does not own and control her body. No woman can call herself free until she can choose consciously whether she will or will not be a mother.

It does not greatly alter the case that some women call themselves free because they earn their own livings, while others profess freedom because they defy the conventions of sex relationship. She who earns her own living gains a sort of freedom that is not to be undervalued, but in quality and in quantity it is of little account beside the untrammeled choice of mating or not mating, of being a mother or not being a mother. She gains food and clothing and shelter, at least, without submitting to the charity of her companion, but the earning of her own living does not give her the development of her inner sex urge, far deeper and more powerful in its outworkings than any of these externals. In order to have that development, she must still meet and solve the problem of motherhood. . . .

The world has been governed too long by repression. . . . The disastrous effects of repressing the sex force are written plainly in the health rates, the mortality statistics, the records of crime and the entry books of the hospitals for the insane. Yet this is not all the tale, for there are still the little understood hosts of sexually abnormal people and the monotonous misery of millions who do not die early nor end violently, but who are nevertheless, devoid of the joys of a natural love life. . . .

As a means of birth control, continence is as impracticable for most people as it is undesirable. . . .

The need of women's lives is not [sexual] repression, but the greatest possible expression and fulfillment of their desires upon the highest possible plane. They cannot reach higher planes through ignorance and compulsion. They can attain them only through knowledge and the cultivation of a higher, happier attitude toward sex. Sex life must be stripped of its fear. This is one of the great functions of contraceptives. That which is enshrouded in fear becomes morbid. That which is morbid cannot be really beautiful.

. . . Knowledge and freedom to choose or reject the sexual embrace, according as it is lovely or unlovely, and these alone, can solve the problem. These alone make possible between man and woman that indissoluble tie and mutual passion, and common understanding, in which lies the hope of a higher race.

HASTE MAKES WASTE
Ida Cox

During the 1920s, blues lyrics expressed women's sexual desires more blatantly than any other source. Like their male counterparts, female blues musicians participated in the Great Migration and achieved tremendous popularity during the 1920s and early 1930s. In fact, women blues artists were the first recorded and among the most popular of the first generation of blues stars.

The overt sexuality of the blues contrasted sharply with reticence about sexual matters among most middle-class black women. Because white people had historically charged black women and men with sexual lasciviousness and then used this accusation to justify white domination of black people, many middle-class black women continued in the 1920s to avoid discussions of their own sexual desire. Even as the dominant culture accepted—even promoted—new sexual identities for middle-class women, black women of this group eschewed the subject.

Not so, female blues artists. The best known composed songs that claimed sexual desire for themselves, criticized irresponsible or violent men, and explored lesbianism. Among these, the most famous were Ma Rainey (1886–1939) and Bessie Smith (1894–1937), but no performer made clearer or more humorous sexual demands of men than Georgia-born Ida Cox (1889–1967) in "One Hour Mama."

How did Cox's lyrics contrast with the sexual propriety of Ida B. Wells or Anna Julia Cooper? Compare her stance on sex with Sanger's. How would Chicago's vice commissioners have responded to her?

I've always heard that haste makes waste,
So, I believe in taking my time
The highest mountain can't be raced
Its something you must slowly climb.

I want a slow and easy man,
He needn't ever take the lead,
Cause I work on that long time plan
And I ain't looking for no speed.

I'm a one hour mama, so no one minute papa
Ain't the kind of man for me.
Set your alarm clock papa, one hour that's proper
Then love me like I like to be.

I don't want no lame excuses bout my lovin being so good,
That you couldn't wait longer, now I hope I'm understood.
I'm a one hour mama, so no one minute papa
Ain't the kind of man for me.

I can't stand no green horn lover, like a rookie goin to war,
With a load of big artillery, but don't know what its for.
He's got to bring me reference with a great long pedigree
And must prove he's got endurance, or he don't mean snap to me.

Source: Ida Cox, "One hour mama," *Mean Mothers.* Rosetta Records, RR 1300, 1980.

I can't stand no crowin rooster, what just likes a hit or two,
Action is the only booster of just what my man can do.
I don't want no imitation, my requirements ain't no joke,
Cause I got pure indignation for a guy whats lost his stroke.

I'm a one hour mama, so no one minute man for me.
Set your alarm clock papa, one hour that's proper,
Then love me like I like to be.

I may want love for one hour, then decide to make it two.
Takes an hour 'fore I get started, maybe three before I'm through.
I'm a one hour mama, so no one minute papa,
Ain't the kind of man for me.

A MORE OR LESS DISTINCT TRACE OF MASCULINITY
Havelock Ellis

One of the defining characteristics of the twentieth century has been the ever greater reliance on experts to direct every aspect of daily life. Shifting authority from religion and tradition to science, Americans increasingly looked to professionals for help with everything from cooking and rearing children to conducting relationships and fighting poverty. Sex did not escape this tendency. During the late nineteenth century, sexologists appeared on the scene and gained wider audiences as the new century progressed.

Among other issues, sexologists studied homosexuality. From their encounters with people who were sexually attracted to others of their sex, sexologists developed a variety of theories about homosexuality. One of these held that true homosexuality grew out of a congenital condition. Believing this, sexologists urged their readers to stop criminalizing same-sex relationships because homosexuals were not responsible for their hereditary condition. Hardly the stuff of gay liberation, the new theory did urge compassion rather than punishment for homosexual acts.

One of these theorists was Havelock Ellis (1859–1939), who in 1897 published *Sexual Inversion*. Ellis worked in England and based the conclusions in this book on cases of homosexuality drawn from the United States as well as Europe. He reached a fairly wide audience in the United States after the turn of the century, but the idea that homosexuality was a permanent aspect of identity probably did not achieve dominant status until the 1920s. Although Ellis's attribution of homosexuality to biology was largely replaced during that decade by Freudian psychological theories, many other elements of Ellis's arguments remained powerful in American culture.

Ellis proposed several categories of homosexuality. At one end of the spectrum were boys and girls who engaged in sex play with members of their own sex and who later found "appropriate" sex partners with members of the other sex.

Source: Havelock Ellis and John Addington Symonds, *Sexual Inversion* (London: Wilson and MacMillan, 1897), pp. 79–80, 82–88, 94–100.

These were not congenital homosexuals but simply curious youngsters whose homosexual experience proved temporary. At the other end of the spectrum were congenital homosexuals: the real thing. The crucial characteristic of a true homosexual was his/her embodiment of qualities associated with the other sex. Female homosexuals were marked by masculine traits; male homosexuals by feminine ones. In other words, true homosexuality was more a matter of gender reversal (sexual inversion, to use Ellis's term) than sexual attraction to members of one's own sex.

Sexual identities defined by gay men and lesbians themselves did not precisely match those articulated by Ellis. Nevertheless, the sex experts' understanding of homosexuality proved a force with which gay men and lesbians had to contend. The following excerpt focuses exclusively on sexual inversion in women. Based on this source, what are some of the ways that lesbian and gay history have diverged? What were the various degrees of inversion, according to Ellis? How did his assumptions match evidence earlier presented on passionate friendships among women?

> ... we know comparatively little of sexual inversion in woman; of the total number of recorded cases of this abnormality, now very considerable, but a small proportion are women, and the chief monographs on the subject devote but little space to women.
>
> I think there are several reasons for this. Notwithstanding the severity with which homosexuality in women has been visited in a few cases, for the most part men seem to have been indifferent towards it; when it has been made a crime or a cause for divorce in men, it has usually been considered as no offence at all in women. Another reason is that it is less easy to detect in women; we are accustomed to a much greater familiarity and intimacy between women than between men, and we are less apt to suspect the existence of any abnormal passion. And allied with this cause we have also to bear in mind the extreme ignorance and the extreme reticence of women regarding any abnormal or even normal manifestation of their sexual life. A woman may feel a high degree of sexual attraction for another woman without realising that her affection is sexual, and when she does realise it she is nearly always very unwilling to reveal the nature of her intimate experience, ...
>
> With girls, as with boys, it is in school, at the evolution of puberty, that homosexuality first shows itself. It may originate either peripherally or centrally. In the first case two children, perhaps when close to each other in bed, more or less unintentionally generate in each other a certain amount of sexual irritation, which they foster by mutual touching and kissing. This is a spurious kind of homosexuality; it is merely the often precocious play of the normal instinct, and has no necessary relation to true sexual inversion. In the girl who is congenitally predisposed to homosexuality it will continue and develop; in the majority it will be forgotten as quickly as possible not without shame, in the presence of the normal object of sexual love. ....
>
> The cases in which the source [of homosexual desire] is central, rather than peripheral, nevertheless merge into the foregoing, with no clear line of demarcation. In such cases a school girl or young woman forms an ardent attachment for another girl, probably somewhat older than herself, often a schoolfellow, sometimes her school-mistress, upon whom she will lavish an

astonishing amount of affection and devotion. This affection may or may not be returned; usually the return consists of a gracious acceptance of the affectionate services. The girl who expends this wealth of devotion is surcharged with emotion, but she is often unconscious of or ignorant of the sexual impulse, and she seeks for no form of sexual satisfaction. Kissing and the privilege of sleeping with the friend are, however, sought, and at such times it often happens that even the comparatively unresponsive friend feels more or less definite sexual emotion (pudendal turgescence with secretion of mucus and involuntary twitching of the neighbouring muscles), though little or no attention may be paid to this phenomenon, and in the common ignorance of girls concerning sex matters it may not be understood. In some cases there is an attempt, either instinctive or intentional, to develop the sexual feeling by close embraces and kissing. This rudimentary kind of homosexual relationship is, I believe, more common among girls than boys, and for this there are several reasons: (1) A boy more often has some acquaintance with sexual phenomena and would frequently regard such a relationship as unmanly; (2) the girl has a stronger need of affection and self-devotion to another person than a boy has; (3) she has not, under our existing social conditions which compel young women to hold the opposite sex at arm's length, the same opportunities of finding an outlet for her sexual emotions; while (4) conventional propriety recognises a considerable degree of physical intimacy between girls, thus at once encouraging and cloaking the manifestations of homosexuality.

These passionate friendships, of a more or less unconsciously sexual character, are certainly common. It frequently happens that a period during which a young woman falls in love at a distance with some young man of her acquaintance alternates with periods of intimate attachment to a friend of her own sex. No congenital inversion is usually involved. . . .

A class of women to be first mentioned, a class in which homosexuality, while fairly distinct, is only slightly marked, is formed by the women to whom the actively inverted woman is most attracted. These women differ in the first place from the normal or average woman in that they are not repelled or disgusted by lover-like advances from persons of their own sex. They are not usually attractive to the average man, though to this rule there are many exceptions. Their faces may be plain or ill-made, but not seldom they possess good figures, a point which is apt to carry more weight with the inverted woman than beauty of face. Their sexual impulses are seldom well marked, but they are of strongly affectionate nature. On the whole, they are women who are not very robust and well-developed, physically or nervously, and who are not well adopted [sic] for child-bearing, but who still possess many excellent qualities, and they are always womanly. . . . So far as they may be said to constitute a class, they seem to possess a genuine though not precisely sexual preference for women over men, and it is this coldness rather than lack of charm which often renders men rather indifferent to them.

The actively inverted woman differs from the women of the class just mentioned in one fairly essential character: a more or less distinct trace of masculinity. She may not be, and frequently is not, what would be called a "mannish" woman, for the latter may imitate men on grounds of taste and habit unconnected with sexual perversion, while in the inverted woman the masculine traits are part of an organic instinct which she by no means always wishes to accentuate. The inverted woman's masculine element may in the least degree consist only in the fact that she makes advances to the woman to whom she is attracted and treats all men in a cool, direct manner, which may not exclude comradeship, but which excludes every sexual relationship, whether of passion or merely of coquetry. . . .

. . . As I have already pointed out, a woman who is inclined to adopt the ways and garments of men is by no means necessarily inverted. . . . There is, however, a very pronounced tendency among sexually inverted women to adopt male attire when practicable. In such cases male garments are not usually regarded as desirable chiefly on account of practical convenience, nor even in order to make an impression on other women, but because the wearer feels more at home in them. . . . And when they still retain female garments these usually show some traits of masculine simplicity, and there is nearly always a disdain for the petty feminine artifices of the toilet. Even when this is not obvious there are all sorts of instinctive gestures and habits which may suggest to female acquaintances the remark that such a person "ought to have been a man". The brusque, energetic movements, the attitude of the arms, the direct speech, the inflexions of the voice, the masculine straightforwardness and sense of honour, and especially the attitude towards men, free from any suggestion either of shyness or audacity, will often suggest the underlying psychic abnormality to a keen observer. . . .

. . . She herself generally feels the greatest indifference to men, and often cannot understand why a woman should love a man, though she easily understands why a man should love a woman. She shows, therefore, nothing of that sexual shyness and engaging air of weakness and dependence which are an invitation to men. . . .

A DISTINCT SEX
Anonymous

By the 1920s, medical doctors and psychologists had largely replaced sexologists as the scientists of sex. Samuel Kahn, a psychiatrist employed by New York City's Department of Correction, was one such investigator. Between 1922 and 1926, Kahn interviewed more than five hundred homosexual women and men who were inmates of either the New York County Penitentiary on Blackwell's Island or the Women's Workhouse. His purpose was to understand homosexuality so that he could more readily diagnose what he considered to be this psychological disorder and thus make it possible for prison officials to segregate homosexual inmates from others.

A decade after the study was completed, Kahn published his findings in *Mentality and Homosexuality*. Included as an appendix to that study was the completed questionnaire of one subject of Kahn's study, an anonymous homosexual prisoner housed in the penitentiary on Blackwell's Island. The following excerpts from that questionnaire, though reported to a professional, reveal more about ideas within a gay community than Ellis's theorizing did. How was gender implicated in the prisoner's understanding of homosexuality? Did he consider every man who engaged in sex with another man to be homosexual? Compare and contrast his views with those of Ellis.

Source: Samuel Kahn, *Mentality and Homosexuality* (Boston: Meador Publishing, 1937), Appendix II, pp. 152–56, 160.

1. What is a homosexual?

   A homosexual is a person whose sex instincts or impulses are unnatural.[2] Nature tells us that a man's instincts are aggressive and positive; a woman's receptive and negative.

   The man whose nature is negative is a homosexual and the woman whose nature is positive is a homosexual.

2. How can a person with the organs of one sex have the sexual inclinations of the other sex?

   The character of a person is composed of a curious mixture of virtues and vices, some of the virtues and vices being essentially masculine and others essentially feminine.

   To illustrate: *Courage* is a masculine virtue, yet there are any number of women who possess it without being queer. *Kindness* is a feminine virtue, still there are many men as kind and merciful as the saints in heaven. *Boastfulness* is masculine, yet many women are boastful. *Vanity* is feminine, still countless numbers of men are vain.

   However, the possession of one, two, three or four feminine attributes in a man does not necessarily imply homosexuality.

   I am not a psychologist, and therefore, do not know how many ethical attributes the average person possesses. But for the sake of convenience let us place the number at fifteen.

   If a man has eight feminine and seven masculine attributes, it naturally follows its logical sequence that his ethical and psychological constitution is predominantly feminine. His point of view on every subject is a feminine point of view. It is particularly so on the question of sex. The fact that he is to all outward appearance a male does not alter the above in as much as his sex, is nine tenths psychological and one tenth physical.

3. Are all homosexuals alike?

   No. They differ from each other in two fundamental respects. First, the outward characteristics and, second, the inward temperament and inclinations.

   We shall take up the outward characteristics first. The homosexuals vary in their outward characteristics all the way from the extreme effeminate to the extreme masculine. It is a mistake to assume that because a homosexual's face, figure, walk, talk and expression is manly that he is not as much of a homosexual as the one whose outward characteristics are distinctly feminine. It is quite possible for a homosexual to look and act like a man and yet possess the soul of a woman. Secondly, their temperaments differ or to be precise, their methods. Some prefer to have their passion sated one way; others a second way; still others a third way and your writer is not trying to be humorous when he says there are a few who use their ingenuity for the purpose of devising new means to sate their passion. Some of them have their passions sated only one way, others use two or three ways.[3] Your writer does not care to be vulgar so he does not enumerate and explain the ways. . . .

---

[2]Notice that what this prisoner calls "sex instincts," we would call gender.

[3]During the early twentieth century, many gay communities assigned sexual identities on the basis of a man's preference for a specific sexual practice and according to his particular role in the sexual relationship. For instance, a gay man might prefer oral or anal sex. This preference was considered part of his sexual identity. Those who liked oral sex were then expected to prefer either to perform oral sex on some else or to be the receiving partner. Each of these preferences was considered part of a permanent sexual identity.

4. Aren't some homosexuals self-made?

No real homosexual is self-made. But for want of a better name, those whom we may call semi-homosexual are made so by circumstances. Some of them overcome it as they grow older; others get worse with time. Most of the semi-homosexuals, your writer thinks, are made so in prison institutions. . . .

5. What is the attitude of the male toward the homosexual?

It is commonly and erroneously assumed that the more masculine a man is the more he despises homosexuals. On the contrary, your writer has observed that the most hostile attitude is that of the semi-homosexuals. Their hostility is caused by their feeling of inferiority to the real homosexuals. It is a well known fact that the secret of a woman's appeal to man is not so much her sex as her effeminacy. There are some women who by a mere smile are capable of kindling the fires of passions in man; others who leave a man emotionless and cold as ice. The attitude of the average man to the homosexual is determined by the degree of effeminacy in the homosexual. Your writer has observed that nine out of ten take favorably to the homosexual. Of course, they seek the eternal feminine in the homosexual and in most cases have no difficulty in finding it. There are some homosexuals so very effeminate that the only way one would believe they are not women is by observing their nude bodies. These feminine homosexuals naturally have the greatest number of admirers. The more masculine of homosexuals, just as that type of woman, has to be content with a lesser number of admirers. Then again there is a surprising number of men who actually prefer the caresses of homosexuals to those of women. . . .

6. Is it possible for a genuine love, such as exists between man and woman to exist between man and homosexual?

With the emphasis on the word possible, I say "Yes." But first let us ascertain the definition of love. Love being somewhat more vague than a piece of cheese for instance, cannot be defined as definitely. However, I think that most definitions of love are some variation of the following: Love is a beautiful friendship developed to the highest degree plus the natural sex attractions. The desires to be with the beloved one, the desire for his happiness and welfare and the jealousy inspired when there is any suspicion of divided affections. A homosexual is capable of any of the above in regards to a man, and vice versa. The answer I reiterate, is yes. A man and homosexual can love each other with all the passionate intensity of man and woman. . . .

7. What is the solution [to homosexuality]?

Punishment isn't. . . . All the jails in the world couldn't cure a real homosexual. . . . The law should treat the homosexuals as a distinct sex, and entitled to the same rights as women are. Let us hope that the day will soon come when the world will be more broadminded and its prejudices will not be its opinions, and its opinions will not be prejudiced.

Anonymous

RECOMMENDED READINGS

Bederman, Gail. "'Civilization,' the Decline of Middle-Class Manliness, and Ida B. Wells's Antilynching Campaign, (1892–94)." *Radical History Review* 52 (Winter 1992):5–32.

Carby, Hazel V. "It Jus Be's Dat Way Sometime": The Sexual Politics of Women's Blues." *Radical America* 20 (1986):9–24.

Chauncey, George. "Christian Brotherhood or Sexual Perversion? Homosexual Identities and the Construction of Sexual Boundaries in the World War One Era." *Journal of Social History* 9 (Winter 1985):189–212.

————. *Gay New York: Gender, Urban Culture, and the Making of the Gay Male World, 1890–1940*. New York, 1994.

Davis, Angela Y. *Blues Legacies and Black Feminism: Gertrude "Ma" Rainey, Bessie Smith and Billie Holiday*. New York, 1998.

Davis, Angela Y. *Women, Race, and Class*. New York, 1981.

Gordon, Linda. *Woman's Body, Woman's Right: Birth Control in America*. New York, 1977.

Hall, Jacquelyn Dowd. *Revolt Against Chivalry: Jessie Daniel Ames and the Women's Campaign Against Lynching*. New York, 1979.

Meyerowitz, Joanne J. *Women Adrift: Independent Wage Earners in Chicago, 1880–1930*. Chicago, 1988.

Peiss, Kathy. *Cheap Amusements: Working Women and Leisure in Turn-of-the-Century New York*. Philadelphia, 1986.

Peiss, Kathy, and Christina Simmons, eds. with Robert A. Padgug. *Passion and Power: Sexuality in History*. Philadelphia, 1989.

FIGURE 7.1
Opponents of women's suffrage sometimes argued that women's voting would disrupt gender relations within families. Women would "unsex" themselves by marking a ballot. This drawing from 1909 depicts that fear. (*Source: Negative Number LC-USZ62-51821, Prints and Photographs Division, Library of Congress, Washington, D.C.*)

CHAPTER 7

Progressive Reform
and World War I

Progressive reform and World War I dominated the political life of Americans between 1900 and 1920. Both reforming campaigns and the prosecution of the war expressed Americans' confusion over gender and sexuality and simultaneously helped to create a modern gender system. Documents in this chapter illuminate some of the gender and sexual implications of political life in the era of progressive reform and war.

Progressive reform comprised a set of reform campaigns that sought to ameliorate the worst effects of industrialization, urbanization, immigration, and gender anarchy by expanding the responsibilities of the state. As reformers saw them, these effects included economic insecurity, the high cost of living, unhealthy working conditions, political corruption, and the loss of economic opportunity for the "little guy." In many ways, progressives' responses to these problems created more intimate relationships between citizens and their government by making the state more responsible for the social and economic welfare of citizens. Mothers' pensions, for example, implemented in nearly every state, provided public stipends to some widows with dependent children; workmen's compensation programs supplied monies to some workers injured on the job. Factory safety laws protected many workers from the worst dangers of industrial employment.

In contrast, progressives simultaneously drove a wider wedge between citizens and the state. They did this partly by diluting the power of the vote in favor of organized interest groups. To make government run more efficiently, they also encouraged the appointment of expert commissions at every governmental level to manage various public problems, which meant that crucial public decisions were often made by officials who were not elected.

This tension between democracy and efficiency was expressed in other progressive initiatives as well. Some reformers, for example, battled for women's suffrage, the referendum, or the direct election of senators while at the same time advocating the replacement of elected city councils with unelected city managers.

131

On the one hand, they aimed to expand democracy and, on the other, to limit it in the interest of efficiency.

Gender shaped progressive reform and was in turn reshaped by it. The ideas that reformers held about the proper roles of women and men and about appropriate sexual behavior informed their legislative proposals. As we have seen, for example, reformers tried to stamp out premarital sex, especially for young women, by regulating dance halls, movie theaters, and other commercial entertainments. Material in this chapter will show further that reformers proposed different kinds of social service programs for women and men. Another way that gender structured progressive reform was by influencing the organizations of reformers: male and female reformers often formed gender-segregated organizations to pursue reforming goals, and they sometimes employed gender-specific tactics to implement their reform agendas.

Gender was also implicated in U.S. participation in World War I. First, because military needs siphoned off so many men, the war temporarily opened new kinds of jobs to women, especially in transportation and industry. Second, it, like the war with Spain in 1898, opened a public dialogue about American manhood—and womanhood. Finally, the government used ideas about manhood and womanhood to encourage support for the war, as shown especially in the series of posters that concludes this chapter.

WHERE WILL INDEPENDENT MANHOOD BE?
Editorialist

While economic policy might seem an unlikely place to look for documents on the history of gender, it turns out to be a fertile field for gender studies. Gender wove through even the public debates over corporate capitalism early in the century. Many commentators worried about the kinds of men that enormous corporations would create.

One of the issues that drove white, male progressives was the "trust." In capital-intensive, mass-producing segments of the economy, gigantic enterprises were absorbing huge portions of the market at the turn of the century. These corporations included U.S. Steel, Standard Oil, and the American Tobacco Company. Referring to virtually all big businesses as "trusts," progressives advocated two different reactions from the state: either break up the trusts or regulate them in the interest of workers and consumers. While the Pure Food and Drug Act (1906) and the Federal Reserve Act (1913) represented attempts at regulation, laws aimed to strengthen the Sherman Anti-Trust Act (1890) exemplified the preference of trustbusters.

Those determined to use the state to dismantle the trusts sometimes justified their demand by pointing to the damage that corporate life inflicted on American manhood. In what ways, according to the following editorial, did gender motivate

Source: "The Menace to Economic Independence," *The Independent* 54 (December 4, 1902), pp. 2908–10.

trustbusters? What version of manhood did they prefer? What kind of economic organization supported that version? How would this writer have responded to the manly ideals of the Pacific Electric Railway employees (Chapter 5)?

Recent developments of trust methods show that the intention of the magnates is to stop at nothing short of a complete control of industry. Recent developments of the trade union methods, on the other hand, show that trade union leaders, on their part, aim at nothing less than the establishment of a despotism which shall deprive non-union workers of any possible opportunity to earn a livelihood, and shall extend to union workers only such opportunities, to earn barely so much income as the union may dictate.

Between these two efforts, that of the trust on the one hand and that of the trade unions on the other hand, economic liberty is in serious danger.

How the greater trusts, like the Standard Oil Company and the United States Steel Corporation, for example, have compelled smaller enterprises to enter the combination under penalty of ruin, is too familiar a story to need repetition. Hitherto trust methods have been employed chiefly within the field of production. Within that field there are left to-day few opportunities for the man who would prefer economic independence to a life of service as a salaried employee. Many thousands of ambitious young business men, who a generation ago would sturdily have fought the battle of existence for themselves, are to-day industrial dependents, receiving fixed salaries and liable to dismissal without warning, not for incompetence only, but merely because a trust decides to modify its plan of operations.

The field of retail business has suffered serious inroads here and there by trust methods. The so-called Cracker Trust, for example, has a grip upon retail trade which is felt by every cross roads and corner grocer in the land. Department stores also, which, under another form, are essentially like trusts in their methods, have been multiplying in every large center of population. Nevertheless, until now there have remained many business opportunities in retail trade to which men of ambition and independent spirit, but possessing only a small amount of capital, have been attracted. That these opportunities are as rapidly as possible to be extinguished in the further evolution of trust methods has of late been made quite clear.

The story of the means by which the American Tobacco Company is driving the retail tobacconist out of business in New York, Boston, Philadelphia, Baltimore, Washington, Chicago and Kansas City, and in scores of smaller towns as well, has recently been told. Having by successive operation secured an effective control of the wholesale tobacco trade and of the manufacture of the various brands of tobacco and cigars, including a very large part of the Cuban output, the American Tobacco Company is now engaged in taking over the retail field; and apparently no expenditure necessary to accomplish the result will be considered too great. Innumerable retail tobacco stores, undoubtedly backed by the trust, are offering cigars, pipes and tobacco at prices which no independent dealer can meet. Thus brought face to face with ruin, the independent dealer is approached by agents of the trust, who offer him a moderate price for his stock and fixtures and a salaried position as a selling agent. If the offer is rejected two stores are opened, one on each side of him, and, regardless of loss, a competition is established which can end only in the speedy ruin of the weaker party.

That these methods will succeed in retail business, as they have succeeded in production, is at least probable. Other trusts are already to some extent embarking upon undertakings similar to that of the American Tobacco Company; and it is alleged that among them may be found even the enterprise that is acquiring control of the cut flower business. It seems certain that before long it will be impossible for any man on his own account to engage in even so simple a business as selling smoking tobacco and cigars, retailing cut flowers, selling newspapers, or even peanuts and bananas on the street corner. Every man who is not a multimillionaire will be a millionaire's man, dependent upon the good will of a superior for his daily bread.

Could there be a more melancholy outcome of our great American attempt to build up a civilization in which every man might be independent and self-respecting?

But this is not the worst. As the number of economic dependents increases, their desperate necessity to resist the arbitrary power of their employers drives employees to methods which are further destructive of individual liberty. At every moment facing the dread possibility of discharge at the decision of a trust, wage earners cling with desperation to "the job," and begin to look with hatred upon the man who would step in and take it for a smaller remuneration or on more humiliating terms. Consumed by this hatred they yield their consent to the employment of any means which their more reckless leaders suggest to maintain the solidarity of the union interest.

What will happen when nine-tenths of those who, under the business conditions of former years, would have been independent business men, find themselves in the same condition that the wage-earner is to-day? There is little risk in predicting that they will unite in organizations that will employ trade union methods, and that we shall see innumerable unions within the salaried class, each striving to bar out competition, to limit the amount and quality of work, and, in short, to maintain a rigorous monopoly of "the job."

And where then will there be any economic liberty? Where will independent manhood be? What manner of people shall we be in this "land of the free and home of the brave?" No more serious problem than this confronts our country to-day.

THE TWO SEXES DIFFER IN THE CAPACITY TO MAINTAIN THE STRUGGLE FOR SUBSISTENCE
Supreme Court of the United States

Whereas some progressives battled for legislation to break up big businesses, others fought for laws that might curb their worst abuses against employees. Such legislation included factory safety laws, workmen's compensation programs, minimum wage and maximum hours laws. State legislatures wrote most of these laws before the 1930s, but the federal Supreme Court was often called in to decide their constitutionality.

Progressives discovered early on that the Supreme Court took a dim view of protective legislation for male workers. Most famously, in *Lochner v. New York* (1905), the Supreme Court ruled unconstitutional a law that restricted the hours of bakers in New York. The Court maintained that the state law interfered with the constitutionally protected freedom of workers to contract for as many hours of work as they chose. Only if the state could prove that baking for long hours constituted a health risk either to the bakers themselves or to the general public could New York invoke its police powers to enforce such a restriction on the freedom of contract. The Court majority did not find such a risk in the bakers' case and overturned New York's law.

Source: *Muller v. Oregon*, 208 U.S. 412 (1908).

Before the *Lochner* decision, many states had already passed maximum hours laws specifically aimed at women workers. One of these states was Oregon, which in 1903 limited the hours of women in industrial work to ten each day. In 1905, Oregon took to court a laundry owner (Curt Muller), who had violated the law. Eventually, Muller took the case to the U.S. Supreme Court, where he expected the reasoning in *Lochner* to result in a rejection of Oregon's law.

Lawyer Louis Brandeis (1856–1941), a future Supreme Court justice hired by the National Consumers' League (NCL), argued Oregon's case. The National Consumers' League, a mostly female organization headed by the fiery reformer Florence Kelley (1859–1932), led the progressive charge for protective legislation for women workers. She hoped that these laws would provide an opening wedge for protective legislation for all workers, a goal realized after Kelley's death in the Fair Labor Standards Act of 1938. For the *Muller* case, she and her colleague, social scientist Josephine Goldmark (1877–1950), aided Brandeis in preparing a precedent-setting brief that provided over one hundred pages of evidence that women workers were peculiarly hurt by long hours and so warranted the exercise of the state's police powers in their defense—even when men did not.

As you will see in the following excerpt of the Supreme Court's decision, the Court accepted this argument. How did ideas about men and women shape this court decision and the dozens of state laws that regulated the hours and conditions of women workers while refusing to protect men? How did those laws, in turn, create or maintain differences between women and men?

. . . We held in *Lochner v. New York*, 198 U.S. 45, that a law providing that no laborer shall be required or permitted to work in bakeries more than sixty hours in a week or ten hours in a day was not as to men a legitimate exercise of the police power of the State, but an unreasonable, unnecessary, and arbitrary interference with the right and liberty of the individual to contract in relation to his labor, and as such was in conflict with, and void under, the Federal Constitution. That decision is invoked by plaintiff in error as decisive of the question before us. But this assumes that the difference between the sexes does not justify a different rule respecting a restriction of the hours of labor . . .

That woman's physical structure and the performance of maternal functions place her at a disadvantage in the struggle for subsistence is obvious. This is especially true when the burdens of motherhood are upon her. Even when they are not, by abundant testimony of the medical fraternity continuance for a long time on her feet at work, repeating this from day to day, tends to injurious effects upon the body, and as healthy mothers are essential to vigorous offspring, the physical well-being of woman becomes an object of public interest and care in order to preserve the strength and vigor of the race.

Still again, history discloses the fact that woman has always been dependent upon man. He established his control at the outset by superior physical strength, and this control in various forms, with diminishing intensity, has continued to the present. As minors, though not to the same extent, she has been looked upon in the courts as needing especial care that her rights may be preserved. Education was long denied her, and while now the doors of the schoolroom are opened and her opportunities for acquiring knowledge are great, yet even with that and the consequent increase of capacity for business affairs it is still true that in the struggle for subsistence she is not an equal competitor with her brother. Though limitations upon personal and contractual rights may be removed by legislation, there is that in her disposition and habits of life which will operate against a full assertion of those rights. She will still be where some legislation to protect her seems necessary to secure a real equality of right. Doubtless there are individual exceptions, and there are many respects in which she has an advantage over him; but looking at it from the viewpoint of the effort to maintain an independent position in life, she is not upon an equality. Differentiated by these matters from the other sex, she is properly placed in a class by herself, and legislation designed for her protection may be sustained, even when like legislation is not necessary for men and could not be sustained. It is impossible to close one's eyes to the fact that she still looks to her brother and depends upon him. Even though all restrictions on political, personal, and contractual rights were taken away, and she stood, so far as statutes are concerned, upon an absolutely equal plane with him, it would still be true that she is so constituted that she will rest upon and look to him for protection; that her physical structure and a proper discharge of her maternal functions—having in view not merely her own health, but the well-being of the race—justify legislation to protect her from the greed as well as the passion of man. The limitations which this statute places upon her contractual powers, upon her right to agree with her employer as to the time she shall labor, are not imposed solely for her benefit, but also largely for the benefit of all. Many words cannot make this plainer. The two sexes differ in structure of body, in the functions to be performed by each, in the amount of physical strength, in the capacity for long-continued labor, particularly when done standing, the influence of vigorous health upon the future well-being of the race, the self-reliance which enables one to assert full rights, and in the capacity to maintain the struggle for subsistence. This difference justifies a difference in legislation and upholds that which is designed to compensate for some of the burdens which rest upon her.

We have not referred in this discussion to the denial of the elective franchise in the State of Oregon, for while that may disclose a lack of political equality in all things with her brother, that is not of itself decisive. The reason runs deeper, and rests in the inherent difference between the two sexes, and in the different functions in life which they perform.

For these reasons, and without questioning in any respect the decision in *Lochner v. New York,* we are of the opinion that it cannot be adjudged that the act in question is in conflict with the Federal Constitution, so far as it respects the work of a female in a laundry, and the judgment of the Supreme Court of Oregon is

Affirmed.

GOVERNMENTAL MATERNALISM
Editorialist

Shortly after the Supreme Court rendered its decision in the *Muller* case—1912, to be exact—the United States Congress created the Children's Bureau, a new agency in the federal Department of Labor and Commerce. Like the *Muller* decision, this

Source: "Our New Mother—the Government," *The Outlook* 105 (September 13, 1913), pp. 60–61.

act of Congress resulted largely from the work of progressive women, who lobbied for a federal bureau to gather information on the nation's children and then to lead in defining the country's child welfare policies.

Women in the settlement movement proved particularly important in the crusade to create a Children's Bureau. Settlements, first appearing in the United States during the 1880s, were places where middle-class women and men lived in the midst of working-class, largely immigrant neighborhoods. Their purpose was to bring the classes closer together. By the turn of the century, settlements existed in most sizable cities, and educated women took the lead in their establishment. Once acquainted with their working-class neighbors, these middle-class women set about creating programs and institutions to provide social services that they believed their neighbors needed. Much of the time, settlement residents piloted local health services, educational series, or recreational programs and then lobbied their municipal, county or state government to provide permanent funding and oversight. In this way, the settlements became leaders in progressive reform.

The idea for a federal agency devoted to child welfare is usually credited to Lillian Wald (1867–1940), head resident of the Henry Street Settlement in New York City. Herself a visiting nurse, Wald participated in creating a reforming network that stretched across the country by 1903, when she first proposed her bureaucratic innovation. Most crucial in her lobbying effort were sister reformers, Florence Kelley, who by then lived at the Henry Street Settlement, and Jane Addams (1860–1935), head resident of Hull House, the nation's foremost settlement, this one located on the south side of Chicago.

The reformers did not rest when Congress passed their bill in 1912. Instead, they initiated a second lobby to push for the appointment of a woman to head the new agency. They argued that, since women had a natural affinity for children, the director of the Children's Bureau ought to be female. This argument, based on particular beliefs about womanhood and manhood, won the day. Julia Lathrop (1858–1932), earliest Chief of the Children's Bureau, was the first female head of a federal bureau. A resident of Hull House, Lathrop hired almost exclusively women to staff the unit.

Mothers' pensions were among the social service programs advocated by professional women in the Children's Bureau. Mothers' pensions were public stipends paid to mothers—usually widows—who found themselves without male support. The purpose of these pensions was to allow impoverished mothers to remain at home with their children rather than having to put them in an orphanage or neglect them while working for wages. Most states created mothers' pensions programs in the 1910s and 1920s. Women in the Children's Bureau much preferred to keep mothers out of the labor market than to encourage waged labor by advocating child care for working mothers. Historians call this commitment to women as mothers—instead of as wage-earning workers—maternalism.

The following editorial from the reforming serial, *The Outlook,* heralded the early work of the Children's Bureau. In what ways did this new bureau embody the modern commitment to expertise? What did it assume were the roles of women and men? How did it change the gendering of the federal government?

Our New Mother—the Government. Any mother understanding English who wishes to be told in simple language what every mother ought to know in preparation for the birth of her child can have the information by simply writing and mailing a letter as follows:

Chief of the Children's Bureau
U.S. Department of Labor
Washington, D.C.

Dear Madam—Please send me a copy of the monograph on "Prenatal Care," Care of Children Series No. 1, Bureau Publication No. 4.

Very truly yours,

and signing her name, with address. This pamphlet, prepared by Mrs. Max West, under the direction of Miss Julia C. Lathrop, Chief of the Bureau, alone is enough to justify the law passed a little over a year ago establishing in the Federal Government a Children's Bureau. If it is circulated and read as it ought to be, an uncountable number of children who would otherwise die will live, and an uncountable number of children who would otherwise be unhappy and unfitted for life because sickly or diseased will be healthy, happy, and vigorous. In this pamphlet the Government has made a beginning of doing for the children of the country what it has done superbly for the country's crops and herds. Through the Department of Agriculture the Government has acted as a volunteer expert farm counselor or consulting farmer. Through the Children's Bureau the Government is now undertaking to act as a sort of expert home-counselor or Consulting Mother. And, whatever one may think of paternalism in government, no one can examine this pamphlet without welcoming most heartily this form of governmental maternalism. The pamphlet might well be called "When a Child is Born." It does not, of course, take the place of physician or nurse, but, on the contrary, enables the mother to co-operate intelligently with both physician and nurse. It starts by telling the mother what are the signs that will inform her that a child is coming to her, and it closes by telling her what she should eat and drink while she is nursing her baby. In between it tells about what should normally be done during pregnancy, what preparations should be made for the period of confinement, what is a sensible outfit for the expected baby, what precautions should be taken for the baby's birth, what may usually be expected at the time of the birth, what should be done in emergencies, how the new-born baby should be cared for, and what the mother should do while lying-in. There is no reason that is not found purely on conventions why this pamphlet should not be read by young girls, and very good reason why it should be. Of course, no father who is worthy of the name can fail to benefit by such information as is contained in this pamphlet—the knowledge of what has to be undergone by the mother of his children. The wide circulation of this pamphlet can also serve a useful purpose in giving the American people a definite idea, at least in part, of what the Children's Bureau really is, and how intimately this new arm of the Government concerns the lives of the people themselves. During the period when the bill creating the Bureau was under debate one eminent official high in the Federal Government persisted in calling it the Child Labor Bureau, as if it was to be devoted to the consideration solely of children in factories. Important as that aspect in the life of children in America is, it is fortunately only one aspect. The Bureau has to do with all the children of America. That the children need the help that such a

Bureau can give is evident from some of the facts stated in the preface of this pamphlet—that "slightly more than 42 per cent of the infants dying under one year of age in the [birth] registration area in 1911 did not live to complete the first month of life, and that of this 42 per cent almost seven-tenths died as a result of conditions existing before they were born or of injury and accident at birth." Such facts, established by the latest reports of the Bureau of the Census, afford ample reason why the new Children's Bureau should undertake the preparation of a series of monographs on the care of children, and why it should begin that series by a pamphlet on care before birth. The existence and availability of this pamphlet should be known to all physicians and nurses, as well as to all mothers.

THE SIGN OF POWER
Dean Benjamin Brawley, Mrs. Carrie Clifford, Miss M. E. Jackson

While white men dominated the public discussion of trusts and white women the push for protective legislation and the Children's Bureau, black and white women and men took up the issue of women's suffrage. Given such widespread participation in the debate over women's suffrage, it stands as one of the central issues in progressive reform.

The campaign for women's suffrage had a long and complicated history. In 1890, through the merger of two older organizations, the National American Woman Suffrage Association (NAWSA) formed. It led the movement for women's suffrage from that point until the victory of the Nineteenth Amendment to the U.S. Constitution in 1920. On the eve of victory, the NAWSA claimed two million members. In the meantime, many local and regional suffrage associations organized in addition to a second, more militant national group called the Congressional Union, and many states granted full or partial suffrage to its women. In fact, by 1919, over half of the states had already granted at least presidential suffrage to women.

The ratification of the Woman's Suffrage Amendment did not automatically enfranchise all American women. While no state could now deny suffrage on the basis of sex, the same measures that disfranchised black men in the South also disfranchised most black women. Not until passage of the Voting Rights Act of 1965 did women's suffrage achieve a complete victory.

Race had previously divided the suffrage movement itself. Hoping to win support of white southerners, leaders in the North refused to admit black women's clubs to the NAWSA and declined openly to advocate the vote for black women. Facing this racism in the white movement, black women formed their own suffrage associations as they simultaneously pushed for the re-enfranchisement of black men in the South.

Arguments for the enfranchisement of women varied dramatically. Some people argued that women deserved the vote because they were rights-bearing individuals just like men; as such, they ought to exercise the right to elect their governors. Others argued that women should have the vote because they were different from

Source: "Votes for Women," *The Crisis* 10 (August 1915), pp. 179, 185, 187.

men. These advocates insisted that, in order to govern best, the state needed the peculiar wisdom of women in addition to that of men. Arguments for women's suffrage, then, embodied varying ideas about women's nature.

In 1915, *The Crisis* published a forum on women's suffrage. More than a dozen black leaders contributed their arguments for women's suffrage. In the process, they revealed many different understandings of womanhood. In the following selections from that forum, identify the assumptions that each author makes about the meaning of womanhood. How did those gender ideals differ? How did the enfranchisement of women materially change the meaning of womanhood in the United States? Compare these arguments with those of Elizabeth Cady Stanton in Chapter 2 and Mary Kenny O'Sullivan in Chapter 3.

POLITICS AND WOMANLINESS
By Benjamin Brawley
Dean of Morehouse College, Atlanta, Ga.

The argument is all for woman suffrage. More and more one who takes the opposing view finds himself looking to the past rather than to the future. Each woman as well as each man is a child of God, and is entitled to all the privileges of that high heritage. We are reminded of the heroine in "A Doll's House": "Before all else you are a wife and mother," says the husband in Ibsen's play. "No," replies Nora, "before all else I am a human being."

There is one objection which many honestly find it difficult to overcome. There are thousands of men in this country who are theoretically in favor of woman suffrage, but who would be sorry to see their wives and sisters at the polls. They cannot overcome the feeling that woman loses something of her fineness of character when she takes her place with a crowd of men to fight out a live issue. Her very need of a protector calls forth man's chivalry; take away that need and the basis of woman's strongest appeal to man is gone.

Even this last objection, merely a practical one, can be overcome. The finest and deepest culture is not that which keeps its possessor forever enclosed in a Doll's House. It is rather that which looks at life in the large, with a just appreciation of its problems and sorrow, and that labors in the most intelligent manner to right the wrongs that are in existence. When once everywhere woman has entered the fray and helped to clean up some of the graft in our cities and to improve the tone of our voting places, even this last fear will disappear.

"VOTES FOR CHILDREN"
By Mrs. Carrie W. Clifford
Honorary President of the Federation of
Colored Women's Clubs of Ohio

It is the ballot that opens the school-house and closes the saloon; that keeps the food pure and the cost of living low; that causes a park to grow where a dump-pile grew before. It is the ballot that regulates capital and protects labor; that up-roots disease and plants health. In short, it is by the ballot we hope to develop the wonderful ideal State for which we are all so zealously working.

When the fact is considered that woman is the chosen channel through which the race is to be perpetuated; that she sustains the most sacred and intimate communion with the unborn babe; that later, she understands in a manner truly marvelous (and explained only by that vague term "instinct") its wants and its needs, the wonder grows that her voice is not the *first* heard in planning for the ideal State in which her child, as future citizen, is to play his part.

The family is the miniature State, and here the influence of the mother is felt in teaching, directing and executing, to a degree far greater than that of the father. At his mother's knee the child gets his first impressions of love, justice and mercy; and by obedience to the laws of the home he gets his earliest training in civics.

More and more is it beginning to be understood that the mother's zeal for the ballot is prompted by her solicitude for her family-circle.

That the child's food may be pure, that his environment shall be wholesome and his surrounding sanitary—these are the things which engage her thought. That his mind shall be properly developed and his education wisely directed; that his occupation shall be clean and his ideals high—all these are things of supreme importance to her, who began to plan for the little life before it was even dreamed of by the father.

Kindergartens, vacation-schools, playgrounds; the movement for the City Beautiful; societies for temperance and for the prevention of cruelty to children and animals—these and many other practical reforms she has brought to pass, *in spite of not having the ballot.* But as she wisely argues, why should she be forced to use indirect methods to accomplish a thing that could be done so much more quickly and satisfactorily by the direct method—by casting her own ballot?

The ballot! the sign of power, the means by which things are brought to pass, the talisman that makes our dreams come true! Her dream is of a State where war shall cease, where peace and unity be established and where love shall reign.

Yes, it is the great mother-heart reaching out to save her children from war, famine and pestilence; from death, degradation and destruction, that induces her to demand "Votes for Women," knowing well that fundamentally it is really a campaign for "Votes for Children."

THE SELF-SUPPORTING WOMAN AND THE BALLOT
By Miss M. E. Jackson
Of the Civil Service of the State of Rhode Island,
President of the R. I. Association of Colored Women's Clubs

Looked at from a sane point of view, all objections to the ballot for women are but protests against progress, civilization and good sense.

"Woman's place is in the home." Would that the poorly paid toilers in field, workshop, mill and kitchen, might enjoy the blessed refreshment of their own homes with accompanying assurance that those dependent upon them might be fed, clothed, properly reared and educated.

Each morning's sun beholds a might army of 8,000,000 souls marching forth to do battle for daily bread. You inquire who they are? Why, the mothers, wives, sisters and daughters of the men of America. "The weaker vessels," the majority of whom are constrained from necessity.

There is no field of activity in the country where women are not successfully competing with men. In agricultural pursuits alone, there are over 900,000. In the ministry, 7,000 dare preach the gospel with "Heads uncovered." And 1,010 possess the courage to invade the field of the Solons, bravely interpreting the laws, although their brothers in all but twelve of the forty-five States (so far as the ballot is concerned), class them with criminals, insane and feeble-minded.

The self-supporting woman out of her earnings, pays taxes, into the public treasury and through church, club and civic organization gives her moral backing unstintingly to her Country.

Imagine if you can the withdrawal of this marvelous economic force,—the working women of America! It is a fundamental necessity of modern civilization.

The laboring man has discovered beyond peradventure that his most effective weapon of defence is the *ballot in his own hand*. The self-supporting woman asks for and will accept nothing less.

NOR FELT MY MANHOOD MORE KEENLY
Alan Seeger

As Carrie Clifford dreamed of a world that would study war no more, some Americans longed for battle. The outbreak of World War I satisfied their longing.

The United States initially tried to stay out of the war that opened in August 1914. Embroiled in the conflagration were Germany, Austria-Hungary, and Turkey on the one side with France, Britain, Russia, Italy, and Japan on the other. Until the United States finally joined the British and their allies as official combatants in April 1917, Americans debated their appropriate role: should they prepare for the possibility of war by building up their military; should they aid one side or the other; should they declare war themselves. One argument for entering the war, according to some, was that battle would create finer men.

Theodore Roosevelt entered the debate with the same arguments he had fashioned during the war against Spain. His book, *The Strenuous Life,* was reissued in 1915, and many younger men, believing as Roosevelt did, enlisted in volunteer units commanded by the French or British.

One of these young men was Alan Seeger. A Harvard graduate filled with romantic notions about war, Seeger joined the French Foreign Legion in 1914. From France, he wrote poems, letters to his parents, and diary entries that were published after he died at war in 1916. One of those letters follows. How did Seeger define manhood? How did his views compare with those in *The Strenuous Life?*

Source: Alan Seeger, *The Letters and Diary of Alan Seeger* (New York: C. Scribner's Sons, 1917), pp. 6–8.

To His Mother
Camp de Mailly, AUBE, France, Oct. 17, 1914

. . . After two weeks here and less than two months from enlistment we are actually going at last to the firing line. By the time you receive this we shall already perhaps have had our *baptême de feu*. We have been engaged in the hardest kind of work,—two weeks of beautiful autumn weather on the whole, frosty nights and sunny days and beautiful coloring on the sparse foliage that breaks here and there the wide rolling expanses of open country. Every day from the distance to the north has come the booming of cannon around Reims and the lines along the Meuse. We have had splendid sham battles, firing dozens of rounds of blank cartridges. Between the *bonds de vingt mètres*, when we lie on the ground, resting the sack on one side and with one's ear in the grass, it has been wonderful to hear this steady pounding of the distant cannonade.

But imagine how thrilling it will be tomorrow and the following days, marching toward the front with the noise of battle growing continually louder before us. I could tell you where we are going but I do not want to run any risk of having this letter stopped by the censor. The whole regiment is going, four battalions, about 4,000 men. You have no idea how beautiful it is to see the troops undulating along the road in front of one in *collones par quatre* as far as the eye can see with the captains and lieutenants on horseback at the head of their companies.

I am keeping a diary in a desultory sort of way, but aside from this I am quite incapable of any such literary effort as you suggest, for one simply has not the time. Tomorrow the real hardship and privations begin. But I go into action with the lightest of light hearts. The hard work and moments of frightful fatigue have not broken but hardened me and I am in excellent health and spirits. Do not worry, for chances are small of not returning and I think you can count on seeing me at Fairlea next summer, for I shall certainly return after the war to see you all and recuperate. I am happy and full of excitement over the wonderful days that are ahead. It was such a comfort to receive your letter and know that you approved of my action. Be sure that I shall play the part well for I was never in better health nor felt my manhood more keenly.

THE PEACE MOVEMENT *IS* A BATTLE
Mrs. J. Malcolm Forbes

Advocates of peace had a tough time responding to Alan Seeger's paeans to war and other promotions for military manhood. Still, they tried, and none more valiantly than members of the Woman's Peace Party.

Source: Mrs. J. Malcolm Forbes, "The Peace Movement and Some Misconceptions," Address delivered at a meeting of the Executive Board of the National Civic Federation (New England Section), May 4, 1916, *Records of the Woman's Peace Party, 1914–1920,* Swarthmore College Peace Collection, Swarthmore College, Swarthmore, Penn.

The Woman's Peace Party organized in January 1915 and later became the United States branch of the Women's International League for Peace and Freedom. Formed by reform leaders like Jane Addams and the president of the National American Woman Suffrage Association, Carrie Chapman Catt (1859–1947), the organization claimed 40,000 members by 1916. It embodied a belief that women were naturally predisposed toward peace in a way that men were not. Still, members knew that they had to convince men of the value of peace or they stood no chance of winning their war against war. Consequently, they had to answer men like Seeger and Roosevelt, who believed that war created better men.

One such response came from Mrs. J. Malcolm Forbes. In an address delivered in 1916, Mrs. Forbes took on the notion that American men needed war to be the best they could be. An excerpt from that speech follows. In what ways did Forbes reject Roosevelt's definition of manhood? Did she appropriate any aspects of his understanding of manhood?

It is a satisfaction to be asked to speak to you of the Cause which I believe the most far-reaching of our generation. I know it is as yet an unpopular Cause, but this is because of misconceptions. . . .

The chief reason for the widespread misapprehension of the Peace Movement has come, I believe, from the name "Peace." Truly a beautiful word, but not suitable for the title of a movement at once radical and bold, formed for the abolition of the war system.

Had the men and women who, in the beginning of the last century, banded themselves together for the overthrow of slavery, called themselves by some title which had a like flavor of piety and finality, I believe that the Anti-Slavery Movement would have met with as many hindrances as has the Peace Movement. Largely because of the word "Peace," persons not yet in the Movement imagine that those who are working to bring about the new order are making use merely of appeals to sentiment, talking in gentle tones of how to bring in the millennium, and crying, Peace! Peace! whereas, the truth is that the *war against war* is and has long been an aggressive campaign of education, its teachings proclaimed in no mincing or uncertain tones. *The Peace Movement is a determined onslaught on the old and barbarous system of war, and a persistent pointing of the way to constructive international relations.* The Peace worker deals not in doves nor olive branches. He must summon all the clearness of thought and logic that he can command; and he must needs stand firm in his faith, heeding neither the ridicule nor the sneers of the unconverted.

When a man new to the Movement hears the words, Peace Society, Peace Advocate and Pacifist, he not unnaturally associates the movement for which they stand, with passive and mild attributes; he thinks he would be ashamed to join a Peace Society, for he says he does "not believe a man is intended to live without fighting." Then the explanation has to be made that the "fighting" he means (healthy struggle and competition) is not synonymous with the killing of men. The Peace Movement *is* a battle. . . .

We Peace workers believe in the Boy Scout Movement of America, and are determined that it shall continue to follow the lines laid down by its founder, General Baden Powell, who has always been emphatically opposed to its being militarized. His basic idea is to train boys for *normal, i.e., civic* citizenship; and to turn their courage and energy into channels of constructive service to their cities and to their countries. It is to be deplored that the other and newer organization, called the United States Boy Scout Movement, is being made essentially military; and it is unfortunate that it should not have chosen a less imitative name.

The accusation sometimes made that Peace teaching is liable to undermine patriotism, can be urged only by persons possessed of but superficial knowledge of the anti-war movement, for when we work to banish the war system from the earth, are we lowering the heroic ideals of manhood? Are we training our boys to be "mollycoddles"? Far from it! We bring up our boys to be ready to die for their country by *serving* humanity's need; and for daily, not occasional, service only.

Are not high forms of courage, devotion, and self-sacrifice found in many of the careers open to both men and women, such as those of missionaries, doctors, nurses, sailors, firemen? It is a grave mistake to assume that the one and highest form of service to one's country is that of the soldier. At best that is only *one* form of service, and in the majority of cases the soldier is not exposed to discomfort, peril and death in the constant way that is the doctor or nurse or life-saver. Many other professions might be named which also are full of opportunity for devotion and self-sacrifice to ideals. . . .

[To those who claim that war is a fine thing] one always wanted to quote the words of William Ellery Channing:

"It is said that without war to excite and invigorate the human mind, some of its noblest energies will slumber, and its highest qualities—courage, magnanimity, fortitude—will perish. To this I answer that, if war is to be encouraged among nations because it nourishes energy and heroism, on the same principle war in our families, and war between neighborhoods, villages and cities ought to be encouraged; for such contests would equally tend to promote heroic daring and contempt of death.

. . . Away then, with the argument that war is needed as a nursery of heroism!"

I LOVE MY OVERALLS
Women Workers in Vermont

Despite the peace movement, of course, the United States eventually entered World War I. Although the government granted deferments from military service to literally millions of men who worked in war industries or had dependents, the labor force lost around 16 percent of its men to military service. With European immigration halted by the war and continued prejudice against Mexican and Asian immigrants, the war opened opportunities for women workers.

The actual numbers of employed women increased very little during the war, but the special circumstances of wartime production shifted workers around within the labor market. As millions of men abandoned their jobs for military service, white women moved into higher paying jobs in offices and heavy industry while black women moved into some of the positions left open by white women in textile mills, domestic service, and other service industries.

Source: Caraola M. Cram, "She Hands Him A Lemon," *Springfield Reporter,* December 5, 1918, p. 2.

FIGURE 7.2
Women answered the call for labor in heavy industry during World War I. Here, they work
in a munitions factory in Frankford, Pennsylvania. Note the poster hanging on the wall.
(*Source: U.S. Army Photos, Negative Number LC-USZ62-76020, Prints and Photographs
Division, Library of Congress, Washington, D.C.*)

Most of the gains made by women workers during the war were short lived.
When soldiers returned from military service, they won their jobs back from
women. Nevertheless, for a moment, the war opened opportunities for some
wage-earning women, who reveled in their new situations. This poem, published
by Vermont women who worked in a machine-tool company during the war, reveals some women's satisfaction with their new status and their annoyance at
men who chastised them for wearing trousers. How did the war transform the
gender system of these women? Might we say that the war created new women
in some places?

My man, you're really out of date,
And now before it is too late,
I'll try to set you right;
We never mixed our bloomers, clown,
They fit just like a Paris gown,
The simple, tender, clinging vine

That once around the oak did twine,
Is something of the past;
We stand erect now by your side,
And surmount obstacles with pride,
We're equal, free, at last.

We're independent now you see,
Your bald head don't appeal to me,
I love my overalls;
And I would rather polish steel
Than get you up a tasty meal.
Or go with you to balls.
Now, only premiums good and big,
Will tempt us maids to change our rig.
And put our aprons on;
And cook up all the dainty things,
That so delighted men and kings
In days now past and gone. . . .

To sit by your machine and chew
And dream of lovely Irish stew,
Won't work today you'll find.
Now, we're the ones who set the pace,
You'll have to hustle in the race
Or you'll get left behind.
We're truly glad we got the chance
To work like men and wear men's pants,
And proud that we made good,
My suit a badge of honor is.
Now, will you kindly mind your "biz"
Just as you know you should.

THE VANISHING POINT
The United States Supreme Court

Historians argue about whether Progressivism survived World War I. Reformers generally encountered more powerful opposition to their legislative campaigns after the war than before, but they continued to achieve some victories at the federal level during the early 1920s (congressional approval of the Maternal and Infant Health Act in 1921 and the Child Labor Amendment in 1924, for instance) and at the state level even later.

One of the new obstacles to progressive legislation was a more conservative Supreme Court than had existed earlier in the century. Before the war, the U.S. Supreme Court had let stand state laws that increasingly interfered with the freedom of contract. After the war, a more cautious Court ended that trend. One indicator of

Source: *Adkins v. Children's Hospital,* 261 U.S. 525 (1923).

this renewed commitment to the freedom of contract came in the Court's decision in *Adkins v. Children's Hospital* (1923).

At issue in *Adkins* was the right of a state to determine minimum wages for women. While the *Muller* decision had allowed states to set maximum hours for women, a subsequent case, *Bunting v. Oregon* (1917) had extended that power over men as well. The *Bunting* case implicitly diminished differences between women and men workers by applying the same legal reasoning and extending the same legal protections to both.

In the *Adkins* decision, the Supreme Court explicitly stated its belief that women and men were now so nearly the same that women rarely qualified for special protective legislation. It made this argument, however, not in service of progressive ends, which would have expanded the power of the state to regulate the labor contract for both women and men as *Bunting* had, but in support of conservative goals: The Court used this doctrine of equality between women and men to invalidate governmental stipulation of minimum wages for either women or men.

Despite its explicit commitment to equality of the sexes, the Court did not overturn *Muller.* The decision of the majority claimed instead that minimum wages and maximum hours constituted entirely different sorts of interference in the labor contract and that states could set maximum hours for women but not minimum wages. It moreover revived *Lochner* and seemed to overturn *Bunting.* In this way, the Supreme Court's decision in the *Adkins* case encapsulated the conflicting tendencies of American thinking about gender in the 1920s. While powerful Americans now believed that women and men were more alike than had been believed in the mid-nineteenth century, they maintained that some differences continued to distinguish the two. Moreover, in law, women and men *were* more alike in the 1920s than they had been previously, despite the maintenance of some differences.

Compare the gender expectations of these justices with those of *Muller.* How did this Court decision embody ideals touted by Dorothy Dunbar Bromley (Chapter 4) or Margaret Sanger (Chapter 6)? How did the gender system advocated here differ from the Victorian ideal?

In the *Muller Case* the validity of an Oregon statute, forbidding the employment of any female in certain industries more than ten hours during any one day was upheld. The decision proceeded upon the theory that the difference between the sexes may justify a different rule respecting hours of labor in the case of women than in the case of men. It is pointed out that these consist in differences of physical structure, especially in respect of the maternal functions, and also in the fact that historically woman has always been dependent upon man, who has established his control by superior physical strength. The cases of *Riley, Miller* and *Bosley* follow in this respect the *Muller Case.* But the ancient inequality of the sexes, otherwise than physical, as suggested in the *Muller Case* (p. 421) has continued "with diminishing intensity." In the view of the great—not to say revolutionary—changes which have taken place since that utterance, in the contractual, political and civil status of women, culminating in the Nineteenth Amendment, it is not unreasonable to say that these differences have now come almost, if not quite, to the vanishing point. In this aspect of the matter, while the physical differences must be recognized in appropriate cases, and legislation fixing hours or conditions of work may properly take them into account, we cannot accept the doctrine that women of mature age, *sui juris,* require or may be subjected to restrictions upon their liberty of contract which could not lawfully be imposed in the case of men under similar circumstances. To do so would be to ignore all the implications to be drawn from the present day trend of legislation, as well as that of common thought and usage, by which woman is accorded emancipation from the old doctrine that she must be given special protection or be subjected to special restraint in her contractual and civil relationships. In passing, it may be noted that the instant statute applies in the case of a woman employer contracting with a woman employee as it does when the former is a man.

The essential characteristics of the statute now under consideration, which differentiate it from the laws fixing hours of labor, will be made to appear as we proceed. . . .

If now, in the light furnished by the foregoing exceptions to the general rule forbidding legislative interference with freedom of contract, we examine and analyze the statute in question, we shall see that it differs from them in every material respect. It is not a law dealing with any business charged with a public interest or with public work, or to meet and tide over a temporary emergency [as was true during World War I]. It has nothing to do with the character, methods or periods of wage payments. It does not prescribe hours of labor or conditions under which labor is done. It is not for the protection of persons under legal disability or for the prevention of fraud. It is simply and exclusively a price-fixing law, confined to adult women. . . , who are legally as capable of contracting for themselves as men.

POSTER ESSAY

During World War I, the United States government and many other organizations (most notably the Red Cross and the Young Men's Christian Association) produced posters to recruit both women and men to various kinds of war work. Those posters drew on common notions about womanhood and manhood to gain support for the war and to persuade women and men to join war service. Looking at these posters through the lenses of gender and sexuality, we see that even the same organization often employed contradictory ideas about womanhood/manhood and sexuality to promote its cause. For instance, some posters depended on young women's open sexuality to entice men to join the military. Other posters tried to lure men into the military by suggesting that women needed protection from the sexual aggression of German soldiers. Moreover, while some posters assumed the heterosexuality of potential male recruits, others hinted that military service might appeal especially to men who preferred homosocial—and perhaps, homosexual—company.

As you examine the following posters produced during World War I, ask yourself what they assume about womanhood, manhood, and sexuality.

Source: National Archives, Still Picture Branch, College Park, Maryland.

FIGURE 7.3

FIGURE 7.4

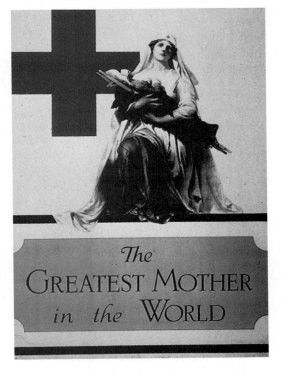

FIGURE 7.5

FIGURE 7.6

FIGURE 7.7

FIGURE 7.8

FIGURE 7.9

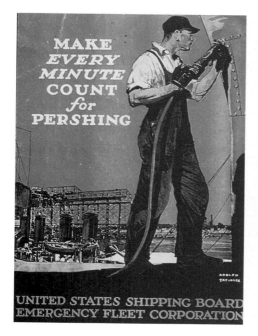

FIGURE 7.10

FIGURE 7.11

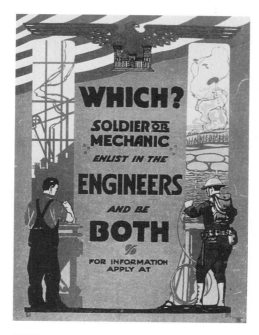

FIGURE 7.12

RECOMMENDED READINGS

Gilmore, Glenda Elizabeth. *Gender and Jim Crow: Women and the Politics of White Supremacy in North Carolina, 1896–1920.* Chapel Hill, N.C., 1996.

Gordon, Linda. *Pitied But Not Entitled: Single Mothers and the History of Welfare.* New York, 1994.

Greenwald, Maurine W. *Women, War, and Work: The Impact of World War I on Women Workers in the United States.* Westport, Conn., 1980.

Kennedy, David M. *Over Here: The First World War and American Society.* New York, 1980.

Koven, Seth, and Sonya Michel, eds. *Mothers of a New World: Maternalist Politics and the Origins of Welfare States.* New York, 1993.

Ladd-Taylor, Molly. *Mother-Work: Women, Child Welfare, and the State, 1890–1930.* Urbana, Ill. 1994.

Muncy, Robyn. *Creating a Female Dominion in American Reform, 1890–1935.* New York, 1991.

————. "Trustbusting and White Manhood." *American Studies* 38 (Fall 1997):21–42.

Skocpol, Theda. *Protecting Soldiers and Mothers: The Political Origins of Social Policy in the United States.* Cambridge, Mass., 1992.

Wheeler, Marjorie Spruill, ed. *Votes for Women! The Woman Suffrage Movement in Tennessee, the South, and the Nation.* Knoxville, Tenn. 1995.

Gender and Inter-National Crises, 1930–1963

Out of gender anarchy had emerged by the 1920s a modern gender system that saw men and women as more similar than the Victorians had believed. According to modern ideals, both women and men had sexual and creative desires that must be satisfied; each belonged in the polling booth and other public places; and both must be able to make a living. Because of the continuing growth of corporate employment, many Americans also accepted a greater degree of economic "dependence" among men than Victorians had, though hope for individual independence continued to inspire many. These beliefs represented a significant change from those predominant in the mid-nineteenth century.

Still, the modern gender system did not maintain that women and men were equal or that they were wholly the same. While both men and women might need to be able to earn wages, for instance, most Americans held fast to the family wage as an ideal. Women's employment was fully accepted as an interim stage between education and marriage or, less fully, as an alternative to marriage. Once wed, however, women were expected to stay home and rear children. Similarly, while both women and men might vote, men held the overwhelming majority of political offices and in many states women could not yet serve on juries. Moreover, despite the new belief that women must have sex to be completely fulfilled, most deplored sexual aggressiveness in women, assuming that men should initiate all sexual encounters.

Almost as soon as this set of ideas achieved widespread acceptance, the United States faced a series of crises that forced change in actual gender relations but discouraged innovations in thinking about gender. The first of these, the Great Depression, began in October 1929, and only World War II, a second international disaster, ended it. The war then set in motion the creation of a system of international rivalries that represented a third crisis: the Cold War.

The Great Depression challenged Americans on every front. Their preference for limited government, faith in volunteerism and localism, and insistence that individuals were responsible for their own destinies, shattered against 25 percent unemployment rates, thousands of bank failures, mass desertions of insolvent farms, and rampant hopelessness and despair. Only if Americans pulled together as a national community could they hope to stave off the worst.

The collapse of so many core American values created political ferment. Both communism and fascism appealed to broad sections of the population, and many new-fangled political schemes like Francis Townsend's old age pensions and Huey Long's Share Our Wealth plan gained considerable constituencies. Pressure from such challengers pushed the administrations of President Franklin D. Roosevelt (1933–1945), to federalize domestic policy and go beyond many social and economic programs fashioned by Progressives, vastly expanding federal responsibility for the welfare of American citizens.

Such profound changes had to affect gender relations. For one thing, general approval of government programs like old-age pensions, farm subsidies, and public works further eroded beliefs in male individualism and independence: In an economy reaching to the farthest corners of the globe, no individual man controlled his own fate. Americans had to acknowledge that men were dependent on impersonal economic trends as well as local corporate policy and even government programs. For another, economic hard times forced millions of married women into the labor market while their husbands remained unemployed, undermining the *practice* of modern gender expectations. Even so, the *ideal* of the family wage and married women's domesticity remained intact—as it would until the 1960s. Similarly, heterosexuality endured as the dominant ideal, but homosexual communities continued to grow.

While Americans struggled to survive in the midst of economic disaster, totalitarian governments in Japan and Germany launched campaigns of international aggression that ultimately sparked the Second World War. Opening in 1939 with Germany's invasion of Poland, World War II eventually pitted Britain, France, the Soviet Union, and the United States against Germany, Italy, and Japan. Although the United States began aiding the Allies long before, it became officially involved when Japan bombed Pearl Harbor in December 1941.

War promptly ended the depression. The military drafted millions of men, and government orders for weapons fired up heavy industry. Unemployment rates plummeted. Just as in World War I, government and industry challenged American women to take up the slack in the labor market, and many women even joined the military. These moves intensified trends well advanced before the war—the formation of gay communities, married women's increasing employment, and even men's decreasing "independence." Especially within the military, men were forced to give up notions of self-direction and individuality in favor of obedience and conformity, prompting literary protests from the likes of James Jones and Norman Mailer and prefiguring the 1950s concern with the "organization man," a corporate employee who gave up independence for security.

The United States and the Soviet Union were allies during the war, but the two countries never trusted each other. American delay in opening a front against Germany in Eastern Europe and refusal to share information on atomic weapons soured their already bad relations. When, after the war, the Soviet Union refused to withdraw from Eastern Europe and began installing communist governments there, the two world powers settled into hostility that defined American foreign policy—and, to some degree, world politics—until the late 1980s.

The Cold War shaped American gender relations in profound and contradictory ways. On the one hand, fifties rhetoric led to a reemphasis on the differences between women and men (witness the change in Hollywood heroines from the boyish figure of Katherine Hepburn to the voluptuousness of Marilyn Monroe) and a fanatic witchhunt against homosexuals. On the other hand, by encouraging the federal government to build a military-industrial complex that required huge numbers of white-collar workers, both male and female, the Cold War sparked the increasing employment of married women and growing absorption of men into expanding bureaucracies.

A transformation of the gender system was in process, but Cold War anxieties—like the depression and hot war before them—prevented most Americans from openly supporting it. Only the relative security of the 1960s would allow direct challenges to existing gender hierarchy and ideologies.

FIGURE 8.1
This etching by Reginald Marsh captured the magnitude of suffering in the early months of
the Great Depression. Why might the majority of those in the breadline be white and male?
(*Source: Reginald Marsh, "Breadline," 1929, Fine Print Collection, Negative Number LC-*
USZ62-77891, Prints and Photographs Division, Library of Congress, Washington, D.C.)

CHAPTER 8

Bread Lines and Gender Lines

The Great Depression was the result of a worldwide economic crisis of unprecedented proportions. The U.S. federal government's response, embodied in the New Deal, represented an extraordinary level of governmental activism. As documents in this chapter will demonstrate, men and women, and white people as well as those of color, experienced both the depression and the New Deal differently.

At the height of the depression, an estimated 25 percent of the labor force was unemployed. Additional workers settled for part-time jobs, and wages fell even for those employed full time. Unemployment varied dramatically by both gender and race. In general, women had lower unemployment rates than men, and black people higher rates than white. In 1931, the Women's Bureau in the Department of Labor estimated an 18 percent unemployment rate among women generally, but black women in some cities endured unemployment rates of 50 percent, which put their unemployment well above that of either white men or white women.

The gender and race segregation of the labor market explained these variations. Among white Americans, men were more likely to be employed in heavy industry than women, and unemployment hit that segment of the economy earlier and longer than it did the service and clerical sectors, in which white women were more likely to be employed. In fact, female-dominated jobs in sales, clerical, and service work disappeared later in the depression and reappeared earlier than the industrial jobs in which white men were overrepresented. Black people and Latinos, still overwhelmingly employed as domestic servants or farm laborers, felt the strain of depression in agriculture and sometimes saw their jobs go to desperate whites.

The New Deal was an attempt to ameliorate the worst effects of the depression. Through a variety of mostly temporary measures, the early New Deal aimed to rejuvenate the economy and in the meantime stave off destitution for millions of suffering Americans. The programs that were part of this effort maintained differences between women and men, between whites and people of color. The highest-paying jobs offered by government employment programs, for instance, were usually reserved for white men, and both women and black men were often paid lower wages for the same work that white men did.

Most permanent New Deal programs came a bit later and included the Social Security Act (SSA) of 1935 and the Fair Labor Standards Act of 1938. Though often urged and even designed by female policymakers, these programs also maintained social hierarchies. For instance, old-age pensions created by the Social Security Act went overwhelmingly to white men because occupations dominated by women or men of color were generally excluded from coverage. The same was true for unemployment insurance, another program mandated by the Social Security Act. SSA also established Aid to Dependent Children (ADC), a federalized version of the mothers' pensions programs originally created during the Progressive era. Particular ideas about women—that they were first and foremost mothers who should be "protected" from wage labor—produced this program and helped to sustain the conflict between mothering and working for wages. Problematic as it was, ADC seldom benefitted women of color, whom local white officials expected to work for wages, whether they had children or not.

Thus, even when neither gender nor race was mentioned in a piece of legislation, it could have very different implications for women and men, whites and people of color. By treating groups of people differently, such programs maintained both distinctions and inequities between races and genders. When the economic crisis finally passed, its legislative legacy remained, privileging some Americans and leaving others to struggle on their own.

WHAT THE HUSBAND AND WIFE OUGHT TO DO AND OUGHT TO FEEL
Katharine Dupre Lumpkin

During the Great Depression, the unemployment of many husbands forced their wives into the labor market. In fact, the number of wage-earning wives increased by 50 percent over the course of the 1930s. This great shift toward married women's wage-earning did not, however, necessarily reflect changed attitudes toward married women's employment. To the contrary, high unemployment among men seems to have increased hostility toward married women workers to such an extent that some companies fired their married, female employees and most school districts refused to hire married women as teachers.

In the early 1930s, sociologist Katharine Dupre Lumpkin studied attitudes toward gender roles among working-class families in New York City. She interviewed forty-six families, most of whom were of Italian descent. Others were native-born. All had experienced economic hard times as revealed by recent visits to a local charity. The following excerpt from Lumpkin's research captures some of the ways that the depression complicated gender arrangements for working-class families. What does Lumpkin's research suggest about the relationship between the actual gender division of labor within families and ideas about men's and women's roles? In light

Source: Katharine DuPre Lumpkin, *The Family: A Study of Member Roles* (Chapel Hill, N.C.: University of North Carolina Press, 1933), pp. 90–99.

of this research, how should we interpret the statistics that show an enormous increase in married women workers during the 1930s?

[The subjects of this study] had very definite ideas about what the husband and wife ought to do and ought to feel about home and family. . . . Husbands and wives knew that the man's role was to provide and rule his household, whether he did these things or not. They had no doubts that the woman's part was to take care of the home and children whatever other duties were thrust upon her. . . .

There was not an out-of-work or ill husband among the group who did not repeatedly express his determined wish to work and support his family. Those who could work and could not find positions reiterated a sense of 'shame' at being out of jobs. It was usually quite painful for them to consider the possibility of wives becoming wage-earners; they had never had to do so since marriage—there spoke the provider part—and should not have to begin now; they were needed to care for home and children. . . .

It might relieve a part of the father's worry when his family was being fed and clothed during his illness or unemployment, but it did not satisfy his role. Mrs. Z earned enough for family support, it is true, when her husband became incapacitated by a chronic illness and had to give up his trade. But Mr. and Mrs. Z spent many an hour trying to devise a plan for earning income so that he could again be the chief wage earner and his wife could remain at home. And except in two or three instances wives were never the providers of family necessities if it was possible for the husbands to be.

It was not just the man who showed this fixity of role concept. The woman reflected it too. Certain wives took occasion to make it known that their husbands had always heretofore been good providers and that it was not their fault they could not do the providing now. A few felt life had disappointed them bitterly when it had foisted upon them husbands who were not doing their part, because they never seemed to keep work long, or to feel real responsibility for their families. Mrs. X declared more than once that if her husband performed his task of family providing as well as she did hers of homemaking, they would not be in their present circumstances. And young Mrs. Y could not understand how her husband really loved his family when he was so unsuccessful at supporting them.

. . . That husbands were always expected to exercise some authority over wife as well as children, came out in any number of ways. There were a few who overtly expressed their feeling that a man should be 'boss' in his own home, that wives should be afraid of husbands. Mr. B represented the type whose earnings were irregular, and who had a much deflated sense of status along with it; he apparently turned to his right to rule to compensate him somewhat, and his irritation was extreme if his wife did not treat him with due respect in that regard.

. . . The home duties devolving upon the husband as ruler differed enormously also, but there were a few general tendencies evident. Clearly, wives were in the habit of not taking steps of any moment except after the husband's stamp-of-approval had been given. They withheld decisions on plans for the household and children until the man had been consulted, and this was usually true for even those homes where relations between man and woman seemed most strained. There were the rare instances where a wife moved without consultation—but this was in homes of strife, and more strife followed.

In child care the father undertook duties of supervision only in an assistant or supplementary capacity. But where training, discipline or plans for the children were in question, then he stood in his position of head. He was threat in time of punishment, the reinforcement of maternal authority. In a few families mothers made regular report of the children's behavior when fathers came home from work. Occasionally it was the father who laid down the more important rules of conduct. Especially was this likely to happen for those routines that came under his eye when he was in the household—table rules, hours of rising and retiring, street play at night, hours of coming in from play, and the like. . . .

The families evidently felt fully as settled about what a wife was meant to do. She sometimes had to do other things as well, of course, but except in a handful of instances this happened only when dire necessity pushed her hard; and the moment conditions permitted, the traditional pattern was back again. There was abundant difference in practice also—in the extent to which the husband felt obligated to help his wife in home duties,—but the fact is that he did it as a helper to her. Even in the homes where the wife aided in family support when her husband could not earn, she ordinarily continued to carry at the same time major responsibility for home duties. In short, homemaking remained the wife's main duty and function. . . .

In two or three families customary role activities had actually been reversed, the wife did fulltime work and the husband the homemaking tasks. Where this was occasioned by ill-health it made a settlement easier, but all felt the woman was having to do an abnormal thing. . . .

There were a number of families where the wife was a wage-earner and apparently had come to adopt it as a routine thing *when* her husband was unemployed. But the real nature of the situation is plain when we learn that except in two or three instances these wives did not continue work after their husbands had regular positions.

There are a few instances of women who expressed satisfaction in a new-found independence and interest from having a position and their own wages. But at the same time, as we shall see, they felt called upon to defend themselves, and except in one or two cases, finally gave up outside work. While they may have longed for the one role, they could rarely reconcile it to the other. . . .

The wife's part, as these women saw it, not only called for concentration upon home tasks but for efficiency and care in them. In many cases they accepted their work as homemaker with pride and seriousness, if we may take home appearance and expressed attitudes as an index. These mothers not only did their work, but a number of them did it exceedingly well, in a sort of professional spirit—planning systematically their days and the children's days, budgeting funds, marketing for the best buys, making over and mending clothes with great care, using left-overs in cooking, planning meals, bearing in mind well-balanced diet. . . .

THESE MARRIED WOMEN . . . ARE CHISELERS
Letter Writers to Government Officials

Lumpkin's research suggested the paradoxical trends in women's labor market participation in the 1930s. It did not, however, reveal the degree of animosity toward married women workers that accompanied the dramatic increase in their wage-

Source: Women's Bureau Records, National Archives, Washington, D.C.

earning. Some Americans mounted a ferocious campaign against married women workers on the grounds that they must be taking jobs away from men, who should receive priority in hiring. As shown in one of the following letters, this campaign found support not only among many men but also among unmarried women workers, one of whom refused to concede that married women should be dignified by the name "worker."

Because of gender segregation in the labor market, married women were not taking jobs away from men. Instead, they were moving into jobs traditionally reserved for women. Demands for workers in these positions increased during the 1930s as the growth of government programs produced more jobs in clerical service, teaching, and social work. Also, many industries mechanized to reduce costs, thereby increasing positions in "light industry" that often went to women.

Still, even women in the highest professional and political positions did not escape vilification, as the following letters reveal. These missives remind us, moreover, that though the 1930s saw very little organized feminist activism, increasing numbers of women found their way into government service. Women were especially strong in the Department of Labor, where in 1933 Frances Perkins (1882–1965) became the first woman to serve as Secretary of Labor. She was in fact the first woman to hold a position in any president's cabinet. She and many other women—among them Grace Abbott, Katharine Lenroot, and Martha May Eliot, all of the Children's Bureau—played central roles in drafting both the Social Security Act and the Fair Labor Standards Act.

What versions of womanhood do the following letters applaud; what versions do they reject?

[Massachusetts Women's Political Club]
President
Miss Florence Birmingham
72 Hobson Street
Brighton, Mass.

                              May 24, 1939

Hon. Arthur D. Healey, M.C.
House of Representatives
Washington, D.C.

My dear Congressman:

   The Massachusetts Women's Political Club, a non-partisan organization, protests the unwarranted, unethical intrusion of Miss Mary Anderson, aide to Madame Perkins, Secretary of Labor, into our fight against the employment of married women in public service. . . .[1]

---

[1]During the 1920s and 1930s, Mary Anderson headed the Women's Bureau in the federal Department of Labor.

. . . In a news dispatch of May 22, Mary Anderson takes an outright stand against our legislation in Massachusetts, and against the same kind of legislation which is being considered by practically every state in the union, according to information we have from correspondence throughout the nation.

In Massachusetts at the last election such legislation was overwhelmingly supported by the electorate. It passed almost four to one in many parts of the state. . . .

Married women should find the self-expression of which she [Frances Perkins] prates through the career which they chose of their own free will—matrimony.

Miss Anderson is wrong when she says we see this issue only from the economic viewpoint. Married women working not only menace the general welfare, but the public health and morals, by their own action in denying children to state and nation, but also by forcing single women and jobless graduates into wrong paths of life. Single girls, denied work, are not permitted to develop their lives and have homes of their own, but are forced into degradation.

In theory, legally and morally, a married woman takes on another, new personality with marriage. She does not retain her identity, as does a man. . . .

There is a change also in her duties to the public health, morals and general welfare. In addition to her new responsibilities, rights accrue to her in law. Her right to support while her husband lives. On his death, her dower and homestead rights, known in the south and southwest as the community property law.

The single girl, on the contrary, has to look out for herself for support, for nobody is legally bound to keep her when she reaches maturity.

These married women cannot be dignified by the name of workers; they are chiselers, deserters from their post of duty, the home. Because of their subsidized state, they offer unfair competition in an already overcrowded labor market. Their resistance to attempts to dislodge them puts us under the rule of a minority. Childless working wives mean falling population, which means falling markets, and reduced production with consequent unemployment.

Economic conditions have changed due to thousands of women who neglect their main duty—motherhood, for a job. . . .

Duplication of jobs within families is poor national economy, and will be responsible for low wages as long as it continues. As long as husband and wife both work and by their combined wages secure an income sufficient to support themselves, just so long will they be contented with that situation, and retard those who are trying to elevate the wage scale of the United States to the place where a married man can secure sufficient income from his own efforts to support his family. . . .

We ask you, as an elected official from this state, to protect the rights of the people of Massachusetts who voted on this legislation, by preventing further interference and activity on the part of Mary Anderson, aide to Frances Perkins, Secretary of Labor, concerning legislation to bar married women from employment in public service.

Sincerely yours for good government,
(Miss) Florence Birmingham

San Carlos Hotel
Pensacola, Florida
3 February 1940

Hon. Frances Perkins
Secretary of Labor
Washington, D.C.

Dear Madame:

    . . . why do you not resign your position and advise all married women who have an income or a husband able to support them, to do likewise.[2] This would be evidence of your interest in the welfare of the working man. If you and the thousands of other married women who have husbands able and willing to support you resign federal positions you are now holding and give the men who are qualified to fill them an opportunity to do so there would be many more happy homes; fewer divorces and juvenile delinquents, and no such thing as unemployment. . . . My two sisters worked from the time they finished high school to the day they married. But not a minute thereafter. Their husbands saw to that. My five daughters went to work as soon as they finished school. Four graduated from the Woman's College. The oldest taught two years and married a young Ensign, now a Lt. Commander. The second secured a position in the office of the city tax collector and work (sic) up to the day of her death which occurred in an automobile accent (sic) just after her 23 birthday. The third and fourth are now teaching; one in high; the other in grammar school. My fifth and only one of the five that did not get a college education took a business course after finishing high school and secured employment at which she worked until her marriage to a young officer in the Marine Corps.

    I am free to admit that our country is in deplorable condition for which the women are largely responsible. The remedy is in the hands of the women. When they decide to let their hair grow long; stop smoking cigarettes and appearing in public scantily clad, or nude, and attend their household duties; husband and children; we will have but little unemployment; less juvenile delinquency and fewer divorces. Cutting out the excessive use of booze will also help materially.

    I heard a priest say after reading the gospel for the day recently, I have heard it said of late that the days of chivalry have passed. He paused a moment and said, the days of chivalry have not passed. Men take women at the price at which they offer themselves—No truer words were ever spoken. The situation as a whole as before stated, is deplorable. The standard of morality is at low ebb and will remain so until made better by our women folk. . . .

    Take the initiative, Madane. (sic) Resign your position and advise the thousands of married women now holding federal positions having husbands able and willing to provide for them, to do likewise and make a home for their husband and children. . . .

Very truly yours,
H. O. Anson

---

[2]One of the special cruelties of this letter is that Secretary Perkins's husband had for years been institutionalized and completely incapable of providing for his family.

THEIR DIFFERENT OCCUPATIONAL DISTRIBUTION
Mary Elizabeth Pidgeon

The National Industrial Recovery Act (NIRA) stood as one of the central programs of the early New Deal. Passed in June 1933, this legislation encouraged related businesses voluntarily to organize themselves in an effort to stabilize the economy. It created the National Recovery Administration (NRA) to oversee these attempts at economic planning. Within only a few months, several hundred business groups produced codes of self-governance in which each enterprise within a particular industry agreed to pay the same wages and charge the same prices, among other things. The NIRA protected the code-writers from anti-trust prosecution.

Although the Supreme Court in 1935 ruled the NIRA unconstitutional, the codes remain powerful witnesses to the ways that gender and race structured the labor market and vice versa. Produced by a large portion of America's big businesses, these codes contained within them common ideas about the differences between women and men, between white people and those of color. In turn, these codes attempted to enforce such differences.

Early on, the federal Women's Bureau analyzed the codes to see how they affected women. Sections of that analysis follow. What does the study reveal about the ways that gender and race structured the labor market and vice versa? How did the codes affect women and men, blacks and whites differently even when neither gender nor race was explicitly mentioned?

It was to be expected that women stood to receive a large share of the gain from the inauguration of so constructive a social policy as that provided for employed persons under the N.R.A., since in the past women have represented one of the chief groups most subject to the vagaries of the labor market, massed heavily in low-wage and long-hour employments, forming large proportions of those having jobs in seasonal industries, of the most part receiving considerably less for their services than men received, in many cases working in insanitary and unhealthful surroundings. . . .

COVERAGE OF CODES ANALYZED

About 570 codes were approved by the N.R.A. by March 1, 1935 (exclusive of various supplementary codes). By January 1, 1934, the Research and Planning Division of that organization estimated that practically 90 percent of the persons who could come under codes had been covered. Several important woman-employing industries were placed under codes in the first half of 1934. The 491 codes that were approved by July 1, 1934, and that have been examined through this survey therefore give a practical representation of the code provisions for women in the life of the first Recovery Act. The codes approved later for the most

Source: Mary Elizabeth Pidgeon, *Employed Women Under N.R.A. Codes* (Bulletin of the Women's Bureau, No. 130) (Washington, D.C., 1935), pp. 3–7, 9, 16–18, 20–24.

part covered few or no women and it has been found that the statements as to proportions of codes falling in certain groups remain substantially the same for a later
as for an earlier analysis.

EXTENT TO WHICH CODES COVERED EMPLOYED WOMEN

Since codes covered only industries in or affecting interstate and foreign commerce, they covered only about half of all employed women, mainly those in the
manufacturing industries, trade, communication, clerical, and certain large service
groups. The chief classes of women that it may be estimated came under codes . . .
may be summarized as follows:

Employment of women estimated to have come under codes

Manufacturing	1,313,792
Clerical	1,244,526
Trade	855,699
Service	683,869
Communication	235,259
	4,333,145

Among the women not covered by codes were those in certain industries in which
the worst employment conditions too often have prevailed. Codes did not cover
household employees ("servants in homes"), nearly 1½ millions, a number approaching the total of all women in manufacturing. This is a group whose conditions
of work in many instances have been very unsatisfactory. Nor could the codes provide for the more than 1½ million women in professional service, whose experience has been that they were paid considerably less than men were paid for work
of the same amount and caliber.

Other large groups not receiving the benefit of code provisions were laun-
dresses not in laundries, dressmakers and seamstresses not in factories, and
women in agriculture and public service. The following list shows that these groups
not coming under codes included well over 4 million women, according to the
census of 1930:

Employment of women not covered by codes

Total for 6 groups	4,391,080
Professional service	1,526,234
Servants in homes	1,422,928
Agriculture	909,939
Laundresses (not in laundries)	356,468
Dressmakers and Seamstresses (not in factories)	157,928
Public Service	17,583

To the foregoing should be added the fact that the largest single occupation group of women other than domestic and personal service—the nearly 2 million clerical workers, who constitute almost one-fifth of all women gainfully employed—either were not under codes, as for example the nearly 150,000 in insurance offices—or received little aid from the codes. While it has been the popular belief that white-collar workers had less need of improved conditions than had factory employees, nevertheless Women's Bureau studies have shown their wages to be very low and their work situation unsatisfactory in other respects. Furthermore, census figures in 1931 indicated that somewhat more than one-tenth of the women clerical workers were without jobs, and available data from public employment offices show applications for such work greatly exceeding the demands. . . .

WAGES

The usual minimum wage fixed in about 15 percent of the codes covered [by this survey] was 40 cents an hour, and in a few cases it was higher. In the codes for all the more important woman-employing industries the minimum wage was not over 30 cents and in several of the largest of these it was 25 cents or less—the equivalent of $10 or less for a 40-hour week, and still less if the plant operation in the week was not full time. The minimum of 30 cents (or $12 for 40 hours) included codes for cotton and other textile industries, hosiery, cotton cloth gloves, boots and shoes, underwear and allied products, and various paper products, while 25 cents or less was the minimum in hotels, retail trade, laundries, restaurants, and canning.

Even these low minima meant wage increases for large numbers of women paid at the lowest levels—for some of them quite considerable increases. In many industries in the past the bulk of the women have been their lowest paid employees, so it is not surprising that their wage increases have been greater than those of men, and the raising of wages for these groups of women has somewhat lessened the sex differentials in pay. . . .

Geographic Differentials in the Minimum Wage

Of codes that made some qualification of the minimum wage, by far the largest number fixed differentials according to geographic location. Something over one-third of the codes fixed a minimum wage lower in the South than in the North. . . .

One of the chief reasons advanced to justify a low wage in the "South" has been the lower cost of living. As a matter of fact, few attempts have been made to ascertain whether this actually was the condition, and such indications as have been presented have not given any conclusive evidence to this effect but have pointed rather to the opposite situation. Economists who have discussed this subject are pretty well agreed that it is not lower costs of living but rather lower standards, something quite different and one of those things the whole theory of N.R.A. activity sought to obviate to such an extent and such steps as were possible. . . .

Negro women were not covered by codes to nearly so great an extent as were white women, due to their different occupational distribution. Much larger proportions of Negroes than of whites live in the Southern States and thus would be subject to the lower minimum wages for the South in codes for industries in which they were at work.

Of nearly 2,000,000 employed Negro women, over one-third are classed by the census as "servants" in homes and more than one-fourth are in agricultural pursuits. In the occupations for Negro women covered by codes—factory work, stores, hotels, restaurants, and laundries—only a little more than 10 percent of the Negro women were employed, as against practically 60 percent of the total number of all gainfully occupied women similarly covered by codes.

An example of the greater effect on Negro than on white women of a minimum wage lower for the South than for other areas is found in the laundry code, where in the 15 States considered as southern . . . well over half of the women are Negro, while in other States—if New York, where about one-third of the women laundry operatives are Negroes, be excepted—Negroes form only about one-fifth of these women. In this code two southern districts were defined, including certain counties in some States. In one of these southern districts the minimum wage for a 40-hour week throughout the entire area averaged only about 62 percent of the rates for the smallest towns in the three northern areas. . . .

Sex Differentials in the Minimum Wage . . .

Despite the many evidences of the skill required in women's work, so strong has been the old attitude of paying women a low wage that it remained in a considerable number of codes, and the differential for women occurred more frequently than any other type of differential with the exception of that relating to the North and South. . . .

Women's wages remained fixed below men's in some 128 codes. . . .

—In addition to the fixing of a minimum lower for women than men, at least two other methods of securing the same result appeared in codes. One set a lower wage for "light, repetitive work", another provided that types of work paid below the code minimum at some earlier date (usually July 1929) still might continue to be so paid.

The phrase "light repetitive work" is very indefinite, and may be used to cover processes requiring much skill or considerable dexterity. Such a phrase would enable a woman doing delicate assembling work on a watch or a typewriter to be paid at a lower rate than a man performing much less skilled work.

CAPABLE OF EXERTING AUTHORITY
Kate Pemberton

The NIRA encouraged organization not only among employers in various industries but also among workers. Section 7a of the act protected unionized workers from prosecution under anti-trust laws that had occasionally been used against workers' organizations. In 1935, after the Supreme Court knocked out the NIRA, Congress immediately passed the National Labor Relations Act (usually called the Wagner Act), which offered permanent legal sanction to unions.

Explicit government support for workers' organizations breathed life into a moribund labor movement. In 1933, less than 6 percent of American workers

Source: "Kate Pemberton's Story." From *Making Do: How Women Survived the 1930s* (Chicago: Follett, 1976), 202–5. Copyright © 1976 by Jeane Eddy Westin.

belonged to unions; by 1939, 17 percent did. Moreover, the kinds of workers who joined unions in the 1930s changed significantly. Whereas most American unions had previously organized white men, especially those in skilled occupations, the union movement spawned by the depression—represented best by the Congress of Industrial Organizations (CIO)—reached out more consistently to allegedly unskilled workers, women, and people of color.

Even though discrimination on the basis of gender and race continued to mark the union movement, the 1930s saw strides toward more equal treatment as revealed in this interview with Kate Pemberton. According to this testimony, how did New Deal programs seek to maintain gender difference? What was expected of women and men in the labor movement? How did that begin to change in this one instance during the 1930s?

I was sixteen on Wednesday, and on Friday I was graduated from Fairview High School. It was May of '32. The mines were shut down, and when the coal mines are down in West Virginia nothing is moving. They had been shut down during the twenties, and there had been a lot of violence. . . .

There were no jobs for sixteen-year-old girls in Fairview. . . .

So I started doing odd jobs . . . anything I could find. I cleaned house and canned tomatoes. The very first job I had was washing jars because I only weighed ninety-five pounds and my tiny hand could get all the way into a jar. . . .

The first big money I made was for addressing envelopes at Fairmont Wallplaster. That lasted two weeks and I got a dollar and a half a day.

After that job which was around Christmas of '34, I didn't work for almost a year. Every day I dressed and hitchhiked into Fairmont and made the rounds. There were always people with twenty years experience standing in the same line I was. . . .

I was always tired. It would be early when I'd leave home—usually with no money for lunch—and dark by the time I got back, pretty worn out and hungry. Discouraged, most of all.

Finally the NYA [National Youth Administration, an agency created by the New Deal] came along, which was like a WPA [Works Progress Administration] for young people. And in the summer of '36 I worked setting up a town library above my Uncle Don's Texaco garage. But the funds ran out before I finished and they just came and took the books away and shut the project down. Then I worked the playground at the grade school for four months. This was NYA, too. We were paid every two weeks and I got six dollars every payday.

About that time the CCC [Civilian Conservation Corps] camps opened and nearly every boy in Fairview signed up. Of course, it was worthwhile, and they took a burden off their families which was a help. But there was nothing comparable for girls. They had an NYA sewing program, I remember. But I never learned to handle a needle. . . .

By 1938 I'd been out of school for six years without a steady job. When I heard they were moving a Westinghouse lamp plant down from New Jersey to Fairmont, I was so excited I got sick. The day they started hiring I was in that line at 5 A.M.

Guess what the first requirement was? You had to be five feet six inches tall. That let me out. I was only five feet one inch and I couldn't fake *that*.

But they soon changed the rule since there weren't ten girls in Fairmont that tall. You know five feet four inches was tall for a woman then. We hadn't had our spinach!

Six months later I got the call and was hired by Westinghouse. Worked there for the next six years. They paid forty cents an hour to start.

After the government got behind the unions, we all joined the United Electrical Workers, CIO. Westinghouse tried to keep us from going union—said they'd take good care of us. But we found out the girls up north had a union and were making a dollar an hour while we only made forty cents. What Westinghouse said after that wasn't very convincing.

The whole plant was predominantly female except for the supervisors. When our local was formed there was only a handful of men, but the women elected all men officers. It never occurred to us that we shouldn't. But there was a gradual change. Our second set of officers had one woman. The third time we elected all women officers and I became business agent.

Well, that was unheard of for a woman because that meant I was chief union negotiator at Westinghouse. And that just didn't happen. It made the papers, and they got me out to WMMN [a local radio station] to talk about it on radio because it was such a big deal.

I was considered very aggressive by some of the other women. But it seemed natural to me, because my father had backed the suffragettes, and he always said Eleanor should have been president because she was smarter than Franklin. And when he was elected mayor of Fairview—on the Socialist ticket, mind you—he appointed Edna Yates as water commissioner. You know the sky fell. A man had always had that job.

Because of my pop, I grew up with a feeling that it was great being a woman.

We sure didn't call ourselves women's libbers, but there *was* a change in the late thirties, especially among union women. We started considering ourselves capable of exerting authority.

LET ME DO THE WORRYING
Jessie Lopez de la Cruz

The Wagner Act did not protect the right of all workers to organize. Like so much other New Deal legislation, it excluded farm workers. This failure disproportionately disadvantaged African Americans and Mexican Americans, who remained overrepresented in agricultural labor. Again, legislation that did not mention race or ethnicity nevertheless effectively maintained race and ethnic hierarchies.

As the depression decreased the price of agricultural products and New Deal programs paid landowners to keep land out of production in order to boost those prices, many agricultural laborers, sharecroppers, and even former landowners were forced into migrant labor camps. Competition from these newly dislocated Americans resulted in the deportation of many Mexican immigrants who had responded to labor shortages in U.S. agriculture during the 1920s.

Source: Jessie Lopez de la Cruz, interview with Ellen Cantarow. Reprinted by permission of The Feminist Press at the City University of New York, from Ellen Cantarow with Susan Gushee O'Malley and Sharon Hartman Strom, *Moving the Mountain: Women Working for Social Change*, pp. 109–11, 114–16. Copyright ©1980 by Ellen Cantarow, Susan Gushee O'Malley, and Sharon Hartman Strom.

Jessie Lopez de la Cruz (1919–) was among roughly 150,000 Mexican Americans who followed the harvests in California during the early 1930s. In the following interview, she recounts the gender division of labor within her family during that depression decade. How were the expectations for women and men different? How were they the same? Compare and contrast these expectations with those of the subjects in Lumpkin's study of workers in New York City.

When I was a girl, boys were allowed to go out and have friends and visit there in the camp, and even go to town. But the girls—the mother was always watching them. We couldn't talk to nobody. If I had a boyfriend, he had to send me letters, drop notes on his way or send them along with somebody. We did no dating. We weren't allowed to. If girls came to visit at my house, my grandmother sat right there to listen to what we were talking about. . . . We were allowed nowhere except out to the field, and then we always worked between my two older brothers [really uncles]. . . . The only one they [her uncles] trusted was Arnold. He's the one I married. He was allowed to come in our house any time of day. He was always joking and talking with my grandmother. Nights, he would come in and sit on the floor with us. . . .

I was fourteen when I met Arnold in 1933. We lived next door to his family, which was a big one. I'd go there and help Arnold's mother make stacks of tortillas. She didn't have time enough to do all the work for the little children. I'd go and help her. When she went to the hospital in 1935, when Arnold's younger brother was born, I cared for the whole family. I'd make tortillas and cook. The little ones we kept in our house and the rest of them stayed in their cabin.

Arnold and I got married in 1938 in Firebaugh, where we'd all moved. We had a big party with an orchestra: some of Arnold's friends played the violin and guitar. But we had no honeymoon. On the second day after our wedding, he went back to his job—irrigating. I'd get up at four o'clock in the morning to fix his breakfast and his lunch. He'd start the fire for me. I did the cooking in his mother's kitchen. We had three cabins in all by this time. His mother had one cabin that was used as a bedroom. There was ours. And the other cabin in front was used as the kitchen for all of us. So in the morning I'd get up and run across and I'd fix his breakfast and his lunch and he'd go off and I'd go back to bed. He'd come home about four or five o'clock and there would be ice around his ears. . . . He worked twelve hours a day.

I felt I was overworked in the house [of Arnold's mother]. . . . I felt sorry for her [Arnold's mother]. She'd worked very hard and she had so many children, and had to wash her clothes in a tub with a rock board and do the ironing by heating the irons on top of the stove. All of us had to do this, but not many families had eight or nine little children.

I cooked with her until May. But I kept after Arnold: "I want my own kitchen!" So in May we drove all the way to Fresno. We got a few spoons and plates and pots and skillets, and I started my own housekeeping. I still went to his mother's to help her during the day when Arnold was working. But I cooked in my own stove.

After I was married, sometime in May, my husband was chopping cotton and I said, "I want to go with you."

"You can't! You have to stay home!"

"I just feel like going outside somewhere. I haven't gone any place. I want to at least go out to the fields. Take another hoe and I'll help you." I went, but only for one or two days. Then he refused to take me. He said, "You have to stay home and raise children." I was pregnant with my first one. "I want you to rest," he said. "You're not supposed to work. You worked ever since I can remember. Now that you're married, you are going to rest." So I stayed home, but I didn't call it rest doing all the cooking for his mother.

Arnold was raised in the old Mexican custom—men on the one side, women on the other. Women couldn't do anything. . . .

Arnold never beat me, or anything like that. But every time I used to talk to him he didn't answer, even if I asked a question. He'd say, "Well, you don't have to know about it." If I asked, "Arnold, has the truck been paid for?" he wouldn't answer. Or I would ask him, "Did you pay the loan company?" he wouldn't answer. Then I'd get kind of mad and say, "Why don't you tell me?" and he'd say, "What do you want to know about it, are you going to pay for it, or what? Let me do the worrying." Now that is all changed; we talk things over. But in the beginning it was different.

The first year we were married, he was home every night. After the first year was up, I guess that was the end of the honeymoon. He would just take off, and I wouldn't see him for three or four days, even more. I didn't even ask, "Where were you?" I accepted it. I wasn't supposed to question him. He would come in and take his dirty clothes off, pile them up, and when I did the wash the next day I'd look through his pockets and find bus ticket stubs of where he'd been to. . . . I really couldn't blame him that much, because when he was young, before we were married, he was never even allowed to go to a dance. So he was trying out his wings.

[Later] he started staying home and he'd say, "Get ready, we're going to Fresno." And both of us would come in, bring the children, go to a show and eat, or just go to the park.

We'd come in about once a month and bring the children with us. . . .

Before I was married, in 1933, we would come and camp by the river in that place where we were picking grapes. After I was married, we still kept on coming there to pick grapes. We would get a blanket and tie it to the limbs of one of the trees, and to the chicken wire fence that divided the horses and cows and rabbits from us. We would sleep under this tree and do our cooking there and fight the flies. For walls, we used what they called sweat boxes. They're about the size of a three-by-five table. After the grapes are dried out in rows, they're picked up and put into sweat boxes. I would nail some of these together as a wall for privacy. Some I would place on the ground and put our mattress on top for a bed. By turning two boxes right side down, and a third on top right side up, I would fill the top one with dirt and put three rocks in a triangle. That would be our stove, where I would cook our meals.

. . . If there was a big rock, we would scrub our clothes there. I'd get a tub and I'd put some water in it, and then I'd put the soap in there and I'd scrub the soap on the shirts or whatever, and I'd scrub on the rub board. When I first started, at around twelve, I got blisters on my knuckles, but later my grandmother taught me how to use the scrub board, and after that it was easy.

. . . My first child was born in 1939. I had five more. I also took Susan, the girl my sister left when she died. . . .

I stopped working toward the last months of my pregnancies, but I would start again after they were born. When I was working and I couldn't find somebody [to stay with the children], I would take them with me. I started taking Ray with me when he wasn't a year old yet. I'd carry one of those big washtubs and put it under the vine and sit him there. I knew he was safe; he couldn't climb out. Arnold and I would move the tub along with us as we worked. . . .

FIGURE 8.2
Migrant workers labored in the fields every day, and women then worked long hours in their quarters. This strawberry picker in Louisiana scrubbed the rough wood floor of her shed; her wood stove reminds us how much more onerous domestic labor was then than now. (*Source: Russell Lee, Farm Security Administration Collection, Negative Number LC-USF34-32866-D, Prints and Photographs, Library of Congress, Washington, D.C.*)

I PERSONALLY AM NOT A COMMON LABORER
African American Letter Writers

In 1935, at just about the same time that the NRA disappeared, President Franklin Roosevelt created the Works Progress Administration (WPA). This agency was supposed to employ destitute Americans rather than dole out "charity." As employees of the WPA, workers were expected to recover the self-respect that came with earning a day's pay, and employed taxpayers were to let go of resentment they might have had at supporting able-bodied, unemployed fellow citizens.

The following letters reveal some of the ways that the administration of the WPA was shaped by gender and race. They were written to various government officials, most especially President and Mrs. Roosevelt, by African Americans. What do these letters as well as Kate Pemberton's oral history reveal about the

Source: Works Progress Administration Collection, Moorland-Spingarn Research Center, Howard University, Washington, D.C.

ways that gender and race influenced the management of the WPA and other work programs? What do they reveal about gender expectations among African Americans themselves?

Philadelphia, Pa.

Dear Mr. Roosevelt:

I am writing to you in hopes that you will help me. I would like very much if you would help me to get a WPA job. I have been waiting for them to send for me for a long while, but it has been over a year. It doesn't seem like they are going to do it. I write to you Mr. Roosevelt because you are a married man and you can understand my situation. I am a young married fellow. I am a colored fellow. I have been married for three years and I haven't had a decent job since I have been married. My wife never says anything directly but she hints around sometimes because she don't have decent clothes to wear. My daughter needs clothes. I get a relief order but it doesn't give enough to get clothes with and then Mr. Roosevelt you can imagine how I feel to have to think that someone else has to take care of me and my family. If I could get a job I would rather work for what I get rather than have them give it to me. Then I would be able to say I am taking care of my family. Here is Christmas coming on and I would love to be able to give my wife and my little girl a present. I have never been able to give them any yet. . . .

Los Angeles, Calif.
October 8, 1935

Hon. Franklin D. Roosevelt
President of the United States
Washington, D.C.

Dear Sir:

I wish to call to your attention the treatment of the Negro through the WPA, here in Los Angeles, California, especially the Negro World War Veterans, of which I am one.

I was called today to be signed up as a clerk in one of the WPA warehouses, myself and 9 others. Everything was alright until our work order reached one Major Dillon, who has charge of the approval of such work orders. Upon receival he immediately cancelled said order, claiming said order was erroneous and that to his knowledge there was nothing available for the Negro at present, but in the near future there would be positions open for them, such as janitors and messengers.

Now, Mr. President, I personally am not a common laborer. I am a graduate of Summer High School, St. Louis, Mo., in June 1916. I enlisted in the U.S. Army, March 6, 1917 and served 22 months over-seas, also I was a quartermasters Property and Stock Record Clerk for the Arizona Sub-District, at Nogales, Arizona, from September 1919 to October 1924, so I feel that owing to the experience I have had and also your words to the U.S. Congress, in your Veto message of the

Soldier's Bonus, that the veterans would be entitled to preference and consideration on all Federal projects.

Now, Mr. President, I and all other Negroes (veterans) ask that we receive said
preference and consideration on the various Federal projects in California. For up
to the present, the Negro veteran and non-veteran has certainly received a *raw
deal* from your representatives of the Federal projects here.

Thanking his Honor the President for any interest in our case, I am,

Very sincerely yours,
R.M.M.

Corinth, Miss.
Feb. 12, 1936

Washington, D.C.
Mr. F. D. Roosevelt

Dear Mr. President

I am writing to you for help and to tell you how we are treated down here in
Corinth, Mississippi [by the WPA] they are doing every thing they can to keep
from giving us Negroes anything at all, the money you send down here for the
relief, we dont get it, if you please send some one down here and see how they
are doing us. They have taken the women out on landscaping in this cold
weather we cannot stand this outside work like men. They let all the white
women stay inside the sewing room put us Negroes out with shovels to dig like
men because we dont go in the snow they have taken our card and tell us we
are cut off from the relief and wont give us nothing to eat nothing wear no coal
to burn.

They promise to give us twenty two dollars a month $22.00. I have not worked
since November. that when they put us out in the cold the last of November and I
am not able to use a big shovel and out in cold like they try to make us do. They
drive us Negroes about like we are cows and horses. You will learn for yourself, Mr.
President if you just send some one down here and see. They wont pay me all what
they owe me they just give $11.00 and wont give me the other $11.00 and wont let
me work at the sewing room out of the cold till it get worm (sic). they know we cant
get anything unless they give it to us. Most all the white women get everything want
and got some one to help them along but we cannot ask them any thing if we do
they us to stay away from them. My case number is 3390-R please answer soon.

Manhattan, Kansas
September 24, 1936

Franklin D. Roosevelt, President,

Dear Sir,

I am writing you in behalf of the needs of our Negro women. We have a sewing
room but there are only two Negro women there and they were working as janitors

up until about a month or so ago and last week they hired one more girl they are all sewing a little now.

There is about 15 or 20 Negro women in Manhattan that really need to be in the sewing room because their little money that they are allowed for groceries will not allow them to feed their children properly. There allowance is from Three to Six dollars a month and no one is able to live on that.

There are several white caseworkers here but they will not work the Negros and white together. It might be that they really don't realize the Negro needs, of course they couldn't know not being around them all the time, and if they do know they ignore us. Now what we need is a Negro Case Worker and I would like to know if I could be a Negro caseworker. I am awaiting your reply.

CITIZENS INVESTIGATION COMMITTEE
414 South Long Street
Charlotte, N.C.

October 2, 1936
Negroes Forced back into Slavery
by Local W.P.A. to accept
Employment in Private Industries
at Starvation Wages.

Hon. Franklin D. Roosevelt
President of the United States
Hone. Harry Hopkins
National W.P.A. Administration,
Washington, D.C.

Gentlemen:

As American citizens and taxpayers, we are appealing to you in regard to a situation that is working a hardship upon citizens of this City and this Section.

Hundreds of colored women employed on W.P.A. Sewing Projects of this City and County are being deprived of employment on Relief Projects by the Local W.P.A. Officials of this City forcing them to accept employment in private industries for wages less than those paid on W.P.A. Sewing Projects.

Hundreds of these women, widows with large families, are being cut off from W.P.A. Sewing Projects and dropped from relief in order that they be forced to accept employment in private industries for less than three dollars a week working from twelve to sixteen hours a day.

We have no objection to accepting employment in private industries as many of us prefer that kind of employment.

Our obligations, such as house rent, food, clothing and other necessities for our children make it necessary for us try to earn enough from our work for a livelihood.

Hundreds of affidavits signed by unemployed women who are widows, with naked children crying for bread, filed petitions and affidavits of their condition with the Local W.P.A. Officials of this City and the State W.P.A. of Raleigh, N.C.

So far, the buck has been passed with a reply as follows:

STATE W.P.A.
Raleigh, N.C.
September 5, 1936

Mrs. A. G., Field Agent
Workers Alliance
821 Popular Street
Charlotte, N.C.

Dear Mrs. G.:

Your letter of September 4, containing signed affidavits from workers on W.P.A. Sewing Room Projects is being referred to the proper persons for investigation of conditions of which you make complaint.

You may rest assured that fair and impartial consideration will be given to the matter.

Very sincerely yours,
Mrs. May E. Campbell
Women's and Professionals Projects

If such investigation has taken place, we do not have any knowledge of it. . . .

The landlords are driving these unemployed women and their children out of their homes, leaving many of them with nothing to go upon and nowhere to go.

Please advise if the Local WPA and Employment Officials have the right to use their authority to deprive citizens of their employment on WPA Projects and push them in private industries at starvation wages?

Shall we be forced back into the days of slavery by these authorities because of our condition and circumstances? . . .

We are bona fide citizens and residents of this City. Our Local Officials deprive us of an opportunity of employment on WPA Sewing Projects and give it to emigrants from elsewhere. We realize that we are poor people in a destitute condition.

We realize again that we have a right to freedom and liberty under the Constitution of our Government.

We also realize that our condition and circumstances were not caused by faults of our own. This is a matter of grave concern to us. We request that you give this situation your immediate attention.

I CANNED EVERYTHIN' THAT WASN'T MOVIN'
Vera Bosanko

As Katharine Lumpkin discovered in New York City, even when women worked for wages, they continued to take responsibility for their households as well. In fact, sometimes women contributed to the family income through domestic labor. To make every penny go farther during the depression, they returned to canning, gardening, and inventing recipes that stretched expensive ingredients farther than be-

Source: "Vera Bosanko's Story." From *Making Do: How Women Survived the '30s* (Chicago: Follett, 1976), pp. 205–6. Copyright © 1976 by Jeane Eddy Westin.

fore. They patched threadbare clothes and turned both collars and cuffs to make every stitch of clothing last just a little longer.

These trends were illustrated in the following life story of Vera Bosanko, interviewed by writer Jeane Westin in the 1970s. In what ways did the depression affect women's work at home, according to this testimony? What was the relation between women's domestic labor and their paid work?

It was 1930 when they closed down the oil fields in Texas. Just stacked the rigs and shut down. My husband lost everything—even his insurance.

'Bout that time Mr. Godwin died. He was my father-in-law so we had all these cattle to look after. Couldn't sell 'em. Weren't worth anything. I kinda cooked for my husband and the boys. Milked the cows and had a garden. I canned everythin' that wasn't movin'. Picked berries that growed out in the wild there. And we had a pecan orchard. Didn't make anything off it, but we had us some real sweet pies.

All of a sudden my husband was killed by a beef. The hired hands, they was going to hang a slaughtered steer up in a tree when one of them let the pulley slip. It hurt my husband inside. He got bad sick, took to hemorrhaging and. . . .

I was pregnant with Jimmy Lou, my youngest girl, so I took the other four children and went over to my aunt's. I was only twenty-four, but I didn't want to live with nobody, nobody at all. I wrote to my cousin up in this small town of St. Jo, Texas, and he let us come up and stay in a little two-room house he had. I raised a beautiful garden. That helped me out. And I washed for milk; washed clothes for a party that had a milk cow. But I finally had to go on WPA. You could sign up and then you got these little slips of paper. With these you could buy all the groceries except tobacco and liquor and such things.

Shortly, WPA put me to work in the canning plants. . . .Then this caseworker from out of Fort Worth came up and told me they needed a real nice lady to take a library job at the high school. This paid forty-two dollars a month. But about every few months they'd come in and say they just didn't have no more money for this project. I'd go on home, and there'd come a telegram in the evening mail telling me to go back to work the next day 'cause they got a bit more money.

That went on for about six years. Well, it was kind of scary. I never knowed where the job was going. Maybe that's the reason why I turned whiteheaded when I was a young age.

POLITICAL MATERNALISM
Clarence Stone

In the 1930s as in other times, Americans ascribed gender to governmental policies and institutions as well as to people. This could prove a powerful strategy for drawing attention and agreement to a particular political position. In this way, gender seeped into discussions that would have seemed not to deal with womanhood or manhood.

Source: Clarence Stone (Arnold, Maryland). Letter to the Editor of *The American Mercury* 43 (March 1938): 381–83. Reprinted by permission to the Enoch Pratt Free Library, Baltimore, Maryland, in accordance with the terms of the will of H. L. Mencken.

Clarence Stone, author of a letter to the editor of the *American Mercury* magazine in 1938, penned one stunning example of this use of gender. Launched in 1924 and originally edited by the curmudgeonly journalist, H. L. Mencken (1880–1956), the *American Mercury* devoted most of its pages to politics and government by the late 1930s. It proudly proclaimed its progressive leanings, commitment to free speech, and support for democracy the world over. Compare the ideas about masculine and feminine qualities in this letter with those in the questionnaire by Samuel Kahn's homosexual subject in the 1920s (chapter 6) and with the assumptions outlined in the earlier editorial, "Our New Mother—the Government (chapter 7)." How does Stone suggest that the feminine outlook is inferior to the masculine?

Adam vs. Eve

Sir: Those who now oppose the New Deal, and those who defend it, are simply taking sides in the latest development of an eternal conflict—the struggle for control between the male attitude toward existence, and the complementary but antagonistic female attitude. The male attitude, though some of its manifestations may seem crude, is found on analysis to be more concerned with issues that arise from the needs of the spirit than with material things. This is true in spite of the fact that many men of ability concentrate on the accumulation of wealth: the deeper truth is that most men of this type have objective minds, and they regard wealth mainly as the evidence of achievement—they become rich not so much because of greed as because the fight to win in a field where riches are the reward of victory. Whatever the field in which it operates, the male mind places a higher value on self-reliant seeking than on any promise of safe living; it stresses the importance of aggressive effort regardless of risk, and insists on freedom from arbitrary restraint.

The female attitude, though some of its manifestations such as sympathy and pity seem spiritually fine, actually gives first place to those material values that offer security and comfort. This outlook on life implies an acceptance of authority—it assumes that the assertion of control by someone, somewhere, carries with it the assurance of protection. The emphasis that women place on safety is, for them, instinctive and necessary —the human race could scarcely continue to exist if those who are or who will be mothers did not demand a sheltered environment in which uncertainty has been reduced as much as is possible.

. . . a fair consideration of the basic male and female attitudes makes it clear that the typical male is chiefly interested in effort and achievement; while the female is more concerned with safeguards, craving the guaranty of an established order.

. . . the New Deal represents a temporary triumph of the female attitude. That is why the present political situation has so aroused the nation—the issues involved reach deeper than politics usually go.

The fact that the New Deal is essentially female in outlook accounts for its instant widespread popularity at the start—it came at a time when the nation needed mothering. And it is obvious that the New Deal is based on the maternal conception of what is most important in life: it sought support, and still seeks it, on the basis of a vast vague emotional promise of security. Hence in the first sensational months of its career, the New Deal probably had the enthusiastic approval of almost all the women in this country. It was introduced and has been persistently advertised in a most beguiling way, with heart throbs always much in evidence. And it still has a strong appeal to a diverse multitude, made up mainly of less discerning women, of the unfortunate of both sexes, and of congenital leaners on others.

Perhaps the male attitude can be summed up, not very precisely, as a preference for being free to take risks in order to win awards and rewards—a self-reliant individualism. The female attitude, on the other hand, reflects an instinctive desire for assurance; this carries with it a willingness to submit to any authority that apparently offers protection and security, an attitude which responds readily and hopefully to large political promises.

In this generation, worn down by a world war and then by a prolonged world depression, great multitudes of people have given up the fight as individuals responsible to and for themselves, and have surrendered to various dictatorial forms of collectivism. . . . A time will come when the repressed need for individual freedom and individual expression must again assert itself.

Today the New Deal may seem so firmly entrenched as to preclude any discussion of its decline. Yet on a tomorrow not so far away, the New Deal will be merely a memory of a fantastic and frightfully expensive adventure in political maternalism. For on some tomorrow, buoyant Adam will once more replace fearful Eve as the dominant force in national affairs.

A VERY INFERIOR SENSE OF HONOR
Irna Phillips

By the 1930s, millions of Americans owned and faithfully listened to their radios. President Franklin Roosevelt used the remarkable medium to broadcast fireside chats, during which entire families gathered around their radios to hear the latest presidential responses to the Great Depression. Radio also made available new varieties of entertainment, one of the most popular being the soap opera.

Originating in the early 1930s as fifteen-minute serial dramas sponsored by soap manufacturers, soap operas found their lasting form in the hands of Irna Phillips (1901?–1974). Phillips was an early twentieth-century New Woman. After growing up in Chicago, she graduated from the University of Illinois and set out to teach school, specializing in storytelling and drama for children. In 1930, she broke into radio and by the end of the decade was simultaneously writing five soap operas, all her own creations!

Her most enduring creation was *The Guiding Light.* Premiered in January 1937 on WMAQ in Chicago, *TGL* focused on a Protestant minister, the Reverend Dr. John Ruthledge, his family, and his parishioners in the small imaginary town of Five Points. Until the mid-1940s, the show made religion the central perspective from which to view controversial issues of the day—unionization, ethnic diversity, war, extramarital sex. Sometimes one sermon constituted an entire episode. Interestingly, in the mid-forties, the kindly minister was replaced by a working-class German immigrant as the focal character of the show, suggesting that the particular version of manhood represented by Rev. Ruthledge had gone out of style.

Source: Irna Phillips, *The Guiding Light,* Script #371, July 5, 1938, Box 3, Original Radio Scripts, Library of American Broadcasting, Hornbake Library, University of Maryland, College Park, Maryland.

In the 1950s, *TGL* made the transition to television, and Irna Phillips moved right along with it, remaining the head writer until 1958. Phillips continued to create and write soaps for television (she was a cocreator of *Days of Our Lives* in 1965, for instance) until her death in 1974. Today, *TGL* is the longest running drama in broadcast history.

What follows is a script from *TGL*. This episode aired on July 5, 1938. In it, Rev. Ruthledge and Mr. Cunningham represent two kinds of middle-class manhood. What were the characteristics of each? Which type do you think the writers of *TGL* favored? Do you see any connections between these conceptions of manhood and the gendered notions of politics discussed in "Adam Vs. Eve"? What does the character of Rose tell us about the role of sexuality in defining "good" womanhood in the 1930s?

ANNOUNCER: And now, the Guiding Light. A great sorrow has entered the heart of Dr. Ruthledge, the Good Samaritan. Ned Holden, the boy whom he reared to manhood, and who seemed destined to carve for himself a great career as newspaperman and author has run away from Five Points. Although we know that at present he is thousands of miles away, his whereabouts are unknown to his mother, Fredrika Lang, and his fiance, Mary Ruthledge. While trying to reconcile himself to Ned's headlong action, another problem came to the attention of the kindly minister, when he learned that Rose Kransky [daughter of working-class Jewish parents] had allowed herself to become involved with a married man. Believing that this young girl was possessed of unusual ability, Dr. Ruthledge had encouraged her to rise above the opportunities which the Melting Pot had to offer her, but he now fears for her future happiness. Although reluctant to interfere in a matter of this kind, he has made up his mind to meet the man with whom Rose is in love, her employer, Mr. Cunningham. Having telephoned for an appointment we find him today just entering the outer office where Rose Kransky sits typing, and as we listen in we hear—

EFFECT: TYPEWRITER, DOOR OPENS AND CLOSES

DOC: Good morning, Rose.

EFFECT: TYPEWRITER STOPS

ROSE: Oh, good morning, Dr. Ruthledge. I'm sorry I didn't hear you come in. Mr. Cunningham will see you in just a minute—won't you sit down?

DR: Thank you.

ROSE: I was a little surprised when Mr. Cunningham told me that you had an appointment with him this morning.

DR: Surprised, Rose?

ROSE: Well yes, in a way—although I guess it isn't anything that concerns me.

PAUSE:

DR: You know, Rose, when I entered this office and saw you sitting at the typewriter, I thought to myself, how proud you ought to be of yourself.

ROSE: Proud?

DR: Yes. When you consider how hard you've worked for an education—how you denied yourself things that other girls had in order that you could attend business college at night, it should be gratifying for you to know that you're capable of filling a responsible position like this.

ROSE: Well, I was never satisfied just to grow up and live in Five Points the way some of the other girls were.

DR: I know you weren't—although somehow I always had an idea that your business career was only a stepping stone to something else.

ROSE: You mean because I used to talk a lot about wanting to go into the theater?

DR: Yes.

ROSE: Well, I did have that idea at one time, but I've kind of forgotten about it now.

DR: Yes I suppose you have.

ROSE: I still love the theater. I've seen quite a few plays in the last six months with Mr. Cunningham.

DR: I see. . . .

ROSE: You've always been so understanding and broad minded about everything, Dr. Ruthledge. I'll never forget all you've done for me in the past. I hope I'll be able to pay you back some day for all your encouragement.

DR: I was well repaid, Rose—at least so I thought—when I learned that you had secured a position as a private secretary.

ROSE: But now you're kind of sorry, huh?

DR: Sorry?

ROSE: Yes—at least I think you are after the way you talked to me the other night about giving up Mr. Cunningham.

DR: We won't talk about that now. I've told you how I feel—I don't suppose I'll change my mind about that.

ROSE: It is about Ned Holden that you want to see Mr. Cunningham today, isn't it? I mean—

DR: Yes, Rose. I promised Mary I'd have a talk with Mr. Cunningham about Ned.

EFFECT: BUZZER.

ROSE: That's Mr. Cunningham now. You can go right in, Dr. Ruthledge.

DR: Thank you, Rose.

ROSE: (FADING) I hope he can help you.

DR: I hope so, too.

EFFECT: DOOR OPENS AND CLOSES.

CHAS: Come right in, Dr. Ruthledge.

DR: Thank you. I don't suppose there's any need for us to introduce ourselves.

CHAS: No. There really isn't. Here, won't you sit down? Do you smoke? Would you care for a cigar?

DR: No. No. Thank you.

CHAS: You said over the phone that you'd like to find out if I could tell you anything about Ned Holden.

DR: I thought there was a possibility that you might know something. I knew that Ned had kept in touch with you ever since your firm had published his book.

CHAS: I'm sorry, but I'm afraid I can't be of any help to you, Dr. Ruthledge. We've been holding several royalty checks for him that were returned to us. Wherever he's gone, he's evidently left no forwarding address.

DR: I see.

CHAS: It seems like a rather strange thing—a young man with everything in the world to live for—a brilliant future ahead of him—haven't you any ideas as to why he should suddenly decide to go away as he did?

DR: Well, that's more or less beside the point.

CHAS: Excuse me. I didn't mean to be inquisitive.

DR: That's quite all right.

CHAS: I understand he was more or less like a son to you.

DR: Yes, he is.

DR: And about to become a son-in-law—my secretary Miss Kransky has told me something about it.

DR: Yes. Rose and Ned have known each other practically all their lives.

CHAS: Rose has spoken of you quite often.

DR: Indeed?

CHAS: Yes, as a matter of fact, one evening when we were out driving, she pointed out your little church down in Five Points. I can't say I envy you your job very much. It must get a little tiresome trying to educate a lot of ignorant foreigners.

DR: They're not ignorant, Mr. Cunningham, and the foreigners among them are doing their best to become good American citizens. They try to rear their sons and daughters in such a way that they can mingle on a more or less equal plane with those who have had the good fortune to be Americans for a greater length of time.

CHAS: Yes, no doubt.

DR: As a matter of fact the children of these foreigners, as you call them, have in a number of cases a much higher code of honor and decency than many of those who have enjoyed greater privileges.

CHAS: Yes, I suppose—although it's always been my opinion that what constitutes honor and decency in one class of society doesn't necessarily apply to another.

DR: I'm afraid we wouldn't see eye to eye on that opinion.

CHAS: Oh come, Dr. Ruthledge, you're an intelligent man, don't tell me that you apply the mass morality idea when you're away from your job of preaching.

DR: Honor and decency apply to each individual Mr. Cunningham. A man with a sense of decency doesn't try to dispense with it simply because of his particular place in society.

CHAS: Oh, I daresay you're right. It isn't a subject in which I'm particularly interested. At any rate it's something which every man has to figure out for himself.

DR: Yes. I would say it amounts to that. So long as every man has a certain number of hours out of the day when he has to live with himself, it would undoubtedly give him an uncomfortable feeling to realize that his sense of honor wasn't all that it should be.

CHAS: Have you any particular definition as to just what constitutes a sense of honor?

DR: I would say that again depends on the individual. It's quite possible that some men might have a very inferior sense of honor and still be able to look at themselves in a mirror with a very contented feeling.

CHAS: Perhaps with an even more contented feeling than many of our so called righteous individuals.

DR: Possibly so.

CHAS: In view of the turn our conversation has taken, I'm inclined to believe that Ned Holden wasn't the only reason for your calling to see me today.

DR: Frankly I was interested in meeting you, Mr. Cunningham.

CHAS: And now that you have?

DR: I'm still willing to give you the benefit of the doubt and say that our little discussion was an impersonal one. I shouldn't like to judge you on the strength of some of the remarks you've made.

CHAS: Please don't be charitable on my account. I assure you, Dr. Ruthledge that your opinion of me, one way or the other, doesn't make the slightest difference to me.

DR: No—there's no reason why it should—well—

CHAS: There's no hurry, Dr. Ruthledge. If you should wish to make any further character analysis of me, I'd be only too happy to have you stay awhile longer.

DR: No. I don't believe that will be necessary. Thank you for allowing me to take up your time.

CHAS: It was a pleasure.

DR: If you should hear anything further from Ned Holden, I'd appreciate your letting me know.

CHAS: I'll be very happy to.

DR: Good day, Mr. Cunningham.

CHAS: Good day, Dr. Ruthledge.

EFFECT: DOOR OPENS AND CLOSES.

ANNOUNCER: So Dr. Ruthledge has finally met Mr. Cunningham, the man to whom Rose is entrusting her future happiness. Apparently Charles Cunningham has taken an immediate dislike to the kindly minister. Was this feeling caused by a somewhat guilty conscience and the knowledge that Rose has told him that Dr. Ruthledge has asked her to discontinue her relationship with him? . . .

LEAD OUT: Tomorrow we again see our new young minister, Tom Bannion. You will hear him discuss with Dr. Ruthledge his ideas for the betterment of Five Points on the Guiding Light.

RECOMMENDED READINGS

Hine, Darlene Clark. "The Housewives' League of Detroit: Black Women and Economic Nationalism." In *Visible Women: New Essays on American Activism,* ed. Nancy Hewitt and Suzanne Lebsock. Urbana, Ill., 1993.

Hoffman, Abraham. *Unwanted Mexican-Americans in the Great Depression: Repatriation Pressures, 1929–1939.* Tucson, Ariz., 1974.

McElvaine, Robert. *The Great Depression: America, 1929–1941.* New York, 1984.

Melosh, Barbara. *Engendering Culture: New Deal Public Art and Theater.* Washington, D.C., 1991.

Milkman, Ruth, ed. *Women, Work, and Protest: A Century of US Women's Labor History.* Boston, 1985.

Ruiz, Vicki. *Mexican Women in Twentieth-Century America.* New York, 1998.

Sanchez, George. *Becoming Mexican-American: Ethnicity, Culture and Identity in Chicano Los Angeles, 1900–1945.* New York, 1993.

Scharf, Lois. *To Work and To Wed: Female Employment, Feminism, and the Great Depression.* Westport, Conn., 1980.

Sitkoff, Harvard. *A New Deal for Blacks: The Emergence of Civil Rights as a National Issue.* New York, 1978.

Wandersee, Winifred. *Women's Work and Family Values, 1920–1940.* Cambridge, Mass., 1981.

Ware, Susan. *Holding Their Own: American Women in the 1930s.* Boston, 1982.

——. *Beyond Suffrage: Women in the New Deal.* Cambridge, Mass., 1981.

FIGURE 9.1
"Wonder Woman," the comic heroine, made her debut
in the early forties, just in time to serve as a symbol for
all the American women who were—both literally and
figuratively—working overtime to fulfill new roles
while keeping up with their old ones. Wonder Woman is
a trademark of DC Comics © 1998. All rights reserved.
Used with permission. (*Source:* Wonder Woman, A Ms.
Book *[New York: Holt, Rinehart and Winston and
Warner Books, 1972] n.p.*)

CHAPTER 9

Homely Heroes and Wonder Women

The social upheaval caused by war exposes the "constructedness" of gender systems, as unusual demands force societies to question and often discard deeply embedded attitudes toward gender roles. World War II was no exception. With men being drafted by the millions, defense industries were compelled to summon American women to take their places. Women moved into all sectors of the economy as well as taking over household finances and playing both father and mother to their children. America's firm commitment to the ideal of the male breadwinner—upheld, as we have seen, even during the depths of the depression—began to crumble. The most popular female icons of the period, Rosie the Riveter and Wonder Woman, suggest that women reigned triumphant. But would these dramatic changes in the gender system outlast the war?

Female labor force participation rose from 27.9 percent in 1940 to a height of 37 percent in 1944. The greatest increase was among married women, who made up almost half of the 6.5 million new women workers. Most women worked for financial rather than patriotic reasons; servicemen's wives, for example, could not afford to live on their military allotments. Mothers of young children, however, tended to remain at home; public opinion, coupled with a scarcity of adequate child care, discouraged them from taking jobs.

Once in the labor force, women faced other obstacles: hostility from male coworkers and trade unions; lack of adequate housing and transportation; long shifts and erratic hours; and shopping problems due to rationing and early store closings. Minority women also confronted discrimination; in manufacturing, for example, African American women seldom got skilled jobs but were instead relegated to janitorial duties. Japanese Americans, men as well as women, were sent to detention centers during the first part of the war, then later released so that men could join the military and women could work in defense plants. Both racial and gender bias awaited the women who entered the military.

While women were challenging men's monopoly on breadwinning and leadership, the war itself put to the test masculinist claims to aggressiveness and bravery. As the country prepared to enter the fray, social commentators worried that the depression, coupled with the transformation of the family from "patriarchal" to "democratic," had turned American men "soft." Postwar studies revealed that in fact a majority of U.S. soldiers did not fulfill the ideal of the fierce, aggressive fighting man; more than three quarters seldom used their weapons, even to return enemy fire. Nevertheless, postwar "prescriptions for Penelope" urged women to honor returning veterans by cheerfully yielding their places as breadwinners and household heads.

Perhaps the war's greatest effect was on gay men and lesbians. The military afforded them unprecedented opportunities to congregate and discover same-sex enclaves around the world. After the war, instead of returning home, many remained in cities on both coasts, where they began to build their own communities.

A FAR LESS VIRILE WORLD

The threat of becoming involved in another global war prompted Americans to engage in a process of social and self-evaluation. Was America prepared to fight? Had the depression rent the nation's social and economic fabric beyond repair—had it lowered the country's morale so greatly that it could not sustain a fighting force?

Much of the public's uneasiness had to do with the disrupted gender relations of the 1930s as well as long-term changes in the American family, both of which were thought to have diminished men's authority and arrested the development of children, particularly sons. In 1939 psychiatrist David Levy identified the pathology of "maternal overprotection," and in his 1942 bestseller *Generation of Vipers,* Philip Wylie denounced what he called "Momism" for producing a cohort of immature young men.

These themes also appeared in a series of articles on the state of American society published by *Harper's Magazine* in 1940 and 1941. Eminent figures including anthropologist Margaret Mead and playwright Archibald MacLeish debated whether America had, indeed, "gone soft," and if so, what had caused this to happen. In excerpts from the first of these articles by novelist Roy Helton, to what does Helton attribute the nation's lack of preparedness? How does he "gender" political events and philosophies? Can you see parallels between Helton's views and those of Clarence Stone in Chapter 8?

> What is happening to our civilization has become abundantly clear in the past decade. The events of this year, however frightful they are, and however harrowing to our humanity, have but added a footnote.
> It may be there are some to-day who still do not believe that anything is happening to us or has happened to us. There have always been wars, and there have always been economic depressions after wars. They say that, and they are

Source: Roy Helton, "The Inner Threat: Our Own Softness," *Harper's Magazine,* 181 (September, 1940) pp. 337–43.

comforted by the fact that the things we experience have familiar names, even though those names are dreadful. What these optimists neglect to consider is that both wars and depressions are growing in violence. The war of 1914 was the bloodiest and most violent war in human history. Yet this present war exceeds it in every dimension but that of time. Nothing like this war was ever seen on earth before. . . .

The real danger is a more serious business even than war. Human civilization is changing its form under the pressure of machinery. Only the most heroic defense can prevent darker ages descending on our race than man has experienced in a thousand years. . . . Can we be more forehanded than our neighbors across the seas? Can we awake sooner than they did to the nature of what threatens democracy? Can we escape underestimating our enemy? We shall not escape that if we consider our enemy to be Stalin or Hitler or Mussolini. Stalin, Mussolini, and Hitler will die. The fabric they are creating will collapse to destroy the future of Germany, Russia, and Italy. But what they mean will not die.

It is very rare that any people is wise enough to look past men into meanings. But we must. For our civilization to survive it must turn its democratic energies toward strength and away from comfort. That is the hard truth which confronts our world and our lives. Every civilization that has avoided facing that truth when the hour came has perished.

For twenty-five years the feminine influence on Western life has mounted into a dominance over every area but that of politics, and even there its power is absolute as to the direction of our purposes. Unquestionably we are a politer people than we were at the turn of the century. The cuspidor has been eliminated from all but the most reactionary of our remoter hotels and barrooms. The cigarette has largely replaced the cigar and the plug. With infinite patience and resolution men have been maneuvered into a position where it is impossible for them to think of anything but women and their wants between the end of each day's work and its beginning the following morning. And it is those wants which with increasing authority have given form to our culture.

Only a fool would say that the result has been unpleasant. We live in a far daintier world than did our fathers, but also a far less virile world. Under urban conditions (and like Great Britain, most of France, Belgium, and Holland, we are now definitely an urban people) women have far more of the rewards of our civilization than men and they completely shape its ideals. Their influence is constant: on the children in the home, in the schools, and then through the period of courtship and marriage. Moreover, our urban population is predominantly a female population and, as any mail-order catalogue will reveal, it is the urban population which sets the direction of public habit and taste. . . .

Who can regard the history of European civilization for the past two years without perceiving that both France and Great Britain have acted on a female pattern and a female philosophy? I am not speaking of the individual and general heroism and fortitude of their armies, but of their official appeasements and submissions, of their thinking and their policy, of their lack of defensive aggression, and of their ability to struggle only when locked in the ravisher's arms, and then the complete and abject submission of France. Some time between 1914 and 1940 John Bull became Britannia and Jacques Bonhomme became La Belle France. And where today is our Uncle Samuel? The probability is high that our national symbol is also becoming a woman. A woman, it is true, with a sword, but a woman. Uncle Sam is not well groomed. He does not any longer fit our notions of ourselves.

The recognition of the fact that women hold the purse strings of the nation has profoundly altered the development of our industry and commerce. Nearly all devices now in general use are being marketed on their feminine and juvenile appeal. Luxury or its imitation is a paramount sales argument.

None of these changes since 1900 is of itself undesirable, but their gross effect is to produce a female world.

Now women are very fine creatures and creatures of superb courage, and no man who is not capable of appreciating that fact has a right to speak out at all. But biological and economic realities, as ancient as humanity, compel them to a selection of values of prime importance to themselves: shelter, comfort, and every attainable advantage for their young. Those are all proper ideals but not adequate to create an enduring society without an equal force in the distinctively male values of enterprise, adventure, and power. The balance of those two sets of factors makes civilization. When the female influence climbs too far into the ascendancy we have comfort, and its sequel, degeneration. When the male influence comes into ascendancy we have war and destruction. . . .

The atmosphere of bright illusion which has enveloped France and Great Britain and the United States concerns itself almost wholly with a future of ease and luxury for all men, a future of unlimited power and unlimited manufactured goods and food conveyed through the air, or over sixteen-lane super-speed highways to eager billions of almost exclusively consuming people whose needs are satisfied by automatic machinery. This vision has been lately heightened by the discovery of an isotope of Uranium which offers a slight possibility of providing the future with an unlimited supply of energy. . . .

Regard it carefully and you will see that every form which the world of tomorrow takes, in fiction, in the daily comics, in grave economic literature, or in the visions of democratic government, is entirely a female dream.

In the model house of any builder's exhibit the male element of family life appears to be a shameful mystery for which no provision can decently be made without killing a sale. This is equally true of our model futures. The male economic function is taken over by Uranium 235, and there is nothing left for men to do but to grow long hair or shake their fists at the planets. A Mr. Lipstick is the end product of our modern industrial romancing; but the future, we may be sure, will not work out along those lines. A female world dream cannot survive in a competitive reality and that is probably not a fact which humanity should deplore. . . .

It must be remembered that this nineteenth-century dream of to-morrow was one in which male constructive efforts were utilized to attain an essentially female ideal. But that was merely a transition. We lost that kind of a future in 1930, and turned from idealizing the creation of a mechanical paradise to the wholly feminine dream of security for our domestic comforts.

Security is the woman's wish, and has always had to be. Its adoption as a goal by men and nations was the final signal of the turning point in the sex of our democratic civilization, and of its future helplessness against any male purpose. . . .

We are a nation of city dwellers. We are largely a sedentary people. For exercise Americans move faster and travel farther under cover and on the seats of their pants than citizens of any other nation in the world. . . .

We indulge our children illimitably. Instead of rearing a race of lusty, weather-conditioned sons and daughters of democracy, we exhaust our private purses to buy gasoline for our racing youth, and strain the resources of our schools and colleges to erect stadia unparalleled since the days of degenerating Rome. We have carried the spectator sports to an excess never witnessed in human life since the days of Augustus. It is true that our younger sons and daughters romp and play like natural human kind, but once in the standard assembly line we have constructed to provide for our future, they must sit out the best Saturday afternoons in the year while twenty-two picked men provide emotion, the sense of achievement, as well as vicarious exercise for twenty-two thousand rooters.

We have constructed motor roads to the tops of our mountains. In our magnificent outdoor training grounds of democracy we have done everything possible to remove any incentive for mature people to use human activity for pleasure. Folk too indolent to climb a seven-foot stepladder can ascend Mt. Mitchell, Mt. Washington, Clingman's Dome or Pike's Peak, sitting down.

. . . For the past twenty years American civilization as represented by its great middle class has appeared to pursue no ideal more world-shaking than the attempt to get harder and harder butter on softer and softer bread. It was so also in the democracies of Europe. To those mild ideals treason is inevitable in the face of a more masculine purpose. To tie such a male purpose to democracy is the only way democracy can survive. . . .

THE BOMBADIER WAS A JEW
Ralph McGill

Since the mass emigration of East European Jews to the United States began in the late nineteenth century, Jewish men had been depicted as effeminate, somehow less manly than "real American men" (while, conversely, Jewish women were characterized as domineering and "unladylike"). Such stereotypes, which had deep roots in the long history of European anti-Semitism, reappeared in Nazi propaganda, casting aspersions on the manhood of American as well as European Jews.

To counter these negative stereotypes in the United States, the National Jewish Welfare Board published the volume *In the Nation's Service,* documenting the military achievements of American Jewish men during the first year of the war. In the following newspaper column, which was reprinted in this volume, what concept of manhood is McGill upholding in his defense of the military record of Jewish men?

DIVIDE AND CONQUER

Facts always interest me. So do emotions. Hitler interests me chiefly because he made clearer than any other of the great warlords of history how effectively propaganda may be made to work for the armed forces.

Hitler wrote for public consumption that one of the best attacks was to tell a lie, the greater the lie the better, against your enemy. If the lie is repeated enough there will be some who believe it.

Source: Ralph McGill, "One Word More," in National Jewish Welfare Board, *In the Nation's Service: A Compilation of Facts Concerning Jewish Men in the Armed Services during the First Year of the War* (New York, 1942), p. 10. Reprinted with permission from *The Atlanta Journal* and *The Atlantic Constitution.*

He said again that one of the best ways to conquer a nation was to divide it. . . .

His agents are busy in this country. Some of them are unwitting dupes who follow the enemy pattern without realizing it.

One of the current enemy agent jobs is to keep going any possible anti-Semitic propaganda. They have as their aim to create suspicion and hatred in this country.

It seems to me that it is a patriotic duty to discuss it and nail the lie, rather than to let it go unchecked. There is a whispering campaign to the effect that Jews are seeking to evade military service. This despite the fact that the percentage of Jews in the armed forces in this war is greater than the percentage of their population in this country. This was true in the first [world] war. The effect of the propaganda has been, in some communities, to remember one case of attempted evasion and to forget all those who went willingly.

A LOOK AT THE RECORD

I had sought, and obtained, some official records which ought to be of interest to fair-minded persons willing to know the truth and to be on guard against the agents of hate and disunion.

The American Bar Association Journal for February reports that the first known fatality among [their] membership . . . was Ensign Robert L. Leopold, of Louisville, Ky.

The first known casualty from the membership of the Chicago Bar Association was Captain Irving Maddelson, who was severely wounded in action while serving with MacArthur on Bataan peninsula. He since has been promoted because of his bravery and ability.

The first Japanese battleship sunk in the war was that one in which Captain Colin Kelly piloted his ship through heavy fire within bombing range. The bombardier in that plane, who aimed the bombs and released them, was a Jew, Corporal Meyer Levin.

The first fatality from Minneapolis was Ensign Ira Jeffrey Weil, who received a posthumous reward for valor.

Among the first fatalities from Chicago was Sherman Levine, an 18-year-old boy who died in action at Pearl Harbor.

Perhaps the youngest boy in action at Pearl Harbor was Morris Samuelson, of New Orleans, who was a gunner on that morning and fired more than 250 rounds at the Japanese. He since has been mustered out because it was discovered he falsified his age when enlisting. He will re-enlist when he is 18. He now is 17. . . .

The first applicant for membership in the American Gold Star Mothers of this war was Mrs. Gertrude Kram, of New York, whose 18-year-old son, a gunner with a Navy crew aboard a tanker, was killed in the torpedoing of his ship. She herself was the daughter of a Gold Star mother.

The first American soldier brought home for burial on American soil was Sergeant Herbert Keilson, of the United States Marines, who was killed aboard a cruiser during the attack on the Gilbert and Marshall Islands some months ago.

One of the youngest war mothers in America is Mrs. Michael Newman, of Oregon, whose 17-year-old son enlisted, with her permission, in the Marines.

Lieutenant Commander Solomon Isquith recently was awarded the Navy Cross "for extraordinary courage and disregard for his own safety" while directing the abandonment of the U.S.S. Utah when it capsized during the attack on Pearl Harbor.

Private Leonard York, of Columbus, recently was honored on the "They Live Forever" program. He received the Order of the Purple Heart for bravery while machinegunning Japanese during the December 7 attack.

Three young Jews were aboard the aircraft carrier Lexington. Lieutenant Commander Max Silverstein was in command of the destroyer Sims when it was sunk in the Coral sea engagement—[he] was killed in the fight. . . .

SOMETHING TO REMEMBER

The list could go on. These are but a few outstanding facts of the war we are in today.

The enemy wants you to dislike some other American group. It is spending money and time in an effort to make you do that.

The enemy wants you to fall into the human error of condemning a whole group by the action of an individual or by the acts of a few individuals.

In time of war emotions are close to the surface.

The best way is to doubt and deny all charges, and some of them are subtle, against a people or an individual until the real facts are known.

The enemy wants you to fall into the error of repeating whispers against other peoples in America.

Don't let Hitler get away with one of his chief weapons.

Don't be repeating one of his lies.

THEY WORKED LIKE DEMONS
Ernie Pyle

One of the most beloved journalists covering World War II was Ernie Pyle (1900–1945), who lived with the troops in both the European and Pacific theatres of war, sending back vivid firsthand accounts of daily life in the trenches and in the jungle. He paid as much attention to what went on behind the lines as to what occurred in the heat of battle, emphasizing the need for teamwork in all parts of the war. Pyle himself lost his life near Okinawa.

Though Pyle's writing was noted for its understatement, he managed to turn the lowly GI into a "homely hero." In the following example of Pyle's journalism, how does Pyle both uphold and undermine conventional notions of heroism? What do his metaphors indicate about the relationship between race and masculinity during this period?

Source: Ernie Pyle, "The Engineer's War," *Brave Men* (New York: Grosset & Dunlap, 1944), pp. 65–72. Reprinted by permission of Scripps-Howard Foundation.

It was on my very first day with the Third that we hit the most difficult and spectacular engineering job of the Sicilian campaign. You may remember Point Calava from the newspaper maps. It is a great stub of rock that sticks out into the sea, forming a high ridge running back into the interior. The coast highway is tunneled through this big rock, and on either side of the tunnel the road sticks out like a shelf on the sheer rock wall. Our engineers figured the Germans would blow the tunnel entrance to seal it up. But they didn't. They had an even better idea. They picked out a spot about fifty feet beyond the tunnel mouth and blew a hole 150 feet long in the road shelf. They blew it so deeply and thoroughly that a stone dropped into it would never have stopped rolling until it bounced into the sea a couple of hundred feet below.

We were beautifully bottlenecked. We couldn't bypass around the rock, for it dropped sheer into the sea. We couldn't bypass over the mountain; that would have taken weeks. We couldn't fill the hole, for the fill would keep sliding off into the water.

All the engineers could do was bridge it, and that was a hell of a job. But bridge it they did, and in only twenty-four hours. . . .

When the first engineer officers went up to inspect the tunnel, I went with them. . . .

It was around 2 P.M. when we got there and in two hours the little platform of highway at the crater mouth resembled a littered street in front of a burning building. Air hoses covered the ground, serpentined over each other. Three big air compressors were parked side by side, their engines cutting off and on in that erratically deliberate manner of air compressors, and jackhammers clattered their nerve-shattering din.

Bulldozers came to clear off the stone-blocked highway at the crater edge. Trucks, with long trailers bearing railroad irons and huge timbers, came and unloaded. Steel cable was brought up, and kegs of spikes, and all kinds of crowbars and sledges.

The thousands of vehicles of the division were halted some ten miles back in order to keep the highway clear for the engineers. One platoon of men at a time worked in the hole. There was no use throwing in the whole company, for there was room for only so many.

At suppertime, hot rations were brought up by truck. The Third Division engineers went on K ration at noon but morning and evening hot food was got up to them, regardless of the difficulty. For men working the way those boys were, the hot food was a military necessity. By dusk the work was in full swing and half the men were stripped to the waist.

The night air of the Mediterranean was tropical. The moon came out at twilight and extended our light for a little while. The moon was still new and pale, and transient, high-flying clouds brushed it and scattered shadows down on us. Then its frail light went out, and the blinding nightlong darkness settled over the grim abyss. But the work never slowed nor halted throughout the night. . . .

The men worked on and on, and every one of the company officers stayed throughout the night just to be there to make decisions when difficulties arose. But I got so sleepy I couldn't stand it, and I caught a commuting truck back to the company and turned in. . . .

It wasn't long after dawn when I returned to the crater. At first glance it didn't look as though much had been accomplished, but an engineer's eye would have seen that the goundwork was all laid. They had drilled and blasted two holes far down the jagged slope. These were to hold the heavy uprights so they wouldn't slide downhill when weight was applied. . . .

At about 10 A.M. the huge uprights were slid down the bank, caught by a group of men clinging to the steep slope below, and their ends worked into the blasted holes. Then the uprights were brought into place by men on the banks, pulling on ropes tied to the timbers. Similar heavy beams were slowly and cautiously worked out from the bank until their tops rested on the uprights.

A half-naked soldier, doing practically a wire-walking act, edged out over the timber and with an air-driven bit bored a long hole down through two timbers. Then he hammered a steel rod into it, tying them together. Others added more bracing, nailing the parts together with huge spikes driven in by sledge hammers. Then the engineers slung steel cable from one end of the crater to the other, wrapped it around the upright stanchions and drew it tight with a winch mounted on a truck.

Now came a Chinese coolie scene as shirtless, sweating soldiers—twenty men to each of the long, spliced timber—carried and slid their burdens out across the chasm, resting them on the two wooden spans just erected. They sagged in the middle, but still the cable beneath took most of the strain. They laid ten of the big timbers across and the bridge began to take shape. Big stringers were bolted down, heavy flooring was carried on and nailed to the stringers. Men built up the approaches with stones. The bridge was almost ready.

Around 11 A.M., jeeps had begun to line up at the far end of the tunnel. They carried reconnaissance platoons, machine gunners and boxes of ammunition. They'd been given No. 1 priority to cross the bridge. . . . Around dusk of the day before, the engineers had told me they'd have jeeps across the crater by noon of the next day. It didn't seem possible at the time, but they knew whereof they spoke. But even they would have had to admit it was pure coincidence that the first jeep rolled cautiously across the bridge at high noon, to the very second.

In that first jeep were [Major] General [Lucian] Truscott and his driver, facing a 200-foot tumble into the sea if the bridge gave way. The engineers had insisted they send a test jeep across first. But when he saw it was ready, the general just got in and went. It wasn't done dramatically but it was a dramatic thing. It showed that the Old Man had complete faith in his engineers. I heard soldiers speak of it appreciatively for an hour.

Jeeps snaked across the rickety bridge behind the general while the engineers kept stations beneath the bridge to watch and measure the sag under each load. The bridge squeaked and bent as the jeeps crept over. But it held, and nothing else mattered. . . .

The tired men began to pack their tools into trucks. Engineer officers who hadn't slept for thirty-six hours went back to their olive orchard to clean up. They had built a jerry bridge, a comical bridge, a proud bridge, but above all the kind of bridge that wins wars. And they had built it in one night and half a day. The general was mighty pleased.

I don't know what it is that impels some men, either in peace or in wartime, to extend themselves beyond all expectation, or what holds other men back to do just as little as possible. In any group of soldiers you'll find both kinds. The work of combat engineers usually comes in spurts, and it is so vital when it does come that the percentage of fast workers is probably higher than in most other branches. I've never seen men work any harder than the engineers I was with. On the Point Calava road crater job there were two men I couldn't take my eyes off. They worked like demons. Both were corporals and had little to gain by their extraordinary labors, except maybe some slight future promotion. And I doubt that's what drove them. Such men must be impelled by the natures they're born with—by pride in their job, by that mystic spark which forces some men to give all they've got, all the time.

These two men were Gordon Uttech, of Merrill, Wisconsin, and Alvin Tolliver, of Alamosa, Colorado. Both were air-compressor operators and rock drillers. Uttech worked all night, and when the night shift was relieved for breakfast, he refused to go. He worked on throughout the day without sleep and in the final hours of the job he went down under the frail bridge to check the sag and strain, as heavier and heavier vehicles passed over it.

Tolliver, too, worked without ceasing, never resting, never even stopping to wipe off the sweat that made his stripped body look as though it were coated with olive oil. I never saw him stop once throughout the day. He seemed to work without instruction from anybody, knowing what jobs to do and doing them alone. He wrastled the great chattering jackhammers into the rock. He spread and rewound his air hose. He changed drills. He regulated his compressor. He drove eye-hooks into the rock, chopped down big planks to fit the rocky ledge he'd created. Always he worked as though the outcome of the war depended on him alone.

I couldn't help being proud of those men, who gave more than was asked. . . .

IT MADE ME LIVE BETTER
Fanny Christina Hill

The defense industry offered women unprecedented employment opportunities; millions flocked into training schools and programs to prepare for skilled jobs paying higher wages than they had ever received before. Minority women, who had long been relegated to the most menial and lowest paid occupations, were especially eager to take advantage of openings in manufacturing, but they found that there, too, ethnic and racial discrimination persisted. One exception to this nationwide pattern was Los Angeles, where the Negro Victory Committee succeeded in convincing the local U.S. Employment Office to open up job training and employment to African Americans. As a result, women like Fanny Hill were able to find excellent jobs in the aircraft industry.

Hill, a young, recently married woman, migrated from Texas to Los Angeles in 1943, when her husband joined the service. Having spent many years doing private domestic work, she was determined to find "a good job," perhaps in a hotel or motel; she soon realized that working for North American Aviation would be even better. She stayed there throughout the war, took time out to have a baby, and then returned to the plant, retiring after forty years. Talking to oral historian Sherna Gluck, Hill described both her factory experiences and her life outside the workplace. She explained how a renewal of discrimination after the war prevented her and other African Americans from progressing at North American as rapidly as they had initially. What resources did she find in the black community of Los Angeles? How did wartime change the course of her life?

Source: "Fanny Christina Hill," in Sherna Berger Gluck, *Rosie the Riveter Revisited: Women, The War, and Social Change* (Boston: Twayne, 1987), pp. 37–42.

I don't remember what day of the week it was, but I guess I must have started our pretty early that morning. When I went there, the man didn't hire me. They had a school down here on Figueroa and he told me to go to the school. I went down and it was almost four o'clock and they told me they'd hire me. You had to fill out a form. They didn't bother too much about your experience in aircraft. Then they give you some kind of little test where you put the pegs in the right hole.

There were other people in there, kinda mixed I assume it was more than men. Most of the men was gone, and they weren't hiring too many men unless they had a good excuse. Most of the women was in my bracket, five or six years younger or older. I was twenty-four. There was a black girl that hired in with me. I went to work the next day, sixty cents an hour.

I think I stayed at school for about four weeks. They only taught you shooting and bucking rivets and how to drill the holes and to file. You had to use a hammer for certain things. After a couple of whiles, you worked on the real thing. But you were supervised so you didn't make a mess.

When we went into the plant, it wasn't too much different than down at the school. It was the same amount of noise; it was the same routine. One difference was there was just so many more people, and when you went in the door you had a badge to show and they looked at your lunch. I gotten accustomed to a lot of people and I knew if it was a lot of people, it always meant something was going on. I got carried away: "As long as there's a lot of people here, I'll be making money." That was all I could ever see.

I was a good student, if I do say so myself. But I have found out through life, sometimes even if you're good, you just don't get the breaks if the color's not right. I could see where they made a difference in placing you in certain jobs. They had fifteen or twenty departments, but all the Negroes went to Department 17 because there was nothing but shooting and bucking rivets. You stood on one side of the panel and your partner stood on this side, and he would shoot the rivets with a gun and you'd buck them with the bar. That was about the size of it. I just didn't like it. I didn't think I could stay there with all of this shooting and a'bucking and a'jumping and a'bumping. I stayed in it about two or three weeks and then I just decided I did not like that. I went and told my foreman and he didn't do anything about it, so I decided to leave.

While I was standing outside on the railroad track, I ran into somebody else out there fussing too. I went over to the union and they told me what to do. I went back inside and they sent me to another department where you did bench work and I liked that much better. You had a little small jig that you would work on and you just drilled out holes. Sometimes you would rout them or you would scribe them and then you'd cut them with a cutters.

I must have stayed there nearly a year, and then they put me in another department, "Plastics." It was the tail section of the B-Bomber, the Billy Mitchell Bomber. I put a little part in the gunsight. You had a little ratchet set and you would screw it in there. Then I cleaned the top of the glass off and put a piece of paper over it to seal off to go to the next section. I worked over there until the end of the war. Well, not quite the end, because I got pregnant, and while I was off having the baby the war was over.

Negroes rented rooms quite a bit. It was a wonderful thing, 'cause it made it possible for you to come and stay without a problem. My sister and I was rooming with this lady and we was paying six dollars a week, which was good money, because she was renting the house for only twenty-six dollars a month. She had another girl living on the back porch and she was charging three dollars. So you get the idea.

We were accustomed to shacking up with each other. We had to live like that because that was the only way to survive. Negroes, as a rule, are accustomed to a lot of people around. They have lived like that from slavery time on. We figured out how to get along with each other.

In the kitchen everybody had a little place where he kept his food. You had a spot in the icebox; one shelf was yours. You bought one type of milk and the other ones bought another type of milk, so it didn't get tangled up. But you didn't buy too much to have on hand. You didn't overstock like I do today. Of course, we had rationing, but that didn't bother me. It just taught me a few things that I still do today. It taught me there's a lot of things you can get along without. I liked cornbread a lot — and we had to use Cream of Wheat, grits, to make cornbread. I found out I liked that just as well. So, strange as it may seem, I didn't suffer from the war thing.

I started working in April and before Thanksgiving, my sister and I decided we'd buy a house instead of renting this room. The people was getting a little hanky-panky with you; they was going up on the rent. So she bought the house in her name and I loaned her some money. The house only cost four thousand dollars with four hundred dollars down. It was two houses on the lot, and we stayed in the small one-bedroom house in the back. I stayed in the living room part before my husband came home and she stayed in the bedroom. I bought the furniture to go in the house, which was the stove and refrigerator, and we had our old bedroom sets shipped from Texas. I worked the day shift and my sister worked the night shift. I worked ten hours a day for five days a week. Or did I work on a Saturday? I don't remember, but I know it was ten hours a day. I'd get up in the morning, take a bath, come to the kitchen, fix my lunch—I always liked a fresh fixed lunch—get my breakfast, and then stand outside for the ride to come by. I always managed to get someone that liked to go to work slightly early. I carried my crocheting and knitting with me.

You had a spot where you always stayed around, close to where you worked, because when the whistle blew, you wanted to be ready to get up and go to where you worked. The leadman always come by and give you a job to do or you already had one that was a hangover from the day before. So you had a general idea what you was going to do each day.

Then we'd work and come home. I was married when I started working in the war plant, so I wasn't looking for a boyfriend and that made me come home in the evening. Sometimes you'd stop on the way home and shop for groceries. Then you'd come home and clean house and get ready for bed so you can go back the next morning. Write letters or what have you. I really wasn't physically tired.

Recreation was Saturday and Sunday. But my sister worked the swing shift and that made her get up late on Saturday morning, so we didn't do nothing but piddle around the house. We'd work in the garden, and we'd just go for little rides on the streetcar. We'd go to the parks, and then we'd go to the picture show downtown and look at the newsreel: "Where it happens, you see it happen." We enjoyed going to do that on a Sunday, since we was both off together.

We had our little cliques going; our little parties. Before they decided to break in to white nightclubs, we had our own out here on Central Avenue. There were a ton of good little nightclubs that kept you entertained fairly well. I don't know when these things began to turn, because I remember when I first came to Los Angles, we used to go down to a theater called the Orpheum and that's where all the Negro entertainers as well as whites went. We had those clip joints over on the east side.

And the funniest thing about it, it would always be in our nightclubs that a white woman would come in with a Negro man, eventually. The white man would very seldom come out in the open with a black woman. Even today. But the white woman has always come out in the open, even though I'm sure she gets tromped on and told about it.

Some weeks before I brought home twenty-six dollars, some weeks sixteen dollars. Then it gradually went up to thirty dollars, then it went up a little bit more and a little bit more. And I learned somewhere along the line that in order to make a good move you gotta make some money. You don't make the same amount everyday. You have some days good, sometimes bad. Whatever you make you're supposed to save some. I was also getting the fifty dollars a month from my husband and that was just saved right away. I was planning on buying a home and car. And I was going back to school. My husband came back, but I was never laid off, so I just never found it necessary to look for another job or to go to school for another job.

I was still living over on the Compton Avenue with my sister in this small little back house when my husband got home. Then, when Beverly was born, my sister moved in the front house and we stayed in the back house. When he came back, he looked for a job in the cleaning and pressing place, which was just plentiful. All the people had left these cleaning and pressing jobs and every other job; they was going to the defense plant to work because they was paying good. But in the meantime he was getting the same the people out there was getting, $1.25 an hour. That's why he didn't bother to go out to North American. But what we both weren't thinking about was that they did have better benefits because they did have an insurance plan and a union to back you up. Later he did come to work there, in 1951 or 1952.

I worked up until the end of March and then I took off. Beverly was born the twenty-first of June. I'd planned to come back somewhere in the last of August. I went to verify the fact that I did come back, so that did go on my record that I didn't just quit. But they laid off a lot of people, most of them, because the war was over.

It didn't bother me much—not thinking about it jobwise. I was just glad that the war was over. I didn't feel bad because my husband had a job and he was also eligible to go to school with his GI bill. So I really didn't have too many plans—which I wish I had had. I would have tore out page one and fixed it differently; put my version of page one in there.

I went and got me a job doing day work. That means you go to a person's house and clean up for one day out of the week and then you go to the next one and clean up. I did that a couple of times and I discovered I didn't like that so hot. Then I got me a job downtown working in a little factory where you do weaving— burned clothes and stuff like that. I learned to do that real good. It didn't pay too much but it paid enough to get me going, seventy-five cents or about like that.

When North American called me back, was I a happy soul! I dropped that job and went back. That was a dollar an hour. So, from sixty cents an hour, when I first hired in there, up to one dollar. That wasn't traveling fast, but it was better than anything else because you had hours to work by and you had benefits and you come home at night with your family. So it was a good deal.

It made me live better. I really did. We always say that Lincoln took the bale off of the Negroes. I think there is a statue up there in Washington D.C., where he's lifting something off the Negro. Well, my sister always said—that's why you can't interview her because she's so radical—"Hitler was the one that got us out of the white folks' kitchen."

LEAVING THEIR CHILDREN IS A TERRIFIC WORRY
The U.S. Children's Bureau

Even before the United States had officially entered the war, government officials began to anticipate the social problems it would cause. In the eyes of some, children would be especially vulnerable, as mothers, eager for well-paying jobs, responded to the demand for defense workers. In 1941 the U.S. Children's Bureau called a conference to discuss ways to address the growing need for child care. The bureau had long regarded maternal employment as harmful to children. Their views were shared by leaders in the field of social work, even including child care advocates, who sought to limit child care services only to families in acute need but opposed maternal employment in general. The U.S. Women's Bureau, by contrast, promoted employment for all women and sought to remove any obstacles that stood in their way.

The differences between these two factions were not really resolved at this conference but continued to dog debates about maternal employment and child care throughout the war. Though government-sponsored child care was ultimately authorized under the terms of the Lanham Act, bureaucratic interventions, including some by the Children's Bureau, delayed delivery of services and many parents had to seek alternatives. Rumors about children locked in cars parked in factory lots and "latchkey children" getting into trouble after school abounded, giving "working mothers" a bad name. The difficulties of obtaining child care discouraged many mothers from seeking work altogether.

In the debate that follows, how did representatives of the different factions frame their positions? How did each side use references to patriotism to support its position?

MISS [Katharine] LENROOT [Chief, U.S. Children's Bureau]. It seemed to me we might discuss the question of what . . . service could be offered to women who are applying for employment or for training, and who if given a chance to discuss the problems of their children with someone might in some instances decide not to go to work, or if they decided to work they might be given some advice as to what provisions, what resources there were for care of the children. . . .

Miss Anderson, do you have any feeling that it might be undesirable to encourage personnel departments of [defense] plants to get this family information, or do you think there would be no reason why they shouldn't?

MISS [Mary] ANDERSON [Chief of the U.S. Women's Bureau]. I don't know whether the companies would want to get it or whether the workers would want them to. I wondered whether or not the woman might think the supervision by a public organization might jeopardize her chances of employment and for that reason not want to give the information. That is particularly true because of the fact that there has been so much done to prevent their getting employment until all the men have employment. We must remember that the women work for the same reason

Source: U.S. Children's Bureau, *Proceedings of Conference on Day Care of Children of Working Mothers with Special Reference to Defense Areas,* held in Washington, D.C. July 31–August 1, 1941; Children's Bureau Publication No. 281 (Washington, D.C.: GPO, 1942), pp. 30–32.

FIGURE 9.2

The Child Service Center at the Kaiser Shipyard in Portland, Oregon represented the state of the art during World War II; architect-designed, it even featured a wading pool. The center was open around the clock to accommodate the night shift and even offered tired workers prepared food to take home with them. Unfortunately, high-quality child care like this was rare. *(Courtesy of the Oregon Historical Society, Negative Number 80379).*

that men work. They work to live. They work to get bread and butter not only for themselves but for dependents, and they are not all child dependents, either; there are older people in the families. For that reason I am not sure that we ought to be so very strict and do all of these counseling things, because I don't believe we could do them anyway, and I wouldn't want to set up any more barriers than there are against women's working.

MISS [Eleanor] NEUSTAEDTER [Community Service Society, New York]. Are we setting up barriers or thinking of ways of offering an opportunity to women who might need this service?

MISS ANDERSON. Suppose here was a woman who had to go to work to support herself and small children. If you could say to her, "Well, now, if you have to go to work and you want to go to work, it may be arranged for someone in the community to look after these little children while you are at work." I am sure she would welcome that suggestion absolutely because I think leaving her children is a terrific worry to her. But approaching the matter in that way is quite different from asking, "Do you have children? How many children do you have? How old are they?" and so on.

MISS LENROOT. Would you think a woman would object if she were asked at a public employment office . . . "Mrs. So-and-so, do you have children and have you made provision for their care, or would you need any service as to what can be done for the children?"

MISS ANDERSON. That depends on the woman. I am sure there are some that would object to it and some that probably wouldn't, some that are in dire need of the help. But the others will say, "They won't take me if I tell them those things." . . .

I think it probably depends on how the questions are asked. They can be told in a sympathetic way, "We are asking these questions only to help you decide these things." . . .

MISS [Elizabeth] CLARK [Executive Director, National Association of Day Nurseries]. . . . I think it is a very delicate thing to do. None of us in the Day Nurseries Association stands for putting any obstacles in the way of defense, but we do want to make sure that we are not creating a lot of emotionally ill and neglected children in the process. Some of us know a little bit about that. . . . It seems terrifically important. I think it is a delicate question to ask, and asking the question isn't enough, we feel, for mothers with children under 2. It is a very serious situation to take those mothers out of the home. Some problems of counseling could certainly be worked out under the leadership of social agencies. . . .

MISS [Edith] ABBOTT [Dean, School of Social Work Administration, University of Chicago]. Isn't it important to get in mind that [child care] should be a public service; that is, . . . something that can hold over after the war. It has been needed for a long time anyway in connection with the schools, and if the schools aren't willing to do it there has to be some other kind of local public agency that will have child centers of the proper kind. I believe the women would be much more willing to give this information if they knew there was public service available for them that they weren't going to have to pay for, any more than they pay to send their children to the public schools. . . .

I THINK THE COMMUNITY OWES ME A LOT
Emi Somekawa and Wilson Makabe

During World War I, German Americans were the target of much hostility from their fellow citizens, but during World War II, this type of spillover hatred of the enemy was directly primarily toward Japanese Americans. By the 1940s there were over 100,000 Japanese Americans, most of them living on the West Coast as merchants, farmers, or truck gardeners. In February 1942, President Roosevelt ordered all of them—resident aliens, naturalized citizens, and native-born Americans alike—to report for "relocation" at various centers away from the coast. They were not allowed to return to their homes until 1945, by which time they had lost most of their property and belongings through theft, vandalism, or mortgage foreclosure.

The following oral histories recount the experiences of two young Japanese Americans who were both rounded up and interned. How did gender determine the particular difficulties each one faced? How did Somekawa use her nursing skills? What did being a soldier mean to Makabe? What impact did their wartime experiences have on the course of their lives after the war?

Source: Emi Somekawa, "Tule Lake," in *And Justice for All: An Oral History of the Japanese American Detention Camps,* ed. John Tateishi (New York: Random House, 1984), pp. 146–51.

At the time of the evacuation, I was married and had one child and was pregnant with another. I was born in Portland, Oregon. My family moved to Salem, Oregon, and was in farming. I graduated from high school in Salem and then went to train as a nurse in Portland, where I met my husband. And we lived there for two years, until the outbreak of the war when we were evacuated to the Portland Assembly Center. I graduated from nursing school in 1939. My husband was in business with his father, the Nichi Bey Fish Company, right in the heart of Japanese Town.

There were three of us Nisei [naturalized or native-born American] nurses then at Emmanuel Hospital. We were received very well. At the time of Pearl Harbor, I was supervising at Emmanuel in the labor rooms. I had my training there, and when evacuation came, the administrator told me that any time I came back to Portland, that job would be there for me. But I wasn't too sure whether I was ever going to come back to Portland. . . .

When we first realized that an evacuation would take place, it was a depressing feeling that's hard to explain to you. My husband's father was an invalid by that time—I think he'd had his third stroke—and so he wasn't able to walk. . . . I thought, well, the only thing that I can do is to take care of my small son and my husband's father. As long as we take care of these two people, I felt that that was the best thing that we could do. I didn't know whether we'd ever come back to our home again, but it was a feeling that all these years we'd worked for nothing. That kind of feeling, you know, that you're just losing everything. . . .

The Portland Assembly Center was terrible. It's just amazing how people can think of putting another group of human beings into a place like that. There was so much horse and cow manure around. We were put into a cubicle that just had plywood walls and it was a horse stall with planks on the floor with about an inch of space between them. You'd find grass growing through the planks already, and it was just terrible. In the corner we saw this folding bed, an army camp cot, with mattress ticking, and we were supposed to go out there and fill it with straw so that we would have a mattress. It's a depressing thing to think that we had to go into a place like that, but we were all there.

This was May of 1942. We were there until September of 1942. We lived in a horse stall from May to September, and my son was born in a horse stall. It was terrible, and that stench that came up from the ground, you know, was just terrible. So of course we didn't want to stay in it any longer than we had to; we'd just go over there and sleep at night. So most of the time people would spend the time right outside the door. Of course, there was a barbed-wire fence, only about five feet from the outside. That was more comfortable than being in our cubicle.

In September we went to Tule Lake. Now the reason we went there was that they needed nurses in the hospital. They did have a few RNs, but they needed more. When we arrived there, they had a message for me saying that they needed me at the hospital right away. They had about three Caucasian nurses. Of course, they took all the top priority jobs, and they didn't do any work. They just kind of watched over us and ran around the halls.

While we were at Tule my father-in-law, who was in Minidoka [another relocation center] became very ill, and we were given permission to go see him. That was a miserable, miserable trip. We were again put on a bus. My two children were still very small. . . . They both needed bottles and baby food, and we didn't have too much priority for seats on the bus. So my husband carried the older one, and I carried the little one, and we traveled that way.

We got to Burns, Oregon, and ran out of milk. Oh, gosh, that was terrible. They knew at the camp that you needed those red tokens to buy anything—canned foods or meat products. Everything was rationed. And of course, we didn't have anything like that when we were in camp. So I thought, well, there's not a thing I can do; I don't have any more. While we were in camp, we were allotted so much canned milk. So, I thought, I'll just have to go to the Safeway store and buy a can anyway, regardless of how much I'm going to have to pay for it. . . . My son was allergic to just any kind of milk, so I had to get this special morning milk for him. I went up to the cashier and I said, "You know, I don't have a red token to buy this, but I need it for my baby because I'm traveling from Tule Lake, California, to another camp. I have no other way of providing him milk." Right then there was this lady right behind me, and she gave me the red token to pay for that milk. You know, right there in Burns, which is a real bad area, I think. There was a lot of discrimination and prejudice. But anyway, I was thrilled to death, because I didn't know how else I was going to ever buy it. I thanked her and bought the milk. It was one of the things that you just can't forget. . . .

The hospital facilities, of course, were very minimal, to say the least. The camp-based hospitals were not furnished with a sufficient number of bedpans, urinals, or washbasins. We never had enough linens, and we'd run around looking for blankets and pillows. The facilities were not there to take care of a hospital full of patients, and I think our base hospital in Tule Lake always had about eighty or ninety patients.

. . . There were a lot of unnecessary deaths in the camp. You wouldn't believe it. It's just that there were not enough people to watch the patients, not enough professionals.

. . . I remember a pregnant woman came in with just terrible pain, and she was having what we call an abruptio placentae, where there's bleeding in the uterus and it's absolutely necessary to operate right away and do a cesarean section. But there was no doctor to do the surgery. The woman died of a hemorrhage without delivering her baby.

I feel very bitter towards the whole thing. Now, this is just my feeling. I can't help but think that if it wasn't for evacuation, maybe I would have had a little different kind of a life. For one thing, when we got married in 1940, my husband didn't have any college education. We were thinking at the time that he would be going on to college while I worked. I felt it was time my husband got some education too. When he didn't have a chance to get that education, I think this was the thing that bothered me most, and that was what I was thinking about when we were put into camp.

Not only was it a most traumatic time in my life, but it was also the most frustrating period, because I felt that all of our accomplishments up to that time were gone. Yet, if it had to be this way with President Roosevelt's orders, we just had to make the best of it. I've often felt that we'd lost several years of my younger life because of being in camp. I'm bitter towards it. I have tried to cope with it the best I can by educating my children, and I've tried to serve the community the best I know how. I hope that something like this will never happen to another group of people or to us ever again. But sometimes I wonder.

I was born in Loomis, Placer County, California, about a hundred miles west of Reno, on January 11, 1919. . . . My father came to this country in 1897, and my mother came in 1903. I had three brothers and four sisters. . . .

Source: Wilson Makabe, "442nd Regimental Combat Team, Italy," in *And Justice for All,* pp. 250–59.

Before the war we had over a hundred acres, a fruit farm that was cleared and in production. We had mostly plums, peaches, and pears, with grapevines planted between the trees. And then we had about thirty acres of straight vineyard. And we were rather proud that we had the finest grapes in the county. . . . December 7 was quite a shock. We were working the back, at the end of the ranch, which is almost a mile from the house. We went in for lunch. . . . Our oldest sister . . . came in to tell us that the Japanese bombed Pearl Harbor.

It was hard for us to believe. But shortly after that, while we were eating, a car pulled up and people got out and identified themselves as being from the FBI. They started talking to us and my father. Then we went into the house. And that's when one of the most amazing things happened: a person who had never been in our house before knew just where to go to look for things. He pulled out correspondence that my father had from Japan. Some old papers from way back, twenty, thirty years before. So, he gathered some things up and he said, "You come with me," and he took my father. My father never had a chance to pack his clothing, or his suitcase, or anything. He went in the car, and that's the last we saw of him until he joined the family in Tule Lake.

When the rest of the family was evacuated, [we] went to a place called Arboga, a camp just being built in the desert . . . in the Sacramento Valley. It was the end of May, and it was hot and dusty. I can remember the tar-paper barracks and the community toilets with bathrooms. We had to help to construct the kitchen facilities and got paid only four dollars or so per month. But I signed up for whatever [work] was available. I ended up as a fireman, and then, when they had an appeal for sugar-beet thinners, I took that on. . . . [Eventually, due to his experience working with his family's fruit trees, Makabe and most of his family got jobs away from the camp at an orchard in Twin Falls, Idaho.]

When we were living and working in Idaho, I heard about the organization of the 442nd [an all-Japanese U.S. Army unit]. That was the latter part of February, 1943. I tried the local draft board, but they didn't even know about it, so I took a bus to Salt Lake City and signed up for the 442nd there. They said, "Go home and we'll let you know when to report." So on June 6 I was notified to report to Fort Douglas, Utah, where I was sworn in. Then I went to basic training at Camp Shelby, Mississippi. But, before I got there, I was given a ten-day pass, plus travel time. I was able to go to Loomis to visit the farm.

I walked from where I got off the train—it was only a short walk—to the fruit house where the manager had his office. While I was in his office, some people—and the worst part of it was that some of them were people I knew and grew up with—joined a bunch of rabble-rousers and wanted to make a riot. So, the manager of the fruit house . . . told me that we had better leave and took me out to the offices of the justice of the peace. . . . I had plans to spend several days in Loomis, to see how the fruit was doing and so on, but instead I left after maybe a couple of hours. I was run out of town, yes.

I remember one girl, a Spanish girl, I never knew her name. She tried to argue with those others telling them that I was in uniform and that I was a soldier, that I was a good citizen and grew up there. Yet some of these people were prominent people, active people, big basketball players who were deferred because they worked on farms.

I got up to Tule Lake and I was able to get a ride from the community up to the camp. They wanted to see my pass and travel orders. An armed MP checked me in at the gate. You could see the guard towers, the barbed-wire fence. Oh, what a depressing scene. To be an American soldier and having to be frisked. Anyway, I spent only one night in Tule Lake. I remember waiting in line with the families. I had two sisters up there. The older sister had four children living in one room; by the time you get six cots in there, you don't have room for anything else. Then my other sister had three children, and I stayed there right on the floor on a blanket and waited in line for dinner. Everybody had to wait in line for the community toilets and the showers. It was sad. When I visited with some of the kids I grew up with, some of them asked me how it was "outside"; others called me a damn fool for volunteering and said, "All you're going to be is cannon fodder". . . .

I saw only about thirty days of combat before I got wounded. I was in northern Italy, up as far as the Arno River across from Pisa.

I really don't know what happened. The last thing I remember was somebody said, "Look out!" I was out for about ten days. When I came to and opened my eyes, someone was working on me in the battalion aid station, a blackout tent. They had flashlights and were working on me. I had both legs in casts. . . . Next time I woke up I was in a hospital fifteen miles back, the field station. . . . Then they got me back to the general hospital near Rome. . . .

The first morning the nurse came to take my temperature which was pretty high, I guess. . . . I remember the doctor came, took one look at my foot, said, "Get him up to surgery." Gangrene had started up on my right leg, my toes were already turning black. I don't know how long I was in surgery, but it was about midnight when I finally came to.

The chief nurse was still on duty and beside my bed. . . . I remember asking that nurse, "How about my back?" I was still groggy. She said, "The back is all right, but we have to take the leg off."

. . . I spent over four months in that general hospital in Rome. They never thought I'd make it. First several months there, every time I opened my eyes, seemed like a chaplain was sitting there by my bed. He came to see me when they finally gave me my orders that I would be heading home. . . . I landed in the States on December 23, 1944. And boy, was I happy when I got back on U.S. soil!

One of the first things they offered me was a free telephone call to any place in the country. So I called my brother, George, in Idaho. That's when I learned that someone had set fire to our house in Loomis. Apparently it was within hours after the radio announcement that the Japanese people could leave the camps and return to their homes on the West Coast. When he told me that . . . oh, you can't describe the feeling. I remember the pain and the hurt, the suffering in the hospitals in Italy—that was nothing compared to this. I cried for the first time. All that time in the hospital I don't remember shedding a tear, but I cried that night. You wonder if it was worth going through all that.

Anyway, in Miami [where Makabe was hospitalized] we were taken to the Orange Bowl game, and were really treated nicely. I remember a retired general saw me. He was a classmate of my original battalion commander at West Point. He said, "You know, it would be a privilege to be able to push you around and take you wherever you want to go." For several days he did just that. He would take me out to any of the places or any place around the hospital that I wanted to see. I still hear from him, General Harris.

[To be near his family, Makabe chose to recuperate at Bushnell Hospital in Utah.] There were quite a few Nisei there. . . . They pushed my bed outside when the girls from Salt Lake City came with all the Japanese food. They had entertainment and everything for us. . . .

I [became] ambulatory about the first of December, 1946, about two and a half years after I got hurt. I had the long brace on my left leg, artificial leg on my right—nothing like the latest things today. I could barely walk, it was painful, but I made up my mind that I was going to walk. The doctor said I would never walk again. I just made up my mind that I wasn't going to have to live in a wheelchair. Well, I stayed there long enough. . . .

[Makabe and the rest of the family returned to Loomis; in 1947, his father became paralyzed and Makabe cared for him until he died.] It became impossible to operate the farm as one unit, so we divided up the property into so many acres each to those of us still living.

We took a beating. My oldest brother was in the Army for two years before they had started the foreclosure. We had about a $1,200 mortgage on fifteen acres in his name—the best vineyard on the property. But he didn't know about that mortgage being foreclosed until he came back in 1946, after five years in the service. He came back and found he didn't have the property he'd heard about. There was a law on the books that Congress had passed called the Soldiers and Sailors Relief Act that said it was illegal to foreclose. The law was commonly called The Moratorium. But by the time he got back he didn't have any money, and he had a young family. Because of the sentiment in Placer County, it would have been impossible for us to get a favorable judgment even if he did try to recover some of that property. . . .

[Later someone tried to buy Makabe's land as part of a freeway project.] This fellow came up and I said I didn't want to sell it for the price he was offering. He had the nerve to say, "Don't you think you owe the community of Loomis an obligation to get that project going?" I didn't sit back, I said, "You said the wrong thing. I served in the Army. I went through hell. I've suffered disabilities all these years, and I got run out of this town by bastards like you that didn't even go into the service, who got deferred because they wanted to stay out. And you say *I* owe the community! I think the community owes me a lot." I said, "I don't feel a *bit* of obligation to community." . . .

One of the fellows had a service station, and when I first came back, I went into this station. I knew the family. The fellow's father was one of the old settlers in Loomis and knew my father well. When he saw me at the service station getting out, struggling to get out of the car, to fill it with gas, he came out. After I was all through he said, "I'd like to talk to you." . . . He said, "Y'know I was one bastard. I had signs on my service station saying 'No Jap trade wanted.'" He said, "Now, when I see you come back like that, I feel so small." And he was crying. That was one of my experiences when I came back.

I'LL SHOW YOU I'M AS GOOD AS YOU ARE
William C. Menninger, M.D.

Perhaps the greatest challenge to gender roles in World War II came with the formation of the women's branches of the military. More than a quarter of a million women volunteered to serve in the Women's Army Corps (WAC) and its counterparts in the Navy (WAVES), Marine Corps (MCWR) and Coast Guard (SPARS). Women had served as nurses during World War I but without receiving military pay

Source: William C. Menninger, M.D., *Psychiatry in a Troubled World: Yesterday's War and Today's Challenge* (New York: Macmillan, 1948), pp. 102–8, 224–28.

or other benefits. In World War II, they became full-fledged members of the military. Though women fulfilled many vital functions, popular opposition to their presence in the armed forces remained high.

One manifestation of this opposition was the vicious "whispering campaign" started in 1943, which accused women in the WAC and the WAVES of having "loose morals." While most of the rumors had to do with heterosexual encounters, some implied that lesbianism was also rampant. Military officials responded by clamping down on all signs of affection among enlisted women. They were, however, somewhat more tolerant of explicit sexual expression among the men, as this document and the following, as well as Figure 9.4, indicate.

William C. Menninger, M.D. (1899–1966), a prominent psychiatrist who served as a consultant to the military during the war, helped set up the Army's screening procedures. Though thousands of draftees were ultimately rejected on psychiatric grounds (many for suspected or admitted homosexuality), thousands of homosexuals, eager to join the military, slipped through the cracks. Menninger was relatively open-minded on some gender issues, but he seemed to have difficulty in accepting the idea that women might have legitimate (that is, nonpathological) reasons for joining the military. By the same token, while tolerant of "innocent" sex play between men, he regarded homosexuality in both women and men as an example of "arrested development."

In the following excerpt, can you detect inconsistencies in Menninger's views? Since he was an influential figure, how do you think his opinions might have affected American attitudes toward gender roles and sexual preferences in the postwar period?

WOMEN IN THE ARMY

Development of femininity. Even in our own democracy the approved feminine role is a passive and dependent one. . . . Before 1942 they were not supposed to fit into a fighting army except as nurses or Red Cross workers. The average man thought of women in an army as mythical Amazons, or the guerilla fighters of revolutions, or camp followers with very specific business purposes. It took World War II with its great need for man power to open the doors of military service, as well as of industry, science and business, to women in any number. Those doors may be hard to close!

The increasing opportunity for American women to modify their traditional position complicates their acceptance of the feminine role. It allows women to choose their pattern of behavior. This is more difficult than it is for men to accept the unchanged concept of the masculine role. Furthermore, our educational philosophy differs from our current standards. The modern girl child in America is not taught to be the passive, dependent individual our culture has conceived of as the norm of adult femininity. So that when grown she is faced with some surprising facts: the "important" work of the world is supposed to be done by men; her early educational, social, and economic preparation for independence conflicts with the limitations of the accepted feminine role; the approved field of her interest seems unbalanced with too much routine for some years and too much leisure in later years.

Furthermore, from childhood on, the girl, whether or not she wishes to do so, is expected to assume the role of a "weaker" sex, because of man's greater physical strength. It is reasonable to assume that a girl educated in the American way has to be "broken in" to being feminine. For she was born into what appears as a "man's world," in which she is supposed to "love, honor, and obey" and to make a home for some man. It is not surprising, therefore, that in our culture women should acquire and retain strong masculine strivings.

Psychological significance of WAC for women. In evaluating the psychological significance of the military service for women, one must keep in mind that all WAC members were volunteers. . . . The appeal of an Army experience in time of war had a special attraction for some women, so that appeal was in itself part of the selective process. One must also recognize that conscious reasons for enlisting, while highly commendable (though possibly in some instances reprehensible), are not the total explanation of motivation.

Emancipation from psychological and environmental shackles certainly was a reason for enlistment in some instances. Here was an ideal opportunity to respond to a patriotic call and at the same time to escape the dependence on a home situation or subjection to its responsibilities. No doubt, it was sometimes an escape from what may be regarded as feminine duties. Many women joined against strong protest of their families—probably the most common problem which they had to solve (or ignore). Patriotism was an airtight rationalization for some women who left excellent jobs or apparently comfortable homes. The unconscious motive could have been a resentment toward their civilian (or feminine?) role or situation.

Identification with a specific male person in the Army, or an unconscious masculine identification, must have been the deciding psychological factor in many cases. War and an army always have been the epitome of a strictly masculine activity. This is as well known and accepted by women as by men. Almost every woman at some time in her life, and perhaps for a long period, has wished she were a boy or a man. Perhaps she was envious of the privileges and the opportunities of men, or irked by having to play the traditional role of a woman. Many women have very definite and strong masculine strivings. Often the motivation for joining an essentially male organization was probably stimulated by an unconscious competition with a consciously loved person—the husband, the brother, or the boy friend. Such competition is often evident in sibling rivalry.

Closely allied to the mechanism of identification is the related motive of protest. This is a denial of the feminine role as if the unconscious were saying, "You see, I can even be a soldier, truly serve in a man's job." Undoubtedly, this sometimes took the form of aggressive behavior as if the unconscious were saying, "See here, husband, brother, father, I'll show you I'm as good as you are. I'll join the Army, too." One might well include in this constellation an aggressiveness against the mother who had different hopes and aspirations for her daughter.

Still another motive may have been the need to find a sense of security. This was sometimes fostered further by a sense of boredom or lonesomeness in the women's civilian role. Joining the WAC was a way of helping the war effort in a commendable fashion which was reasonably safe. It would also give her something to do and provide her, as it does all soldiers, with the security and satisfaction of passively receiving food, a job, and clothing.

Some women joined the WAC merely as another escape from numerous previous unsuccessful attempts to adjust themselves in civilian life. These were maladjusted individuals who had never been able to fit into their environment and used the Army as an opportunity to make another trial. These were the problem personalities of the WAC.

Probably an unrecognized motive in a certain number of women was the desire to enlist in order to be with other women. Perhaps a very small number were overtly homosexual, though this problem was never a serious one in the WAC. It was anticipated that it would be more prevalent than it actually was. The reaction to homosexuality was interesting. Many women were ignorant of it prior to their coming into the WAC. Some were overconscious of it as a possibility. There was a strong tendency toward "witch-hunting" on the part of some prudish or sadistic officers, who suspected normal friendships of being tinged with homosexuality. On the other hand, it was a surprise to many persons, in and out of the WAC, to learn that some of the most efficient and admirable women had homosexual tendencies.

Finally, a motive in some cases was the search for an opportunity to express femininity. One must suspect, on the basis of psychological knowledge, however, that this was less frequently operative. Some women could have assumed, justifiably, that here was a chance to do an important job within a woman's capacity which would spare a man for a strictly masculine job. They must have hoped that, like Army nurses, they might play something of the mother or the sister role. Normal feminine urges to do secretarial and clerical work, housekeeping and cooking, could find expression in enlistment, regardless of what other desires might have been present. Another aspect of this same motive was seen in those who sought masculine company and felt that the Army was obviously the place to find it.

In considering these various conscious and unconscious motivations, one cannot and should not ignore the external pressure of the country being at war. It needed man power badly; women could replace men and thus free them for other duty. The fact that psychiatric experience gave an insight into unconscious motivation should not in any sense impugn the women who contributed so much to the success of the war effort. The unconscious motives, however, do throw light on some events that transpired in the Women's Army Corps during the war.

Psychological significance of the WAC for men. The initial attitude of many of the male personnel in the Army toward the WAC was that the Army was very considerate in providing a female contingent! This psychological response was based in part on the narcissism of the male who too often assumes that women exist to serve him; in part on the automatic exaggeration of the sexual interest in women in an all-male society; and in part on the need for an antidote to the unconscious, vague fears of impotency that exist in a strictly one-sex group. . . .

In spite of the general opinion that the WAC did a very capable job, its existence was accepted by the men with ambivalence; that is, while consciously recognizing its accomplishments, male officers and soldiers denied its value emotionally.

This was indicated by [a] Gallup poll [which showed that many] men were willing only that women of whom they were not fond should come into the Army. In some way this attitude was less threatening to their supremacy or possibly to their concept of femininity. Undoubtedly it was an expression of their own unconscious simultaneous desires to possess and protect women. In essence it was an expression of their own struggle with the double standard for men and women.

Many men will of necessity be forced by the success of the experiment to make a readjustment in their concepts of the feminine role. Maskin and Altman

FIGURE 9.3
Cartoons like this one frequently appeared in army newspapers, providing "escape valves" for male objections to women's presence in the military. *(Source: Department of Defense files, rpt. in Mattie E. Treadwell,* The Women's Army Corps *[Washington, D.C.: Office of the Chief of Military History, Department of the Army, 1953] p. 196).*

[two psychiatrists], who discussed this point, believed that this experience will ultimately beget a new, freer, collaborative and democratic relationship between men and women. This sounds a little optimistic, but among those couples where wives were in the WAC, there is likely to be a new alignment. This will apply equally to families in which wives gained a wider horizon by experience in industry. . . .

HOMOSEXUALITY

Due to their emotional blind spot, some people assume that a man who goes into the Army must become asexual, certainly so if he is married. However, no amount of wishful thinking will change the fact that he does not. Human nature is not like that. When individuals are forced into a homosexual society, mature as well as immature personalities have to find outlets or sublimations for their normal sexual energies, drives, and interests. Many soldiers found direct outlets, whether auto-erotic, homosexual, or heterosexual. This group probably included almost as many married as unmarried men, if they had been separated from home for a long period. The armies of some other countries have a different attitude than does ours, and provide "comfort girls." In America, we placed from 50,000 to 100,000 healthy young men in a camp and in essence told them to forget the most powerful drive in their lives. They were supposed somehow to adjust to an exclusively male society and remain completely continent and abstinent. This did not happen. Some thought they had to have physical substitutes; others managed with psychological substitutes.

The physical substitutes were varied: many men discovered satisfaction in a physical interest in other men, which often surprised them; others resorted to masturbation; still others, including many married men, found "women" to satisfy their need. The Army did not sit in moral judgment on the non-marital sexual relations of the soldier as long as these were with women, except when they interfered with his effectiveness. However, great efforts were made to control venereal diseases.

There were numerous psychological substitutes used: possession of "pin-up girl" photographs; an increased interest in "dirty" stories, in profanity, and in homosexual buffoonery. Another substitute was writing and receiving frequent letters to and from a wife or sweetheart (or often sweethearts). A most important substitute had to be the satisfaction the soldier derived from the comradeship and fellowship of his associates—his male friends—a disguised and sublimated homosexuality.

The gallery of pin-up girls had a double value. It gave evidence of its owner's virility to all those who viewed it, in addition to the individual's enjoyment. . . . Similarly, a connection with a woman, however shabby and perfunctory, was recounted in an adventurous spirit and in terms that never failed to do credit to the subject's virile capacities.

. . . "Homosexual buffoonery" [was] one of several common methods by which a soldier relieved his emotional tension. In the barracks, usually when the men were getting undressed, one frequently observed play-acting in which various persons "kiddingly" assumed the role of overt homosexuals. One soldier, returning from the shower room in the nude was greeted with catcalls, salacious whistling, and comments like, "Hey, Joe, you shouldn't go around like that—you don't know what that does to me." Joe responded by coyly draping a towel around himself and wriggling his hips in feminine fashion. Some of the men joined in the buffoonery by playing the role of the appreciative spectator: "Ain't he hot stuff though!" "C'mon, take it off." Others acted the part of active solicitors for sexual favors: "How much do you want for sleeping with me tonight?"; "Come into my bed and I'll give you the time of your life."

. . . The spirit in which the homosexual role was acted was unquestionably that of "kidding around." The buffoonery was carried to such extremes that no one participating in it ever considered in his own mind the disturbing possibility of any seriousness in it. It was as if the individual thought, "I really have no inclinations of this sort at all; otherwise I would never be so free about kidding around in this way." . . . When the entire group participated in the acting out of homosexual play it served to eliminate individual feelings of guilt.

Sometimes, however, there is homosexuality which represents an arrest in psychosexual development. Instead of the normal progress from one stage to another, a personality may stop at the homosexual level or regress back to it so that a preference for members of the same sex to the exclusion of interest in the opposite sex persists into adult life. When the ultimate in gratification in sexual relations is found with one of the same sex it is regarded as pathological.

The "problem" of homosexuality in the Army, as it referred to the overt sexual relationships between men, was not nearly so large as one might have judged from the emotional discussions of the subject by some officers. Some figures for 1943 showed that 20,620 men in the Army were diagnosed as "constitutional psychopaths." Of these 1,625 were presumably of the "homosexual type." In the same year among 3,175 patients diagnosed as "constitutional psychopaths" in overseas theaters, 327 were designated as being homosexual. These figures, however, are probably of little if any importance as an indication of either the true incidence or significance of the problem. . . .

Probably for every homosexual who was referred or came to the Medical Department, there were 15 or 20 who never were detected. Those men must have performed their duty satisfactorily, whether assigned to combat or to some other type of service. This is always surprising to those who so heatedly condemn the homosexual. Such critics also assume that feigning homosexuality to escape service is a very common procedure. They fail to see that if a man does wish to malinger he has a far easier time of it if he chooses a simple expedient like a backache or headache. No doubt there were some warped personalities who hoped to avoid service by claiming to be overt homosexuals, but this surely was a very small number of the antisocial personalities, who would have been poor military material in any event. . . .

STRAIGHT YET WILLING TO PLAY
Bob Basker

As even William Menninger conceded, the army's screening procedures were imperfect at best when it came to homosexuals; moreover, as historian Allan Bérubé has pointed out, many gay men were eager to join the military, not only because they were patriotic, but also because they were more than willing to join an all-male

Source: "Bob Basker." Reprinted with permission from *Quiet Fire: Memoirs of Older Gay Men* by Keith Vacha, pp. 47–51. Copyright © 1985. Published by Crossing Press, Freedom, Calif.

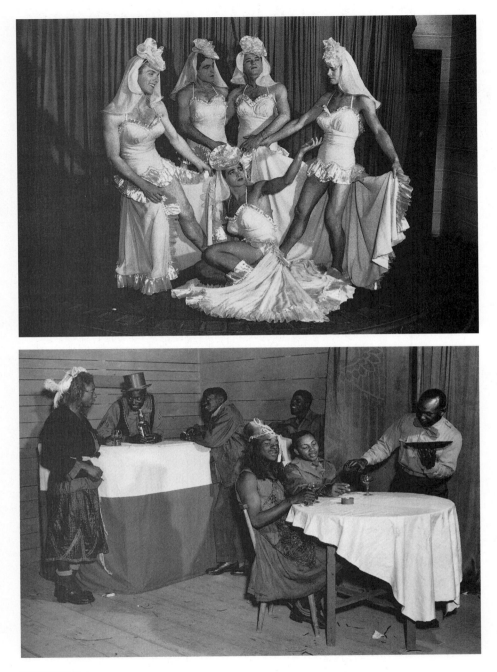

FIGURE 9.4
Because regulations barred WAC soldiers from performing in the same shows with men, the Army had to rely on men to play female roles. Gay soldiers often volunteered for these parts, which allowed them to do female impersonations without arousing suspicion. These scenes show dancers from "This Is the Army," the war's most popular production, and black performers in "Jumping with Jodie." *(Courtesy of the Library of Congress)*

community. What opportunities did the army offer Bob Basker? What were the prevailing views of male homosexuality, and how did they serve as a kind of camoflauge for men like him? Do Basker's recollections confirm or contradict Menninger's interpretation of "homosexual buffoonery"?

... Then the war broke out and I enlisted.

For several years, from '41 to '44, I was stationed in the New York area and then I went overseas to Plymouth, England. I really enjoyed it there. I loved the gay life in England even though the people there were very uptight as far as gay life went. After a while my unit moved to Antwerp, Belgium, where we were under the rocket bombs and V-2's. I was buried alive twice in buildings that collapsed on me, but I never got a scratch so I didn't earn a Purple Heart. Never could get a service-related disability either.

One time in Wales I had sex with some nineteen-year-old kid in the YMCA. It was really great. He shipped out on a merchant ship and the next day I found out I had gonorrhea. I felt terrible because I might have given it to him, but I had no way of getting in touch with him. At that time the way you got rid of it was to have your urethral canal irrigated and then take sulfa pills. It was a lot more complicated then than now.

We were never taught about VD in the proper way back then. We were taught to avoid sex because we'd get VD, and I'm sure many of us developed psychological problems about sex as a result. . . .

I had sex with different people three to four times a week, starting at the age of fourteen. So if you figure out three times a week, fifty weeks a year, that's at least a hundred and fifty partners. Over a period of twenty years, three thousand partners. That creates a tremendous amount of sophisticated sex, if one is sensitive to the needs of others. In a way it gives us an advantage over straight people, our ability to have this multiplicity of experiences. For instance, one time in Paris with a young Frenchman, we had sex in a private box at the Paris Opera. Afterwards I couldn't remember what opera it was—we used to laugh about that. Another time we had sex in the garden of Versailles. I think straight people rarely have or take advantage of these types of situations.

During the years that I was with my army unit, of the four hundred men in it I must have had sex with a hundred of them. But I never developed a reputation of being gay. Sex was on an individual basis, in the shower room, in different ways. There were a few gay ones among them, but most of them were straight yet willing to play. How it worked was you'd get in the shower, around one o'clock in the morning after you'd been out on the town, taking a shower before you went to bed. My technique was to say to the guy next to me, "Hey, would you do me a favor and soap my back?" And the guy would soap my back and I'd say, "Thanks" and then I'd say, "Here, let me do your back." I wouldn't ask, I'd just assume, and start to soap his back. If he didn't flinch, I'd start soaping his chest and if he didn't flinch then, I'd start soaping his stomach. Then I would do one leg, then the other, then start soaping his balls, then maybe his ass. Generally, by this time, they'd have a hard on. If they flinched anywhere along the line, they'd say, "Thanks," and move away. Only one time did someone come to me who must have heard something from someone else and approached me to have sex. Other than that I never had any problems.

During the time I was stationed in Antwerp I became acquainted with an older group of gay men. One night at dinner I was introduced to a man who was much older than I was. I was twenty-six and this man, Pierre Rinehart, was fifty-one. He was a restaurant owner and he fascinated me. Apparently I fascinated him too,

The fighting man thinks that the jump back to civilian life will be easy. Perhaps you think so, too. But it won't be, depend upon it. After the first joy of reunion, you will see him restless, uncertain, critical of the home he's dreamed of. Rooms on these five pages have been planned for the days after Johnny comes marching home

LIVING ROOM FOR A RETURNING GENERAL WAS CREATED BY LORD AND TAYLOR, NEW YORK

FIGURE 9.5
Popular magazines offered scores of what historian Susan Hartmann calls "prescriptions for Penelope"—advice to women about how to handle returning veterans. This article told housewives, "home must be the greatest rehabilitation center of them all." *(Source: Marion Gough, "Home Should Be Even More Wonderful than He Remembers It."* House Beautiful, *vol. 87, no. 1 [January 1945], pp. 28.)*
Reprinted by permission from House Beautiful, *copyright © January, 1945. Hearst Communications, Inc. All Rights Reserved.*

being an American soldier who spoke several different languages and was interested in his culture.

Pierre not only had an apartment in Antwerp, he had one in Brussels, too. I went to this apartment and I was overwhelmed. The apartment was full of flowers, the most beautiful flowers, gladiolas, everything, trays of liquors, and this beautiful music playing from Samson and Delilah, "My Heart at Thy Sweet Voice." It was very romantic and I was *really* overwhelmed. We had sex and I enjoyed it very much. We were very compatible. . . . And the guy was just insatiable at fifty-one. Well, not insatiable but capable of a tremendous amount of potency. . . . I don't remember. And when the sex was over, he made all these sauces and exquisite food. He was a real French chef and he really spoiled me.

But the first time we were together one of the things he did was shove a bunch of bills into my pocket. I was highly indignant, I was insulted. I didn't go there for money, I went there because the man had the right vibrations as far as I was concerned. I had a wonderful time and I enjoyed the attention I was getting. He insisted I take the money, though. I thought it was very rude of him to do that. But I kept it. And I got even with him. I thought, "Well, fuck him. If he's got that kind of money, I'm going to insist that he pay me as much as the Army pays me." So I told him how much I wanted and there was no problem. I think it was like four hundred Belgian francs . . . a month! That was about forty-four francs to the dollar back then. I made all kinds of money. I didn't have any expenses. The Army took care of one part of my life and I lived at Pierre's apartment when I didn't have to stay over on base. I'd send money orders back to my brother in the States to hold for me. . . . By the time I came back to this country I had saved about $10,000 so I could go into business for myself.

Pierre offered to send me to medical school, which is what I wanted to do. He offered to get me a car and everything, but I finally decided to take my discharge in Europe and become an American civilian working for the Army. I was discharged in November of '45 and stayed in Europe until the summer of '46. Then my job ended. . . . After that, I had a great time. I went to Nice and Monte Carlo on vacation and took Pierre along with me. I did a lot of traveling. . . .

RECOMMENDED READINGS

Adams, Michael C. C. *The Best War Ever: America and World War II*. Baltimore, 1994.

Anderson, Karen. *Wartime Women: Sex Roles, Family Relations, and the Status of Women during World War II*. Westport, Conn., 1981.

Bérubé, Allan. *Coming Out Under Fire: The History of Gay Men and Lesbians in World War II*. New York, 1990.

Cooke, Miriam, and Angela Woollacott, eds. *Gendering War Talk*. Princeton, N.J., 1993.

Gabin, Nancy. *Feminism in the Labor Movement: Women and the United Auto Workers, 1935–1975*. Ithaca, N.Y., 1990.

Hartmann, Susan M. *The Home Front and Beyond: American Women in the 1940s*. Boston, 1982.

Higonnet, Margaret, Jane Jenson, Sonya Michel, and Margaret Weitz, eds. *Behind the Lines: Gender and the Two World Wars*. New Haven, Conn., 1987.

Honey, Maureen. *Creating Rosie the Riveter: Class, Gender, and Propaganda during World War II*. Amherst, Mass., 1984.

Kesselman, Amy. *Fleeting Opportunities: Women Shipyard Workers in Portland and Vancouver During World War II and Reconversion.* Albany, N.Y., 1990.

Lemke-Santangelo, Gretchen. *Abiding Courage: African American Migrant Women and the East Bay Community.* Chapel Hill, N.C., 1996.

Meyer, Leisa. *Creating GI Jane: Sexuality and Power in the Women's Army Corps During World War II.* New York, 1996.

Milkman, Ruth. *Gender at Work: The Dynamics of Job Segregation during World War II.* Urbana, Ill., 1987.

Tuttle, William M., Jr. *"Daddy's Gone to War": The Second World War in the Lives of American Children.* New York, 1993.

FIGURE 10.1
With their "big hair" and suggestive lyrics, the "girl groups" of the 1950s such as the Shirelles (left) and Ronettes (right) broke through many gender stereotypes. Asking "Will You Love Me Tomorrow?" the Shirelles explicitly addressed the question of the double standard. (*Courtesy of Movie Still Archives.*)

CHAPTER 10

The Unquiet Fifties

With suburban sprawl, the rise of giant corporations, the Cold War abroad, and McCarthyism at home, the fifties have gained a reputation as a period of conformity and suppression, particularly when it came to women and homosexuals. In studying this decade, however, it is important not to mistake *prescription* for *description*. Though both the media and public policy converged upon a norm of middle-class heterosexual domesticity, it was not universally accepted. For many women—and men—the fifties was a time of self-discovery and rebellion, either individually or as part of a burgeoning social movement.

On the surface, the new suburban lifestyle appeared seamless. Contented nuclear families (mom, dad, and the requisite 3.2 kids), surrounded by their many material comforts, became symbols of all that was right with the American way—the country's weapon of choice against the Communist threat. Harvard sociologist Talcott Parsons claimed that American families had developed an ideal division of labor that distributed duties along "instrumental" and "expressive" axes, with husbands concentrating on breadwinning and wives on managing the emotional economy of the home. This new "professionalized" family functioned smoothly in a corporate world that demanded flexibility on the part of employees—and their dependents.

But the reality, historians have discovered, was considerably different. Not all married women were full-time housewives. Between 1950 and 1960, the proportion of mothers with children under age 16 who were employed rose from 10 percent to 24 percent; this pattern was common among middle-class as well as low-income families. Nor did all Americans adhere to prescribed norms of premarital virginity, monogamy, and heterosexuality. As the pioneering sexologist Alfred Kinsey discovered, nearly 50 percent of women engaged in sex before marriage, while a third of the men and more than a quarter of the women had had some homosexual experience. Lesbians and gay men, building on networks created during World War II, formed tight-knit communities in cities across the country. Despite (or perhaps because of) persistent persecution, these communities became stronger and more confrontational, though it would take another decade before homosexuals felt ready to "come out of the closet."

Fifties prescriptions also obscured differences of race and class in the trend toward suburbanization. Though mass construction backed by federal financing dramatically expanded home ownership, it was still beyond the reach of the poorest Americans, many of them minorities who continued to encounter discrimination and segregation. But African Americans, empowered by their wartime experiences and hard-won educational advances, were on the move, with women forming the organizational backbone that gave the young civil rights movement much of its strength.

Thus the era that appeared on the surface to be complacent and conformist was actually one of individual and collective challenges to gender norms and restrictions—challenges that would become even louder in the decade to come.

LET'S DRINK TO THE LADIES
Richard Nixon and Nikita Khrushchev

The Cold War occurred on several fronts simultaneously. The United States and the Soviet Union, while adding to their nuclear arsenals, waged an ideological battle on the terrains of diplomacy and culture. No matter where or when they met, Soviet and American leaders seldom passed up an opportunity to score propaganda points off of each other. One such occasion was the opening of the American National Exhibition in Moscow in July, 1959, with Vice President Richard M. Nixon and his wife Pat on hand to do the honors. Nixon was the highest-level American official to visit the Soviet Union in peacetime, and Soviet Premier Nikita Khrushchev hoped that by putting on a display of hospitality, he would garner an invitation to hold talks with President Dwight D. Eisenhower in Washington.

But neither Nixon nor Khrushchev, both volatile individuals, was able to hold his tongue, and the deep conflicts between the two superpowers quickly rose to the surface. While blaming each other for the military build-up that had brought the entire world to the brink of disaster, each leader also sought to gain the ideological advantage by proving that his system yielded a higher standard of living—butter as well as guns. Nixon, defending capitalism against the charge that it produced gross inequalities between the classes, claimed that all of the goods on display—a model split-level home, a car, a television set—were well within the purchasing power of the average American factory worker. Khrushchev rejoined that Soviet people were not slaves but also enjoyed a comfortable lifestyle.

One of the unspoken issues of these famous "kitchen debates" was the contrast in attitudes toward wage-earning women. American suburban domesticity depended, of course, on the presence of full-time housewives, while all Soviet women, regardless of marital status or number of children, were expected to work outside the home. From Khrushchev's comments, does it seem that employment brought Soviet women greater respect and independence?

Source: "Encounter," *Newsweek*, vol. 54, no. 5 (August 3, 1959), pp. 16–17.

Khrushchev (*taking Nixon's arm*): "In another seven years, we shall be on the same level as America. . . . In passing you by, we shall wave. We can stop and say: If you want capitalism you can live that way, we feel sorry for you."

Nixon: "You may be ahead of us . . . in the thrust of your rockets. . . . We may be ahead . . . in color television."

Khrushchev (*breaking in*): "No, we are up with you on this too. . . . We have bested you in one technique and also in the other."

Nixon: "You see, you never concede anything."

Khrushchev: "I do not give up."

Nixon (*pointing to a panel-controlled washing machine*): "In America, these are designed to make things easier for our women."

Khrushchev: "A capitalist attitude."

Nixon: "I think this attitude toward women is universal."

Khrushchev (*jeering at the products on display*): "Don't you have a machine that puts food into the mouth and pushes it down? These are merely gadgets. . . .

Nixon began chatting about the pushbutton kitchen.

Khrushchev: "Newly built Russian houses have all this equipment right now. In America, if you don't have a dollar you have the right to [sleep] on the pavement."

Nixon: "If you were in the Senate, we would call you a filibusterer—you do all the talking and don't let others talk."

Khrushchev: "On political problems, we will never agree with you. For instance, Mikoyan likes very peppery soup. I do not. But this does not mean that we do not get along."

Then, noting that Nixon was looking approvingly at some girls, modeling bathing suits, he added with a wink, "You are for the girls, too."

Nixon (*showing the Russian a model American house*): "We hope to show our diversity and our right to choose. We do not wish to have decisions made at the top by government officials. . . . Would it not be better to compete in the merits of washing machines than in the strength of rockets?" . . .

That night, as the two men stood at the microphones for the formal opening of the exhibition, their argument was renewed when Khrushchev proposed a toast, in U.S. wine, "to elimination of all bases in foreign lands." Nixon countered with a toast to peace.

Khrushchev: "We stand for peace [but] if you are not willing to eliminate bases then I won't drink this toast."

Nixon: "He doesn't like American wine."

Khrushchev: "I like American wine, not its policy. . . . I defend . . . peace. How can peace be assured when we are surrounded by military bases?"

Nixon: "We'll talk about that later. Let's drink to talking . . . not fighting."

Khrushchev approved of that but suddenly pointed to a waitress and suggested: "Let's drink to the ladies."

Nixon agreed: "We can all drink to the ladies."

PERVERSION AND SUBVERSION
U.S. Senate

In the highly charged atmosphere of McCarthyite America, any deviation from the heterosexual norm came to be perceived as a national weakness and an opening for Communist subversion. While social commentators cast homosexuals as a threat to youth and family life, politicians argued that the infiltration of gay men and lesbians into both the civilian and military branches of the government opened a major breach in the country's defenses. In 1950 the U.S. Senate called for investigations into the prevalence of homosexuals within the federal government.

Politicians' homophobic zeal was fueled by dubious police methods. One Washington, D.C. lieutenant estimated that there were more than 5,000 homosexuals in Washington, three quarters of whom worked for the federal government. He had arrived at this number by multiplying the number of homosexuals cited in police records by five, on the assumption that "every one of these fellows has friends."

In the following excerpts, what is the implicit theory about the origins or causes of homosexuality? What, in the view of the senators, makes homosexuals a threat to national security?

. . . It was determined that even among the experts there existed considerable difference of opinion concerning the many facets of homosexuality and other forms of sex perversion. Even the terms "sex pervert" and "homosexual" are given different connotations by the medical and psychiatric experts. For the purpose of this report the subcommittee has defined sex perverts as "those who engage in unnatural sexual acts" and homosexuals are perverts who may be broadly defined as "persons of either sex who as adults engage in sexual activities with persons of the same sex." In this inquiry the subcommittee is not concerned with so-called latent sex perverts, namely, those persons who knowingly or unknowingly have tendencies or inclinations toward homosexuality or other types of sex perversion, but who, by the exercise of self-restraint or for other reasons, do not indulge in overt acts of perversion. This investigation is concerned only with those who engage in overt acts of homosexuality or other sex perversion.

The subcommittee found that most authorities agree on certain basic facts concerning sex perversion: . . . that sex deviation results from psychological rather than physical causes, and in many cases there are no outward characteristics or physical traits that are positive as identifying marks of sex perversion. Contrary to a common belief, all homosexual males do not have feminine mannerisms, nor do all female homosexuals display masculine characteristics in their dress or actions. The fact is that many male homosexuals are very masculine in their physical appearance and general demeanor, and many female homosexuals have every appearance of femininity in their outward behavior.

Generally speaking, the overt homosexual of both sexes can be divided into two general types: the active, aggressive or male type, and the submissive, passive or female type. The passive type of male homosexual, who is often effeminate in his mannerisms and appearance, is attracted to the masculine type of man and is friendly and congenial with women. On the other hand the active male homosexual often has a dislike for women. He exhibits no traces of femininity in his speech or mannerisms which would disclose his homosexuality. This active type is almost exclusively attracted to the passive type of homosexual or to young men or boys who are not necessarily homosexual but who are effeminate in general appearance. The active and passive type of female homosexual follow the

Source: *Employment of Homosexuals and Other Sex Perverts in Government,* Committee on Expenditures in the Executive Departments, Subcommittee on Investigations, 81st Congress, 2nd Sess., Senate Document No. 241, December 15, 1950.

same general patterns as their male counterparts. It is also a known fact that some perverts are bisexual. This type engages in normal heterosexual relationships as well as homosexual activities. These bisexual individuals are often married and have children, and except for their perverted activities they appear to lead normal lives.

Psychiatric physicians generally agree that indulgence in sexually perverted practices indicates a personality which has failed to reach sexual maturity. The authorities agree that most sex deviates respond to psychiatric treatment and can be cured if they have a genuine desire to be cured. However, many overt homosexuals have no real desire to abandon their way of life and in such cases cures are difficult, if not impossible. The subcommittee sincerely believes that persons afflicted with sexual desires which result in their engaging in overt acts of perversion should be considered as proper cases for medical and psychiatric treatment. However, sex perverts, like all other persons who by their overt acts violate moral codes and laws and the accepted standards of conduct, must be treated as transgressors and dealt with accordingly. . . .

Those charged with the responsibility of operating the agencies of Government must insist that Government employees meet acceptable standards of personal conduct. In the opinion of this subcommittee homosexuals and other sex perverts are not proper persons to be employed in Government for two reasons: first, they are generally unsuitable, and second, they constitute security risks. . . .

Overt acts of sex perversion, including acts of homosexuality, constitute a crime under our Federal, State, and municipal statutes and persons who commit such acts are law violators. Aside from the criminality and immorality involved in sex perversion such behavior is so contrary to the normal accepted standards of social behavior that persons who engage in such activity are looked upon as outcasts by society generally. The social stigma attached to sex perversion is so great that many perverts go to great lengths to conceal their perverted tendencies. This situation is evidenced by the fact that perverts are frequently victimized by blackmailers who threaten to expose their sexual deviations.

Law enforcement officers have informed the subcommittee that there are gangs of blackmailers who make a regular practice of preying upon the homosexual. The modus operandi in these homosexual blackmail cases usually follow the same general pattern. The victim, who is a homosexual, has managed to conceal his perverted activities and usually enjoys a good reputation in his community. The blackmailers, by one means or another, discover that the victim is addicted to homosexuality and under the threat of disclosure they extort money from him. These blackmailers often impersonate police officers in carrying out their blackmail schemes. Many cases have come to the attention of the police where highly respected individuals have paid out substantial sums of money to blackmailers over a long period of time rather than risk the disclosure of their homosexual activities. The police believe that this type of blackmail racket is much more extensive than is generally known, because they have found that most of the victims are very hesitant to bring the matter to the attention of the authorities.

In further considering the general suitability of perverts as Government employees, it is generally believed that those who engage in overt acts of perversion lack the emotional stability of normal persons. In addition there is an abundance of evidence to sustain the conclusion that indulgence in acts of sex perversion weakens the moral fiber of an individual to a degree that he is not suitable for a position of responsibility.

Most of the authorities agree and our investigation has shown that the presence of a sex pervert in a Government agency tends to have a corrosive influence upon his fellow employees. These perverts will frequently attempt to entice normal individuals to engage in perverted practices. This is particularly true in the case of young and impressionable people who might come under the influence of a pervert. Government officials have the responsibility of keeping this type of corrosive influence out of the agencies under their control. It is particularly important that the thousands of young men and women who are brought into Federal jobs not be subjected to that type of influence while in the service of the Government. One homosexual can pollute a Government office.

Another point to be considered in determining whether a sex pervert is suitable for Government employment is his tendency to gather other perverts about him. Eminent psychiatrists have informed the subcommittee that the homosexual is likely to seek his own kind because the pressures of society are such that he feels uncomfortable unless he is with his own kind. Due to this situation the homosexual tends to surround himself with other homosexuals, not only in his social, but in his business life. Under these circumstances if a homosexual attains a position in Government where he can influence the hiring of personnel, it is almost inevitable that he will attempt to place other homosexuals in Government jobs. . . .

The lack of emotional stability which is found in most sex perverts and the weakness of their moral fiber, makes them susceptible to the blandishments of the foreign espionage agent. It is the experience of intelligence experts that perverts are vulnerable to interrogation by a skilled questioner and they seldom refuse to talk about themselves. Furthermore, most perverts tend to congregate at the same restaurants, night clubs, and bars, which places can be identified with comparative ease in any community, making it possible for a recruiting agent to develop clandestine relationships which can be used for espionage purposes. . . .

MY RIGHTS AS A GAY PERSON
"Pat" and "George"

Because of the virulence of its language, historian Martin Bauml Duberman calls "Employment of Homosexuals and Other Sex Perverts in Government" the "key document" of the Cold War period when it came to the persecution of gay Americans. Indeed, it appears to have set off a nationwide "witch hunt" for homosexuals. In the District of Columbia, the Senate investigation generated widespread publicity which, in turn, led to a police crackdown on "sex perverts." Soon, police departments in cities and towns across the country followed suit, and no place was safe. In fact, homosexuals were more vulnerable in areas where the local gay community was small. One of the harshest campaigns occurred in Boise, Idaho in 1955.

Lesbians and gay men responded to persecution by organizing both formally and informally. In 1951 Henry (Harry) Hay, a teacher of musical history, started the

Source: Interviews with "Pat" and "George" in Nancy Adair and Casey Adair, *Word Is Out: Stories of Some of Our Lives* (New York and San Francisco: New Glide Publications and Dell Publishing, 1978), pp. 61–63, 71–73. Copyright © 1978 by Adair Films/Nancy Adair and Casey Adair. Used by permission of Dell Books, a division of Bantam Doubleday Dell Publishing Group, Inc.

Mattachine Society, whose purpose was to unite homosexuals, educate the public about homosexuality, and lead a struggle against right-wing attacks. Though the Mattachine was theoretically open to women, lesbians felt uncomfortable in the organization, so in 1955 they formed their own group, the Daughters of Bilitis, under the leadership of San Francisco couple Del Martin and Phyllis Lyon. These organizations gave political expression to the gay and lesbian communities that were springing up everywhere.

As you read the following memoirs, consider the impact of persistent harassment. Did it succeed in deterring homosexuality, as the government had intended, or did it serve to sharpen lesbians' and gays' sense of identity and strengthen their networks?

"PAT"

[Peter (interviewer)]: *San Francisco, even then, was known as a gay town?*

[Pat]: Oh, yeah. Especially right after the war. There were five gay bars on Broadway and dancing—you could go from bar to bar. The GIs would wait outside and try to beat you up. They got mad that they couldn't dance with the girls—the girls were gay. We would announce this to them. "Go away, I'm a lesbian, I'm a queer. Get out of my life." We all lived on Bush Street in this old two-story house. It was a very exciting place to be, because, as I said, we were in bars every night. You never wanted to work because you might miss something. But you had to work in order to get money to go to bars at all. So we worked part-time.

I remember—oh, God!—Blum's fruitcake factory. You couldn't work in any office job because there you were in your costume. I was in my shaved-over-the-ears, sideburn stage, and you could hardly go down to work in an office in that garb—nobody would hire you. And you'd look pretty funny on the street. So we went to work in the factory. We got bandanas and tied them over our heads so nobody could see our short haircuts. There were about three of us. Nancy—a tiny, diminutive type who had to have all her clothes made for her, like itsy-bitsy pin-striped pants and infinitesimal suspenders with her initials in gold—even had a little itsy-bitsy tuxedo. She was barely five feet tall, very blond, with short, short hair. And she would stomp, stomp. She really wasn't butch at all, but it was a good act. When we got out of work at the fruitcake factory, we got into a cab and went to the gay bar. You'd rip off your bandana, and there you were!

P: *Did you live in a sort of communal way?*

[Pat]: Yeah. It was fun because we were allowed to be together and to have fun and play with being gay and to put on our different costumes for being gay. We had a big loyalty code. If anyone said anything bad about one of your buddies, you took her outside and got into a fight with her. We shared our money, and if you came home in the middle of the night with a woman that you'd picked up at the bar and you wanted something to eat, we had a basket on a pulley. You'd scream out of the window, "Eggs," and somebody in the house would have eggs and put them in the basket. You'd pull up the basket and get your stuff to share with your girlfriend or whoever else you managed to drag home.

P: *Was there much role playing?*

[Pat]: . . . [S]ome of the girls were butches, like Nancy, and others were femmes, like me. Everybody had their allotted tasks; butches had to do all the heavy work. They didn't have laundromats, so I'd wash the sheets in the one bathroom and put a board across the bathtub and sit on it and (*stamping her feet up and down*) read and wash the sheets—that was the femme's job. Then the butches would take over and wring out the sheets. So there was itty-bitty Nancy wringing out the sheets, and then the butches would hang them up. We femmes were supposed to be too weak to do that.

Femmes were few and far between. It was hard to get a good femme, because once she was around dykes for a while, she turned into a dyke, anyway. It was fierce for me because I didn't belong either place, really. I might have belonged more in the traditional women's role, but who needs that? If you were going to be gay, you wanted to be like a guy because they were the ones who could get things on. The masculine role was the one to play—to do all the asking, all the picking and choosing.

"GEORGE"

[Peter (interviewer)]: *How did you end up in San Francisco?*

[George]: I felt the need to get out of Los Angeles, so I just took a Greyhound bus for San Francisco with thirty dollars in my pocket. I didn't know a soul when I came to town, and I wandered around, ran into a police officer, and I said, "Where is a gay bar?" (*laughs*) He told me about this bar called the Black Cat. And so that year I began to get oriented to the gay community, and I used to go to the Black Cat every Sunday afternoon. (*In this description of the Black Cat, George cried, then pulled himself together, cried again, and laughed. Toward the end, his tears and laughter seemed to become one strong emotion.*) This was about 1952 or 1953, somewhere in there. I found out that they had a satirical opera done in a comical way on Sundays. They had an entertainer named José, and he used to put on crazy women's hats and do *Carmen*—you know, the opera *Carmen*—using these crazy outfits, and he had a pianist who'd play. Like, Carmen would be in Union Square, which is a main downtown park, and would be dancing around the park, you know, and obviously you knew Carmen was . . . what he was saying was a guy was Carmen. And then he would do Carmen with this crazy hat, dancing around the stage trying to hide from the vice squad who were in the bushes trying to capture Carmen. The best thing was that he did it very deliberately, with a spirit of unity. There used to be maybe two-hundred people would fill this bar, and they would all cheer his satire, which was basically the beginning of gay liberation. The really exciting part was at the end of each opera he would sort of informally joke with the audience, and in those comments was my beginning of my awareness of my rights as a gay person because I get very emotional about this. . . . It was the beginning of my awareness that I was not only a gay person but that I should come out of my person and be in a broader sense aware of other gay people and their rights too. Because José would say, "Let's unite."

You must realize that the vice squad was there. At that time they used to park their police cars outside of gay bars, and they used to take down the names of people when they entered. They used to come in and stand around and just generally intimidate people and make them feel that they were less than human. It was a frightening period. I am very stirred by this, because at that time there was no place to go for your freedom, and you were very much aware that there was no freedom and that your freedom was in a gay bar, and when you got out on the streets you were Mr. Straight or Miss Straight.

But José would make these political comments about our rights as homosexuals, and at the end of them—at the end of every concert—he would have everybody in the room stand, and we would put our arms around each other and sing, "God Save Us Nelly Queens." I get very emotional about this, and it sounds silly, but if you lived at that time and had the oppression coming down from the police department and from society, there was nowhere to turn . . . and to be able to put your arms around other gay men and to be able to stand up and sing, "God Save Us Nelly Queens." We were really not saying, "God Save Us Nelly Queens." We were saying, "We have our rights too." José is still very much with us in the community here in San Francisco, and we treasure José to this day for making us aware in a lot of ways.

WORKING WOMEN HAVE BEEN BLAMED FOR EVERYTHING
Elizabeth Pope

In her 1963 book *The Feminine Mystique,* Betty Friedan argued that by promoting the image of "the happy housewife heroine," the mass media had made American women a false promise. Instead of living happily in their tract houses, cleaning, cooking, and caring for their families, millions of housewives were suffering from "the problem with no name." In fact, many women were already heading into the labor force, enough so that journalists and family experts felt compelled to address a very different problem: the impact of wage-earning mothers on family life. As the following article indicates, experts could not reach a consensus on this issue. Friedan argues that magazine editors were part of a de facto conspiracy to sell women a bill of goods about the joys of domesticity. Based on your reading of the document, where do you think the author and editors of *McCall's* came down on this issue?

Like it or not, the fact is that American wives and mothers are becoming wage earners.

Ever since World War II, when for the first time vast numbers of women were exposed to the seduction of the weekly pay check, more and more wives have been taking full-time jobs outside the home. Today more than ten million—better than one out of four—are working as homemakers and wage earners at the same time.

It's a tough assignment. At best it means getting up earlier and going to bed later. It means rushing through housework on weekdays, spending evenings and weekends trying to catch up on loose ends. It means double responsibility, double worries.

Is it worth it? Do the personal and dollar gains outweigh the difficulties?

Working women have been blamed for everything from juvenile delinquency to divorce. They have been charged with neglecting their babies, bulldozing their husbands, neglecting their homes. It's hard to think of a social problem ranging from inadequate breakfasts to world unrest which someone at some time or another hasn't dumped into their laps.

Source: Elizabeth Pope, "Is a Working Mother a Threat to the Home?" *McCall's,* 82, 10 (July 1955), pp. 29, 70, 72, 73.

The question, of course, concerns not only the working women themselves, but every other member of their families, especially their children. There are more than five and a half million mothers of children under eighteen among the ranks of working wives. What happens to those children, big and little, when Mother goes out to work? In the long run are they helped or hurt? Is there any truth in the argument that the little ones are being deprived of their emotional birthright? Or in the even more widespread notion that there is some connection between juvenile delinquency and the employment of mothers?

Leading psychiatrists don't agree at all over the question "Are babies and preschoolers emotionally damaged if their mothers go out to work?" Dr. Leo H. Bartemeier, prominent Catholic leader in psychiatry and medical director of Baltimore's Seton Institute, answers this question with an emphatic *yes.* A small child doesn't know or care why his mother works, Dr. Bartemeier says. All he knows is that day after day she goes away and leaves him. Without the continuous care of his mother he feels unloved and unsatisfied, and he may carry the scars of this experience for life. Even granting that truly satisfactory arrangements can be made for a baby's care while his mother works, Dr. Bartemeier sees no way out of the underlying emotional problem.

"Until children are at least six," he says, "motherhood is a twenty-four-hour job and one that no one can do for you. A mother who runs out on her children to work—except in cases of absolute necessity—betrays a deep dissatisfaction with motherhood or with her marriage. Chances are, she is driven by sick, competitive feelings toward men, or some other personality problem. She does a grave disservice to her children, although the harm may not show up for years."

These are fighting words to Dr. Lauretta Bender, Senior Psychiatrist in charge of Children's Services at New York's Bellevue Hospital. Dr. Bender believes that from the moment of birth a mother's value to her child depends on the *quality* and continuity of her relationship with him, not on the *quantity* of time spent together. To her mind there are as many unloving mothers who stay at home all day as go out to work. "It's lack of love that leaves scars, not Mother's workday absences. Having a job actually increases some women's capacity to love and also their children's awareness of being loved." . . .

The working mothers whom *McCall's* talked to across the country seem to share Dr. Bender's opinion. Many of them work because they want the money and enjoy their jobs, because they find housework lonely and monotonous. "I get a big kick out of my job and I'm tickled to death to see the kids when I come home," says Grace Farnham, salesclerk in a Southern city. "Before I worked I used to be tired all the time and snap at the children for no reason at all. I enjoy being with people, and long hours of housecleaning all by myself certainly didn't improve my disposition."

If the children of working mothers are emotionally deprived, their mothers don't know it. "When I took care of them all the time," one mother told us, "the kids always seemed to be whining. Now that they're in nursery school they're much happier and more independent."

Working women who believe their children don't suffer from their absence are just whistling in the dark, according to Dr. Bartemeier. "There is an enormous amount of evidence," he says, "that, prior to the age of four, children should not be separated from their mothers. Even after they have begun school they continue to need their mothers in the home. Every experienced schoolteacher in the lower grades has observed the striking difference between those children whose mothers work for wages and those who reflect the trust and security of a mother devoted to her home."

Some experienced teachers may observe "the striking difference" Dr. Bartemeier mentions. The experienced teachers *McCall's* interviewed for this article, however, felt that there were no significant emotional differences between the children of working and nonworking mothers. The emotional difficulties they encountered in their pupils, they said, could be traced to many causes which didn't necessarily include mothers' having jobs.

If a first-rate substitute takes over when Mother's away and if the mother herself has a good relationship with her children, it may even help a child for Mother to work. This is the consensus among the staffs of the Child Welfare League of America, the Bank Street College of Education and the Mills College of Education, all of which are in close contact with children of stay-at-home as well as employed mothers.

It is also the opinion of Millicent Carey McIntosh, President of Barnard College and one of America's most distinguished educators. Mrs. McIntosh has been a working woman for thirty-three years, a working wife for twenty-three, a working mother for twenty-one. Her husband is a prominent pediatrician and they have five children. Understandably, Millicent McIntosh has little sympathy for a point of view like Dr. Bartemeier's.

In her long experience with schools, Mrs. McIntosh has seen many mother-daughter relationships, many patterns of full-time, part-time and no employment. She thinks no one pattern is necessarily better for children than any of the rest. Each woman, she believes, should chart her course individually, according to what's right for her, not only as a mother but as a human being. The only course she would not advocate is for any woman to tether herself unhappily to her own hearthstone out of a sense of duty. "The woman who does this is likely to over-organize her household and end up pushing her husband and children around for want of adequate outlets. I've seen many daughters become either deeply resentful or slavishly dependent on such a mother. And it all goes back to the silly notion that a 'good' woman stays home all the time." . . .

[Opponents of maternal employment assume] that the children of working mothers are by definition neglected emotionally. According to this reasoning, if you think it's all right to work you also think it's all right for children to be emotionally neglected.

Neither Dr. Bender nor Mrs. McIntosh, needless to say, are defending the emotional neglect of children. Their point is simply that a child's emotional health does not depend on whether his mother has an outside job; it depends on the over-all *quality* of her feeling for him, whether she is home all day or not. There is one point, however, on which all the experts agree. Small babies should have their mothers with them full time if possible. . . .

Judge Justine Wise Polier, of the Domestic Relations Court of New York City . . . asks, "Is it possible that there may be even less likelihood of delinquency when mothers work than when they don't?" . . . [She] feels that delinquency is the result of a tragic combination of social, economic, and psychological difficulties which bear down heavily on the children involved. It is most prevalent in very low-income families—especially those in which parents have given up the struggle to better themselves.

If the woman in such a situation has enough gumption and self-respect to go out to work—on top of her regular housework—it means she's still struggling. Her children have something to cling to. There is some hope in their lives. "There are plenty of things that are worse for children," says Judge Polier, "than finding Mother at work when you come home from school. Perhaps the worst is finding her resigned to hopelessness."

Judge Polier hates to hear the question argued as if working or not working were always a matter of free choice. So does Marie Jahoda, Associate Director of New York University's Research Center for Human Relations. Dr. Jahoda says that the overwhelming majority of working mothers can't afford to choose. They work because they need the money. More than a million (about one out of five) of all employed mothers are widowed, divorced or separated from their husbands and have to work to support their children. Many others are married to men whose earnings fall below the Labor Department's health and decency level. Most of them are in factory and clerical jobs and their median wage is about $1400 a year.

Does a working mother gain enough in personal satisfaction to outweigh the difficulties of doing two jobs?

Experts are unanimous in prefacing their answer to this question with the words "That depends." It depends on what kind of person she is and why she gets a job, on how old her children are and what they are like, on the attitude of her husband and the family's financial situation. . . .

Perhaps the most succinct answer to the questions of whether or not—and if so, when—mothers should work comes from Mirra Komarovsky, head of the Sociology Department of Barnard College. Dr. Komarovsky's view encompasses the entire sweep of a woman's life. "It is a continuous process," she says. "In the beginning, when there are babies, it takes a very exceptional woman and very exceptional circumstances to be able to do a good job as a mother and a worker at the same time. As children grow older, the task becomes easier. Finally, when they are away from home much of the day, the entire situation has been reversed. By then it is the exceptional woman who can maintain her own and her family's equilibrium *without* a job." . . .

WOMANLY YEARNINGS
La Leche League

Though the focus on family and domesticity tended to associate women closely with motherhood, it was not necessarily a disadvantage. By self-consciously accepting responsibility for motherhood, many women found that it could be the basis for neo-maternalist mobilization and individual self-empowerment. One of the most successful neo-maternalist organizations was the La Leche League, whose goal was to promote and disseminate information about breastfeeding, a practice that had gone out of favor with the introduction of bottle feeding earlier in the century.

The idea for the League was hatched when twelve suburban Chicago mothers met in the fall of 1956 to share their joys and problems in nursing their infants. They believed that while breastfeeding was an entirely natural function, it did not come naturally to modern mothers, who often felt isolated in their decision to nurse and needed assistance to do so successfully. They set out to teach other mothers about pregnancy, breastfeeding techniques, and child care.

In 1958 the League gathered their store of practical advice and maternalist philosophy in the first edition of *The Womanly Art of Breastfeeding*. By 1961, they had

Source: La Leche League, *The Womanly Art of Breast Feeding* (La Leche League: Franklin Park, Ill., 1958), pp. i, 1–2, 5.

organized 43 mothers' groups; five years later, there were 430; and by 1976, 3,000, with several dozen more abroad. Though the founders were too modest to claim credit, their work certainly had something to do with the significant increase in breastfeeding in the United States from 20 percent of mothers of newborns in the mid-fifties to 60 percent by the mid-eighties.

Hardly a radical organization, La Leche League nevertheless challenged the medical establishment's advice to mothers, contending that bottles, formulas, and schedules alienated mothers from their infants. Some members rejected not only bottles but all forms of "mother-substitutes," such as high chairs, playpens, and, of course, pacifiers. Many also supported the move toward natural childbirth.

With an average of seven children each, the founders (all of whom were Catholic) believed that mothers should stay at home, and for many years the organization remained ambivalent on the issue of maternal employment. Like turn-of-the-century maternalists, the League endorsed motherhood as women's special vocation, portraying breastfeeding as a "moral imperative" which was invested with a "higher civic purpose."

Though its method anticipated by more than a decade the "consciousness-raising groups" that became the vehicle for the women's liberation movement, many feminists initially criticized the League because of its unquestioning acceptance of motherhood as women's destined role. Eventually, however, the women's health movement came to recognize in the organization an approach which, while different from their own, could help women seeking to regain control of their own bodies. For this reason, historian Lynn Weiner has aptly called the League "both prologue and counterpoint" to the wave of feminism that followed. Do you think members of the League intended to empower women?

All the points discussed in our booklet are those which are discussed at our meetings. This booklet is written by mothers for mothers. It is not intended as a substitute for the writings of the various members of the medical profession who have done valuable research in this field. The mothers of La Leche League are familiar with many books, pamphlets, and articles written by doctors and nurses. We quote these sources in many instances and recommend many of them to the mothers for reading. . . .

How did Eve manage? Certainly she didn't join a league. Eve had it easy. Her baby came. The milk came. She nursed her baby. . . . Eve, of course, did not have well-meaning but not too well-informed friends and relatives questioning her ability to breast feed her baby. Eve—and you—nourished this baby completely for nine months in the womb, why any sudden doubts now? Her ability to nurse was taken for granted. Similarly, we take our ability to walk for granted. Imagine, though, our loss of confidence, perplexity, and perhaps complete failure of this natural function if it were constantly being questioned or criticized?

Also, Eve had no choice. There just weren't bottles and formulae. And the bottles and formulae we have today are good, thank God. So let's consider them for a bit. The medical profession in its role of assisting or substituting for Nature, tackled the problem of finding an acceptable milk for the baby who could not get breast milk. And with the help of refrigeration, sterilization, and the rubber company, the modern formula was delivered. It worked, and though still only a substitute . . . was better than nothing in the exceptional case. Then somehow the exception became the rule. Perhaps because it was talked about—it was new. Don't we all at times angle to try something just because it is new and being talked about? . . . And to alter old established positions a bit more, bottle feeding often led to a whole new manner of "mothering."

So many more new decisions had to be made—which formula to use, how to prepare it, how much, to hold the baby or not—a mother could easily begin to regard her baby as a most complex digestion system instead of a most dependent, but "feeling" *person.* In the midst of scales and charts, mother began to lose confidence in her own abilities, to miss the easy natural enjoyment of a new baby.

Time, however, and strong often unfilled womanly yearnings are now demanding we take another look at our babies and our "mothering." Psychiatrists are pointing out clinical proof that the natural inclinations of a mother to hold and nurse her baby should not be ignored as inconsequential. And that the manner in which a baby's early needs are met often greatly determines his good or bad response to people and things in later life. "The original plan for care and feeding" bears reexamining. Many forward looking doctors are taking a backward glance, and realizing the unique good of breast feeding are recommending it. And many new mothers give it a try, but are often disappointed. Why? Possibly because the doctor, who is necessarily well grounded in prescribing formula, has had very little opportunity to learn about the woman's role in breast feeding. Nursing is strictly a woman's art, to be passed on from mother to daughter by association. Doctors in Grandma's—or Great-grandmother's—day actually had little to do in the matter, because as the majority of nursing mothers will attest to, once established, the breast feeding itself requires a minimum of medical attention. (No quality or quantity changes to be made. They're automatic!)

Most likely things didn't go just right for you in your past attempts to breast feed because it is a lonely practice. There weren't the other women to exchange experiences with, pass on a hint or two, encourage and reassure. And, except for Eve, a woman needs that sort of thing! The sort of thing the mothers of La Leche feel they can give.

When you subscribe to the League, you'll meet another nursing mother who will personally consider your situation. She has the combined experiences of all the other mothers of the League to draw on plus access to a great deal of the new material written on the subject in recent years. Most of all this mother assigned to you hopes to share with you the "spirit" of nursing that comes from experiencing the quick, strong love-ties so natural between a nursing mother and her baby; from her sure understanding of her baby's needs and her joy and confidence in herself to satisfy them; and from seeing the happy dividends from this good relationship as the baby grows up. It is a "spirit" first sensed, gradually understood and absorbed, finally realized by a mother as she nurses her own new baby.

Our goal is to help you successfully breast feed your babies and so successfully mother them. . . . Putting your infant to your breast is your very first act of love for him after you deliver him into the world. It is the second important step in your role as mother. Thus the intimate sharing of your body which you and your baby experienced while you carried him in your womb is somewhat prolonged for another few months. And in so prolonging you thereby start ever so slowly and gently, as befits a baby's pace, the gradual process of growth from complete dependence in the womb to independence—a process of growth which will continue until he is an adult.

A FORM OF SOCIAL LAG
Frankenstein Smith

Though Kinsey's research suggested that by the 1950s, young women had become nearly as sexually active as men, popular advice literature divided sharply along gender lines, prescribing diametrically opposing values and strategies to each sex. While a spate of guides for female adolescents such as *Secrets of Charm* and the *Teen-Age Popularity Guide* warned young women against appearing to be too "available," the newly founded *Playboy* published articles such as "Will She or Won't She" and "Some Guys Get It," offering strategies for seduction. In what ways did both types of advice converge to reinforce a norm of heterosexuality? What limits did *Playboy* set for male sexual behavior?

All sophisticated playboys are interested in virginity. We trust that the matter of your own virginity has already been satisfactorily taken care of. You must now face up to the problem of virginity in your female friends and acquaintances.

Most men recognize that virginity is an unpleasant little matter to be disposed of early in life. They appreciate that it's troublesome, a bother, and all things considered, just isn't worth having around. Unfortunately, this important information has been withheld from a large part of our female population. Some men, shirking their responsibilities, might shrug this off as none of their concern. If you've a social conscience, however, you realize, of course, that it is up to enlightened members of the community to get the facts to the uninformed.

The most pleasant, satisfying, and generally successful method of spreading the good news is through demonstrations. You will, of course, meet a certain amount of intellectual resistance from young ladies who have been previously misguided by Smith [College], narrow minded mothers, teachers, maiden aunts, etc. The purpose of this article is to show you how such resistance to learning (a form of social lag) can be most easily overcome.

First of all, what is virginity? Those wise in the ways of women know that it is far more a state of mind than a state of being. Each girl seems to have her own peculiar and rather precise idea of just how far she can go without losing it. And, since it is primarily a state of mind, you will most often meet with success by attacking the mind, not the body. Your attitude is extremely important and will affect your entire approach to the problem. Remember (and this is very important) you are actually doing the girl a *service*. Some may suggest that you are trying to deprive them of something—trying to take from them a cherished possession. This is nonsense. Actually, you are *giving* them a new freedom—a means of enjoying life more fully—a greater appreciation of life and its many pleasures. You must be fully convinced on this point yourself before attempting to convince anyone else. Such a healthy, clean-minded, all-American attitude on the subject cannot help but favorably impress members of the opposite sex.

Some difficulties have arisen because of the confusion (in female minds) between virginity and purity. The two having nothing to do with one another, and it is important that you point this out at the proper moment. Some of the most impure women we've ever known have been virgins and will doubtless die that way. On the

Source: Frankenstein Smith, "Virginity: An Important Treatise on a Very Important Subject," *Playboy* 1, 10 (Sept. 1954), pp. 9, 40, 50.

All-purpose areas give this three-bedroom house spaciousness far beyond its size.

ONE-STORY HOUSE
with double-duty features

By CAROL L. MERCADO

Double-duty rooms cut the high cost of living space in this handsome house. Folding doors in the family zone make three rooms of one, or one room of three, with no effort at all. Doors fold to the walls to produce a huge play area; unfold the doors, and it becomes a sunny breakfast room, a spacious family room, a breezy porch.

The three-way fireplace separates family room from formal living area; living-room windows open onto a plant-edged raised terrace. The patio, three steps down, is another double-duty area. For three seasons it's a sheltered play yard; its concrete floor is made to order for bicycles, skates, doll carriages. In winter the toys move indoors, and the ground-level patio becomes a bad-weather carport (a gravel drive provides parking space the rest of the year).

Baths are partitioned to reduce rush-hour traffic; the laundry is strategically placed near children's rooms and kitchen, where most of the washday work is produced. Estimates for building this house range from $16,000 to $25,000, depending upon local costs.

B — BATH
C — CLOSET
K — KITCHEN
S — SINK
DW — DISHWASHER
R — REFRIGERATOR
□□ — RANGE
U & L — UTILITY AND LAUNDRY

COVERED PATIO

PLANT BOX

TERRACE

BEDROOM 13'8" x 10'6"

U & L 6' x 10'6"

B'FAST 6'9" x 7'2"

BEDROOM 9'9" x 11'6"

DINING– FAMILY ROOM 14'2" x 21'6"

K 8'6" x 14'2"

LIVING ROOM 23'6" x 17'3"

MASTER BEDROOM 10'3" x 14'3"

ENTRY

PORCH

Write to us for information on how to obtain plans.

FIGURE 10.2

These two architectural plans show how space could express different concepts of gender relations. One might imagine the senior male occupant of the "One-Story House with Double-Duty Features" fantasizing about the "Playboy Penthouse Apartment." (*Sources: Ladies Home Journal, vol. 73, no. 5 [May 1956], p. 53; and Playboy, vol. 3, no. 9 [September 1956], p. 158.*)

238

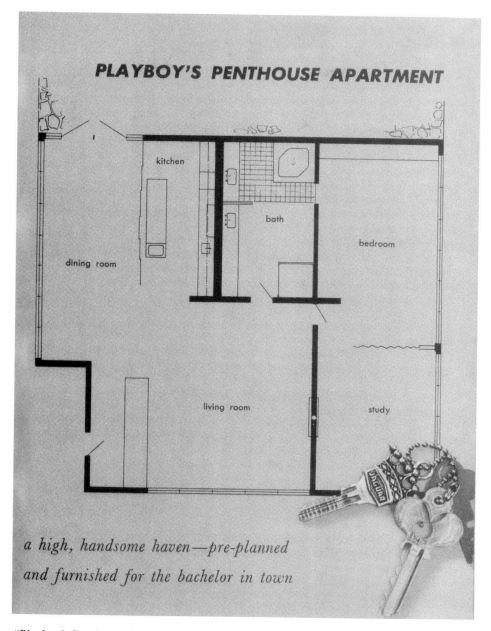

"Playboy's Penthouse Apartment" reproduced by Special Permission of *Playboy* Magazine. Copyright © 1956 by Playboy. The Rabbit Head Design is a Trademark of Playboy Enterprises, Inc. and used with permission.

other hand, we regularly share friendly intimacies with one of the sweetest, purest young things in all creation.

Thus armed with our convictions, we are ready to begin. First, of course, we must select a suitable subject and, these days, that can sometimes be more of a problem than you might assume. Often you may find the young lady you have chosen for enlightenment has already been enlightened a few times by others. And while there may be a certain amount of enjoyment involved in this discovery, it robs you of the special pleasure of spreading the good news—and that, after all, is what this article is about.

Once we've found our subject we are ready for the *approach*. In theory, we suppose, there are as many different approaches as there are women, since each requires a technique slightly different than the next. Indeed, a method that works like a charm on Monday evening may get you a clout in the snout with a different miss on Tuesday. It is obviously impossible to consider all the various possible techniques but we will spend some time on a few of the more basic ones.

The Physical Approach. Boys are bigger than girls. And some guys figure that's all the advantage they need to make any seduction a success. Trouble is, that ain't seduction. If you're going to play the game according to the rules, you've got to win over the lady's mind first. The muscle method is too often confused with a dirty four letter word spelled r-a-p-e. The girl may not fully understand that you have only her best interests at heart. Such goings on can lead to misunderstandings, strained relationships, and long jail sentences.

The Alcoholic Approach. This isn't really an approach at all. Liquor, by itself, never seduced anybody. You can, however, dissolve a good many inhibitions in the proper amount of alcohol. A few drinks will usually help along any of the standard approaches, but we emphasize—a *few* drinks. It is possible to reach a point of diminishing returns when imbibing. The girl may lose all interest in sex, you may discover—at the last moment—that you are not up to the occasion, the girl may get sick, you may get sick, she may lose consciousness, (Ground Rule 32b: It is unfair to take liberties with a lady who is unconscious. This cannot be properly considered seduction since she has pretty well lost her freedom of choice. Some will argue that any amount of alcohol robs a person of a certain amount of free choice in such matters. We prefer to believe that liquor only gives a lady the courage to do what she would very much like to do when cold sober, but hasn't the nerve for.)

The Intellectual Approach. In its purest forms this technique is best suited to librarians and girls working on their Ph.D.s. With this approach, sex never even enters the conversation until the very end of the evening. Much time is spent, instead, in discussing the world's great writers, the philosophy of Aristotle, the pros and cons of world government, progressive education, Einstein's theory of relativity, etc. Throughout the evening, the emphasis is intellectual rather than physical. You compliment, not the girl's good looks or her 38 inch bust, but her mind. By the time you get around to the young lady's virginity, the physical side of life seems so completely unimportant, she will comply with scarcely a second thought.

The Freudian Approach. Here's a real favorite. Sigmund and Dr. Kinsey . . . have done more for sex than any other men who ever lived. Explain to the lady that her virginity is really stuck up someplace in her superego, and not the spot where she thinks she keeps it. Explain that sex is a perfectly normal drive, like hunger, thirst, Hydromatic. Hint darkly about the dangers of frustrating the libido—mention neuroses, psychoses, halitosis, and anything else you can think of to throw in. By evening's end, the poor creature will be begging you to save her from a life of frigidity, a traumatic-schizophrenic-oedipus-complex or worse, and, big man that you are, you'll do just that.

The Atomic Age Approach. This technique has the advantage of being as up-to-date as tomorrow's headlines. Mumble something morose about the shape the world is in, talk about U.S.-Russian relations, mention the Hydrogen Bomb, spend some time discussing the effect one H-Bomb would have if it fell, just for the sake of conversation, on the roof of a particular bar in which you're drinking. If this doesn't get to her, start talking about flying saucers and invasion from Mars. When you've got her in the properly pessimistic frame of mind, slug down a stiff one and say, "We might as well live for tonight, baby, 'cause who knows where the hell we'll be tomorrow."

This is actually a variation on the very successful wartime technique that ran to something like, "Love me tonight, 'cause tomorrow I'm getting blown to bits on the fighting fronts of the world." The advantage of this new approach is obvious since you've two corpses to contemplate instead of just one. . . .

The Persistent Approach. Some girls attempt to avoid most of the standard approaches by simply changing the subject whenever it gets around to s-e-x. For these we suggest persistence, with a capital "P." No matter what she talks about, *you* talk about sex.

For example, you're sitting in a restaurant. You've just ordered drinks and are looking over the dinner menu. Your date notices you eyeing her rather low cut dress.

"Do you like me in this dress?" she asks, "It's new." "Very much," you reply politely, "and I'd like you even better without it."

Somewhat flustered by this, she tries to change the subject to the weather.

"It's been an awfully hot summer, hasn't it?" she says. "Not as hot as I am for you right now," you counter in a voice suggesting both sincerity and quiet emotion.

Staring at her menu, "The fish looks good."

Ignoring your own menu, staring at her boldly, "Did you know that male fish fertilize the eggs *after* the female has laid them and that they never have bodily contact with one another? This has been suggested as the basis for the expression 'poor fish.'"

She, "May I have the cherry from your Tom Collins?"

And so on.

Eventually she will become thoroughly undone, will find it impossible to avoid the subject any longer and you will be on your way.

We have offered here, as we said in the beginning, only a few of the more basic techniques. With a little experimentation, you will undoubtedly be able to add a number of equally successful methods of your own. If you hit on any really good ones be sure to let us know.

A JOY SHE DARED NOT REVEAL
Jo Ann Gibson Robinson

Rosa Parks is justly famous for her courageous act of defiance, which set off the Montgomery bus boycott of 1955 and, with it, the civil rights movement. Less well known are the names of other African American women, young and old, who, in the years leading up to the boycott, were rebuked or also arrested for "talking back" to

Source: Reprinted by permission of The University of Tennessee Press. From *The Montgomery Bus Boycott and the Women Who Started It: The Memoir of Jo Ann Gibson Robinson*, edited with a foreword by David J. Garrow, pp. 15–17, 20–21, 36–37, 45–47, 98–119, 162. Copyright © 1987 by The University of Tennessee Press.

drivers, not having the correct change, or, like Parks, refusing to surrender their seats to white riders. Among these are Geneve Johnson, Viola White, Katie Wingfield, Claudette Colvin, Mary Louise Smith, and Jo Ann Gibson Robinson. Though their suffering was well known within the black community, most of these women (as well as countless other African Americans, both male and female) endured their humiliating encounters with segregation quietly and, having no alternative, went on riding the buses. In Robinson's case, however, the experience left her with a lasting pain that eventually prompted her to take political action.

Robinson was the youngest of twelve children born to a rural Georgia farming family and the first to graduate from college. She went on to earn a master's degree in English from Atlanta University. In 1949 she took a teaching position at Alabama State in Montgomery, where she joined the Dexter Avenue Baptist Church, the home institution of Martin Luther King, Jr., and also became active in the Women's Political Council, a black professional women's civic organization which had been founded as an alternative to the segregated local chapter of the League of Women Voters.

Though Robinson frequently defers to King and other male leaders of the civil rights movement, her memoir shows that it was the Council that had originally conceived of the boycott and made precise plans for carrying it out. She reveals that it was her personal decision to take action that set the plans in motion. These details help balance the historical record of the civil rights movement by documenting women's vital behind-the-scenes contributions. How did gender shape African Americans' experience of segregation and their responses to it?

I was as happy as I had ever been in my life that Saturday morning before Christmas in December 1949 as I prepared to leave the campus of Alabama State College in Montgomery for the holidays. I had been a member of the English faculty at the college since September of that year, and I had loved every minute of it.

I boarded an almost empty city bus, dropped my coins into the proper place, and observed the passengers aboard, only two—a white woman who sat in the third row from the front, and a black man in a seat near the back. I took the fifth row seat from the front and sat down, immediately closing my eyes and envisioning, in my mind's eye, the wonderful two weeks' vacation I would have with my family and friends in Ohio.

From the far distance of my reverie I thought I heard a voice, an unpleasant voice, but I was too happy to worry about voices, or any noise for that matter. But the same words were repeated, in a stronger, unsavory tone, and I opened my eyes. Immediately I sat up in that seat. The bus driver had stopped the bus, turned in his seat, and was speaking to me!

"If you can sit in the fifth row from the front of the other buses in Montgomery, suppose you get off and ride in one of them!" I heard him, but the message did not register with me. My thoughts were elsewhere. I had not even noticed that the bus had come to a full stop, or I had subconsciously surmised that passengers were getting on or off.

Suddenly the driver left his seat and stood over me. His hand was drawn back as if he were going to strike me. "Get up from there!" He yelled. He repeated it, for, dazed, I had not moved. "Get up from there!"

I leaped to my feet, afraid that he would hit me, and ran to the front door to get off the bus. I even stepped down to the lower level, so that when the door was opened, I could step off the bus and hide myself, for tears were falling rapidly from my eyes. It suddenly occurred to me that I was supposed to go to the back door to get off, not the front! However, I was too upset, frightened, and tearful to move. I never could have walked to the rear door. Then the driver opened the front door, and I stumbled off the bus and started walking back to the college. Tears blinded my vision; waves of humiliation inundated me; and I thanked God that none of my students was on that bus to witness the tragic experience. I could have died from embarrassment.

My friends came and took me to the airport, but my holiday season was spoiled. I cried all the way to my destination and pretended to have a headache when my relatives met me at the airport in Cleveland five or six hours later. In all these years I have never forgotten the shame, the hurt, of that experience. The memory will never go away.

Even now, when segregation has been abolished and riders sit where they please on public transportation lines, memories like mine will not fade away. Although almost thirty years have gone by, black people have not forgotten the years leading up to the boycott of 1955—the suffering, the abuse they endured at the hands of arrogant white bus drivers. It was during the period of 1949–1955 that the Women's Political Council of Montgomery—founded in 1946 with Dr. Mary Fair Burks as president and headed from 1950 on by me—prepared to stage a bus boycott when the time was ripe and the people were ready. The right time came in 1955. . . .

At 5:30 A.M. Monday, December 5, 1955, dawn was breaking over Montgomery. Early morning workers were congregating at corners. There, according to the plan, Negroes were to be picked up not by the Montgomery City Lines, but by Negro taxis driving at reduced rates of ten cents per person, or by some two hundred private cars which had been offered free to bus riders for Monday only.

The suspense was almost unbearable, for no one was positively sure that taxi drivers would keep their promises, that private car owners would give absolute strangers a ride, that Negro bus riders would stay off the bus. And then there was the cold and the threat of rain!

The black Women's Political Council had been planning the boycott of Montgomery City Lines for months, but the plans had only been known publicly for the past three days. The idea itself had been entertained for years. Almost daily some black man, woman, or child had had an unpleasant experience on the bus and told other members of the family about it at the supper table or around the open fireplace or stove. These stories were repeated to neighbors, who re-told them in club meetings or to the ministers of large church congregations.

At first the ministers would soothe the anger of their congregations with recommendations of prayer, with promises that God would "make the rough ways smooth" and with exhortations to "have patience and wait upon the Lord."

The members had been patient and had waited upon the Lord, but the rough ways had gotten rougher rather than smoother. As months stretched into years, the encounters with some of the bus drivers grew more numerous and more intolerable.

Very little or nothing tangible had ever been done on the part of the darker race to prevent continuous abuse on city transit lines, except to petition the company and the City Commission for better conditions, . . . but nothing came of it. . . .

The Women's Political Council, over a long period, tried to ascertain why there was so much killing, cutting, intoxication, and burglary, etc., on weekends among black children and adults. We discovered that all the pent-up emotions resulting from bitter experiences on local transportation lines often were released upon husbands, wives, or children, resulting in injuries that necessitated hospital care.

Grown men frequently came home on particular evenings, angry from humiliating experiences on buses, to pick fights with their wives and children. They needed a target somewhere, a way to relieve internal conflict. These quarrels often ended in cuttings or killings, divorce or separation. When these men were later approached in a kind, understanding manner by some WPC member and asked why such crimes had occurred, these grown men—hard, tough and penitent—would cry with body-shaking sobs as they tried to explain, without really knowing why, what had made them do such things. If women were involved, they gave their children unnecessary beatings. Children, imitating the adults in their lives, resentfully fought other children, robbed stores or houses, stole bicycles, or played hooky from school. They often beat their pets severely for no apparent reason.

In 1956, the superintendent of a local hospital, which customarily treated many weekend fight victims, told a reporter that since the boycott began, the hospital had had fewer such patients. Thus the hospital official corroborated the WPC's findings that bitter bus experiences could have caused, or greatly contributed to, serious weekend fights in the home. After December 5, 1955, the people were able to release their suppressed emotions through the boycott movement, which allowed them to retaliate directly for the pain, humiliation, and embarrassment they had endured over the years at the hands of drivers and policemen while riding on the buses. And there was no need for family fights and weekend brawls.

The number of Negro men walking increased during 1954 and early 1955. They walked to and from work, to town, to movies, to see their girlfriends, because of fear of riding the buses. At no time did a single man ever stand up in defense of the women. Although it hurt to be called "coward," perhaps they were cowards, except for a very few men who challenged authority and paid the price. For, at the very first hint of conflict, the men left at the nearest exit. They didn't dare to challenge the bus operators, who possessed police powers. The men feared and did not expect to get justice in the courts. They had wives and children and could not afford to lose their jobs or to go to jail. If they were on the bus when trouble started, they merely got up and got off. Or they avoided getting on the bus in the first place. They rode when forced to, walked when they did not get rides or could not afford taxi fare. But they were tired, and they murmured! . . .

[The immediate cause of the boycott was the arrest of Mrs. Rosa Parks on December 1, 1955. Her trial was scheduled for Monday, December 5. Jo Ann Robinson decided the time had come to act.]

I made some notes on the back of an envelope: "The Women's Political Council will not wait for Mrs. Parks's consent to call for a boycott of city buses. On Friday, December 2, 1955, the women of Montgomery will call for a boycott to take place on Monday, December 5."

Some of the WPC officers previously had discussed plans for distributing thousands of notices announcing a bus boycott. Now the time had come for me to write just such a notice. I sat down and quickly drafted a message and then called a good friend and colleague, John Cannon, chairman of the business department at the college, who had access to the college's mimeograph equipment. When I told him that the WPC was staging a boycott and needed to run off the notices, he told me that he too had suffered embarrassment on the city buses. Like myself, he had been hurt and angry. He said that he would happily assist me. Along with two of my most trusted senior students, we quickly agreed to meet almost immediately, in the middle of the night, at the college's duplicating room. We were able to get three messages to a page, greatly reducing the number of pages that had to be mimeographed in order to produce the tens of thousands of leaflets we knew would be needed. By 4 A.M. Friday, the sheets had been duplicated, cut in thirds, and bundled. Each leaflet read:

Another Negro woman has been arrested and thrown in jail because she refused to get up out of her seat on the bus for a white person to sit down. . . . This has to be stopped. Negroes have rights, too, for if Negroes did not ride the buses, they could not operate. Three-fourths of the riders are Negroes, yet we are arrested, or have to stand over empty seats. If we do not do something to stop these arrests, they will continue. The next time it may be you, or your daughter, or mother. This woman's case will come up on Monday. We are, therefore, asking every Negro to stay off the buses Monday in protest of the arrest and trial. Don't ride the buses to work, to town, to school, or anywhere on Monday. You can afford to stay out of school for one day if you have no other way to go except by bus. You can also afford to stay out of town for one day. If you work, take a cab, or walk. But please, children and grown-ups, don't ride the bus at all on Monday. Please stay off all buses Monday.

Between 4 and 7 A.M., the two students and I mapped out distribution routes for the notices. Some of the WPC officers previously had discussed how and where to deliver thousands of leaflets announcing a boycott, and those plans now stood me in good stead. We outlined our routes, arranged the bundles in sequences, stacked them in our cars, and arrived at my 8 A.M. class, in which both young men were enrolled, with several minutes to spare. We weren't even tired or hungry. Just like me, the two students felt a tremendous sense of satisfaction at being able to contribute to the cause of justice.

After class my two students and I quickly finalized our plans for distributing the thousands of leaflets so that one would reach every black home in Montgomery. . . . Some of our bundles were dropped off at schools, where both students and staff members helped distribute them further and spread the word for people to read the notices and then pass them on to neighbors. Leaflets were also dropped off at business places, storefronts, beauty parlors, beer halls, factories, barber shops, and every other available place. Workers would pass along notices both to other employees as well as to customers.

During those hours of crucial work, nothing went wrong. The action of all involved was so casual, so unconcerned, so nonchalant, that suspicion was never raised, and neither the city nor its people ever suspected a thing! We never missed a spot. And no one missed a class, a job, or a normal routine. Everything was done by the plan, with perfect timing. By 2 o'clock, thousands of the mimeographed handbills had changed hands many times. Practically every black man, woman, and child in Montgomery knew the plan and was passing the word along. No one knew where the notices had come from or who had arranged for their circulation, and no one cared. Those who passed them on did so efficiently, quietly, and without comment. But deep within the heart of every black person was a joy he or she dared not reveal. . . .

[The boycott was highly effective.] The merchants began to feel the squeeze. Some businesses began closing or going bankrupt. "Closed" was seen on many storefronts where "Open for Business" had been seen before.

The truth was that the buses had no riders, and the bus company was financially distressed. The company had survived from December 5 until December 22, about seventeen days, almost without passengers. Following the holidays, service resumed on routes in basically white areas, but the continuing loss of revenue was tremendous. . . .

In mid-December 1955, the black people of Montgomery were calm, proud, content, and strangely peaceful. They faced the birthday of Christ with grim determination to continue their passive resistance. . . .

[Jo Ann Robinson was arrested for boycotting on February 22, 1956. She was booked and then sent home. The Montgomery Improvement Association, representing the black population, sued the city of Montgomery on the grounds that] racially segregated seating on city buses violated the 14th Amendment's guarantee of equal government treatment of all citizens, irrespective of race, as the Supreme Court already had ruled on with regard to schools in its 1954 landmark opinion in *Brown v. Board of Education of Topeka*. . . . [O]n June 5, [a three-judge federal court] announced that they had voted two to one against the constitutionality of segregated seating on Montgomery's city buses. Relegating black riders to the rear of city buses, or forcing them to stand over empty seats reserved for whites, or making them surrender seats to white passengers, were all unconstitutional practices. . . .

RECOMMENDED READINGS

Breines, Wini. *Young, White, and Miserable: Growing Up Female in the Fifties,* Boston, 1992.

D'Emilio, John. *Sexual Politics, Sexual Communities,* Chicago, 1983.

———. "The Homosexual Menace: The Politics of Sexuality in Cold War America." In *Making Trouble: Essays on Gay History, Politics, and the University,* New York, 1992.

Douglas, Susan J. *Where the Girls Are: Growing Up Female with the Mass Media,* New York, 1994.

Ehrenreich, Barbara. *The Hearts of Men: American Dreams and the Flight from Commitment,* Garden City, N.Y., 1983.

Gerassi, John. *The Boys of Boise: Furor, Vice and Folly in an American City,* New York, 1968.

Harrison, Cynthia. *On Account of Sex: The Politics of Women's Issues, 1945–1968,* Berkeley, 1988.

Harvey, Brett. *The Fifties: A Women's Oral History,* New York, 1993.

Kennedy, Elizabeth Lapovsky, and Madeline D. Davis. *Boots of Leather, Slippers of Gold: The History of a Lesbian Community,* New York, 1993.

McFadden, Margaret T. "America's Boy Friend Who Can't Get a Date: Gender, Race, and the Cultural Work of the Jack Benny Program, 1932–1946," *Journal of American History,* vol. 80, no. 1 (June 1993):113–34.

May, Elaine Tyler. *Homeward Bound: American Families in the Cold War Era,* New York, 1988.

Meyerowitz, Joann, ed. *Not June Cleaver: Women and Gender in Postwar America,* Philadelphia, 1994.

Rupp, Leila J., and Verta Taylor. *Survival in the Doldrums: The American Women's Rights Movement, 1945 to the 1960s,* Columbus, Ohio, 1990.

Timmons, Stuart. *The Trouble with Harry Hay: Founder of the Modern Gay Movement,* Boston, 1990.

Warren, Carol B. *Madwives: Schizophrenic Women in the 1950s,* New Brunswick, N.J., 1987.

Weiner, Lynn. "Reconstructing Motherhood: The La Leche League in Postwar America," *Journal of American History,* vol. 80, no. 4 (March 1994):1357–81.

Gender in Revolution, 1963–Present

By the 1960s, it was clear that traditional gender ideology could no longer contain changing social roles and structures. While men continued to struggle with the lack of autonomy and disincentives to creativity that characterized large bureaucratic organizations (both military and civilian), women gained new independence through increased labor force participation and higher education. Later marriages and fewer children afforded women more time and energy for pursuing careers or activities outside the house. Families were also reshaped, as the proportion of two-parent households declined and more women lived alone or headed their own households.

As the previous section indicates, some of these trends had been visible by the late fifties—*before* the emergence of the protest movements of the sixties and early seventies. But it was the movements for women's liberation and gay and lesbian rights that gave voice to the glaring contradictions between rhetoric and reality, challenging the values that underlay the American gender system and presenting new visions of how women and men might live—both separately and together—in American society.

Though each of these movements had its own sources, social location, ideology, and set of claims, their roots were also deeply entwined and had links to other political mobilizations of the day. Many of the founders of women's liberation had cut their political teeth in the civil rights movement; feminists, in turn, lent support to gay liberation; and lesbian feminists became affiliated with both groups. A majority of gender activists also considered themselves to be part of the antiwar movement. At times, all the groups blurred into one, the "New Left"; to those for whom activism had become a way of life, it was simply "the movement."

The driving force of the movement came from the "baby boom" generation; now college students and young adults, they had grown up in relative affluence and attended college as a matter of course. But they were not too comfortable to acknowledge the persistent gap between rich and poor pointed out by sociologist Michael Harrington in his startling 1962 report, *The Other America*. One fifth of all

Americans (30 million), including African Americans, Latinos/Latinas, Native Americans, rural and urban alike, lived below the poverty line. Class inequality, along with racial and gender oppression, became one of the enduring themes of movement politics.

The "discovery of poverty" not only energized the New Left but also led to the crafting of government programs on a scale that had not been seen since the New Deal. John F. Kennedy had begun to address this issue during his truncated presidency, but it was Lyndon B. Johnson who launched a full-scale "War on Poverty," initiating dozens of innovative programs costing billions of dollars. Though he failed to eradicate poverty, LBJ left a significant legislative legacy to America's disadvantaged in the form of Head Start, Medicaid, Medicare, and the Food Stamp program, as well as the Civil Rights Act of 1964 and the Voting Rights Act of 1965.

Despite these dramatic efforts on the part of liberal Democratic administrations, throughout the sixties the movement gained in momentum and militancy. How can we explain this? Many sociologists argue that liberalism often spawns radicalism by creating space on its left for oppositional politics and also by raising expectations. Indeed, the mood during these heady days was one of infinite possibility. But optimism turned to anger with the assassinations of Dr. Martin Luther King, Jr. and Malcolm X, precipitating a shift from the nonviolent tactics of the civil rights movement to "Black Power." Similarly, the persistence of a war they regarded as morally reprehensible drove a minority of antiwar activists "underground." Others succumbed to the counterculture, with its "back-to-nature" antimaterialism and invitations to experiment with sexuality and drugs; for this group, politics now took the form of "lifestyle protest."

It came as a shock to many activists that not all Americans shared their values or were eager to refashion society from the ground up. As the movement reached the peak of its power, its members encountered opposition from forces just as determined and often better mobilized than they: the "New Right."

Like its left-wing counterpart, the New Right was composed of multiple groups organized around specific issues, most of them oppositional. The right took on court-ordered busing, compulsory school integration, anti-poverty programs and government expansion. Defending traditional gender roles, conservatives targeted feminist issues such as abortion rights, child care, and affirmative action. They vociferously condemned homosexuality as "unnatural," citing Biblical texts as their authority. And claiming a monopoly on "the American way," they characterized the antiwar movement as unpatriotic.

With the election of Richard M. Nixon in 1968, right and left became increasingly polarized, and backlash set in. Riding the wave of antitax, antigovernment sentiment, a series of Republican presidents systematically dismantled most of LBJ's "Great Society" programs and undermined many of the gains made by the women's movement, including abortion rights and antidiscrimination legislation. With the political spectrum shifted to the right, only two moderate Democrats, Jimmy Carter and Bill Clinton, have been able to win the Presidency since the 1960s.

Older, sobered, and somewhat more willing to work with the system rather than against it, many on the left hoped that Clinton, despite his centrist platform, would turn the political tide. But they have been sadly disappointed. While upholding the principle of affirmative action, Clinton has ended welfare entitlements for the poor and limited the rights of homosexuals in the military. Among the most vocal of Clinton's left-wing critics have been feminists, who decried "welfare reform" as an attack on women, and gay and lesbian liberationists, who see danger in the policy of "don't ask, don't tell." Though much of the movement has dispersed, feminists, gays, and lesbians have remained mobilized, with much work still to be done.

FIGURE 11.1
Antiwar demonstrators clashed with police in Chicago during the 1968 Democratic
Convention. Many versions of manhood met during those protests. (*Source: Warren K.
Leffler, U.S. News and World Report Magazine Collection, LC-U9-19773, frame 24, Prints
and Photographs Division, Library of Congress, Washington, D.C.*)

CHAPTER 11

Gender and Protest

The social contradictions that had been brewing beneath the surface of the fifties burst forth in the sixties. Millions of Americans—black and white, Mexican American and Indian American, young and old, male and female—protested against racism, economic exploitation, and war, against the dehumanization advanced by bureaucratic institutions and mass culture. With the movement for racial justice always in the lead, most of these efforts to reform American society and government initially took the form of nonviolent protest. By mid-decade, however, many protest organizations split as some members chose to take up arms against injustice.

We might divide 1960s protest movements roughly into two groups: those demanding political change and those focused on cultural revolution. Political revolutionaries included those involved in the struggle for racial justice for African Americans, Mexican Americans, and American Indians. They also included members of Students for a Democratic Society (SDS) and the antiwar movement. While each movement had a distinctive agenda and set of tactics, all strove in one way or another for self-determination, understood as taking power back from oppressive corporations, the government, schools, and the military.

Hippies represented the more exclusive focus on cultural revolution. Sporting unkempt hair, tie-dyed T-shirts, and necklaces of withering flowers, many young people rejected what they saw as the stultifying norms of bourgeois society: the nuclear family, corporate employment, and competitive consumerism. They wanted to replace the Cold War culture of the 1950s with peace and love. Seeking intense physical and spiritual experience as opposed to the deadening conformity they believed characteristic of the earlier decade, youth in the 1960s turned to hallucinogenic drugs, unfettered sex, and rock and roll. More young people participated at least tangentially in the cultural revolt of the 1960s than in organized political dissent.

Both cultural and political protesters pushed for dramatic change of one kind or another but ironically remained conservative on the issue of gender hierarchy. As you will see in the following documents, women who were risking their lives in the struggle for civil rights or who had clearly demonstrated leadership qualities in SDS or the antiwar movement had a hard time being recognized as leaders and often wound up taking the minutes and making the coffee at organizational meetings. The same was true in the Chicano movement that erupted a bit later in the decade.

If anything, many social movements became decreasingly hospitable to women over the course of the decade. As the war in Vietnam escalated after 1965, and the antiwar movement with it, young war-resisting men feared their manhood was being compromised by their defiance of both the corporate work ethic and military service, two pillars of post-war American manhood. Their search for manly identity led some to emphasize unbounded sexual experience and dominance over women as foundations of their manhood. We see this strikingly in the common war resisters' motto: "Girls say yes to guys who say no." The same direction was evident in organizations where violence replaced nonviolence as an explicit tactic. Often, more militant tactics worked against the leadership and visibility of women.

Ultimately, experience in these movements led many women to initiate the second wave of feminism. Indications of that direction are evident even in the documents in this chapter, which seeks to illustrate the gender division of labor and confusion about gender in several movement organizations.

THEY WERE NOT TAKING ORDERS FROM WOMEN
Jessie Lopez de la Cruz

The 1960s movement for self-determination among Mexican Americans began in the fruit and vegetable fields of California. There, in 1962, union organizer César Chávez began urging rural workers to join the Farm Workers Association (later the United Farm Workers, AFL-CIO). Once organized, he insisted, farm laborers could demand better pay, housing, and work conditions, which had not changed substantially since Jessie Lopez de la Cruz began her career in the fields during the 1930s.

The farm workers' cause soon spread beyond the grape and lettuce ranches of California. In addition to organizing strikes among workers, the United Farm Workers (UFW) mobilized consumer boycotts against products raised on targeted farms. To get families all over the United States to stop buying nonunion grapes and lettuce, organizers often spoke to housewives, encouraging women of all ethnicities to see the public power inherent in their roles as consumers. Not since the early twentieth century, when the National Consumers' League raised women's consciousness about the public power of purchasing had consumption taken on such explicit, national political implications.

Source: Jessie Lopez de la Cruz interview with Ellen Cantarow. Reprinted by permission of The Feminist Press at The City University of New York, from Ellen Cantarow with Susan Gushee O'Malley and Sharon Hartman Strom, *Moving the Moutain: Women Working for Social Change.* Copyright ©1980 by Ellen Cantarow, Susan Gushee O'Malley, and Sharon Hartman Strom, pp. 134, 136–37, 141–43.

Moreover, the ethnic consciousness built by the UFW swept into the barrios of cities in the Southwest, where a younger generation of Mexican Americans began to call themselves Chicanos and to speak of La Raza as a people oppressed and ripe for liberation. They campaigned, among other things, for improved education, better housing, access to political power, humane immigration and naturalization laws, and the creation of Chicano studies programs on college campuses.

Lopez de la Cruz, first introduced in Chapter 8, was among the earliest of Chávez's converts to unionism. She enthusiastically took on the role of union organizer. How does the following interview with Lopez de la Cruz illuminate gender struggles in the early union as well as the gender division of labor in the fields?

But then late one night in 1962, there was a knock at the door and there were three men. One of them was César Chávez. And the next thing I knew, they were sitting around our table talking about a union for the farmworkers. Arnold [de la Cruz's husband] had already told me about a union for the farmworkers. He was attending their meetings in Fresno, but I didn't. I'd either stay home or stay outside in the car. But then César said, "The women have to be involved. They're the ones working out in the fields with their husbands. If you can take the women out to the fields, you can certainly take them to meetings." So I sat up straight and said to myself, "*That's* what I want!"

When I became involved with the union, I felt I had to get other women involved. . . . Then some women I spoke to started attending the union meetings, and later they were out on the picket lines. . . .

It was very hard being a woman organizer. Many of our people my age and older were raised with the old customs in Mexico: where the husband rules, he is king of his house. The wife obeys, and the children, too. So when we first started it was very, very hard. Men gave us the most trouble—neighbors there in Parlier [,California]! They were for the union, but they were not taking orders from women, they said. When they formed the ranch committee at Christian Brothers—that's a big wine company, part of it is in Parlier—the ranch committee was all men.[*] We were working under our first contract in Fresno County. The ranch committee had to enforce the contract. If there are any grievances they meet with us and the supervisors. But there were no women on the first committee.

That year, we'd have a union meeting every week. Men, women and children would come. Women would ask questions and the men would just stand back. I guess they'd say to themselves, "I'll wait for someone to say something before I do." The women were more aggressive than the men. And I'd get up and say, "Let's go on, let's do it!"

When the first contract was up, we talked about there being no women on the ranch committee. I suggested they be on it, and the men went along with this. And so women were elected.

The women took the lead for picketing [at selected grocery stores], and we would talk to the people. It got to the point that we would have to find them, because the men just wouldn't go and they wouldn't take their wives. So we would say,

---

[*]On every farm, the union created a ranch committee elected by the workers. The committee is the grass-roots base of the union. If you have an on-the-job complaint, you bring it to the ranch committee, which then discusses the complaint with the supervisor. . . .

"We're having our picket line at the Safeway in Fresno, and those that don't show up are going to have to pay a five-dollar fine." We couldn't have four or five come to a picket line and have the rest stay home and watch tv. In the end, we had everybody out there[†]. . . .

In '68, while we were in Parlier, I was put in charge of the hiring hall. My house was right next to the office, and I had an extension to the office phone in my house. I could do the housework and take care of the children, but I could take care of the office, too. Before the contract, the hiring hall was just a union office, where people came to learn about the union. When they got the first contracts, we began dispatching people out to work.

It was up to me to get all the membership cards in order alphabetically. When the grower came to us to ask for workers, I'd look for the ones who were in the union longest, and also working under the Christian Brothers contract. I'd call them: "Can you be ready Monday or Wednesday morning? Be there on time, because you're going to start working for Christian Brothers." One of the things we had to explain over and over to people who had been working for a ranch many years was that no one was going to take their jobs away. The growers told them, "If you sign up for Chávez's union we'll fire you." But the union contract guarantees that the people working here have the right to stay here, so we always made a list of names of people who were working at the ranch. And when the union organizes them, they have the highest seniority, they're the first ones hired.

The hiring hall was also a place where people could meet and talk. A lot of people were migrants who needed to get to know each other. The people who were there all the time [permanent workers] were against the migrants. I said, "We have to get these people together. We can't be divided." I was at the hall all day. People would drop by and I'd introduce them.

The second year we had a contract I started working for Christian Brothers. The men were doing the pruning on the grape vines. After they did the pruning, the women's crew would come and tie the vines—that was something we got changed. We made them give pruning jobs to women.

I was made a steward on the women's crew. If there were any grievances, it was up to me to listen and then enforce the contract. For example, the first time we were paid when I started working, during the break the supervisor would come out there with our checks. It was our fifteen-minute break, which the contract gave us the right to. He always came then! We had to walk to the other end of the row; it took us about five minutes to get there, the rest of the fifteen to get our checks, and walk back, and we'd start working. This happened twice. The third time I said, "We're not going to go after our checks this time. They always come during our break and we don't get to rest." So when we saw the pickup coming with the men who had the checks I said, "Nobody move. You just sit here." I walked over to the pickup. I said to the man inside, "Mr. Rager, these women refuse to come out here on their break time. It's their time to rest. So we're asking you, if you must come during our rest period, you take the checks to these ladies." From that day on, every payday he would come to us. That was the sort of thing you had to do to enforce the contract.

[†]The picket lines at the Safeway chain were set up to keep consumers from shopping at a store that sold nonunion grapes. The picket lines at the ranches were set up to keep workers from working.

LAUGHABLE TO MOST
Mary King

The struggle for racial justice among African Americans represented the prototypical political movement of the 1960s. Building on a century-long struggle that picked up considerable momentum during World War II, the civil rights movement of the early 1960s strove to turn back Jim Crow and the disenfranchisement of black people in the South.

One of the most important civil rights associations in the 1960s was the Student Nonviolent Coordinating Committee (SNCC). Organized in 1960 by activist college students in the South, SNCC sought through nonviolent direct action (such as sit-ins and freedom rides) to end segregation and through voter registration drives to empower southern black people in electoral politics. During the early 1960s, black and white women and men participated in these dangerous campaigns, suffering illegitimate jail terms, brutal beatings, and even death at the hands of those who would stop at nothing to maintain white supremacy.

Mary King and Casey Hayden were two of the white women who worked for SNCC in the early 1960s. For a staff retreat in 1964, they anonymously prepared the following position paper. According to this document, what was the particular gender hierarchy operating in this organization explicitly devoted to equality and empowerment?

SNCC POSITION PAPER, NOVEMBER 1964
(Name withheld by Request)

1. Staff was involved in crucial constitutional revisions at the Atlanta staff meeting in October. A large committee was appointed to present revisions to the staff. The committee was all men.
2. Two organizers were working together to form a farmers league. Without asking any questions, the male organizer immediately assigned the clerical work to the female organizer although both had had equal experience in organizing campaigns.
3. Although there are women in the Mississippi project who have been working as long as some of the men, the leadership group in COFO [Council of Federated Organizations] is all men.
4. A woman in a field office wondered why she was held responsible for day-to-day decisions, only to find out later that she had been appointed project director but not told.
5. A fall 1964 personnel and resources report on Mississippi projects lists the number of people in each project. The section on Laurel, however, lists not the number of persons but "three girls."
6. One of SNCC's main administrative officers apologizes for appointment of a woman as interim project director in a key Mississippi project area.
7. A veteran of two years' work for SNCC in two states spends her day typing and doing clerical work for other people in her project.

Source: [Mary King and Casey Hayden], "SNCC Position Paper, November 1964," in Mary King, *Freedom Song: A Personal Story of the 1960s Civil Rights Movement* (New York: William Morrow, 1987), pp. 567–69.

8. Any woman in SNCC, no matter what her position or experience, has been asked to take minutes in a meeting when she and other women are outnumbered by men.

9. The names of several new attorneys entering a state project this past summer were posted in a central movement office. The first initial and last name of each lawyer was listed. Next to one name was written: (girl).

10. Capable, responsible, and experienced women who are in leadership positions can expect to have to defer to a man on their project for final decision making.

11. A session at the recent October staff meeting in Atlanta was the first large meeting in the past couple of years where a woman was asked to chair.

Undoubtedly this list will seem strange to some, petty to others, laughable to most. The list could continue as far as there are women in the movement. Except that most women don't talk about these kinds of incidents, because the whole subject is not discussable—strange to some, petty to others, laughable to most.

The average white person finds it difficult to understand why the Negro resents being called "boy," or being thought of as "musical" and "athletic," because the average white person doesn't realize that *he assumes he is superior.* And naturally he doesn't understand the problem of paternalism. So too the average SNCC worker finds it difficult to discuss the woman problem because of the assumption of male superiority. Assumptions of male superiority are as widespread and deep-rooted and every much as crippling to the woman as the assumptions of white superiority are to the Negro. Consider why it is in SNCC that women who are competent, qualified, and experienced are automatically assigned to the "female" kinds of jobs such as: typing, desk work, telephone work, filing, library work, cooking, and the assistant kind of administrative work but rarely the "executive" kind.

The woman in SNCC is often in the same position as that token Negro hired in a corporation. The management thinks that it has done its bit. Yet, every day the Negro bears an atmosphere, attitudes, and actions which are tinged with condescension and paternalism, the most telling of which are seen when he is not promoted as the equally or less skilled whites are.

This paper is anonymous. Think about the kinds of things the authors, if made known, would have to suffer because of raising this kind of discussion. Nothing so final as being fired or outright exclusion, but the kinds of things which are killing to the insides—insinuations, ridicule, overexaggerated compensations.

This paper is presented anyway because it needs to be made known that many women in the movement are not "happy and contented" with their status. It needs to be made known that much talent and experience are being wasted by this movement, when women are not given jobs commensurate with their abilities. It needs to be known that just as Negroes were the crucial factor in the economy of the cotton South, so too in SNCC, women are the crucial factor that keeps the movement running on a day-to-day basis. Yet they are not given equal say-so when it comes to day-to-day decision-making.

What can be done? Probably nothing right away. Most men in this movement are probably too threatened by the possibility of serious discussion on this subject. Perhaps this is because they have recently broken away from a matriarchal framework under which they may have grown up. Then, too, many women are as unaware and insensitive to this subject as men, just as there are many Negroes who don't understand they are not free or who want to be part of white America. They don't understand that they have to give up their souls and stay in their place to be accepted. So, too, many women, in order to be accepted by men, on men's terms, give themselves up to that caricature of what a woman is—unthinking, pliable, an ornament to please the man.

Maybe the only thing that can come out of this paper is discussion—amidst the laughter—but still discussion. (Those who laugh the hardest are often those who need the crutch of male supremacy the most.) And maybe some women will begin to recognize day-to-day discriminations. And maybe sometime in the future the whole of the women in this movement will become so alert as to force the rest of the movement to stop the discrimination and start the slow process of changing values and ideas so that all of us gradually come to understand that this is no more a man's world than it is a white world.

NOT SURE OF MY ROLE
Mike Hoffman

In the same year that SNCC formed, Robert "Al" Haber, a graduate student at the University of Michigan, revitalized an old leftist student organization and renamed it Students for a Democratic Society (SDS). This heir to turn-of-the-century American socialism attempted to coordinate student protest movements on northern college campuses. Led by men, this organization of the New Left nonetheless invited the participation of young women, many of whom developed a commitment to community organizing, democratic participation, and the empowerment of submerged groups in American society and the world.

Like so many other protest organizations, SDS grew phenomenally during the mid-1960s and then factionalized later in the decade. In 1964, it reported 27 campus chapters and 1,200 members; by 1966, it claimed 151 chapters; and in 1968, 100,000 members. Membership grew in conjunction with the escalation of the Vietnam War between 1965 and 1968. Having begun the decade focused on issues of poverty and racism, the movement became associated overwhelmingly with antiwar protest. Eventually one splinter group, Weatherman, decided to eschew nonviolence and go "underground" in order to wage violent assaults on what they saw as the U.S. war machine. By 1971, SDS no longer had a national presence.

Initially, SDS rejected both communism and corporate liberalism as they existed in the postwar world. Both of these political economies seemed to create gigantic bureaucratic institutions that were racist, imperialist, and in every way hierarchical. They took power away from individuals and local communities, forcing everyone into molds that served the interests of the powerful elite. SDS enunciated a creed it believed subversive of this order. As revealed in the following poem by SDS member Mike Hoffman, however, these commitments left some young men wondering what it would mean to be a man in a world not dominated by corporate employment and television. What did Hoffman believe constituted manhood for the previous generation? Why could he not accept that version of manhood for himself?

Source: Mike Hoffman, "What's Offered?" *New Left Notes* 1 (April 22, 1966), p. 6.

I stand in a black hole
Sensing life and the world above
not sure of my role
feeling all emotions but love

Oft my niche was delegated
And always it I deluded
Not sure the role relegated
Not wishing to be deluded

At times I start to step
To be part of the stream
Then seeing who before leapt
My being wants to scream

Masses rushing from TV to debt
Not knowing themselves, least others
Nothing, but nothing, have they yet
Soon they'll not know their mothers.

To this I'm urged to join
To become a part of this life
Satisfying what I feel in my loins
To be a part of this eternal strife

Who I ask is the fool
I, for not embracing this pseudo life
When sheer quantity, not quality is the rule
And sex is equated with wife

Nowhere can one turn for protection
All is shadows and formless
All sensual, striving for permanent erection
This life is killing and far from harmless

Having this day decided to go
Make my way, refusing to bank
And my own seed sow
Trying to be a man

A LOT OF MANHOOD EMERGED IN CHICAGO
Stewart Albert

The year 1968 stood as the high point of the decade's protest and anti-protest. In April, Dr. Martin Luther King, Jr. was assassinated, sparking race riots in major cities all over the country. That same month, students shut down Columbia University. In June, presidential candidate Robert Kennedy was assassinated, and two months later police riots tore apart the Democratic National Convention in Chicago. To some, the United States seemed to be teetering on the brink of violent disintegration.

Source: Stewart Albert, "Chicago Retrospective," *Berkeley Barb* 7 (September 6–12, 1968), p. 9.

One group that participated joyfully in the mayhem was the Youth International Party, members of which were called YIPpies. Led by Jerry Rubin (1938–1994) and Abbie Hoffman (1936–1989), Yippies bridged the cultural and political revolt of the 1960s. They advocated illicit drugs as aids in creating an alternative to the stultifying effect of mass society, and they used wacky street theater to highlight the absurdities and baseness of corporate capitalism. During the 1968 Democratic Convention, they staged a Festival of Life in Lincoln Park while other groups soberly demonstrated closer to convention headquarters.

The following article reports experiences at the convention from a YIPpie perspective. During the convention, while delegates in the Hilton Hotel battled over the party's position on the Vietnam War, Chicago police gassed and clubbed thousands of demonstrators who had flocked to Chicago in hopes of pushing the Democratic Party to nominate antiwar candidate Senator Eugene McCarthy and/or include an antiwar plank in the platform. They were disappointed in every hope. How does the author of the following article define YIPpie manhood? How does his language effectively erase women from the scene in Chicago and even from the history of protest?

> In Chicago, teargas was a very democratic experience. On the last two nights, it impartially choked throats of Yippies, Women for Peace, TV cameramen, and even some delegates to the Democratic Convention.
>
> The moderate forces tried to lead orderly marches on the sidewalk policed by monitors who must have taken a semester of piggery at some academy. Dick Gregory made an appearance, as did Eugene McCarthy, but it served for nothing.
>
> Richard Daley saw every demonstrator in Chicago as Ho Chi Minh with a reefer in his mouth, out to rape his daughter.
>
> The marches were broken up by teargas, rifle-butts (the National Guard occasionally joining the pigs), and nightsticks. We all went back into the streets, breaking store windows, throwing rocks at cops and tossing garbage.
>
> The action centered around the heavily guarded Hilton Hotel, in which the delegates hoped to avoid any contact with Chicago.
>
> It did not work. The teargas seeped through the airconditioning and even Hubert Humphrey got sick and had to take a bath.
>
> The teargas scenes were grotesque—people running, vomiting, burning, choking and praying for some decency that it all stop.
>
> Chicago was a revolutionary wet-dream come true. One night a thousand longhairs joined at the picket-line of striking black bus drivers. On the following night, striking cab-drivers left a picket-line to join the march on the Amphitheatre. The white working-class motorcycle gangs . . . were either free neutrals or with us in Lincoln Park.
>
> What happened that week [in Chicago] was the prototypical formation of the alliance necessary to bring the man down and keep him down. It all happened without a single leaflet being given to anyone and without a single white missionary getting a factory job.
>
> This wasn't the way I was told it would happen. The catechism of orthodox American Leninism is to shave off your beard, get a haircut and stop smoking pot. A revolutionary act is to give leaflets to dockworkers.[1]

---

[1]SDS had in the summer of 1968 suggested that members get summer jobs in factories in order to participate in and perhaps help to spark revolution among workers.

The Progressive Labor Party, for example, sends its best people into factories and they recruit a couple of new members each year—and we are the dropout freaks doing everything we were not supposed to do, out on the same rock—throwing things as the workers, and not a single Freddy in sight.

We must realize that the fragmentation dumb-dumbs of repression fired at us in Chicago finally explode in the paycheck prisons of nine-to-five average America.

The best way we can push the workers into revolution is not by sharing in their factory slavery but by creating our own liberated communities in every major city.

We will constantly confront the man in the battle for the street, parks and living space needed for us to humanize in. Occasionally we must interrupt the pigs' highest ceremonies by dumping a huge pile of shit on their best rug.

We did this in Chicago, and maybe we can follow it up at Richard Nixon's inauguration. It is nothing like going into the man's churches on his high holy days barefooted and smelly, to make him fire his Madison Avenue front group and show off his southern sheriff soul to NBC.

It is by our example of rebellion that we will steer the workers into realizing their own dreams. We won't do it by collapsing before the mediocratic clean-shaven alcoholic conformities and telling the prolies to read this after they have read that.

We found out in Chicago that the military man of imperialism might have at least one clay foot. There were 43 soldiers at Fort Hood who refused to come to Chicago. The National Guard obeyed orders, but they had faces and not pig-snouts. We went up and down the line telling them not to let their officers kick them around and to behave with more humanity than the Russians did in Prague. The reaction was one of embarrassed presence and rationalization. There were few true believers in the crowd.

At first, our own reaction was one of terror and frenzied running. Then a more confident move-just-as-far-back-as-you-have-to walk, and finally the discovery that tear gas cannisters could be hurled back and a cop-car taken out of action if enough people surrounded it. A lot of manhood emerged in Chicago, and for that we must be ironically grateful to the Democratic Party.

Our revolution is going to be a chaotic, funky mud type of thing, not fitting any Germanic isms of somebody else's historical necessity. It is being made in the streets right now. On its appearance, you laugh with joy at its absolute originality.

In Chicago, it was a street-tough with a swastika tattooed on his arm, waving an NLF flag and giving skin to a Blackstone Ranger who had just called for the overthrow of the government. It was a Cleveland suit-and-tie sociologist belting out a pig.

It was a bloodied NBC photographer telling us the National Guard was coming and where there were rocks to throw at them. It was bearded OM-ing hippies breaking windows of scabbing buses.

And finally, it was a busload of ten-year-old black children exchanging revolutionary fists and victory signs with me, and the proud look on the face of an on-looking, and saluting black woman.

Our revolution is a movable feast. You can sup of it wherever you make your scene. All it takes is the guts to be free.

A REAL MANHOOD IS BASED ON HUMANISM
Bobby Seale

Among those demonstrators arrested in the aftermath of the Democratic Convention was Bobby Seale (1936–), a leader in the Black Panther Party (BPP). The BPP formed in 1966, when Seale and his friend, Huey P. Newton (1942–1989), drafted a ten-point program defining economic and social justice for all of America's oppressed. Headquartered in Oakland, California, the BPP soon opened chapters in cities all over the United States. The emergence and popularity of the BPP epitomized changes in protest movements generally in the late 1960s.

The central goals of the early civil rights movement seemed to have been met when Congress passed the Civil Rights Act in 1964 and the Voting Rights Act in 1965. The former ended segregation in public facilities and forbade racial discrimination in employment; the latter sought to end disenfranchisement. But stopping legal discrimination could not wipe out social and political inequities that rested on economic inequality between black people and white. Beginning in 1964, urban riots in the North reminded all Americans that racial injustice was built into institutions other than the law.

In the wake of these riots and the savage repression that met all antiracist activism in the United States, many black activists gave up on integration as the goal and nonviolence as the method of their movement. Believing that violence must be met with violence, some finally "picked up the gun." According to one male militant, to remain nonviolent in the face of murderous assaults "was odious to us and I personally thought it was a challenge to my manhood." The very tactic of nonviolence, then, had become for some a betrayal of manly identity.

The Black Power movement that in 1966 began to grow away from the nonviolent, integrationist civil rights movement emphasized pride in blackness and encouraged black people to give up on acceptance by whites. The goal of the liberation struggle should instead be to free black people from white domination in the United States and in every part of the globe. Black Power advocates offered support to groups striving to overthrow European and American imperialism all over the world.

The Black Panther Party, though it appealed to black nationalist groups in its rejection of nonviolence, was not itself a nationalist group. Under the leadership of Newton and Seale, the BPP shared the New Left's analysis of oppression, believing that all oppressed people—of every color—must unite to overthrow capitalism. Capitalism was the enemy; not white people per se. In their opposition to capitalism, Panthers adopted Marxist rhetoric as well as concepts, for instance, labelling economic classes as bourgeois or proletarian.

In the following excerpts from Bobby Seale's autobiography, we see a complicated definition of Panther manhood that included not only the willingness to use violence in the struggle for liberation but also a commitment to practical social services such as free breakfasts for poor children and political education for urban youth. What set of characteristics did Seale believe constituted Panther manhood?

Source: Bobby Seale, *Seize the Time: The Story of the Black Panther Party and Huey P. Newton* (New York: Random House, 1970), pp. 34, 64–65, 102–3, 105, 368–69, 380, 401–3.

How did he expect Panther men to treat Panther women? What versions of manhood were the Panthers fighting, according to Seale? Did all recruits to the BPP share Seale's definition of manhood? Finally, how did Seale's version of manhood compare with that of Henry MacNeal Turner (Chapter 2) or W.E.B. DuBois (Chapter 5)?

Huey and I . . . talked and emphasized the necessity of arming the people with guns. The cultural nationalists and many of the leading white liberals, they look at it like, "You can't pick up guns." . . . But Huey said, "No, you must pick up guns, because guns are key." . . .

Huey wanted brothers off the block [for the Party]—brothers who had been out there robbing banks, brothers who had been pimping, brothers who had been peddling dope, brothers who ain't gonna take no shit, brothers who had been fighting pigs—because . . . Huey P. Newton knew that once you organize those brothers, you get niggers, you get black men, you get revolutionaries who are too much. . . .

When we started passing the platform around the poverty center there [in Oakland], . . . [people would] ask, "Why do you want to be a vicious animal like a panther?"

Huey would break in. "The nature of a panther is that he never attacks. But if anyone attacks him or backs him into a corner, the panther comes up to wipe that aggressor or that attacker out, absolutely, resolutely, wholly, thoroughly, and completely." . . .

So Huey [also] organized what he called a Junior Panther group. He would never let these young brothers come into the office, because we always had guns in the office at Fifty-sixth and Grove. He said we were going to set up a place—one of the churches maybe—where we could teach them some Black history and some revolutionary principles. . . . These young brothers began at twelve, thirteen, or fourteen. Junior Panthers. Everyone from sixteen years of age and up was treated like a man. If he wasn't a man, he could get on out of the Party.

Some [public school] teachers got together and said that Huey was teaching young kids to use *guns.* They lied to the parents. Huey didn't let kids in the office. He didn't let them in because we had guns there. He told them they had to learn Black history and revolutionary principles and grow up to be men, and defend their people in the black community.

Another problem at that time [early in the BPP history] was that the brothers identified *only* with the gun. When we started the Party, Huey and I didn't have any intention of having them identify only with the gun. We knew that we had to teach them that the gun was only a tool and it must be used by a mind that thinks. When we first started out, the very first members had to go to political education classes. Included was one hour of field stripping of weapons, safety and cleaning of weapons in the home, etc. Then we had one or two hours of righteous political education and study. The third area was work, coordinating various activities, and understanding the political significance of various actions we took, like . . . when we went to the sheriffs' office and tried to enter armed with guns, along with community people, to protest murder and police brutality. . . .

A true revolutionary will get up early in the morning and he'll go serve the Free Breakfast for Children. Then when that's done he'll go and he'll organize a boycott around a specific issue, to support Breakfast for Children, or support any other kind of program [that serves the community]. He'll do revolutionary work in the community. He'll propagandize the community, he'll pass out leaflets. As a citizen in the community and a member of the Black Panther Party, he'll go to the firing range

FIGURE 11.2
This image of Huey P. Newton, co-founder of the Black Panther Party, became a familiar sight in the late 1960s. What aspects of Panther manhood did this visual image emphasize? Did this image in any way contradict the sort of manhood that Bobby Seale prescribed in his autobiography? (*Source: Courtesy of the Huey P. Newton Foundation, Inc.*)

and take firing practice, but he'll follow all the gun laws and he won't conceal his weapon, or other jive stuff. He'll follow the rules and be very dedicated. He is constantly trying to politically educate himself about the revolutionary principles and how they function, to get a broad perspective. He'll also defend himself and his people when we're unjustly attacked by racist pigs. . . .

The problems between the brothers and sisters relate to past conditioning. In a situation where a brother and sister are lying beside each other, past social conditioning has taught that brother that he can use force on the sister, and take her without caring about her feelings in the matter. Now the brother must learn that he has no right to use any kind of force on that sister. . . .

We had to make more rules in the Party because a number of . . . incidents came up. One of those rules was that the brothers had better not use any force on any sister in the Party. It hasn't been all smooth and easy, getting these rules across. A year and a half ago, when this started, it even got to the point where a sister was hit by a brother. She fell back and her heel was cut by a piece of glass that broke when she fell on it. It was a struggle to stop this kind of thing.

When the sister was previously regulated [sic] to typing and cooking and stuff like this, we broke up those roles in the Party. That was a struggle, too. We even had to deal with the way brothers talked to sisters, because every once in a while we'd catch a brother talking to a sister in such a harsh manner that it really scared her, enough so she'd do anything he said. The sisters brought these complaints up, and we told the brothers, "We're tired of that. We're not going to have that in the Party." . . .

In our Party, the sister is not told to stay home. If she's got a job, they take all the babies over to one house and one person, male or female, takes care of them all. We do that quite often, for the sisters who have children. Then of course there's the Liberation School, which brothers and sisters run; and sisters have to learn to shoot just as well as brothers. . . .

These principles came from Huey. Huey has always talked about the fact that he believed in equality for men and women. You'll find some women's organizations that are working strictly in the capitalist system. But the very nature of the capitalistic system is to exploit and enslave people, all people. So we have to progress to a level of socialism to solve these problems. We have to *live* socialism.

So where there's a Panther house, we try to live it. When there's cooking to be done, both brothers and sisters cook. Both wash the dishes. The sisters don't just serve and wait on the brothers. A lot of black nationalist organizations have the idea of regulating [sic] women to the role of serving their men, and they relate this to black manhood. But a real manhood is based on humanism, and it's not based on *any* form of oppression.

MALE CHAUVINISM AND ALL OF ITS MANIFESTATIONS ARE BOURGEOIS
Panther Sisters

As Bobby Seale's autobiography suggested, sexism and violence against women sometimes marked the efforts of the Black Panther Party in its earliest years—as they did many protest organizations in the 1960s. By 1969, however, women in the Party were forcing discussion of this form of oppression, and during the mid-1970s, Elaine Brown (1943–) took over leadership of the Party.

In fact, women occupied many positions of authority within the BPP during its stormy history. Some commentators insist that the increasing absence of male leadership due to incarceration or exile opened doors for female leadership in the 1970s. Moreover, although Panther women joined men in self-defense training, women seemed especially attracted to the Party's social services: alternative schools, health care, and programs for senior citizens. During the 1970s and early 1980s, women maintained these services despite harassment from law enforcement officials, declining support from white allies, and battles within the Panther leadership itself.

In 1969, the Panther newspaper published an interview with several unnamed Panther women. Excerpts from that interview follow. What do you make of the anonymity of these interviewees? How does their analysis of women's oppression compare or contrast with that of SNCC's King and Hayden in 1964? How does their representation of women's roles in the BPP compare or contrast with Seale's?

Editorial Note:
    Within the Movement, debate rages over organizational and political strategy for the women's liberation movement. This debate rarely includes the ideas of black women. So we rapped with six women, members of the Black Panther Party, about some of the issues raised by the women's liberation movement and their own ex-

Source: "Sisters," *The Black Panther,* 3 (September 13, 1969), (special section). *Underground Newspaper Collection,* reel 16-1, Bell and Howell, Wooster, Ohio.

perience with women's liberation inside the Black Panther Party. (Technical note: A large space between paragraphs means that a different sister is speaking.)

MOVEMENT: How has the position of women within the Black Panther Party changed? How have the women in the Party dealt with male chauvinism within the Party?

PANTHER WOMEN: . . . There used to be a difference in the roles (of men and women) in the party because sisters were relegated to certain duties. This was due to backwardness and lack of political perspective on the part of both sisters and brothers. Like sisters would just naturally do the office-type jobs, the clerical-type jobs. They were the ones that handled the mailing list. You know all those things that go into details. They were naturally given to the sisters and because of this, because the sisters accepted it so willingly because they had been doing this before, this is the type of responsibilities they've had before, it was very easy for male chauvinism to continue on. The only examples we had of sisters taking responsibility were probably in Kathleen [Cleaver] or one or two people who exercised responsibility in other areas of Party work.

We've recognized in the past 4 or 5 months that sisters have to take a more responsible role. They have to extend their responsibility and it shouldn't be just to detail work, to things women normally do. This, I think, has been manifested in the fact that a lot of sisters have been writing more articles, they're attending more to the political aspects of the Party, they're speaking out in public more and we've even done outreach work in the community, extensive outreach work in that we've taken the initiative to start our own schools—both brothers and sisters now work in the liberation schools. It's been proven that positions aren't relegated to sex, it depends on your political awareness.

I can remember that when I came into the Party over a year ago at that time David Hilliard was National Headquarters Captain, and there was another sister in the Party who was the National Captain for women and even though most of the people related to David Hilliard as being National HQ Captain, most of the women related to this other sister for directives because she was the National Captain for women. Under her were sergeants and lieutenants who were all sisters and in their ranks were other sisters. There was almost a separation between the brothers and the sisters.

When that was abolished, when there were no longer any separate positions for sisters and brothers, when we all had to relate to the brothers or sisters who were in specific positions, there wasn't just a reaction on the part of certain brothers [but also on the part of the sisters]. . . .

And I can see since the time I joined the Party that the Party has undergone radical change in the direction of women leadership and emancipation of women. Even though Ericka Huggins provides us with a very good example, it's not so much Ericka and the realization that Ericka poses a strike (sic) example. It's the fact that the political consciousness and the political level of members of the Party have risen very much since I joined the Party and because of the fact that we're moving toward a proletarian revolution and because we have come to realize that male chauvinism and all its manifestations are bourgeois and that's one of the things we're fighting against. . . .

MOVEMENT: No, they [some women] say the movement doesn't deal with their special oppression.

PANTHER WOMEN: . . . I think that's one place where women who are already advanced are going to have to take a strong stand. The fact is because of objective conditions in this society women are more backwards, because of their positions in their home, or in school, even working women who are more exposed to what's happening in the world, are still relegated at home and to the family jobs to the children, etc., etc., and their perspective in terms of the world is more limited. So it's very important that women who are more advanced, who already understand revolutionary principles, go to them and explain it to them and struggle with them. We have to recognize that women are backwards politically and we have to struggle with them. And that can be a special role that revolutionary women can play.

. . . A revolution cannot be successful simply with the efforts of the men, because a woman plays such an integral role in society even though she is relegated to smaller, seemingly insignificant positions.

I think conditions outside the Party have forced us to realize that we have to get rid of male chauvinism. As Panthers, we cannot separate ourselves and divide ourselves and work as Pantherettes, and on the other hand have brothers work as Panthers and expect to present a United Front against Fascism or against the enemy or against outside forces. There has to be unity within the Party. We can't be divided on the basis of sex and we can't be divided on the basis of principles or anything.

Ericka [Huggins] became a good example because the pigs realized she was a revolutionary. Maybe we didn't realize that, in the sense that we thought about it at the time or brought her up as an example of a strong woman. But, I think the pigs realize that and this outside condition has forced us to realize that we can't operate as two halves, separate, apart from each other—we have to be united.

MOVEMENT: Black women are considered to be the most oppressed group in the US, as blacks and as women. That special oppression gives them a special, even vanguard role. Do you want to talk about that a little?

PANTHER WOMEN: I think, historically, even at this time, even for women in the Party, to say we want full share and full responsibility is kind of difficult and kind of touchy because of our society. Our men have been sort of castrated, you know. The responsibilities that they rightfully should have had before, were taken away from them—to take away their manhood. We've had to fight all of this before. Our men are constantly thinking or saying that maybe if we [women] assume a heavier role, a more responsible role, that this, in turn, will sort of take away their responsibility and it's such a touchy thing that we have to be very sure that the roles are evenly divided. . . .

I think it's important that within the context of that struggle that black men understand that their manhood is not dependent on keeping their black women subordinate to them because this is what bourgeois ideology has been trying to put into the black man and that's part of the special oppression of black women. Black women as generally a part of the poor people of the US, the working class, are more oppressed, as being black, they're superoppressed, and as being women they are sexually oppressed by men in general and by black men also. . . .

MOVEMENT: What are your ideas on the strategy for women's liberation in terms of separate women's organizations, the priority of women's liberation in relation to other issues like imperialism and racism?

PANTHER WOMEN: . . . To the extent that women's organizations don't address themselves to the class struggle or to national liberation struggles they are not really furthering the women's liberation movement, because in order for women to be truly emancipated in this country there's going to have to be a socialist revolution. . . .

RECOMMENDED READINGS

Brown, Angela D. "Black Panther Party." In *Black Women in America: An Historical Encyclopedia,* ed. Darlene Clark Hine. Brooklyn, 1993.

Brown, Elaine. *A Taste of Power: A Black Woman's Story.* New York, 1992.

Carson, Clayborne et al., eds. *Eyes on the Prize: America's Civil Rights Years.* New York, 1987.

———. *In Struggle: SNCC and the Black Awakening of the 1960s.* Cambridge, Mass., 1981.

Evans, Sara. *Personal Politics.* New York, 1979.

Freeman, Jo, ed. *Social Movements of the Sixties and Seventies.* New York, 1983.

Jenkins, J. Craig. *The Politics of Insurgency: The Farm Workers Movement in the 1960s.* New York, 1985.

Knapper, Karl. "Women and the Black Panther Party: An Interview with Angela Brown." 26, 1 *Socialist Review* (1996):25–67.

Majka, Linda C., and Theo J. Majka. *Farm Workers, Agribusiness, and the State.* Philadelphia, 1982.

Matusow, Allen J. *The Unraveling of America: A History of Liberalism in the 1960s.* New York, 1984.

McAdam, Doug. *Freedom Summer.* New York, 1988.

Rose, Margaret. " 'Woman Power Will Stop Those Grapes': Chicana Organizers and Middle-Class Female Supporters in the Farm Workers' Grape Boycott in Philadelphia, 1969–1970." *Journal of Women's History* 7 (Winter 1995):6–36.

Rothschild, Mary Aiken. *A Case of Black and White: Northern Volunteers and the Southern "Freedom Summers."* Westport, Conn., 1982.

Ruiz, Vicki L., and Susan Tiano, eds. *Women on the U.S.-Mexico Border: Responses to Change.* Boston, 1987.

Swerdlow, Amy. *Women Strike for Peace: Traditional Motherhood and Radical Politics in the 1960s.* Chicago, 1993.

The mountain-moving day is coming.
I say so, yet others doubt.
Only a while the mountain sleeps.
In the past
All mountains moved in fire,
Yet you may not believe it.
Oh man, this alone believe,
All sleeping women now will
                    awake and move.

Yosano Akiko, 1911*

FIGURE 12.1
The women's movement was not monolithic, but often divided along class, racial, and ethnic lines. In the early 1970s, Asian women at the University of California, Berkeley began to organize. They contacted other Asian women's groups in the Bay Area and across the country, started a journal, and held demonstrations like this one. *(Photograph by Nikki Arai, from Asian Women's Journal,* Asian Women *[Los Angeles: Asian Studies Center, University of California, Los Angeles, 1975], p. 1.)*

268

CHAPTER 12

Gender as Protest

Historians find it difficult to write about the movement known as "second-wave feminism" because it was so diffuse. Was there one movement or many? When did it start? When did it end? Which groups should be included? While the documents collected in this chapter offer no definitive answers to these questions, they are intended to suggest some of the many forms feminism (or, more properly, feminisms) assumed in the 1960s and 1970s. But they make no claim to being comprehensive, for many groups produced few written records and their activities are only now being captured in oral histories and interviews.

As we noted in Chapter 10, stirrings of gender unrest could be found in the 1950s in groups like La Leche League and the Daughters of Bilitis. Most historians, however, would argue that the momentum of second-wave feminism began building in 1962, when President Kennedy appointed his Commission on the Status of Women. Though somewhat hampered by its official trappings and moderate membership, the commission affirmed women's right to choose among life courses, pointed to social, cultural, and legal barriers to women's progress, and called for legislation and social policies that would open up educational and employment opportunities for women. With the formation of the "National Organization for Women" (NOW) in 1966, and its offshoot, the Women's Equity Action League (WEAL) in 1968, the struggle for equal rights for women continued.

The women who came of age politically in the New Left had a different vision of social change. Unlike equal rights or liberal feminists, they argued that legislation could not eliminate inequality because the sources of women's oppression lay buried much deeper in American society and culture. Socialist feminists, who attributed gender inequality to the combined effects of capitalism and "male chauvinism," called upon men as well as women to undergo "consciousness-raising" and work to transform the fundamental structures of American society. Radical feminists blamed patriarchy for women's oppression. Convinced that women and men were essentially different, they believed that the only solution was for women to withdraw from society and create separate communities.

Though both radical and socialist feminists tended to eschew formal organization, their ideas spread rapidly from one sector of American society to another. Soon theologians and nurses were scrutinizing the rhetoric and practices of their professions, Girl Scout leaders were revamping their manuals, and wage-earning women were demanding entry into "non-traditional" occupations such as firefighting and plumbing. But working-class women, women of color, and lesbians felt excluded by the "one-size-fits-all" notion of universal womanhood emanating from the women's movement. Through their own actions and rhetoric, they exposed its underlying white, middle-class, and heterosexual assumptions. Yet, despite multiple tensions within the movement, feminism has remained one of the most vital political legacies of the 1960s.

AN INVITATION TO ACTION
President's Commission on the Status of Women

The idea for convening a panel to investigate the status of women came from Esther Peterson, a longtime advocate for the rights of working women who was President Kennedy's choice for chief of the Women's Bureau. Eleanor Roosevelt was appointed chair of the President's Commission on the Status of Women (PCSW), but it was Peterson who directed its research and influenced the crafting of policy recommendations. Members included educators, lawyers, academics, and civic leaders.

The commission issued its report in 1963, the same year Betty Friedan published *The Feminist Mystique,* a startling exposé of mass-media efforts to brainwash American women into thinking that their only option was to play the role of wife and mother. Though the PCSW's language was far more temperate, it nonetheless presented a systematic analysis of the ways in which culture and society had limited women in the postwar era. Moreover, it spawned numerous state commissions on the status of women which provided further and more detailed documentation of gender-based discrimination.

While some historians argue that the purpose of the PCSW was simply to preempt more radical feminist demands, the commission's work had concrete results. It led to passage of the Equal Pay Act of 1963, which barred private employers from paying women less than men for the same jobs. Even more important, it opened the way for inclusion of gender discrimination in the Civil Rights Act of 1964, laying the foundations for affirmative action and litigation against sexual discrimination and harassment.

To see how far the PCSW had come politically, it is useful to compare its positions and rhetoric with what preceded it as well as what came later. Compare and contrast this document with the others in this chapter, as well as those in Chapter 10. What did the PCSW identify as the causes or sources of women's inequality? What kind of solutions did it propose? Why do you think the commission used liberal rhetoric to frame feminist demands?

Source: U.S. President's Commission on the Status of Women, *American Women: Report of the President's Commission on the Status of Women* (Washington, D.C.: GPO, 1963), pp. 1–7.

This report is an invitation to action. When President John F. Kennedy appointed our Commission, he said: . . . *we have by no means done enough to strengthen family life and at the same time encourage women to make their full contribution as citizens. . . . It is appropriate at this time . . . to review recent accomplishments, and to acknowledge frankly the further steps that must be taken. This is a task for the entire Nation. . . .*

Certain tenets have guided our thinking. Respect for the worth and dignity of every individual and conviction that every American should have a chance to achieve the best of which he—or she—is capable are basic to the meaning of both freedom and equality in this democracy. They have been, and now are, great levers for constructive social change, here and around the world. We have not hesitated to measure the present shape of things against our convictions regarding a good society and to note discrepancies between American life as it is in 1963 and as it might become through informed and intelligent action.

The human and national costs of social lag are heavy; for the most part, they are also avoidable. That is why we urge changes, many of them long overdue, in the conditions of women's opportunity in the United States. . . .

We believe that one of the greatest freedoms of the individual in a democratic society is the freedom to choose among different life patterns. Innumerable private solutions found by different individuals in search of the good life provide society with basic strength far beyond the possibilities of a dictated plan.

Illumined by values transmitted through home and school and church, society and heritage, and informed by present and past experience, each woman must arrive at her contemporary expression of purpose, whether as a center of home and family, a participant in the community, a contributor to the economy, a creative artist or thinker or scientist, a citizen engaged in politics and public service. Part and parcel of this freedom is the obligation to assume corresponding responsibility.

Yet there are social as well as individual determinants of freedom of choice; for example, the city slum and the poor rural crossroad frustrate natural gifts and innate human powers. It is a bitter fact that for millions of men and women economic stringency all but eliminates choice among alternatives. . . .

Economic expansion is of particular significance to women. One of the ironies of history is that war has brought American women their greatest economic opportunities. In establishing this Commission, the President noted: "In every period of national emergency, women have served with distinction in widely varied capacities but thereafter have been subject to treatment as a marginal group whose skills have been inadequately utilized."

Comparable opportunity—and far more varied choice—could be provided by full employment in a period without war.

The Council of Economic Advisers had estimated that between 1958 and 1962 the country's productive capacity exceeded its actual output by some $170 billion, or almost $1,000 per person in the United States. Had this potential been realized, lower rates of unemployment and an impressive supply of additional goods and services would have contributed to national well-being. The currently unused resources of the American economy include much work that could be done by women. . . .

But while freedom of choice for many American women, as for men, is limited by economic considerations, one of the most pervasive limitations is the social climate in which women choose what they prepare themselves to do. Too many plans recommended to young women reaching maturity are only partially suited to the second half of the twentieth century. Such advice is correspondingly confusing to them.

Even the role most generally approved by counselors, parents, and friends— the making of a home, the rearing of children, and the transmission to them in their earliest years of the values of the American heritage—is frequently presented as it is thought to have been in an earlier and simpler society. . . .

Similarly, women's participation in such traditional occupations as teaching, nursing, and social work is generally approved, with current shortages underscoring the nation's need for such personnel. But means for keeping up to date the skills of women who continue in such professions are few. So, too, are those for bringing up to date the skills of women who withdraw in order to raise families but return after their families are grown.

Commendation of women's entry into certain other occupations is less general, even though some of them are equally in need of trained people. Girls hearing that most women find mathematics and science difficult, or that engineering and architecture are unusual occupations for a woman, are not led to test their interest by activity in these fields.

Because too little is expected of them, many girls who graduate from high school intellectually able to do good college work do not go to college. Both they as individuals and the nation as a society are thereby made losers.

The subtle limitations imposed by custom are, upon occasion, reinforced by specific barriers. In the course of the twentieth century many bars against women that were firmly in place in 1900 have been lowered or dropped. But certain restrictions remain. . . .

Some of these discriminatory provisions are contained in the common law. Some are written into statute. Some are upheld by court decisions. Others take the form of practices of industrial, labor, professional, or governmental organizations that discriminate against women in apprenticeship, training, hiring, wages, and promotion. We have identified a number of outmoded and prejudicial attitudes and practices.

Throughout its deliberations, the Commission has kept in mind certain women who have special disadvantages. Among head of families in the United States, 1 in 10 is a woman. At least half of them are carrying responsibility for both earning the family's living and making the family's home. Their problems are correspondingly greater; their resources are usually less.

Seven million nonwhite women and girls belong to minority racial groups. Discrimination based on color is morally wrong and a source of national weakness. Such discrimination currently places an oppressive dual burden on millions of Negro women. The consultation held by the Commission on the situation of Negro women emphasized that in too many families lack of opportunity for men as well as women, linked to racial discrimination, has forced the women to assume too large a share of the family responsibility. Such women are twice as likely as other women to have to seek employment while they have preschool children at home; they are just beginning to gain entrance to the expanding fields of clerical and commercial employment; except for the few who can qualify as teachers or other professionals, they are forced into low-paid service occupations.

Hundreds of thousands of other women face somewhat similar situations: American Indians, for instance, and Spanish-Americans, many of whom live in urban centers but are new to urban life and burdened with language problems.

While there are highly skilled members of all these groups, in many of the families of these women the unbroken cycle of deprivation and retardation repeats itself from generation to generation, compounding its individual cost in human indignity and unhappiness and its social cost in incapacity and delinquency. This cycle must be broken, swiftly and at as many points as possible. The Commission strongly urges that in the carrying out of its recommendations, special attention be given to difficulties that are wholly or largely the products of this kind of discrimination. . . .

Eight out of ten women are in paid employment outside the home at some time during their lives, and many of these, and others as well, engage in unpaid work as volunteers.

The population contains 13 million single girls and women 14 and over. A 20-year-old girl, if she remains single, will spend some 40 years in the labor force. If after working for a few years, she marries and has a family, and then goes back into the labor force at 30, she is likely to work for some 23 more years. Particularly during the years when her children are in school but have not yet left home permanently, the work she seeks is apt to be part-time. Inflexibility with regard to part-time employment in most current hiring systems, alike in government and in private enterprise, excludes the use of much able and available trained womanpower; practices should be altered to permit it. . . .

MOVEMENT WOMEN, TOO, HAVE BECOME DISILLUSIONED
Kathy McAfee and Myrna Wood

Asked to define a socialist-feminist, author Barbara Ehrenreich once quipped, "someone who has to go to twice as many meetings." Indeed, as the following document indicates, socialist-feminists did feel compelled to negotiate between two camps—the left and the women's movement. This strand of women's liberation arose from within—and ultimately in opposition to—the male-dominated ranks of the New Left, and its writings bore the earmarks of women's struggle to come to terms with their intellectual and political origins. On the one hand, feminist activists such as Kathy McAfee and Myrna Wood, members of the Boston-based collective Bread and Roses, found useful many elements of the New Left's analysis of American society. But on the other hand, they felt constrained by its Marxist insistence on focusing on class as the source of oppression—to the exclusion of gender. At the same time, socialist-feminists, though largely white and middle-class, anticipated many of the critiques later made by working-class women and women of color.

In what ways do "socialist" and "feminist" ideas work against one another in this document? In what ways do they reinforce one another? What do McAfee and Wood mean by a "revolutionary women's movement"? Are there any points on which they would concur with the President's Commission on the Status of Women?

A great deal of confusion exists today about the role of women's liberation in a revolutionary movement. Hundreds of women's groups have sprung up within the past year or two, but among them, a number of very different and often conflicting ideologies have developed. The growth of these movements has demonstrated the desperate need that many women feel to escape their own oppression, but it has

Source: Kathy McAfee and Myrna Wood, "Bread and Roses," *Leviathan* #3 (June 1969), pp. 8–11, 43–44.

also shown that organization around women's issues need not lead to revolution-ary consciousness, or even to an identification with the left. (Some groups mobilize middle class women to fight for equal privileges as businesswomen and acade-mics; others maintain that the overthrow of capitalism is irrelevant for women.)

Many movement women have experienced the initial exhilaration of discover-ing women's liberation as an issue, of realizing that the frustration, anger, and fear we feel are not a result of individual failure but are shared by all our sisters, and of sensing—if not fully understanding—that these feelings stem from the same op-pressive conditions that give rise to racism, chauvinism and the barbarity of American culture. But many movement women, too, have become disillusioned af-ter a time by their experiences with women's liberation groups. More often than not these groups never get beyond the level of therapy sessions; rather than aiding the political development of women and building a revolutionary women's movement, they often encourage escape from political struggle.

The existence of this tendency among women's liberation groups is one rea-son why many movement activists (including some women) have come out against a women's liberation movement that distinguishes itself from the general move-ment, even if it considers itself part of the left. A movement organized by women around the oppression of women, they say, is bound to emphasize the bourgeois and personal aspects of oppression and to obscure the material oppression of working class women *and men*. At best, [according to Bernadine Dohrn], such a movement "lacks revolutionary potential." In SDS [Students for a Democratic Society, a New Left organization], where this attitude is very strong, questions about the oppression and liberation of women are raised only within the context of current SDS ideology and strategy; the question of women's liberation is raised only as an incidental, subordinate aspect of programs around "*the* primary struggle," anti-racism. (Although most people in SDS now understand the extent of black peo-ple's oppression, they are not aware of the fact that the median wage of working women [black and white] is lower than that of black males.) The male domination of the organization has not been affected by occasional rhetorical attacks on male chauvinism and most important, very little organizing of women is being done.

Although the reason behind it can be understood, this attitude toward women's liberation is mistaken and dangerous. By discouraging the development of a revo-lutionary women's liberation movement, it avoids a serious challenge to what, along with racism, is the deepest source of division and false consciousness among workers. By setting up (in the name of Marxist class analysis) a dichotomy between the "bourgeois," personal and psychological forms of oppression on the one hand, and the "real" material forms on the other, it substitutes a mechanistic model of class relations for a more profound understanding of how these two aspects of op-pression depend upon and reinforce each other. Finally, this anti-woman's libera-tionist attitude makes it easier for us to bypass a confrontation of male chauvinism and the closely related values of elitism and authoritarianism which are weakening our movement.

Before we can discuss the potential of a women's liberation movement, we need a more precise description of the way the oppression of women functions in a capitalist society. This will also help us understand the relation of psychological to material oppression.

1) *Male Chauvinism—the attitude that women are the passive and inferior servants of society and men—sets women apart from the rest of the working class.* Even when they do the same work as men, women are not considered workers in

the same sense, with the need and right to work to provide for their families or to support themselves independently. They are expected to accept work at lower wages and without job security. Thus they can be used as a marginal or reserve labor force when profits depend on extra low costs or when men are needed for war.

Women are not supposed to be independent, so they are not supposed to have any "right to work." This means, in effect, that although they do work, they are denied the right to organize and fight for better wages and conditions. Thus the role of women in the labor force undermines the struggles of male workers as well. The boss can break a union drive by threatening to hire lower paid women or blacks. In many cases, where women are organized, the union contract reinforces their inferior position, making women the least loyal and militant union members. . . .

In general, because women are defined as docile, helpless, and inferior they are forced into the most demeaning and mindrotting jobs—from scrubbing floors to filing cards—under the most oppressive conditions where they are treated like children or slaves. Their very position reinforces the idea, even among the women themselves, that they are fit for and should be satisfied with this kind of work.

2) *Apart from the direct, material exploitation of women, male supremacy acts in more subtle ways to undermine class consciousness.* The tendency of male workers to think of themselves primarily as men (i.e., powerful) rather than as workers (i.e., members of an oppressed group) promoted a false sense of privilege and power, and an identification with the world of men, including the boss. The petty dictatorship which most men exercise over their wives and families enables them to vent their anger and frustration in a way which poses no challenge to the system. The role of the man in the family reinforces aggressive individualism, authoritarianism, and a hierarchical view of social relations—values which are fundamental to the perpetuation of capitalism. In this system we are taught to relieve our fears and frustration by brutalizing those weaker than we are: a man in uniform turns into a pig [the pejorative New Left term for police]; the foreman intimidates the man on the line; the husband beats his wife, child, and dog.

3) *Women are further exploited in their roles as housewives and mothers, through which they reduce the costs (social and economic) of maintaining the labor force.* All of us will admit that inadequate as it may be American workers have a relatively decent standard of living, in a strictly material sense, when compared to workers of other countries or periods of history. But American workers are exploited and harassed in other ways than through the size of the weekly paycheck. They are made into robots on the job; they are denied security; they are forced to pay for expensive insurance and can rarely save enough to protect them from sudden loss of job or emergency. They are denied decent medical care and a livable environment. They are cheated by inflation. They are "given" a regimented education that prepares them for a narrow slot or for nothing. And they are taxed heavily to pay for these "benefits."

In all these areas, it is a woman's responsibility to make up for the failures of the system. In countless working class families, it is mother's job that bridges the gap between week to week subsistence and relative security. It is her wages that enable the family to eat better food, to escape their oppressive surroundings through a trip, an occasional movie, or new clothes. It is her responsibility to keep her family healthy despite the cost of decent medical care; to make a comfortable home in an unsafe and unlivable neighborhood; to provide a refuge from the alienation of work and to keep the male ego in good repair. It is she who must struggle daily to make ends meet despite inflation. She must make up for the fact that her children do not receive a decent education and she must salvage their damaged personalities.

A woman is judged as a wife and mother—the only role she is allowed—according to her ability to maintain stability in her family and to help her family "adjust" to harsh realities. She therefore transmits the values of hard work and conformity to each generation of workers. It is she who forces her children to stay in school and "behave" or who urges her husband not to risk his job by standing up to the boss or going on strike.

Thus the role of wife and mother is one of social mediator and pacifier. She shields her family from the direct impact of class oppression. She is the true opiate of the masses.

4) *Working class women and other women as well are exploited as consumers.* They are forced to buy products which are necessities, but which have waste built into them, like the soap powder, the price of which includes fancy packaging and advertising. They also buy products which are wasteful in themselves because they are told that a new car or TV will add to their families' status and satisfaction, or that cosmetics will increase their desirability as sex objects. Among "middle class" women, of course, the second type of wasteful consumption is more important than it is among working class women, but all women are victims of both types to a greater or lesser extent, and the values which support wasteful consumption are part of our general culture.

5) *All women, too, are oppressed and exploited sexually.* For working class women this oppression is more direct and brutal. They are denied control of their own bodies, when as girls they are refused information about sex and birth control, and when as women they are denied any right to decide whether and when to have children. Their confinement to the role of sex partner and mother, and their passive submission to a single man are often maintained by physical force. The relative sexual freedom of "middle class" or college educated women, however, does not bring *them* real independence. Their sexual role is still primarily a passive one; their value as individuals still determined by their ability to attract, please, and hold on to a man. The definition of women as docile and dependent, inferior in intellect and weak in character cuts across class lines.

A woman of any class is expected to sell herself—not just her body but her entire life, her talents, interests, and dreams—to a man. She is expected to give up friendships, ambitions, pleasures, and moments of time to herself in order to serve his career or his family. In return, she receives not only her livelihood but her identity, her very right to existence, for unless she is the wife of someone or the mother of someone, a woman is nothing. . . .

All women, even including those of the ruling class, are oppressed as women in the sense that their real fulfillment is linked to their role as girlfriend, wife or mother. This definition of women is part of bourgeois culture—the whole superstructure of ideas that serves to explain and reinforce the social relations of capitalism. It is applied to all women, but it has very different consequences for women of different classes. For a ruling class woman, it means she is denied real independence, dignity, and sexual freedom. For a working class woman it means this too, but it also justifies her material super-exploitation and physical coercion. Her oppression is a total one. . . .

It is true, as the movement critics assert, that the present women's liberation groups are almost entirely based among "middle-class" women, that is, college and career women; and the issues of psychological and sexual exploitation and, to a lesser extent, exploitation through consumption, have been the most prominent ones.

It is not surprising that the women's liberation movement should begin among bourgeois women, and should be dominated in the beginning by their consciousness and their particular concerns. Radical women are generally the post war middle class generation that grew up with the right to vote, the chance at higher education and training for supportive roles in the professions and business. Most of them are young and sophisticated enough to have not yet had children and do not have to marry to support themselves. In comparison with most women, they are capable of a certain amount of control over their lives.

The higher development of bourgeois democratic society allows the women who benefit from education and relative equality to see the contradictions between its rhetoric (every boy can become president) and their actual place in that society. . . .

Few radical women really know the worst of women's condition. They do not understand the anxious struggle of an uneducated girl to find the best available man for financial security and escape from a crowded and repressive home. They have not suffered years of fear from ignorance and helplessness about pregnancies. Few have experienced constant violence and drunkenness of a brutalized husband or father. They do not know the day to day reality of being chained to a house and family, with little money and lots of bills, and no diversions but TV.

Not many radical women have experienced 9–11 hours a day of hard labor, carrying trays on aching legs for rude customers who may leave no tip, but leave a feeling of degradation from their sexual or racist remarks—and all of this for $80–$90 a week. Most movement women have not learned to blank out their thoughts for 7 hours in order to type faster or file endless numbers. They have not felt their own creativity deadened by this work, while watching men who were not trained to be typists move on to higher level jobs requiring "brain-work."

In summary: because male supremacy (assumption of female inferiority, regulation of women to service roles, and sexual objectification) crosses class lines, radical women are conscious of women's oppression, but because of their background, they lack consciousness of most women's class oppression. . . .

I BECAME A LESBIAN BECAUSE OF WOMEN
Rita Mae Brown

In the spring of 1970, several hundred women were seated in a public school auditorium in New York City, waiting for the Second Congress to Unite Women to begin. These women saw themselves as the vanguard of women's liberation; veterans of the New Left and members of consciousness-raising groups, they were fully engaged in thrashing out feminist ideas and applying them to their own lives. Yet few were prepared when the doors at the rear of the auditorium flew open and several dozen women wearing T-shirts emblazoned with the slogan "Lavender Menace" ran down the aisles. The confrontation between straight women and lesbians that followed would radically alter the course of women's liberation.

As part of the moving force behind Lavender Menace, Rita Mae Brown went on to help found The Furies, a lesbian collective based in Washington, D.C. whose

Source: Rita Mae Brown, "Take a Lesbian to Lunch," from *A Plain Brown Rapper* (Oakland, CA: Diana Press, 1976), pp. 79–80, 86–95.

members believed that only women who were erotically and emotionally committed to one another could commit themselves completely to the principles of socialist feminism. A poet and author as well as political activist, Brown has published numerous novels, including the bestselling *Rubyfruit Jungle,* introducing the broader public to the experience of coming out.

In the essay excerpted below, Brown narrates her troubled passage through the feminist world of the late sixties and early seventies. How did her experience as a lesbian expose the contradictions and weaknesses of the various feminist and gay groups she encountered? To what extent were her views also shaped by her class background?

Before there was a [Women's Liberation Movement] there were always a number of women who questioned the system and found it destructive to themselves. Those women became women-identified. I am one of those women. The male culture's word for this kind of woman is Lesbian. This is a narrow definition so typical of the male culture's vulgar conceptual limitations. In their world, the term applies only to sexual activity between women. In our world, to be a *political* Lesbian means to be a woman-identified woman. It means you move toward women and are capable of making a total commitment to women. The male party line concerning Lesbians is that women become Lesbians out of reaction to men. This is a pathetic illustration of the male ego's inflated proportions. I became a Lesbian because of women, because women are beautiful, strong and compassionate.

Secondarily, I became a Lesbian because the culture that I live in is violently anti-woman. How could I, a woman, participate in a culture that denies me my humanity? How can any woman in touch with herself participate in this culture? To give a man support and love before giving it to a sister is to support that culture, that power system, for men receive the benefits of sexism regardless of race or social position. The higher up they are on the color line and the salary line the more benefits they receive, but all men benefit by sexism at some level.

Proof of the pudding is that the most rabid man haters are heterosexual women, and with good reason—they are directly oppressed by individual men. The contradiction of supporting the political system that oppresses you and the individuals who benefit by that system, men, is much more intense for the heterosexual woman than for the homosexual woman. Lesbians are oppressed by the male power system but not by individual men in the same intimate, insidious fashion. Therefore, we Lesbians are the ultimate insult to the sexist male and the world he has built up around his weaknesses. Why? Because we ignore him, because we are the ultimate insult, we pay and we pay heavily. . . .

When the rumblings of the just born Women's Liberation Movement reached me, I was filled with hope. I was off to find and join Women's Liberation and to conquer sexism once and for all. What I found was that sexism exists between women in the movement and it is potentially as destructive as the sexism between men and women.

I came to Women's Liberation via a political homosexual group, the Student Homophile League, which three women and about ten men helped to found in 1967 at Columbia University and [New York University]. I left the homosexual movement because it was male dominated. Homosexual men (with few exceptions) are like heterosexual men in that they don't give a damn about the needs of women. As soon as I heard of it, I went to the National Organization for Women. N.O.W. is not the same as Women's Liberation, but at the time I didn't know that. I went to a few business meetings where the women conducted themselves in a parliamentary manner and played polite power games with each other. . . . Eventually a woman did talk to me. I questioned her on the Lesbian issue and she bluntly told me that the word Lesbian was never to be uttered. "After all, that is exactly what the press wants to say we are, a bunch of Lesbians." She then went on to patronizingly say, "What are you doing worrying about Lesbians, you must have a lot of boyfriends." Okay, sister, have it your way. I kept silent for a few more months. Finally N.O.W. had what it termed a rap session for new women. It was at the apartment of a woman lawyer and was full of stock-brokers, editors, art directors and others of similar professional privilege or aspiring to similar professional privilege. I showed up, too, minus the privilege, but I figured that I was a new woman and that's what counts. . . . The rap session droned on. Women bitched about job discrimination, the pill, etc. . . . By this time I had a few months to review the political issues at stake and to come up with the firm conclusion that N.O.W. was, to make a long story short, full of shit. A women's movement is for women. Its actions and considerations should be for women not for what the white, rich, male heterosexual media finds acceptable. In other words, Lesbianism definitely was an important issue and should be out in the open.

I stood up and said something that went like this: "All I've heard about tonight and in the other meetings is women complaining about men, in one form or other. I want to know why you don't speak about other women? Why you deliberately avoid Lesbianism and why you can't see anything but men? I think Lesbians are ahead of you." . . . What followed my short remarks resembled a mass coronary. One woman jumped up and declared that Lesbians want to be men and that N.O.W. only wants "real" women. This kind of thing went on for a bit. Then the second wave set in—the sneaky, sly curiosity that culminates in, "Well, what do you do in bed?" (I paint myself green and hang from the rafters.) After approximately one hour of being the group freak and diligently probed, poked and studied, these ladies bountiful decided that, yes, I was human. Yes, I did resemble a young woman in her early twenties. Yes, I even looked like what young women in their early twenties were supposed to look like. . . . There were other Lesbians in the room and they too looked like what women are supposed to look like. The difference between them and me was that I opened my mouth and fought the straight ladies. I was even angrier at my silent sisters than at these incredibly rude, peering, titillated heterosexual wonders. Lesbian silence is nothing new to me, but it never fails to piss me off. I know all the reasons to be quiet in front of the straight enemy, and I find them false. Every time you keep your mouth shut you make life that much harder for every other Lesbian in this country. Our freedom is worth losing your job and your friends. If you keep your mouth shut you are a coward; you silently assert heterosexual imperialism; you allow it to go on by not fighting back. The women in that room were cowards. They thought they could pass for straight. . . .

In the room, somehow, a few women got beyond the label, Lesbian, and tried to see me as a person. At the next general meeting, some of them came over and talked to me. They were trying to break down the barriers between us. The N.O.W. leadership was another story. They would in no way recognize the issues of Lesbianism as relevant to the movement. Secretly, a few of them called me and "confessed" to being Lesbians themselves. They were ashamed of their silences but their logic was, when in Rome do as the Romans do. They were busy playing straight because they didn't want to lose their positions in the leadership. They asked me not to reveal them. There were hints that I could have a place in the leadership if I would play my cards right (shut up). . . .

As women began to be comfortable with me and see that I was a fairly decent human being, they began to turn on to me. It was very painful for me because when they experienced warm or sexual feelings they began to treat me as a man. All these women knew was men. The old seduction game we learned in pre-school sex-role training—that's what I was getting. I can't respond to that kind of thing. Some of the women were hurt, some angry and some vicious. Then there was the most manipulative woman of all, the one who was going to liberate herself on my body. She could then pass herself off as a right on brave feminist, because she had slept with a woman. It was pretty confusing. As you can see, the women still thought of Lesbianism as a sexual activity only. This is the way in which men define it. The women couldn't understand that Lesbianism means a different way of living. It means, for me, that you dump all roles as much as possible, that you forget the male power system, and that you give women primacy in your life—emotionally, sexually, personally, politically. It doesn't mean that you look at girlie magazines or pinch the bottoms of passers-by. . . .

By this time, I had discovered women of the other groups. I went to Redstockings, an organization which pushed consciousness raising and the pro-woman line. Redstockings was not too pro-woman when it came to Lesbians. They could empathize with the prostitute, support the housewife, encourage the single woman and seek child care for the mother, but they wouldn't touch the Lesbian. The token Lesbian once more, I became more and more depressed. At least, I had enough insight to realize that this was not my personal problem. It was and still is the crucial political issue, the first step toward a coherent, all-woman ideology. . . .

Lesbianism is the issue that deals with women reacting positively to other women. All other issues deal with men and the society they have built to contain us. . . . If we cannot look at another woman and see a human being worth making a total commitment to—politically, emotionally, physically—then where the hell are we? If we can't find another woman worthy of our deepest emotions then can we find ourselves worthy of our own emotion or are all commitments reserved for men, those that benefit by our oppression? . . . A few Redstockings tried to deal with these issues. They received no support from the other women. By this time I was tired and too wise to spend much energy on the straight ladies. . . .

The next move was to Gay Liberation [GLF], a radical group for homosexuals which began in 1969–70. It supposedly is for men and women. I knew from my previous experience that I wouldn't work with homosexual men again unless something wonderful happened inside their heads and in their system of priorities. But there were gay women there with little women's consciousness and I thought maybe I could push a more feminist understanding among them. It would be a positive step for them as well as me as I needed to be among other Lesbians. Gay Liberation contained women who were highly politicized concerning homosexual oppression so if they could get a consciousness of woman oppression and connect the two, it would be a step forward.

There are good reasons many Lesbians have no political consciousness of woman oppression. One of the ways in which many Lesbians have protected themselves from the pain of woman oppression is to refuse to see themselves as traditional women. Society encourages this view because if you are not a traditional woman, then you must be some kind of man. This is the other side of the male-identified coin: Heterosexual women live through their men and thereby identify with them, gaining heavy privilege; some Lesbians assume a male role and thereby become male identified, although they receive no political-economic privilege. . . . Other Lesbians feel themselves as women, know intensely that they are not imitation men but stay away from Women's Liberation which could develop their political consciousness. They know from direct experience that straight women cannot be trusted with Lesbian sensibilities and sensitivities. Many of the women in GLF fell into that group. They would rather work with male homosexuals and endure male chauvinism than expose themselves to a more obviously hostile element, the heterosexual woman. More hostile because if her man suspects she is trucking with Lesbians she loses the privileges she gains through association with him. . . .

When I suggested consciousness raising to the women in GLF they were suspicious. They thought I was a Pied Piper wooing them into Women's Liberation instead of fighting homosexual oppression by working through GLF. . . .

In spite of their suspicions, they did form consciousness raising groups. A sense of woman oppression was developed and many were well along the way because of their increasing anger over how the gay men mistreated them. They saw that Lesbian oppression and male homosexual oppression have less in common than they formerly thought. What we have in common is that heterosexuals of both sexes hate and fear us. The similarity stops there because that hate and fear take on vastly different forms for the Lesbian than for the male homosexual. . . .

The first explosion from this new direction came at the Second Congress to Unite Women when the Lesbians (40 in number) confronted the women there. For the first time, straight women were forced to face their own sexism and their complicity with the male power structure.

Since the Congress, in the spring of 1970, Lesbians have come out in ever increasing numbers and the backlash has increased proportionally. Many Lesbians have come to the conclusion that they can no longer work with straight women, women who remain tied to men ideologically as well as individually.

This is a call for a separatist movement of Lesbians? Yes and No. No, (speaking for myself) because I do not want to be separate from any women. Yes, because until heterosexual women treat Lesbians as full human beings and fight the enormity of male supremacy with us, I have no option but to separate from them just as they have no option but to be separate from men until men begin to change their own sexism. Separatism is the heterosexual woman's choice by default, not mine.

Separation is what the ruling rich, white male wants: female vs. male; black vs. white; gay vs. straight; poor vs. rich. I don't want to be separate from anyone— that just keeps the Big Man on top of all of us. But I can't work with people who degrade me, don't deal with behavior that is destructive to me and who don't share their privileges. The last thing that I want is separatism. We can only achieve reformist changes for our subgroup if we remain separatists. Together we can change the entire society and make a better life for ourselves individually and collectively.

IT'S MY BODY
Boston Women's Health Book Collective

With its inherent skepticism, women's liberation prompted feminists to examine critically every institution, every source of authority in their lives. One of the most important of these was health care. In the late sixties a group of Boston women—

Source: Boston Women's Health Book Collective, "Managing the Obstetrician-Gynecologist," *Our Bodies, Ourselves,* New York: Simon and Schuster, 1973, pp. 249–52.

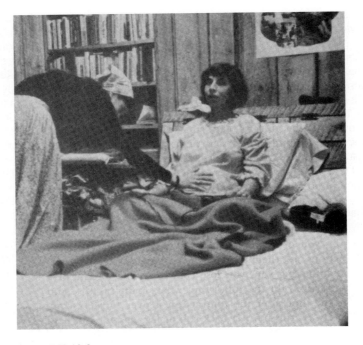

FIGURE 12.2
The feminist health movement advocated the "demedicalization" of childbirth, urging women to treat it as a natural event, not an illness. As a result, many mothers-to-be chose to give birth at home rather than in the hospital. This woman, resting on her own bed, is in the early stages of labor with a midwife (rather than a doctor) in attendance. *(Photograph by Edna Katz, from the Boston Women's Health Book Collective,* Our Bodies, Ourselves *[New York: Simon & Schuster, 1971], p. 200.)*

few of them trained professionals, but all of them experienced patients—began to explore the whole system of health care from training through delivery. The first edition of their pathbreaking feminist health care manual, *Our Bodies, Ourselves,* printed on newsprint in 1971, sold over 200,000 copies. In 1973 the first mainstream edition appeared; since then it has undergone multiple revisions, and the collective has also put out a manual for adolescent women, *Ourselves and Our Bodies,* and for older women, *Ourselves Growing Older.*

Compare the tone of *Our Bodies, Ourselves* with that of the La Leche League (Chapter 10). How did feminism affect women's views toward physicians? Toward their own bodies?

While doing the research for this book several of us came upon certain sections in major medical texts—the kind that medical students study and doctors use as references—which offer medical opinions about the character of female patients. In one text on gynecology there is a long section on the psychology of women in which the doctor is advised to interview the woman patient when he first sees her and to measure what might be called her "femininity" quotient. He is told to pay attention to how the patient responds to his questions, whether "in a feminine way or whether she is domineering, demanding, masculine, aggressive or passive in her attitude." What these value-laden terms mean exactly is not clear. Is being demanding the same as asking the doctor to explain what he is doing? . . .

There is great irony in the fact that doctors are socially sanctioned as sexual counselors and advisors, and yet are astoundingly ignorant of female sexuality. In one obstetrics book, in discussing female orgasm, the author-doctor avers that "it is as variegated as thumbprints and not at all contingent on mechanical and muscular stimuli but rather on how a woman feels about her husband." He goes on to say that the only important question to ask a woman with regard to her lack of sexual satisfaction is, "Does she really love her husband?" That certainly simplifies the counseling process for the doctor.

These attitudes toward women remind us again that many male doctors, like many other men, have created myths about the female character and personality which blind them to us as a group and as individuals. What is frightening is how much power male doctors hold over many aspects of our lives, and how their *official* ideas about women affect the medical care we get and thus our very survival. . . .

The notion that there are some ob-gyn specialists who are greatly superior to others is often a myth. The fact that many of us have a need to believe that we are in the hands of superior physicians is one of the problems we need to be liberated from. . . .

I knew that my doctor had a reputation for being one of the best in the city, and it made me feel good when I said his name and other people would say, "Oh, right, I've heard of him." I felt he was great and I was one of his lucky patients, even though I was rarely comfortable with him and always felt belittled when I went to him: I'd have to wait a very long time, or he wouldn't answer my questions, or I'd feel sometimes too timid to even ask any questions.

***

While I was learning a lot of things about my body I went to see a gynecologist for my yearly check-up. I thought, This time I won't feel intimidated. But it happened anyway. One of the things I remember really clearly is when he asked me how long my menstrual cycle was, and I told him, he looked surprised and just said, "That's interesting." I asked him if it was unusually long (I've since found out it is), if my hormones were out of whack, if he could even tell anything at all. He just sidestepped or didn't answer my questions. I wouldn't have cared so much if he had said he couldn't tell, or didn't know, or even if he just wasn't interested in menstrual problems. But he talked to me as if I shouldn't know. It's my body, and I felt defeated in trying to learn about it. I decided that the next time I would go with another woman, who could help me ask questions and also see what the doctor was doing during the actual examination.

***

Remember too: The doctor is no longer a god-figure; that's the price we pay for our developing independence. A too close doctor-patient relationship during pregnancy, for example, may actually retard or disrupt your own growth and/or developing relationship with the man in your life at a time when it needs all the strengthening it can get.

***

I'd had a lot of trouble conceiving and my doctor had operated to remove ovarian cysts. Four months after the operation I became pregnant. My doctor was very happy too. I remember we both felt he had been responsible for my pregnancy, and my husband had merely been the vehicle for my doctor's success. My husband felt excluded. I know I played along with that whole game, not really aware of what I was doing or why.

***

The first time I met him I thought he was so cold, clinical, and businesslike. Then all his "charm" made me feel dependent on him. I respected that he was going to do the best job he could possibly do. If he criticized me, I shrank inside. Sometimes I'd be annoyed that I had to travel so far for him to look at my stomach. But the mysteries still held: He was going to give me the baby. Once he confused me with someone else and I was very depressed.

Remember: Obstetricians don't provide continuity. Don't choose them to depend on emotionally. During pregnancy you really need to lean on someone who will also be there after the baby is born. Find someone else to share the whole experience with, for the doctor disappears from the scene right after your baby is born, and you don't see him again for six weeks or so.

Many of us are still looking for an authoritarian figure, for a father in our doctor. And doctors foster our dependency. . . .

At one level it is possible to think of the ob-gyn as a friend who is helping to protect you against unwanted pregnancy or venereal disease or death and disaster in childbirth. But at another level it's possible to see him as someone whose main concern is to keep you healthy and maintain you in your place as a sex object for your man, or for men: "clean," the right size, in good working order, and free from fear of disease or pregnancy; or pregnant, but to be returned to the prepregnant state "as good as new" and as quickly as possible, almost as if the pregnancy had never happened. Sometimes it seems as if one reason why many ob-gyn men are negative (subtly or not so subtly) about breast-feeding, for example, is that they have identified with a man's sense of sexual possessiveness about the breasts and want to preserve these exclusively for him and in nearly virginal condition for as much of the time as possible. The same may be true for the use of forceps and the practice of routine episiotomies, or the oft-repeated caution that a woman should not get overtired, which can—on the surface—seem so solicitous.

Certainly, we may want all of these things, too, for our own reasons. When we want sex we want to feel ready for it in every way and protected against pregnancy if we choose to be, but not because we see this as our exclusive or even our primary function as women, and especially not because our first "duty" is to be in shape for a man whenever he might want us. Similarly, we know that children have needs too, but especially we as women have many other needs. The doctor, and the ob-gyn in particular, can be viewed as society's representative in identifying us to ourselves and to others as creatures whose only needs appear to be meeting the needs of others. Our medical care thus sometimes seems directed toward those purposes. . . .

OUR EARLY SISTERS WOULD HAVE WANTED THE ERA
Sonia Johnson

As women in even the most conservative pockets of American society attempted to apply the principles of feminism to their own lives, conservative men began to mobilize in opposition. Few confrontations were more dramatic than the one between Sonia Johnson, a Mormon housewife from Utah, and Orrin Hatch, a Republican Senator and Mormon churchman from the same state. The occasion was a hearing on extending the ratification period for the Equal Rights Amendment in August, 1978.

The amendment had initially passed Congress in 1972. After an initial burst of ratifications, the process had languished, compelling feminists to return to Congress and plead for an extension. Though they gained the extra time, ERA supporters could never obtain the necessary ratifications and the bill lapsed in 1982.

In her memoir, *From Housewife to Heretic* (1981), Johnson describes her state of mind at the Senate hearings. While waiting to speak, she was "trembling so that without looking directly at it, I could see my skirt dancing across my knees." But she became calmer as she spoke, and as the following excerpt revealed, clearly had her wits about her in a sharp exchange with Senator Hatch. What sources of authority does Johnson invoke? How does her style and tone compare to that of the other feminists in this chapter?

Mrs. JOHNSON. Wherever we go with our bumper stickers, our buttons, our signs and banners that proclaim us Mormons who support the ERA, we are greeted with disbelief and amazement. This, in turn, amazes us. So few people remember that the church was once in the forefront of the equal rights movement, and that Mormon feminists played a significant part in that movement. . . .

The question we are most often asked is: How is it philosophically possible to remain affiliated with the church and still support the ERA?

Early Mormon feminists demonstrated that the movement for equal rights could be compatible with Mormon doctrine. That they are compatible is eminently clear to us. . . .

The church teaches that our Father in Heaven knows that many of us will make self-limiting and destructive choices, but that his greatest desire is that we should one day become like him. He understands that for such growth it is essential for us to have full options, to take responsibility for choosing, to live somehow through the consequences of our choices, and to learn from them what constitutes full humanity. He treats us with this precious gift, not because he thinks we will all use it wisely, but because he loves us so much he is willing to take the risk.

The leaders of the church, though great and good men, are nevertheless mortal and not yet like our Father in the fullness of love. Because they love us less, they are less willing to risk, less willing to trust us to make wise decisions. They have chosen to tamper with our agency, to attempt to compel us to do what they believe is right through the use of fear and of their considerable authority. Unlike the Lord, they are afraid now, having taught us correct principles, to let us govern ourselves.

Source: *Equal Rights Amendment Extension,* Hearings before the Subcommittee on the Constitution of the Committee on the Judiciary, U.S. Senate, 95th Cong., 2nd Sess., August 4, 1978, pp. 307–9; 320–21.

The rhetoric of the modern church sounds much like that of former times, but there is one critical difference—women are supported in word only, not in deed, a practice which confuses and blinds many church members. In their official statement opposing the ERA, the leaders of the church affirm the "exalted role of woman in our society," and then proceed to withdraw support from an amendment which would give her equal protection under the law. . . .

We firmly believe that what our early sisters would have wanted, what they would be working for if they were here today, what constitutes the whole loaf with which they would be contented, is ratification of the equal rights amendment. . . .

Senator [Birch] BAYH [D-Indiana]: Is there any difficulty in being philosophically sympathetic to the ERA as you are, and being affiliated with the church?

Ms. JOHNSON. I hope there will not be.

Senator BAYH. So do I.

Senator HATCH. So do I. I doubt that there will be. . . .

Senator HATCH. Ms. Johnson, how many people do you represent in the Mormons for ERA? How many women do you represent?

Ms. JOHNSON. I have no idea. We have not taken a poll.

Senator HATCH. Is it a large number?

Ms. JOHNSON. It is a steadily growing number of women. I think—I am sure there are more than we have any idea about. I think the numbers are growing.

Senator HATCH. I think that you would have to admit that in the Mormon Church, almost 100 percent of the women are against the equal rights amendment, right?

Ms. JOHNSON. Oh, my goodness. . . . I do not have to admit that. It simply is not true.

Senator HATCH. I think it is true.

Ms. JOHNSON. You say it is true and I say it is not. I am a woman and I know many women and I know many organizations—

Senator HATCH. I notice in your letter to the legislature that you had 20 women listed.

Ms. JOHNSON. There were not just women on that list. You realize yourself that it is a difficult position and many people who are for it are not willing to put their names on letters. . . .

I know personally three or four times that many in this area alone who are very happy about the ERA and share my views. But because they hold positions and because their wives hold a position in the church and because they are afraid of what the church might do to them, they will not lend their assistance by giving us their names. But they will give us money. They will give us support. They will call and say, "Onward, onward, ever onward, shoulder to shoulder," and so on.

I get lots of that kind of feedback. . . .

The point here is that numbers of adherence have never proven an issue true or false.

Senator HATCH. That is a good point.

Ms. JOHNSON. You yourself belong to a church of only 3 million members which purports to be the only true church in the world. That is a pretty precarious position. I am accustomed to being one of the few and in the right.

Senator HATCH. I notice you are very self-confident that you are right and everybody else is wrong. I would have to admit that the majority can be wrong but on the other hand I have also seen the minority wrong many times. You may very well be wrong here, as confident as you are.

Ms. JOHNSON. You may very well be wrong, as confident as you are.

Senator HATCH. That is true, and I am very confident. As a matter of fact, I am very confident that I am right.

Ms. JOHNSON. And so am I. . . .

IT'S NOT MERELY ARITHMETIC—IT'S GEOMETRIC
Barbara Smith

The relationship between women of color and second-wave feminism was often a vexed one. To many women of color, women's liberation appeared at best irrelevant, at worst, another likely site for prejudice and misunderstanding. A few minority women participated individually in early feminist organizations (for example, Dorothy Height, president of the National Council of Negro Women, was a member of the President's Commission of the Status of Women and probably responsible for references to the issue of race in its final report), but at the height of the movement, women of color were notable chiefly by their absence.

As oral historian Sherna Gluck has argued, however, the fact that women of color were not visible, either individually or collectively, within white, middle-class women's liberation organizations, does not mean that they were not concerned with feminist issues. Some attempted to organize separate feminist groups such as the National Black Feminist Organization, founded in 1973, but met with lukewarm success. Most preferred to remain in groups organized primarily around racial or ethnic agendas. Though their feminist actions may not have been obvious to the casual observer at the time, oral histories reveal that women were pushing steadily for greater recognition, respect, and gender equality within these organizations.

Though white feminists frequently deplored the gap between themselves and women of color, there was little they could do to change it on their own. By the late seventies, women of color began to engage the issues that divided them from white feminists. Barbara Smith was part of a group of highly articulate authors that included Audre Lorde, Cherríe Moraga, bell hooks, and Gloria Anzaldúa. As the selection below indicates, for minority women, speaking out involved risks on all sides. What does Smith see as the relationship between gender and racial oppression? Does she believe that feminism will ultimately benefit women of color?

Black and other Third World women's relationships to the systems of oppression in this society are, by definition, different from those of other oppressed groups who do not experience both racial and sexual oppression at the same time. The effect of this double, actually triple oppression because of class, is not merely arithmetic—one plus one plus one—but geometric. There is such a thing as racial-sexual oppression which is neither solely racial nor solely sexual. A good example is forced sterilization of Third World women: racism and imperialism determine the

Source: Barbara Smith, "Notes for Yet Another Paper on Black Feminism, or Will the Real Enemy Please Stand Up?" *Conditions, Five: The Black Women's Issue,* ed. Lorraine Bethel and Barbara Smith (1979), pp. 123–27.

racial or nationality group to be oppressed and sexism and misogyny determine that women are the appropriate targets of abuse. . . .

Feminism is potentially the most threatening of movements to Black and other Third World people because it makes it absolutely essential that we examine the way we live, how we treat each other and what we believe. It calls into question the most basic assumption about our existence and this is the idea that biological, i.e., sexual identity determines all, that it is the rationale for power relationships as well as all other levels of human identity and action. An irony is that among Third World people biological determinism is rejected and fought against when it is applied to race, but generally unquestioned when it applies to sex.

Rigid sex roles, sexism, and violence towards women seem entrenched in Black society and culture, perhaps even more deeply than in white society and culture, as indicated by the fact that there has been much resistance to the examination of our oppression until this point. Black and other Third World women are sexually oppressed every day of our lives, but because we are also oppressed racially and economically, sexual oppression has not been considered a priority. It has been rendered falsely invisible.

By naming sexual oppression as a problem it would appear that we would have to identify as threatening a group we have heretofore assumed to be our allies— Black men. This seems to be one of the major stumbling blocks to beginning to analyze the sexual relationships/sexual politics of our lives. The phrase "men are not the enemy" dismisses feminism and the reality of patriarchy in one breath and also overlooks some major realities. If we cannot entertain the idea that some men *are* the enemy, especially white men and in a different sense Black men too, then we will never be able to figure out all the reasons why, for example, we are being beaten up every day, why we are sterilized against our wills, why we are being raped by our neighbors, why we are pregnant at age twelve and why we are at home on welfare with more children than we can support or care for. Acknowledging the sexism of Black men does not mean that we become "man-haters" or necessarily eliminate them from our lives. What it does mean is that we must struggle for a different basis of interaction with them. That if we care about them and ourselves we will not permit ourselves to be degraded or manipulated.

. . . There are many problems inherent in trying to reach a viable Black feminist analysis of what goes on in Black women's lives. I want to briefly discuss two of them here.

The first is economics. I am in essential agreement with the Marxist analysis that it is our material conditions which most clearly affect what we are able to do in our lives. These determine to a huge extent the content and quality of our lives: for example, the amount of access we have to the basic necessities of food, clothing, housing and health care as well as what we are able to think, what we are taught to believe and what we are allowed to do. If, for example, a poor Black woman were no longer poor, she probably would no longer be a welfare mother. She would still, however, be a mother, suffering the sole responsibility for the care of her children, the isolation and overwork inherent in that role under patriarchy. She also might very well still be raped, beaten, sterilized, or pregnant against her will since these kinds of oppression are not solely motivated by economic causes. She would also still be Black whatever else occurred. Sexism and racism are inherently part of all that happens to Black women, indeed are just as central to our material conditions as class oppression.

I realize that little will change in our lives until capitalism is destroyed and economic conditions and relationships radically changed. I also realize that while struggling for survival we cannot always examine and fight all the forces that make our lives intolerable. But this does not mean that these forces do not exist. Therefore those of us who try to examine and fight these forces must not hesitate to do so merely in order to maintain political "correctness" and a false sense of solidarity. I do not believe that socialism will resolve political conflicts that do not spring solely from an economic root. It may provide an atmosphere in which these situations can be criticized and worked upon, but it does not appear to contain the answers to nor an analysis of phenomena which are based more directly in realms other than the economic. I think it is essential to struggle against sexism and racism just as we struggle against economic oppression. These are not trivial oppressions but very real ones which pre-date capitalism and therefore will not necessarily disappear when capitalism disappears.

The second major problem is how we think about men. White males are the primary oppressor group in American society. They oppress Black people, they oppress working people, they oppress women, they oppress Black women. They also oppress each other. To say that men are not the enemy, that it is instead the ruling class is sophistry. In this country, white men *are* the ruling class, the ruling class *are* white men. It is true that not all white men are capitalists or possess extreme class privilege, but it is safe to assume that 99 44/100% of them are racists and sexists. It is not just rich and powerful capitalists who inhibit and destroy life. Rapists, murderers, lynchers, and ordinary bigots do too and exercise very real and violent power because of their white-male privilege. . . .

White males are the group who most often have the opportunity to oppress everybody, but Black and other Third World men can oppress women too and do so quite effectively and cruelly. One thing that Black feminism does is to be quite specific about naming the oppressor/enemy. This is another way of saying that the personal is political, a reality that many people do not want to accept. It is much less threatening on a gut level to call the oppressor the "Ruling Class" and to ignore everything and everyone else who is making your life intolerable and unfree. . . .

Let me make it clear that I am not saying that feminism will solve everything, that it is the only road to "salvation." Black feminism, if it is to provide sound analysis of Black women's situation, must incorporate an understanding of economic oppression and racism as well as of sexism and heterosexism. What I am saying is that a deeply serious analysis of sexual oppression cannot be left out of revolutionary politics, that to ignore the pervasive and killing results of sexism as a trivial concern of Black and other Third World women is naive and false. As women all of us know how our lives have been undermined and broken because we are women, whether we consciously acknowledge it or not. This is why those of us who are Black and feminists must be committed to struggle and to learn with each other so that we can better understand the nature of the triple oppression we face. Only when we begin to understand and to practice the politics that come out of this understanding will we have a hope of becoming truly free.

March 8, 1976

Author's Postscript

I wanted to share with readers how I feel and have always felt about ". . . Will the Real Enemy Please Stand Up?" Saying what I've said and having it in print scares me. This is because the essay so specifically addresses in a critical way the reality of violence against Black women by Black men. This has been a deeply taboo subject judged politically "incorrect" in different historical eras and by people of many different political persuasions. Even with the murders of twelve Black women in my own community (Boston) in a four-month period this year, I still fear that what I've said here will be misunderstood and dismissed by those who most need to hear it. Yet, I stand by the accuracy and integrity of my analysis and have always felt that it belonged in a Black feminist publication. I wanted readers to know that writing this and having it published were difficult and challenging decisions for me.

Second Postscript

This paper was initially written in order to clarify some ideas for myself, as a result of attending an International Women's Day Program in 1976, sponsored by a Third World mixed-left sectarian group. That day the analysis of feminism was constantly rejected, the reality of patriarchy denied, and the phrase "men are not the enemy" repeated many times.

RECOMMENDED READINGS

Backhouse, Constance, and David Flaherty, eds. *Challenging Times: The Women's Movement in Canada and the United States.* Montreal, 1992.

Castro, Ginette. *American Feminism: A Contemporary History.* New York, 1990.

Deslippe, Dennis A. "Organized Labor, National Politics, and Second-Wave Feminism in the United States," *International Labor and Working-Class History* 49 (1996):143–65.

Echols, Alice. *Daring to Be Bad: Radical Feminism in America, 1967–1975.* Minneapolis, 1989.

Evans, Sara. *Personal Politics: The Roots of the Women's Liberation Movement in the Civil Rights Movement and the New Left.* New York, 1979.

Gluck, Sherna, with Maylei Blackwell, Sharon Cotrell, and Karen S. Harper. "Whose Feminism, Whose History? Reflections on Excavating the History of (the) U.S. Women's Movement." In Nancy Naples, ed. *Community Activism and Feminist Politics: Organizing Across Race, Class, and Gender.* New York, 1998.

Harrison, Cynthia, *On Account of Sex: The Politics of Women's Issues, 1945–1968.* Berkeley, 1988.

King, Katie. *Theory in Feminist Travels: Conversations in U.S. Women's Movements.* Bloomington, Ind., 1994.

Nicholson, Linda, ed. *The Second Wave: A Reader in Feminist Theory.* New York, 1997.

Shreve, Anita. *Women Together, Women Alone: The Legacy of the Consciousness-Raising Movement.* New York, 1989.

Taylor, Verta, and Leila J. Rupp. "Women's Culture and Lesbian Feminist Activism: A Reconsideration of Cultural Feminism." In Nancy Naples, ed. *Community Activism and Feminist Politics: Organizing Across Race, Class, and Gender.* New York, 1998.

Thom, Mary. *Inside Ms.: 25 years of the Magazine and the Feminist Movement.* New York, 1997.

Watkins, Bonnie, and Nina Rothchild, eds. *In the Company of Women: Voices from the Women's Movement.* St. Paul, Minn., 1996.

FIGURE 13.1
By 1971, some gay men, calling themselves Effeminists, had
withdrawn from the Gay Liberation Front. They made common cause
with feminists, arguing that male supremacy oppressed both gay men
and women. (*Photo by Bettye Lane, Studio 501D, 463 West St. New
York, NY.*)

CHAPTER 13

The Trials and Triumphs of Gay and Lesbian Liberation

The last liberation struggle to emerge in the 1960s was gay liberation. It knitted together many strands of protest spun during the decade: the New Left rejection of hierarchy, the feminist insistence that gender was created rather than natural, and the countercultural suspicion of monogamy and corporate culture.

This movement also drew on a quieter history of resistance and community formation. Since military experience during World War II had brought many gay men and lesbians into contact with each other as documented in Chapter 9 and prompted veterans to form homosexual communities in cities like San Francisco and New York, gay men and lesbians had been creating institutions, identities, and organizations that helped them to survive violent police raids, McCarthyite hunts, and a generally homophobic culture. Two of the most important 1950s gay organizations were the Mattachine Society and the Daughters of Bilitis, noted in Chapter 10, both of which insisted that homosexuality was not a condition to be overcome.

Moved by the struggle for racial justice, these homophile groups began openly to protest discrimination against gay people in the 1960s. They demonstrated against the ban on federal employment that McCarthy had aimed so viciously to enforce during the 1950s; they protested police brutality against gay men and lesbians; and they argued against the medical classification of homosexuality as a psychological disorder. These middle-class and older protesters were joined in 1969 by a younger group that called itself the Gay Liberation Front.

The struggle for gay liberation made much headway during the 1970s. Activists won repeal of sodomy laws in thirty-four states; in 1974, the American Psychiatric Association wiped homosexuality off its roster of psychiatric disorders. Thousands of gay and lesbian organizations formed over the course of the decade; openly gay people ran for political office—and sometimes won. In general, American society saw much greater openness about homosexuality (and heterosexuality) than before.

The next decade, however, ushered in new challenges for gay liberationists. The eruption of AIDS provided a rationale for a backlash that threatened the triumphs of the

1970s, and it forced a rethinking of gay manhood among those who had rooted their identities in sexual freedom. Some activists suggested that sexual expression be moved away from the center of gay men's identification. At the same time, sexual freedom edged *closer* to the center of lesbian identity. During the 1970s, lesbian feminists often downplayed the importance of sex as a component of lesbianism, emphasizing instead egalitarian care as the heart of lesbian identity. The 1980s saw a small but visible group contest what they saw as sexual repression in this dominant lesbian feminist community.

The founding in 1984 of *On Our Backs,* a magazine of lesbian pornography, evinced the trend. Playing on the title of *off our backs,* a serial founded in 1969 by radical feminists, the new publication proclaimed 1984 "the year of the lustful lesbian." *On Our Backs* celebrated varieties of sexual experience. It rejected what it saw as the stuffy sexual morality of 1970s feminism, insisting that even sado/masochism need not be sexist or imperialist, as earlier feminists had concluded, but could be simply fun and exciting.

This chapter documents some of the gender analyses prevalent in the gay liberation movement in the 1970s and the challenges to those analyses mounted in the 1980s. Backlash against the movement will be discussed in subsequent chapters.

THE STUD, THE TOOLBOX, THE BARN
Allen Young

Historians pin the opening of the gay liberation movement to a police raid on the Stonewall Inn. Stonewall was one of many gay bars in New York's Greenwich Village, long a haven for social rebels. Police often shut down the bars that catered to gay and lesbian customers, but on June 27, 1969, patrons of the Stonewall defied the routine: they fought back. They resisted arrest and, for an entire weekend, rioted against New York's men in blue. This uprising sparked the formation of the Gay Liberation Front, an organization devoted to ending the oppression of gay people in America.

Allen Young, a former member of SDS, joined the Gay Liberation Front in 1970. In the article excerpted here, he analyzed the Stonewall riot and the power of gender in creating gay identities before Stonewall. According to Young, where did gender roles come from? What did they have to do with gay identity? Compare his gender analyses with those of women in the feminist movement. What would he have thought of the gay prisoner surveyed by Samuel Kahn in the 1920s; of Pat and George in the 1950s? What would full sexual liberation mean?

> On a June evening in 1969 police began what seemed like a routine raid on the Stonewall Inn, Greenwich Village's most popular gay men's bar. But the raid didn't go off as planned. We fought back. The gay liberation movement was born.
>
> I am smiling ironically as I write "we." I wasn't there, and it took me more than six months before I even began to take part in the gay liberation movement. I was a "closet case," an oppressed homosexual, oppressed in America, oppressed in the movement [for social change].

Source: Allen Young, "Out of the Closets, Into the Streets," in Karla Jay and Allen Young, eds., *Out of the Closets: Voices of Gay Liberation* (New York: Douglas/Links, 1972), pp. 6–31.

I might well have been on Christopher Street—home of the Stonewall—that June night. I had been to the Stonewall several times that spring and the previous winter. But the Stonewall was a dancing bar, favorite hang-out of the freest of the gay people—those most likely to be labeled "fag" and "drag queen." I wasn't comfortable there: I preferred the more up-tight and sedate (read "masculine") crowd at Danny's, a few blocks closer to the waterfront. . . .

Our struggle as gays is to eliminate oppressive patterns that straights have burdened us with. Many gay men play either male or female roles. Some people think that this only has to do with what happens in bed. Although sex may be a factor, role-playing permeates all areas of human interaction. I was socialized into playing a male role. It didn't come easy: I knew that I threw a baseball "like a girl," and I have always been worried about my femininity. But a time did come when I could feel comfortable about my ability to pass for a "real man." Most important, I could hide my gayness. . . .

The worst thing about being gay is experiencing the anti-homosexualism of the society. To survive in a hostile environment, most gays hide their homosexuality. The result is the fear associated with the possibility of discovery, and the shame and guilt associated with homosexual dreams, daydreams, desires, and acts. For an important minority of homosexuals—those who are identified as such because they have the mannerisms, clothing or speech pattern usually reserved for the other sex—the oppression takes on different forms. The blatantly gay are often subject to verbal abuse, physical brutality from police and other thugs, and the knowledge that even those who can tolerate discreet homosexuality will not tolerate this turn-around of sex-determined roles.

Most male homosexuals are still trapped by notions of masculinity. It is a familiar story—the oppressed worships the oppressor. Listen to the names of some of America's gay men's bars—The Stud, The Tool Box, The Barn. What passes for gay men's art—including murals in these bars—often depicts such masculine characters as the Body-Builder, the Motorcyclist, the Cowboy. What goes on inside most of these gay bars often preserves the notion that the people inside are "real men," too. The billiard table, the sawdust on the floor, the leather vest on the bartender, and, most of all, the standing around with carefully groomed indifference while quaffing their beer (just like good collegians or dockworkers). The gay man's quest for masculinity, or exaggerated masculinity, cannot be dismissed as mere evidence of his sexism. Beyond that, it is evidence of oppression, evidence of how a minority is overwhelmed by the values and style of the majority.

Some additional observations about gay bars are necessary. On one level, these gathering places are products of a system we are striving to eliminate. First, they perpetuate male supremacy; second, most of them are owned by greedy gay capitalists or greedier criminal syndicates. It is impossible, however, to escape a crucial fact: aside from the meetings of gay organizations, these bars are the only places where large numbers of gay people get together. Until I went to a gay liberation meeting in January, 1970, for example, I had never been in a roomful of homosexuals—with the exception of a gay bar. As congregating places for gay people (particularly gay men, although there are a handful of lesbian bars in the biggest cities), the gay bars are the focal points of conflict between our new spirit of liberation and the forces which would keep us in our place. In other words, they are community institutions, as the community is now constituted. . . .

While fully recognizing the oppressive nature of dimly-lit bars in out-of-the-way streets such as Greenwich Street in New York and Folsom Street in San Francisco, we will continue to preserve the bars as temporary gay turf where there is at least minimal freedom for gay people. This campaign goes on simultaneously with attempts to provide alternative meeting grounds, such as coffee houses and community centers. Such places, along with gay liberation meetings, communal houses and apartments, already offer such an alternative to thousands of gays in nearly 100 localities. . . .

For gay people, the essential point is to see limited sexuality as an end result of male supremacy and sex roles. Gay, in its most far-reaching sense, means not homosexual, but sexually free. This includes a long-ranged vision of sensuality as a basis for sexual relationships. This sexual freedom is not some kind of groovy life style with lots of sex, doing what feels good irrespective of others. It is sexual freedom premised upon the notion of pleasure through equality, no pleasure where there is inequality. . . . Heterosexual relationships are encumbered by notions of how men and women are supposed to behave. It is a system which has male supremacy built in. Homosexuals committed to struggling against sexism have a better chance than straights of building relationships based on equality because there is less enforcement of roles. We have already broken with gender programming, so we can more easily move toward equality. . . .

As I develop a gay identity, I feel much more in touch with my humanity than when I was regularly passing for straight. I am swept up in a process of change which allows me to define myself in terms other than some masculine ideal. I have a growing awareness of myself and my relationships to other people which is exhilarating and deeply satisfying. My revolutionary fervor is more real than it ever was. I dance more, I laugh more, I am learning how to listen to others. I have sex less often but find it infinitely more satisfying. I am finding out how to love my brothers and sisters, how this love is the vital revolutionary force we all need.

THE IMPRISONING AND ARTIFICIAL LABELS OF GAY, STRAIGHT, AND BI
Third World Gay Revolution and Gay Liberation Front (Chicago)

The Stonewall rebellion clearly detonated long-standing resentments among gay and lesbian Americans. Soon after the first Gay Liberation Front formed in New York City, local cells organized in cities throughout the country. That these associations coalesced so quickly was evidence that the gay community was already well-organized, sometimes in formal organizations and sometimes around those community institutions—like bars—noted by Allen Young.

The language and analyses of liberationists also suggested that organizers had been involved in earlier political movements of the 1960s. How did the following manifesto, issued jointly by Chicago's Gay Liberation Front and Third World Gay Revolution, echo the thinking of Bobby Seale and the Panther women? How did it draw on concepts shared with YIPpie, Stewart Albert? How were gender and sexual identities/hierarchies related, according to this document? What was the goal of gay liberation, and how was it related to other liberation struggles?

Source: Third World Gay Revolution (Chicago) and Gay Liberation Front (Chicago), "Gay Revolution and Sex Roles," first published as "Statement," in *Chicago Gay Pride,* June 1971 and reprinted in Jay and Young, *Out of the Closet* (New York: Douglas/Links, 1972), pp. 252–59.

Gay liberation is inherently revolutionary. Most of homosexual oppression, and of the oppression all society receives as feedback, grows from the assumption that people are inborn heterosexual. That is acknowledged as false by even the most pig shrinks by now. . . .

With the assumption of inborn heterosexuality come the assumptions of whole package deals of inborn traits of women and of men. Everyone by now recognizes these as programmed role-playing. The recognition hasn't much weakened their rule. If you challenge their tyranny over you, you're "confusing gender identity." (No normal person would question his or her normal roles, so your failure to adjust is latent homosexuality—keep your place!) To maintain sex roles, heterosexual standards had to manufacture artificial definitions of male and female. A "real man" and "real woman" are not so by their chromosomes and genitals, [according to these artificial definitions,] but by their respective degrees of "masculinity" and "femininity," and by how closely they follow the sex-role script in their relationships with individuals and society. Heterosexual "normality" demands all-or-nothing outlines of "masculine" and "feminine" and denial of half the self.

Sex roles are so institutionalized that "normal" heterosexual relationships are so unequal, so exploitative, so possessive, so noncommunicative, so manipulative, so competitive, so non-respectful, so tied up in power struggle and with fulfilling roles that a ridiculously unloving standard of love is accepted. . . .

A gay person who accepts straight standards will associate "masculinity" with men and "femininity" with women. He or she will accept definitions of "real man" and "real woman" by that and by their proper relationships to the proper sexes. She or he will accept labeling of many of his or her feelings (which have nothing to do with being gay—just being human) as characteristic only of the opposite sex. He or she will accept that there are only the straights' two alternatives—mutually exclusive "manhood" and "womanhood." Thus has sexist brainwashing actually *created* a correlation between homosexuality and transsexualism. Though "gender identity," being entirely artificial, has little to do with sexual orientation, this is another way gay oppression is used to keep people in line. Anyone should be allowed to do anything with his or her appearance. Everyone should be allowed to integrate his or her personality. But, by straight standards, a person cannot like certain modes of appearance for their own sake, or give rein to some aspects of her or his personality, without violating her inborn sex-determined tendencies toward different appearances, interests, emotions, etc.; and therefore identifying with the opposite sex, and therefore being homosexual and therefore sick.

The oppression of women and that of gay people are interdependent and spring from the same roots, but take different forms. Women and children are oppressed by how they fit into the sex-class structure. Gay people are persecuted because we don't fit into that structure at all. Every effort has been made to exterminate us. (This is not to say that gay people are more oppressed than women or vice versa. It is counterrevolutionary to try to rank oppressed peoples in the order of the viciousness of their oppression, or to claim that one liberation movement is more important than another.) . . .

But individuals refusing to keep their places do not equally threaten a class structure (whether it be of economic class, sex, race, or whatever.) It can easier afford to allow an individual from a lower stratum to try to enter upper strata than vice versa. This reinforces the preeminence of the ruling group and keeps the oppressed divided and competing. For he or she must concede the superiority and desirability of the upper stratum. . . .

This somewhat neutralizes the threat to male supremacy that homosexual women's not needing men represents. Male homosexuals, however, have partly relinquished male privilege (though it wasn't voluntary, which is why male supremacist values still infect many homosexual men). So homosexual men are actively, openly persecuted by straight male-society—the persecution a magnification of straight men's insane reactions to fear of their own homosexuality—and of anything else within them, such as the "femininity" they attribute to homosexual men, that might imperil their power and privilege. Sexism's vertical one-dimensional class structure is also why *any* deviation from "normal" interests, feelings, etc. for one's sex is often attributed to transsexual tendencies (thus homosexuality). This is a major reason for the personality-typing of gay people. It is also why, for example, women's liberationists are accused of wanting to be men, and why terms such as "faggot" are thrown at a boy who doesn't suppress his "feminine" interests or characteristics. A "feminine" male threatens other males by in effect partially renouncing privilege, and thus threatening their own privilege, not only by mirroring a suppressed part of them but by weakening male-ruling-class position. So, as a defense of male position, he is separated from his maleness—"not a real man." Male supremacy is directly responsible for the more active persecution of male than of female homosexuals and transvestites.

The dependency of male privilege on "masculinity" and male role-playing is the means by which sexist "normality" requires men to "prove their masculinity" by obsession with possessions and with power, whether on the level of the sexual or the international. Male values are societal values in a male-dominated society, and "masculinity"-tripping is the anti-human values of the death culture. So it's even more important for society to compel men than women to suppress half of themselves. . . .

Though to us as individual gay people gay represents potential for love with equality and freedom, that's only the first level of gay is good. After all, the imprisoning, artificial labels of gay, straight, and bi would be meaningless without the sex roles and "correct gender identification" and isolation and channeling and antihumanism that sexism imposes. (As Judy Grahn said, "If anyone were allowed to fall in love with *anyone,* the word 'homosexual' wouldn't be needed.") A higher level of gay is good is as a tool to break down enforced heterosexuality, sex roles, the impoverished categories of straight, gay, and bisexual, male supremacy, programming of children, ownership of children, the nuclear family, monogamy, possessiveness, exclusiveness of "love," insecurity, jealousy, competition, privilege, individual isolation, ego-tripping, power-tripping, money-tripping, people as property, people as machines, rejection of the body, repression of emotions, antieroticism, authoritarian anti-human religion, conformity, regimentation, polarization of "masculine" and "feminine," categorization of male and female emotions, abilities, interests, clothing, etc., fragmentation of the self by these outlines. . . .

WOMEN-IDENTIFIED WOMEN HAVE BEEN AROUND A LONG TIME
Audre Lorde

While gay liberationists insisted that ranking oppressions was counter-revolutionary, many activists in other movements persisted in doing precisely that. In the following article, poet Audre Lorde [1934–] argued against this tactic, contending, as did the

Source: Audre Lorde, "Scratching the Surface: Some Notes on Barriers to Women and Loving," *The Black Scholar,* 9, 7 (April 1978), pp. 31–35.

FIGURE 13.2
Many African Americans and Latino(a)s seceded from white-dominated gay liberation organizations during the 1970s. In June 1977, the Salsa Soul Sisters marched in New York's Gay and Lesbian Rights Parade. (*Photo by Bettye Lane, Studio 501D, 463 West St. New York, NY.*)

Chicago activists, that various forms of oppression supported each other. Only by standing against them all would liberation be possible for anyone.

Lorde, a prolific writer and teacher, suggested the centrality that black Africa had come to play in the struggle for justice and identity among African Americans. In order to legitimate lesbianism among African American women, for instance, she cited a range of relationships among women in Africa. The implication was that, if African women enjoyed this spectrum of relationships with each other, then similar relationships ought to find acceptance in the United States.

As you will see, Lorde sometimes folded lesbians into a larger category of women-identified women. Why? How did that strategy fit and/or undermine the goals of gay liberation as defined by Allen Young and the Chicago activists? How did some black men and heterosexual black women use homophobia to keep women subordinate to men? How did this illuminate the ways that gender and sexual *systems* interacted?

> Racism: The belief in the inherent superiority of one race over all others and thereby the right to dominance.
>
> Sexism: The belief in the inherent superiority of one sex and thereby the right to dominance.
>
> Heterosexism: The belief in the inherent superiority of one pattern of loving and thereby its right to dominance.

Homophobia: The fear of feelings of love for members of one's own sex and therefore the hatred of those feelings in others.

The above forms of human blindness stem from the same root—the inability to recognize or tolerate the notion of difference as a beneficial and dynamic human force, and one which is enriching rather than threatening to the defined self.

To a large degree, at least verbally, the black community has moved beyond the "two steps behind her man" mode of sexual relations sometimes mouthed as desirable during the [nineteen] sixties. . . .

For black women as well as black men, it is axiomatic that if we do not define ourselves for ourselves, we will be defined by others—for their use and to our detriment. The development of self-defined black women, ready to explore and pursue our power and interests within our communities, is a vital component in the war for black liberation. The image of the Angolan woman with a baby on one arm and a gun in the other is neither romantic nor fanciful. Black women in this country coming together to examine our sources of strength and support, and to recognize our common social, cultural, emotional, and political interests, is a development which can only contribute to the power of the black community as a whole. For it is only through the coming together of self-actualized individuals, female and male, that any real advances can be made. The old sexual power-relationships based on a dominant/subordinate model between unequals have not served us as a people, nor as individuals.

Black women who define ourselves and our goals beyond the sphere of a sexual relationship can bring to any endeavor the realized focus of a completed and therefore empowered individual. Black women and black men who recognize that the development of their particular strengths and interests does not diminish the other, do not diffuse their energies fighting for control over each other. We focus our attentions against the real economic, political, and social forces at the heart of this society which are ripping ourselves and our children and our worlds apart. . . .

Today, the red herring of homophobia and lesbian-baiting is being used in the black community to obscure the true double face of racism/sexism. Black women sharing close ties with each other, politically or emotionally, are not the enemies of black men. Too frequently, however, an attempt to rule by fear tactics is practiced by some black men against those black women who are more ally than enemy. These tactics are sometimes expressed as threats of emotional rejection: "Their poetry wasn't too bad but I couldn't take all those lezzies (lesbians)." The man who says this is warning every black woman present who is interested in a relationship with men—and most black women are—that (1) if she wishes to have her work considered she must eschew any other allegiance except to him and (2) any woman who wishes his friendship and/or support had better not be "tainted" by woman-identified interests. . . .

Instead of keeping our attentions focused upon the real enemies, enormous energy is being wasted in the black community today by both black men and heterosexual black women, in anti-lesbian hysteria. Yet women-identified women—those who sought their own destinies and attempted to execute them in the absence of male support—have been around in all of our communities for a long time. As Yvonne Flowers of York College pointed out in a recent discussion, the unmarried aunt, childless or otherwise, whose home and resources were often a welcome haven for different members of the family, was a familiar figure in many of our childhoods. . . .

The black lesbian has come under increasing attack from both black men and heterosexual black women. In the same way that the existence of the self-defined black woman is no threat to the self-defined black man, the black lesbian is an emotional threat only to those black women who are unsure of, or unable to express their feelings of kinship and love for other black women, in any meaningful way. For so long, we have been encouraged to view each other with suspicion, as eternal competitors, or as the visible face of our own self-rejection.

But traditionally, black women have always bonded together in support of each other, however uneasily and in the face of whatever other allegiances which militated against that bonding. We have banded together with each other for wisdom and strength and support, even when it was only in relationship to one man. We need only look at the close—although highly complex and involved—relationship between African co-wives; or at the Amazon warriors of ancient Dahomey, who fought together as the Kings' main and most ferocious bodyguard. We need only look at the more promising power wielded by West African Market Women Associations of today, and those governments which have risen and fallen at their pleasure.

In a verbatim retelling of her life, a 92-year-old Efik-Ibibio woman of Nigeria recalls her love for another woman:

> I had a woman friend to whom I revealed my secrets. She was very fond of keeping secrets to herself. We acted as husband and wife. We always moved hand in glove and my husband and hers knew about our relationship. The villagers nicknamed us twin sisters.[1]

The Fon of Dahomey still have 12 different kinds of marriage, one of which is known as "giving the goat to the buck," where a woman of independent means marries another woman who then may or may not bear children, all of whom will belong to the blood line of the other woman.[2] Some marriages of this kind are arranged to provide heirs for women of means who wish to remain "free," and some are homosexual relationships. Marriages of this kind occur throughout Africa, in several different places among different peoples.[3]

In all of these cases, the women involved are recognized parts of their communities, evaluated not by their sexuality but by their respective places within the community. . . .

If the recent hysterical rejection of lesbians in the black community is based solely upon aversion to the idea of sexual contact between members of the same sex (a contact existing for ages in most of the female compounds across the African continent, from reports) why then is the idea of sexual contact between black men so much more easily accepted, or unremarked? Is the reality of the imagined threat the existence of a self-motivated, self-defined black woman who will not fear nor suffer some terrible retribution from the gods because she does not necessarily seek her face in a man's eyes. . . .

---

[1] Andreski, Iris. *Old Wives Tales: Life-Stories of African Women.* Schocken Books, New York, 1970, p. 131.

[2] Herskovits, Melville. *Dahomey.* Northwestern University Press. Evanston, 1967. 2 volumes. I, pp. 320–21.

[3] *Ibid.,* I, p. 322.

WHEN YOU DENY THAT ROLES EXIST
Amber Hollibaugh and Cherríe Moraga

During the 1980s, divisive sexual issues came to the fore among lesbian feminists. To some, it seemed that feminists in the 1970s expected perfect equality—defined by sameness—in lesbian relationships. This expectation hid and made it impossible to discuss the complicated gender and sexual issues in real lesbian relationships and in fact made taboo every sort of difference within a sexual relationship.

Liberationists in the 1970s hated the gender "roles" that they believed earlier generations of gays had played: men assuming the role of effeminate fairy or macho stud, for instance, and women playing the role of butch or femme. By the 1980s, however, some lesbians claimed that butch/femme "roles" were more than self-conscious performance; they were integral parts of identity. Others insisted that playing the part of femme or butch could be fun and erotic, not dangerous and oppressive.

Discussion of "roles" within lesbian relationships, widespread in the 1980s, was nowhere more sensitively presented than in the following conversation between feminists Cherríe Moraga [1952–] and Amber Hollibaugh [1947–]. How did gender figure in the sexual identities and experiences of these discussants? How did their ideas about gender roles within gay relationships differ from those expressed by Allen Young and Chicago's Third World Gay Revolution? Compare Moraga's understanding of herself as "butch" with the analyses of Havelock Ellis.

This article was derived from a series of conversations we entertained for many months. Through it, we wish to illuminate both our common and different relationship to a feminist movement to which we are both committed.

THE CRITIQUE

In terms of sexual issues, it seems feminism has fallen short of its original intent. The whole notion of "the personal is political" which surfaced in the early part of the movement . . . is suddenly and ironically dismissed when we begin to discuss sexuality. We have become a relatively sophisticated movement, so many women think they now have to have the theory before they expose the experience. It seems we simply did not take our feminism to heart enough. This most privatized aspect of ourselves, our sex lives, has dead-ended into silence within the feminist movement.

Feminism has never directly addressed women's sexuality except in its most oppressive aspects in relation to men (e.g. marriage, the nuclear family, wife battering, rape, etc.). . . .

. . . but we didn't learn what's *sexual*. . . .

What grew out of this kind of "non-sexual" theory was a "transcendent" definition of sexuality where lesbianism (since it exists outside the institution of heterosexuality) came to be seen as the practice of feminism. It set up a "perfect"

Source: Amber Hollibaugh and Cherríe Moraga, "What We're Rollin Around in Bed With: Sexual Silences in Feminism: A Conversation Toward Ending Them," *Heresies,* 3, 4 (1981), pp. 58–62.

vision of egalitarian sexuality, where we could magically leap over our hetero-sexist conditioning into mutually orgasmic, struggle-free, trouble-free sex. We feel this vision has become both misleading and damaging to many feminists, but in particular to lesbians. . . . There is little language, little literature that re-flects the actual sexual struggles of most lesbians, feminist or not.

The failure of feminism to answer all the questions regarding women, in partic-ular women's sexuality, is the same failure the homosexual movement suffers from around gender. It's a confusing of those two things—that some of us are both female and homosexual—that may be the source of some of the tension between the two movements and of the inadequacies of each. When we walk down the street, we are both female and lesbian. We are working-class white and working-class Chicana. . . .

THE CONVERSATION

CM: *In trying to develop sexual theory, I think we should start by talking about what we're rollin' around in bed with. We both agree that the way feminism has dealt with sexuality has been entirely inadequate.*

AH: Right. Sexual theory has traditionally been used to say *people have been forced to be this thing; people could be that thing.* . . . It hasn't been able to talk re-alistically about what people *are* sexually.

I think by focusing on roles in lesbian relationships, we can begin to unravel who we really are in bed. When you hide how profoundly roles can shape your sex-uality, you can use that as an example of other things that get hidden. There's a lot of different things that shape the way people respond—some not so easy to see, some more forbidden, as I perceive S[ado]/M[asochism] to be. . . . The point is, that when you deny that roles, S/M, fantasy, or any sexual differences exist in the first place, you can only come up with neutered sexuality, where everybody's got to be basically the same because anything different puts the element of power and devi-ation in there and threatens the whole picture.

CM: *Exactly. Remember how I told you that growing up what turned me on sex-ually, at a very early age, had to do with the fantasy of capture, taking a woman, and my identification was with the man, taking? Well, something like that would be so frightening to bring up in a feminist context . . . fearing people would put it in some sicko sexual box. And yet, the truth is, I do have some real gut-level misgivings about my sexual connection with capture. It might feel very sexy to imagine "tak-ing" a woman, but it has sometimes occurred at the expense of my feeling, sexu-ally, like I can surrender myself to a woman; that is, always needing to be the one in control, callin the shots. It's a very butch trip and I feel like this can keep me pri-vate and protected and can prevent me from fully being able to express myself.*

AH: But it's not wrong, in and of itself, to have a capture fantasy. The real ques-tion is: Does it *actually* limit you? For instance, does it allow you to eroticize some-one else, but never see yourself as erotic? Does it keep you always in control? Does the fantasy force you into a dimension of sexuality that feels very narrow to you? If it causes you to look at your lover in only one light, then you may want to check it out. But if you can't even dream about wanting a woman in this way in the first place, then you can't figure out what is narrow and heterosexist in it and what's just play. After all, it's only *one* fantasy.

CM: *Well, what I think is very dangerous about keeping down such fantasies is that they are forced to stay unconscious. Then, next thing you know, in the actual sexual relationship, you become the capturer, that is, you try to have power over your lover, psychologically or whatever. If the desire for power is so hidden and un-acknowledged, it will inevitably surface through manipulation or what-have-you. If you couldn't play capturer, you'd be it.*

AH: Part of the problem in talking about sexuality is *it's so enormous* in our culture that people don't have any genuine sense of dimension. So that when you say "capture," every fantasy you've ever heard of from Robin Hood to colonialism comes racing into your mind and all you really maybe wanted to do was have your girlfriend lay you down.

But in feminism, we can't even explore these questions because what they say is, in gender, there is a masculine oppressor and a female oppressee. So whether you might fantasize yourself in a role a man might perform or a woman in reaction to a man, this makes you sick, fucked-up, and you had better go and change it. . . .

For example, *I think the reason butch/femme stuff got hidden within lesbian-feminism is because people are profoundly afraid of questions of power in bed.* And though everybody doesn't play out power the way I do, the question of power affects who and how you eroticize your sexual need. And it is absolutely at the bottom of all sexual inquiry. . . .

CM: *But what is femme to you? I told you once that what I thought of as femme was passive, unassertive, etc., and you didn't fit that image. And you said to me, "Well, change your definition of femme."*

AH: My fantasy life is deeply involved in a butch/femme exchange. I never come together with a woman, sexually, outside of those roles. Femme is active, not passive. It's saying to my partner, "Love me enough to let me go where I need to go and take me there. Don't make me think it through. Give me a way to be so in my body that I don't have to think; that you can fantasize for the both of us. You map it out. You are in control."

It's hard to talk about things like giving up power without it sounding passive. I am willing to give myself over to a woman equal to her amount of wanting. I expose myself for her to see what's possible for her to love in me that's female. I want her to respond to it. . . .

CM: *I feel the way I want a woman can be a very profound experience. Remember I told you how when I looked up at my lover's face when I was making love to her (I was actually just kissing her breast at the moment), but when I looked up at her face, I could feel and see how deeply every part of her was present? That every pore in her body was entrusting me to handle her, to take care of her sexual desire. This look on her face is like nothing else. It fills me up. She entrusts me to determine where she'll go sexually. And I honestly feel a power inside me strong enough to heal the deepest wound.*

AH: Well, I can't actually see what I look like, but I can feel it in my lover's hands when I look the way you described. When I open myself up more and more to her sensation of wanting a woman, when I eroticize that in her, I feel a kind of ache in my body, but it's not an ache to *do* something. I can feel a hurt spot and a need and it's there and it's just the tip of it, the tip of that desire and that is what first gets played with, made erotic. It's light and playful. It doesn't commit you to exposing a deeper part of yourself sexually. Then I begin to pick up passion. And the passion isn't butch or femme. It's just passion.

But from this place, if it's working, I begin to imagine myself being *the woman that a woman always wanted.* That's what I begin to eroticize. That's what I begin to feel from my lover's hands. I begin to fantasize myself becoming more and more female in order to comprehend and meet what I feel happening in her body. I don't want her not to be female to me. Her need is female, but it's butch because I am asking her to expose her desire through the movement of her hands on my body and I'll respond. I want to give up power in response to her need. This can feel profoundly powerful and very unpassive.

A lot of times how I feel it in my body is I feel like I have this fantasy of pulling a woman's hips into my cunt. I can feel the need painfully in another woman's body. I can feel the impact and I begin to play and respond to that hunger and desire. And I begin to eroticize the fantasy that *she can't get enuf of me.* It makes me want to enflame by body. What it feels like is that I'm in my own veins and I'm sending heat up into my thighs. It's very hot. . . .

CM: *But don't you ever fantasize yourself being on the opposite end of that experience?*

AH: Well, not exactly in the same way, because with butches you can't insist on them giving up their sexual identity. . . . That's why roles are so significant and you can't throw them out. You have to find a way to use them, so you can eventually release your sexuality into other domains that you may feel the role traps you in. But you don't have to throw out the role to explore the sexuality. There are femme ways to orchestrate sexuality. I'm not asking a woman not to be butch. I am asking her to let me express the other part of my own character, where I am actively orchestrating what's happening. I never give up my right to say that I can insist on what happens sexually. . . . Quite often what will happen is I'll simply seduce her. Now, that's very active. The seduction can be very profound, but it's a seduction as a femme.

CM: *What comes to my mind is something as simple as you comin over and sittin on her lap. Where a butch, well, she might just go for your throat if she wants you.*

AH: Oh yes, different areas for different roles! What's essential is that your attitude doesn't threaten the other person's sexual identity, but plays with it. That's what good seduction is all about. I play a lot in that. It's not that I have to have spike heels on in order to fantasize who I am. Now that's just a lot of classist shit, conceiving of femme in such a narrow way.

CM: *Well, I would venture to say that some of these dynamics that you're describing happen between most lesbians. Only they may both be in the same drag of flannel shirts and jeans. My feeling, however, is . . . and this is very hard for me . . . what I described earlier about seeing my lover's face entrusting me like she did, well,* I want her to take me to that place, too.

AH: Yes, but you don't want to have to deny your butchness to get there, right?

CM: *Well, that's what's hard. To be butch, to me, is not to be a woman. The classic extreme butch stereotype is the woman who sexually refuses another woman to touch her. It goes something like this: She doesn't want to feel her femaleness because she thinks of you as the "real" woman and if she makes love to you, she doesn't have to feel her own body as the object of desire. She can be a kind of "bodiless lover." So when you turn over and want to make love to her and make her feel physically like a woman, then what she is up against is QUEER. You are a woman making love to her. She feels queerer than anything in that. Get it?*

AH: Got it. Whew!

CM: *I believe that probably from a very early age the way you conceived of your-self as female has been very different from me. We both have pain, but I think that there is a particular pain attached if you identified yourself as a butch queer from an early age as I did. I didn't really think of myself as female, or male. I thought of myself as a hybrid or somethin. I just kinda thought of myself as this free agent un-til I got tits. Then I thought,* oh oh, some problem has occurred here. . . . *For me, the way you conceive of yourself as a woman and the way I am attracted to women sexually reflect that butch/femme exchange—where a woman believes herself so woman that it really makes me want her.*

But for me, I feel a lot of pain around the fact that it has been difficult for me to con-ceive of myself as thoroughly female in that sexual way. So retaining my "butchness" is not exactly my desired goal. Now that, in itself, is probably all heterosexist bullshit—about what a woman is supposed to be in the first place—but we are talkin about the differences between the way you and I conceive of ourselves as sexual beings.

AH: I think it does make a difference. I would argue that a good femme does not play to the part of you that hates yourself for feelin like a man, but to the part of you that knows you're a woman. Because it's absolutely critical to understand that femmes are women to women and dykes to men in the straight world. *You and I are talkin girl to girl.* We're not talkin what I was in straight life.

I was ruthless with men, sexually, around what I felt. *It was only with women I couldn't avoid opening up my need to have something more than an orgasm.* With a woman, I can't refuse to know that the possibility is just there that she'll reach me some place very deeply each time we make love. That's part of my fear of being a lesbian. I can't refuse that possibility with a woman.

You see, I want you as a woman, not as a man; but, I want you in the way *you* need to be, which may not be traditionally female, but which is the area that you ex-press as *butch.* Here is where in the other world you have suffered the most dam-age. My feeling is part of the reason I love to be with butches is because I feel I repair that damage. I make it right to want me that hard. Butches have not been al-lowed to feel their own desire because part of butch can be perceived by the straight world as male. I feel I get back my femaleness and give a different defini-tion of femaleness to a butch as a femme. That's what I mean about one of those unexplored territories that goes beyond roles, but goes through roles to get there.

CM: *How I fantasize sex roles has been really different for me with different women. I do usually enter into an erotic encounter with a woman from the kind of butch place you described, but I have also felt very ripped off there, finding myself taking all the sexual responsibility. I am seriously attracted to butches sometimes. It's a different dynamic, where the sexuality may not seem as fluid or comprehensible, but I know there's a huge part of me that wants to be handled in the way I described I can han-dle another woman. I am very compelled toward that "lover" posture. I have never to-tally reckoned with being the "beloved" and, frankly, I don't know if it takes a butch or a femme or what to get me there. I know that it's a struggle within me and it scares the shit out of me to look at it so directly. I've done this kind of searching emotionally, but to combine sex with it seems like very dangerous stuff.*

AH: Well, I think everybody has aspects of roles in their relationships, but I feel pretty out there on the extreme end. . . . I think what feminism did, in its fear of het-erosexual control of fantasy, was to say that there was almost no fantasy safe to have, where you weren't going to have to give up power or take it. . . .

CM: *Oh, of course when most feminists talk about sexuality, including lesbianism, they're not talkin about Desire. It is significant to me that I came out only when I met* *a good feminist, although I knew I was queer since eight or nine. That's only when I'd risk it because I wouldn't have to say it's because I want her [sexually]. I didn't have to say that when she travels by me, my whole body starts throbbing.*

AH: Yes, it's just *correct.*

CM: *It was okay to be with her because we all knew men were really fuckers and there were a lot of "okay" women acknowledging that. Read: white and educated. . . . But that's not why I "came out." How could I say that I wanted women so bad, I was gonna die if I didn't get me one, soon! You know, I just felt the pull in the hips, right?*

AH: . . . So it [feminism] became this really repressive movement, where you didn't talk dirty and you didn't do dirty. It really became a bore. So after meetings, we *ran* to the bars. You couldn't talk about wanting a woman, except very loftily. You couldn't say it hurt at night wanting a woman to touch you. . . .

Yes, we're not just accusing feminism of silence, but our own participation in that silence has stemmed from absolute terror of facing that profound sexual need. Period.

There is no doubt in my mind that the feminist movement has radically changed, in an important way, everybody's concept of lesbianism. . . . Lesbianism is certainly accepted in feminism, but more as a political or intellectual concept. It seems feminism is the last rock of conservatism. It will not be sexualized. . . .

Well I won't give my sexuality up and I won't *not* be a feminist. So, I'll build a different movement, but I won't live without either one. . . .

A CONTRADICTION IN TERMS: GAY FREEDOM AND CLOSE THE BATHS
Guy Straight

At the same time that a new analysis of gender roles and sexual difference divided America's lesbian feminists, a new disease syndrome unsettled the gay men's community. In the early 1980s, Acquired Immune Deficiency Syndrome (AIDS), unfamiliar and unexplained, began its devastating march through gay male enclaves in urban areas like San Francisco and New York. By mid-decade, it took lives in outlying areas and was clearly not confined to the gay population but was now known to be caused by the Human Immunodeficiency Virus (HIV), an agent passed between people by transfer of blood or semen. Anal sex and intravenous drug use were two practices especially prone to transmit the virus.

While many gay men in the early 1980s lived in monogamous relationships, some, maintaining gay liberation's countercultural perspectives, rejected monogamy as an oppressive institution and gloried in the sexual freedoms made possible by city life. Specifically gay male institutions like bathhouses and sex clubs, providing opportunities for recreational sex, symbolized for many a gay male identity based on sexual freedom. Although only a small minority of gay men even in urban areas actually frequented these institutions, the bathhouses and clubs represented for many the liberation they had fought hard and risked much to achieve. The AIDS epidemic called these freedoms into question and, as a result, threatened hard-won identities.

Source: Guy Straight, "Would Rather Have AIDS," Letter to the Editor, *Bay Area Reporter,* 13, 23 (June 9, 1983), p. 8.

The power of that threat was captured in the following letter to San Francisco's *Bay Area Reporter.* It was written early in the epidemic, when the evidence that HIV was sexually transmissible was not so compelling as it would be later. For this writer, what was the foundation of gay male identity?

Never before in the history of man have so many words been said regarding a subject which no one admits to knowing anything about: AIDS.

In the caterwauling to the general public, the governmental entities, and the homosexual community, the "Gay Press" has accomplished something that the Roman Catholic Church, St. Peter, St. Paul, St. Augustine, the Rev. Jerry Falwell [leader of a fundamentalist Christian group that condemned homosexuality], Anita Bryant [anti-gay activist], and the thundering of hellfire and damnation have not been able to accomplish: cutting down on the amount of head given to relative strangers and forcing a decline in old-fashioned sodomy. . . .

In this morning's paper I read of a "leader" of the gay community who has suggested that the bathhouses be closed during Gay Freedom Day. What a contradiction in terms: Gay Freedom and Close the Baths. . . .

In howling SOMEBODY DO SOMETHING, the Chicken Littles of our community have provided the Queer Baiters with ammunition far beyond their wildest dreams of repression.

The compilers of the statistics of AIDS have never been known to favor the homosexual community and have in fact twisted figures time and time again to bring as bad a light as possible to the health hazards of same-sex relations. . . .

Summed up: The AIDS thing will come and go and bureaucrats and media will get a bundle of dollars through advertising revenue and grants plus some well-meaning fundraisers. AIDS then will be conquered by expert researchers working on their own for a well-financed drug lab without fanfare.

The real loser in the AIDS Affair will be the freedom of men to choose their particular form of sex expression with as many sex partners as they choose (or are able to perform).

Let us return sex back into homosexuality and leave the rabble-rousing to the rednecks. For one, I'd rather take my chances with AIDS than with the politicians (professional and gay) looking into my private life and I am sure my friend Jim Burge, AIDS victim, would be the first to back me up.

Guy Straight
San Francisco

WE MEN MUST CHANGE OUR SEXUAL LIFESTYLE
Ron Huberman, Cleve Jones, Bill Kraus

The opinions of Guy Straight would soon claim few adherents as AIDS proved genuinely catastrophic for America's gay male community. By the mid 1980s, even gay men previously committed to multiple sex partners in anonymous settings were reinventing themselves as sexually restrained AIDS activists. Many commentators

Source: Ron Huberman, Cleve Jones, and Bill Kraus, "Three Gay Figures Join the AIDS Debate," *Bay Area Reporter,* 13, 21, (May 26, 1983), p. 4.

observed that AIDS had created new priorities among many gay men: health, intimacy, and responsibility for the whole community. One referred to these new aspects of gay identity as a "feminization" of gay men.

Among the first to outline this new set of ideals were San Francisco activists
Ron Huberman, Bill Kraus, and Cleve Jones. According to their 1983 manifesto, excerpted here, what would the characteristics of a new gay male identity be? How
would it differ from the gay identity forged through gay liberation in the 1970s?

> We three Gay men are convinced that the AIDS epidemic means that we men
> must—temporarily, we hope—change our sexual lifestyles in order to save our
> lives. Still, despite all the evidence, despite the suffering we see around us, despite
> the pleadings of the doctors who care for AIDS patients and are trying to avert a
> full-scale epidemic—there are those who insist on believing that there is no rela-
> tionship between AIDS and sexual contact.
>
> But what a peculiar perversion it is of Gay liberation to ignore the overwhelm-
> ing scientific evidence, to keep quiet, to deny the obvious—when the lives of Gay
> men are at stake.
>
> What a strange concept of our Gay movement it is to care more about what
> straight people think of us, and to worry more about what they may do to us, than
> about the need to spread the news about this disease to our people so that we can
> protect each other.
>
> Can anyone who believes passionately that we must respect and love one an-
> other be so afraid to see this epidemic for what it is—and to say so—that we re-
> main silent while thousands of Gay people come here from all over the
> world—especially during Lesbian/Gay Freedom Week—without knowing what is
> happening here?
>
> Are we so insecure about homosexuality that we don't understand that telling
> the theories about sexual transmissibility will save Gay people's lives, but implies
> nothing bad about being Gay at all? Don't we understand that the fact that this
> disease agent is loose among us is no more a condemnation of being Gay than
> keeping people out of the ocean during a severe undertow is a condemnation of
> swimmers? . . .
>
> We are not moralists, and we are not homophobes. We have worked for Gay
> liberation for years—with Harvey Milk [gay city supervisor who was murdered by an
> anti-gay assassin], with No on 6 [anti-gay ballot initiative], and in many of the strug-
> gles against oppression, including the effort to rescue the Jaguar Book Store [a gay
> bookstore in San Francisco].
>
> We are Gay men who have lived the San Francisco lifestyle. We do not have
> lovers with whom to retire to a cozy home and wait out the epidemic. We face the
> same choices that other Gay men face.
>
> And we have decided not to be passive victims of this epidemic, but to take
> steps to protect ourselves by making serious changes in our sex lives.
>
> We have stopped going to the baths and similar places. We have greatly re-
> duced the number of our sexual partners. We have decided to spend more time with
> our friends, and to get to know our sexual partners better.
>
> We have decided to take better care of our health—to drink less and sleep more.
>
> We have decided to listen to the doctors who say that the risk of transmission
> of AIDS is through bodily fluids—urine, semen, blood, fecal matter—and to avoid
> sexual practices that involve contact with or ingesting these fluids. . . .

What's left to do? Is there life after AIDS? We can't say that the adjustments in lifestyle are easy. We miss some of the old ways, and look forward to the time when they will be safe again. But there are ways in which we Gay men can transform this epidemic into our finest hour.

There is nothing bad about taking care of our health. And there's nothing bad about getting to know people better, about re-emphasizing our friendships, about helping to take care of one another.

This difficult time will bring us closer together, and it will help to forge a Gay community which has been developing over decades of struggle.

As individuals and as a community, we have survived all of the crises which have confronted us in what is still a homophobic society. We have fought it alone, in our private lives in coming out; and we have fought it together, in the streets when they killed Harvey and on the ballot when they tried to take our rights away.

And out of that shared pain and triumph, and the overwhelming desire to be free, we have built a community.

Now that community will sustain us—and, ultimately, help lead us to another victory—in this crisis which is more grave than all the other crises.

What we have learned is to respect and care for ourselves and each other—to value our lives—and in the next year we will have the opportunity to deepen that respect and caring.

We will learn that there is something we share that is deeper than quick and easy sex—and once again, we will survive. . . .

RECOMMENDED READINGS

Blasius, Mark, and Shane Phelan, eds. *We Are Everywhere: A Historical Sourcebook of Gay and Lesbian Politics.* New York, 1997.

Cruikshank, Margaret. *The Gay and Lesbian Liberation Movement.* New York, 1992.

Deitcher, David, ed. *The Question of Equality: Lesbian and Gay Politics in America Since Stonewall.* New York, 1995.

Duberman, Martin B. *Stonewall.* New York, 1993.

Faderman, Lillian. *Odd Girls and Twilight Lovers: A History of Lesbian Life in Twentieth-Century America.* New York, 1991.

Nestle, Joan. *Persistent Desire: A Butch-Femme Reader.* Boston, 1992.

Shilts, Randy. *And the Band Played On: Politics, People, and the AIDS Epidemic.* New York, 1987.

———. *Conduct Unbecoming: Lesbians and Gays in the United States Military: Vietnam to the Persian Gulf.* New York, 1993.

Thompson, Mark, ed. *Long Road to Freedom: The Advocate History of the Gay and Lesbian Movement.* New York, 1994.

Remember that you're worth waiting for!

FIGURE 14.1
The sexual revolution, as well as the gender revolution, were targets of conservative backlash. Through their own sex education programs, conservative sex educators sought to reach young people with a message of chastity. (*Source: Coleen Kelly Mast,* Sex Respect: The Option of True Sexual Freedom *[Bradley IL: Respect, Inc., 1990], n.p.; reprinted with permission).*

CHAPTER 14

Backlash

To many Americans, the visions of feminists and gay and lesbian activists did not presage liberation but rather a deep threat to their way of life and to American society as a whole. Echoing the rhetoric of the Cold War, they claimed that radical changes in the gender system would lead to the disintegration of the male-headed family and with it, the country's strongest defense against Communism. These Americans mobilized to prevent ratification of the Equal Rights Amendment (passed by Congress in 1972) and weaken the implications of *Roe* v. *Wade* (the 1973 Supreme Court decision that legalized abortion), forming a loose coalition that came to be known as the New Right.

Hardly monolithic, the New Right combined vociferous objections to social innovations such as child care, abortion on demand, and open homosexuality, with opposition to governmental expansion, long one of the hallmarks of American laissez-faire conservatism. Right-wing religious activists ranging from Roman Catholic to evangelical and fundamentalist Christians joined forces with urban whites opposed to court-ordered school busing, Sun Belt populists seeking to block federal regulation of the environment, and Southern Californians in revolt against taxes.

In the mid-1970s the right began to coalesce into large umbrella organizations like the Moral Majority and the Christian Coalition. While charismatic, politically-minded, and media-savvy evangelists Pat Robertson and Jerry Falwell stirred up emotions and defined issues, communications wizard Richard Viguerie organized vast telephone networks and channeled moral outrage into contributions, votes, and letter-writing campaigns.

One of the few women who gained prominence in this movement was Phyllis Schlafly, a Harvard-trained lawyer and mother of four who founded the Eagle Forum. Most women on the right remained anonymous—housewives who set aside their domestic duties to lobby, picket, and run for local office such as schoolboard member, where they could work on behalf of conservative issues. These women believed that liberalized abortion, along with "the pill" (first introduced in 1960), made both premarital sex and adultery too easy. While right-wing ideology prescribed only a narrow role for women, it also granted them moral support for their insistence on marital fidelity.

The backlash was not entirely confined to the organized right. Much of the hostility against feminists, gays, and lesbians took the form of taunts and spontaneous outbursts. Resentment toward the gender revolution combined with frustration over America's defeat in Vietnam to produce extreme expressions of "machismo" such as the *Rambo* films. According to cultural analysts, these were part of an effort to "remasculinize" American society.

In addition to opposition from the right, feminism and gay activism were also weakened by disillusionment on the part of middle-of-the-road Americans. As conservative gender ideology gained respectability under the Reagan and Bush administrations, the ERA was defeated and struggles for access to abortion, employment equity, and gay rights lost considerable ground.

MEN WANT TO MARRY HORSES
Illinois State Legislators

The Equal Rights Amendment (ERA) became the lightning rod for every objection to feminism and gay liberation. To many opponents, it was the devil incarnate, and they seemed to take a certain delight in painting dire pictures of the social decay and gender chaos that would ensue if the amendment was ratified.

Feminist activists, faced with determined and well-orchestrated opposition to the ERA, realized they must abandon some of their countercultural distaste for electoral politics if they were to succeed. But they did not change tactics fast enough; the ERA was defeated largely by conservative forces based in churches across key states.

The following excerpts are taken from debates in the Illinois legislature in the mid-1970s, where the amendment was being hotly contested and was eventually defeated. Why do you think the speakers selected particular images? How did they attempt to turn the issue from a political into a moral one?

Webber Borchers: ". . . I would just like to tell one story with what I personally saw with the Russian Army. And, I would like to point out that, in my opinion, that this is a direct blow . . . this is a direct blow against the home and the family and could be disastrous to our Country. I saw in May of 1945 across the Elbe River, with my own eyes, the mixed units, male and female in the Russian Armies. They are equal. Now, crudeness is a bad thing, but sometimes, crudeness can explain what your grand

Source: Illinois General Assembly, House of Representatives, *Debates,* May 1, 1972, pp. 213–14 [Borchers]; May 16, 1972, pp. 200–2 [Hyde]; May 1, 1975, pp. 36–37 [Hanahan]; May 16, 1975, pp. 45–46 [Cunningham]. Note: these excerpts are taken from verbatim transcripts; the errors are the transcriber's.

daughters and your daughters may be confronted with in a case out of the serving in the United States' Army or . . . or the Military Units of the United States. I personally saw an open latrine trench. I have personally seen women and men soldiers of the Russian Army squatting over those trenches. Now, visualize your daughters, your grand daughters in that position. . . . If that is the direction in which you wish to take the culture of our country, fine. But, not for me. I want to see the idea of the sanctity and the protection continue as we've always had in this Country. But, think of the crudeness of it. But, this is what you are asking for because that is a necessary Military Service. And, you can't carry two latrine trenches and two latrine ah . . . canvas protection in the field in the front line of an Army in combat. And, you are asking for that very thing. I won't repeat any more of the rest, Pal. Vote 'no.' "

Henry Hyde: ". . . Such obvious differential treatment for women as exemption from the draft, exclusion from the Service Academies and more restrictive standards for enlistment will have to be brought into conformity with the Amendment's basic prohibition of sex discrimination. A woman will register for the draft at the age of eighteen as a man does. Under the Equal Rights Amendment, the Woman's Army Corps will be abolished. There is no reason to prevent women from doing these jobs in combat zone[s]. Look at Criminal Law, statutory Rape Law will go out the window. The Courts may be expected to hold that Laws which confine liability for prostitution to women are invalid, under this Amendment. Of course, we'll legalize pimping because the Pandering Statute will again will become, of course, unconstitutional. The . . . Equal Rights Amendment would invalidate Prostitution Laws. . . . Let's look at domestic relations. [In] 90 percent of the custody cases, the Mother is awarded the custody of her child. The Equal Rights Amendment would prohibit any statutory or common law presumptions about which parent was the proper guardian based on the sex of the parent. In all States, Husbands are primarily liable for the support of their Wives and Children. Child-support Sections of the Criminal Non-support Laws could not be sustained where only the male is liable for support. How about the protective labor Legislation? Under the Equal Rights Amendment, Courts are not likely to find any justification for the continuance of Laws which exclude women from certain occupations. And, in Illinois, women aren't supposed to work in the Coal Mines. But, I guess that they want the right to do that. Now, there will be no . . . discrimination in schools, in public schools. There will be no more girls schools. The House of the Good Shepherd for wayward girls, I suppose can be inhabited by anybody looking for a room for the night. Ah . . . convents, I don't know what will become of them, but they'll be unconstitutional, I suppose. States which grant jury service exemptions to women with children will either extend the exemption to men with children or abolish the exemption altogether. So, try and get a jury sometime. They'll be composed of bachelors, I suppose, and not if they tell the truth. . . . The YWCA and the Girl Scouts, of course, will have no meaning and the League of Women Voters will have to tear up its charter. . . . Divorced, separated and deserted Wives, struggling to support themselves and their children through whatever work they can get, may find their claims of support from the Father harder to enforce than they do right now. Now, to talk to the Women's Lib types, that's alright with them. But, I've talked to some married women who aren't trained to make a living in the world. They're housewives. They don't know shorthand. They don't know typing.

They don't know structural engineering. And, to say to them that you have [no] rights to support for you or your children, superior to man. That's just what this Amendment is going to do. Most sex discrimination is a matter of private practice, not public Law. Now, we have the 14th Amendment in the Supreme Court in the Reid case has said that, 'Women may not be discriminated against invidiously,' but at the same time, there are discriminations in favor of women that are . . .very important. This is really an attack on the home. It's an attack on Motherhood. It says that for a woman to have to be a Mother and have to be a housewife is somehow degrading. I submit that the problem with this Society today is that the home is being attacked and assaulted and no longer wields any influence. And, this is one more step, however well intentioned the Sponsors are, to attack the beauty, the sanctity, and the essentialness of having the home the center of life and society. . . ."

Thomas J. Hanahan, Jr.: "The family unit made this country great and if you want to see something destroyed, a family unit, pass E.R.A. Put it on the heads of your children and your grandchildren and watch and witness the decline of the United States of America. A great country that was founded on the principal of family units. In Colorado, where they passed E.R.A., men want to marry horses. Homosexuals marry homosexuals there. This is what you're talking about with E.R.A. . . . Some people think that E.R.A. is going to answer all the problems that we've got in sex discrimination. . . . I suggest that if you've listened to the women and listened with your heart and your mind instead of the loud braggings of a bunch of braless, brainless broads, you'll vote 'no' on E.R.A."

Roscoe D. Cunningham: ". . . I have nothing against E.R.A., except I believe that the horde of kooks and carpetbaggers who have swarmed into Illinois in its behalf, to stampede its passage in recent days represent a considerable threat to that grand American tradition called 'Family and Home.' You and I know that the honored head of that block of the national foundation is the wife of the breadwinner, the mother of the children, the queen bee around whom all life can happily revolve, and yet, the grand madam of E.R.A., one glorious dynam [Gloria Steinem!] has often publicly described these extraordinary housewives and mothers as 'prostitutes.' On behalf of my mother, my wife, my daughters and yours I resent glorious dynam, her ilk and every alien philosophy that they espouse. I have never met a rabbit gun-hoe libber' [rabid gung-ho libber] who was happily married, and that somber fact...should be noticed to the thousands of dedicated ladies all be it misguided in the State of Illinois and the honored Members of this House and the many hundreds of super-fine ladies in my district who have striven so mightily for E.R.A.'s ratification that it does attract the strangest of bedfellows. Equal opportunity under the law for everyone to make his or her life reach its maximum potential is the solemn obligation of decency, [happiness], the books are full of laws that are designed and proven effective for that high purpose, and the greatest of these is the Federal Equal Pay Act of 1963. If there be a lady anywhere in the United States of America who is discriminated against in her employment on account of her sex, her remedy is as close as the nearest courthouse. If we will but enforce the present existing statutes, we can and will bring equality for all, and we will not destroy the national fabric in the process. We can have our cake and eat it, too. It is time, Ladies and Gentlemen, it is time to quit tampering with our Constitution. . . . I invite you to return to the faith of your fathers and of your mothers by voting 'no.' "

OUR FEMALE NATURE AFFORDS US DISTINCT CAPABILITIES
Women for Faith and Family

One of the most divisive gender issues—and a powerful cause of backlash—was abortion. Feminists' insistence on legalized abortion drove many women, even those who espoused other aspects of feminism, into antiabortion or "right-to-life" organizations. Their ranks were filled not only with Catholics but with women from across the religious spectrum who believed freer sexuality would unleash male passions and undermine the family. By casting the demands of women's liberation as an attack on morality, the religious right sought to discredit the entire movement.

Surprisingly, Catholics were not unanimous in opposing abortion. In October 1984, a group of nearly 100 Catholic women, including nuns and self-identified feminist theologians, signed an advertisement in *The New York Times* arguing that opposition to abortion was not "the only legitimate Catholic position," and that "a large number of Catholic theologians hold that even direct abortion, though tragic, can sometimes be a moral choice."

In response to the ad and to other perceived feminist inroads into the Church, a small group of Catholic women from St. Louis formed Women for Faith and Family. Their initial goal was to "provide a means whereby the voices of women faithful to the church could be heard." They drafted a statement, "Affirmation for Catholic Women" (excerpted below) and began to circulate it. Within three years they had collected over thirty thousand signatures in the United States and the statement had been translated into seven different languages and circulated widely abroad as well.

Though the statement was written by and for Catholic women, its principles reflect the thinking of many women on the religious right. What is the relationship between feminism and morality in this statement? Do you think its authors regard women as inferior or subordinate to men? What similarities do you see between this position and that of, say, the Woman's Christian Temperance Union (Chapter 3)?

By signing this affirmation women pledge their loyalty to the teaching of the Catholic Church. The names will be forwarded to the Pope.

Because of the assaults against the Christian Faith and the family by elements within contemporary society which have led to pervasive moral confusion, to damage and destruction of families and to the men, women and children which comprise them . . .

Because we are cognizant of our obligations as Christian women to witness to our faith, being mindful that this witness is important to the formation of the moral conscience of our families and of humanity, we wish to make this affirmation:

1. We believe that through God's grace our female nature affords us distinct physical and spiritual capabilities with which to participate in the Divine Plan for creation. Specifically, our natural function of childbearing endows us with the spiritual capacity for nurture, instruction, compassion and selflessness, which qualities are necessary to the establishment of families, the basic and Divinely ordained unit of society, and to the establishment of a Christian social order.

Source: "Affirmation for Catholic Women," quoted in Helen Hull, "Women for Faith and Family: Catholic Women Affirming Catholic Teaching," in *Being Right: Conservative Catholics in America*, ed. Mary Jo Weaver and R. Scott Appleby (Bloomington, IN: University of Indiana Press, 1995), pp. 177–78.

2. We believe that to attempt to subvert or deny our distinct nature and role as women subverts and denies God's plan for humanity, and leads to both personal disintegration and ultimately to the disintegration of society. Accordingly, we reject all ideologies which seek to eradicate the natural and essential distinction between the sexes, which debase and devalue womanhood, family life and the nurturing role of women in society.

3. We affirm the intrinsic sacredness of all human life, and we reject the notion that abortion, the deliberate killing of unborn children, is the "right" of any human being, male or female, or of any government. Such a distorted and corrosive notion of individual freedom is, in fact, inimical to authentic Christianity and to the establishment and maintenance of a just social order.

4. We accept and affirm the teaching of the Catholic Church on all matters dealing with human reproduction, marriage, family life and roles for men and women in the Church and in society.

5. We therefore also reject as an aberrant innovation peculiar to our times and our society the notion that priesthood is the "right" of any human being, male or female. Furthermore, we recognize that the specific role of ordained priesthood is intrinsically connected with and representative of the begetting creativity of God in which only human males can participate. Human females, who by nature share in the creativity of God by their capacity to bring forth new life, and, reflective of this essential distinction, have a different and distinct role within the Church and in society from that accorded to men, can no more be priests than men can be mothers.

6. We recognize and affirm the vocations of women who subordinate their human role of motherhood and family life in order to consecrate their lives to the service of God, His Church and humanity. Such women's authentic response of consecrated service to the physical, spiritual and/or intellectual needs of the community in no way diminishes or compromises their essential female nature, or the exercise of inherent attributes, insights and gifts peculiar to women. Rather, it extends the applications of these gifts beyond the individual human family.

7. We stand with the Second Vatican Council which took for granted the distinct roles for men and women in the family and in society and affirmed that Christian education must impart knowledge of this distinction: "In the entire educational program [Catholic school teachers] should, together with the parents, make full allowance for the difference of sex and for the particular role which Providence has appointed to each sex in the family and in society." . . .

YOU CAN STOP
Coleen Kelly Mast

In the view of many on the right, the attack on family values came from multiple sources—not only feminist and gay liberation, but the media and even the educational system, through programs in sex education. To defend against this ubiquitous onslaught, conservative educators devised their own sex education curricula, which emphasized chastity instead of premarital sex and the use of contraceptives and marital

Source: Coleen Kelly Mast, *Sex Respect: The Option of True Sexual Freedom* (Bradley, IL: Respect, Inc., 1990), pp. 90, 92; reprinted with permission.

SECONDARY VIRGINITY.

Secondary virginity is the decision to stop having sex until after marriage and the acting out of that decision.

Any person who wants it can have it by:
-- deciding to change.
-- detaching himself from old habits, from people, places, and situations which weaken self-control.
--developing new, non-physical ways to share.

So, even though you may have lost your physical virginity, you can still return to the qualities of psychological virginity and all its advantages. Don't buy the myth that once you've given in to them you can no longer control your sexual impulses. After all, if you gain ten pounds during Thanksgiving break, it doesn't mean you have to gain another ten during spring break. If you take money from someone else's locker, it doesn't mean you have to keep stealing money the rest of the school year.

FOR ME, IT'S RIGHT TO START OVER!

You can stop. It won't be easy, but neither is studying for a test rather than cheating, cooling off instead of punching someone, or telling the truth instead of lying when you're in a tight spot. It's not always easy to do the right thing; but it can make you feel a sense of self-confidence, self-worth, and self-control in a way nothing else can.

WHAT DO YOU THINK?

1. The following are some reasons people give for choosing secondary virginity. What others can you think of?

"I didn't like being used. "
"We were so much into sex that we never became friends."
"The worry wasn't worth it."
"Frankly, I was scared of getting herpes."

_____

_____

2. Bill, after having been sexually involved with Marcie for several months, has decided to choose secondary virginity. Marcie calls him a wimp, a fool, and a few names that are not printable here. She tells him he's not normal to deny himself his sexual freedom. What can Bill say in defense of his sensible choice?

_____

3. Be prepared! Make a list of ways to draw the line on sexual activity tactfully and effectively.

_____

_____

4. What kind of peer support would help a person practice secondary virginity?

_____

_____

TWENTY-FIVE WAYS TO SAY "NO!"

1. Prove you love ME by waiting.

2. I'm busy working on my reputation.

3. I'd rather take a cold shower; it's safer.

4. I look much better with my clothes on.

5. Sex is not a game. No score.

6. I want to make sure you like me for myself.

7. That's the same line people have been using throughout history. It's not going to work on this modern, progressive person!

8. If you think I'm going to fall for that, you obviously don't know me as well as you think you do.

9. I'd hate to lose my virginity; I heard it's hard to find.

10. I'd rather dance.

11. I wish you cared enough to keep your hands to yourself.

12. Real men don't even ask.

13. If we ever go out again, please bring your self-control.

14. Of course you can wait; you're not a rabbit.

15. I'd rather break up than break out with herpes.

16. Maybe they do on TV, but this is real life, not fiction.

17. I've got to stand up for something, so I don't fall for anything.

18. I may be a square today, but at least I'll be around tomorrow.

19. Of course it's part of our nature; so are germs.

20. I love you too, and that's why I'm saying no.

21. Curiosity killed the cat.

22. We'll each have to look ourselves in the mirror tomorrow.

23. All of my zippers are locked anyway.

24. No, I won't change my mind next week either.

25. I spent all week deciding what to wear tonight and three hours getting ready. If you think you are going to mess any of this up, you are sadly mistaken.

fidelity instead of serial monogamy. Ultra-conservative parents objected that even this type of sex education usurped their role as the primary moral instructors of their children. Nevertheless, workbooks like Coleen Mast's *Sex Respect* found a large market in church-based youth groups and denominational schools. What techniques does Mast use to put her message across? How do you think modern students would respond?

AS A MEMBER OF THE MALE SPECIES
Quarterback of the Statutory Rapists

Much of the opposition to the gender revolution, particularly on the part of men, took the form not of organized political protest but of gut-level challenges that often contained threats of violence. As gay men and lesbians increasingly claimed public space and the right to express their sexuality openly, these threats took the form of gay-bashing. Antifeminist men regarded women who asserted themselves as fair game for sexual violence.

It has been difficult to trace the origins or exact date of the following document, but its raw emotion suggests that it was written around the time the women's movement was at its height in the early seventies. How does the author justify his position?

To Whom It May Concern—Which I'm sure is no one of any importance

I don't believe in petitions.
I don't believe in the feminist movement.
I don't even believe in authority.
Since joining the intramural football team known as THE STATUTORY RAPISTS during their second year of regular play, I have felt that the name lacked intelligence and creativity. However disgusting I find such a label I do, however, strongly believe in the concept behind it and as a member of the male species I feel that it has been both my prerogative and my pleasure. Recognizing that I can not speak for my team and my team captain, and realizing what little loss there is, I can only say that some of us will play under no other name.

I make no apology.

Quarterback of THE STATUTORY RAPISTS

Source: "Quarterback of the Statutory Rapists," "I Make No Apology," Football Team of the College of Law, Ohio State University; reprinted from *The Ohio State Lantern,* n.d., with permission.

OURS IS A SOCIETY THAT PRESUMES MALE LEADERSHIP
Daniel Patrick Moynihan

In some sectors of American society, female employment had been the norm long before the advent of second-wave feminism. As we have seen in earlier chapters, this

Source: [Daniel Patrick Moynihan], *The Negro Family: The Case for National Action* (Office of Policy Planning and Research, U.S. Department of Labor, March 1965), pp. 29–35, 38, 47.

The Rhodesian Army offers you an interesting and varied career with new allowances for fighting troops

For further details contact:
The Army Careers Officer
Phone: 707087 Salisbury
WRITE:
Philips House,
Gordon Ave,
Box 8138 Causeway.

Replica of Rhodesian Army Recruiting Poster. 17″ x 22″, $3.00.

Soldier of Fortune, Box 693, Boulder, CO 80302

FIGURE 14.2
Though many Vietnam veterans attempted to put the war behind them as quickly as possible, others felt a need to restore America's reputation as a world power—and their own images as "real men"—through assertions of military prowess. Arms sales went up and paramilitary magazines were established. The most successful was *Soldier of Fortune: The Journal of Professional Adventurers,* founded in 1975 by Robert K. Brown, a former member of the U.S. Special Forces in Vietnam. This ad for a replica of a Rhodesian Army recruiting poster appeared in an early issue. (*Source:* Soldier of Fortune, *vol. 2 [Fall 1976], p. 81; Courtesy of the Rare Book Room, Main Library, University of Illinois at Urbana-Champaign.*)

was certainly the case in the African American community, where both women and men had to work in order to keep their families afloat. In the mid-1960s this pattern came to the attention of social reformers seeking to understand the high rate of poverty among African Americans. In a controversial report, Daniel Patrick Moynihan, then Assistant Secretary of Labor, argued that women's employment led to a form of matriarchy which demoralized men and produced a "tangle of pathology" within black households. Black poverty would end only when men became breadwinners and claimed their rightful places as heads of households.

"The Moynihan Report," as it came to be called, generated heated debate when it was released and continues to raise a number of knotty questions. Why was Moynihan critical of matriarchy? Was his position anti-feminist? In what ways did Moynihan's diagnosis of the causes of black poverty dictate his solution (a policy supporting male employment)? Was this the only alternative?

> That the Negro American has survived at all is extraordinary —a lesser people might simply have died out, as indeed others have. That the Negro community has not only survived, but in this political generation has entered national affairs as a moderate, humane, and constructive national force is the highest testament to the healing powers of the democratic ideal and the creative vitality of the Negro people.

But it may not be supposed that the Negro American community has not paid a fearful price for the incredible mistreatment to which it has been subjected over the past three centuries.

In essence, the Negro community has been forced into a matriarchal structure which, because it is so out of line with the rest of the American society, seriously retards the progress of the group as a whole, and imposes a crushing burden on the Negro male and, in consequence, on a great many Negro women as well.

There is, presumably, no special reason why a society in which males are dominant in family relationships is to be preferred to a matriarchal arrangement. However, it is clearly a disadvantage for a minority group to be operating on one principle, while the great majority of the population, and the one with the most advantages to begin with, is operating on another. This is the present situation of the Negro. Ours is a society which presumes male leadership in private and public affairs. The arrangements of society facilitate such leadership and reward it. A subculture, such as that of the Negro American, in which this is not the pattern, is placed at a distinct disadvantage.

Here an earlier word of caution should be repeated. There is much evidence that a considerable number of Negro families have managed to break out of the tangle of pathology and to establish themselves as stable, effective units, living according to patterns of American society in general. E. Franklin Frazier has suggested that the middle-class Negro American family is, if anything more patriarchal and protective of its children than the general run of such families. Given equal opportunities, the children of these families will perform as well or better than their white peers. They need no help from anyone, and ask none. . . .

It might be estimated that as much as half of the Negro community falls into the middle class. However, the remaining half is in desperate and deteriorating circumstances. Moreover, because of housing segregation it is immensely difficult for the stable half to escape from the cultural influences of the unstable one. The children of middle-class Negroes often as not must grow up in, or next to the slums, an experience almost unknown to white middle-class children. They are therefore constantly exposed to the pathology of the disturbed group and constantly in danger of being drawn into it. . . .

In a word, most Negro youth are in *danger* of being caught up in the tangle of pathology that affects their world, and probably a majority are so entrapped. Many of those who escape do so for one generation only: as things now are, their children may have to run the gauntlet all over again. That is not the least vicious aspect of the world that white America has made for the Negro.

Obviously, not every instance of social pathology afflicting the Negro community can be traced to the weakness of family structure. If, for example, organized crime in the Negro community were not largely controlled by whites, there would be more capital accumulation among Negroes, and therefore probably more Negro business enterprises. If it were not for the hostility and fear many whites exhibit towards Negroes, they in turn would be less afflicted by hostility and fear and so on. There is no one Negro community. There is no one Negro problem. There is no one solution. Nonetheless, at the center of the tangle of pathology is the weakness of the family structure. Once or twice removed, it will be found to be the principal source of most of the aberrant, inadequate, or antisocial behavior that did not establish, but now serves to perpetuate the cycle of poverty and deprivation.

It was by destroying the Negro family under slavery that white America broke the will of the Negro people. Although that will has reasserted itself in our time, it is a resurgence doomed to frustration unless the viability of the Negro family is restored. . . .

A fundamental fact of Negro American family life is the often reversed roles of husband and wife.

Robert O. Blood, Jr. and Donald M. Wolfe, in a study of Detroit families, note that "Negro husbands have unusually low power," and while this is characteristic of all low income families, the pattern pervades the Negro social structure: "the cumulative result of discrimination in jobs . . . , the segregated housing, and the poor schooling of Negro men." In 44 percent of the Negro families studied, the wife was dominant, as against 20 percent of white wives. "Whereas the majority of white families are equalitarian, the largest percentage of Negro families are dominated by the wife."

The matriarchal pattern of so many Negro families reinforces itself over the generations. This process begins with education. Although the gap appears to be closing at the moment, for a long while, Negro females were better educated than Negro males, and this remains true today for the Negro population as a whole. . . .

In 1960, 39 percent of all white persons 25 years of age and over who had completed 4 or more years of college were women. Fifty-three percent of the nonwhites who had attained this level were women.

However, the gap is closing. By October 1963, there were slightly more Negro men in college than women. Among whites there were almost twice as many men as women enrolled. . . .

Inevitably, these disparities have carried over to the area of employment and income.

In 1 out of 4 Negro families where the husband is present, is an earner, and someone else in the family works, the husband is not the principal earner. The comparable figure for whites is 18 percent.

More important, it is clear that Negro females have established a strong position for themselves in white collar and professional employment, precisely the areas of the economy which are growing most rapidly, and to which the highest prestige is accorded.

The President's Committee on Equal Employment Opportunity, making a preliminary report on employment in 1964 of over 16,000 companies with nearly 5 million employees, revealed this pattern with dramatic emphasis.

In this work force, Negro males outnumber Negro females by a ratio of 4 to 1. Yet Negro males represent only 1.2 percent of all males in white collar occupations, while Negro females represent 3.1 percent of the total female white collar work force. Negro males represent 1.1 percent of all male professionals, whereas Negro females represent roughly 6 percent of all female professionals. Again, in technician occupations, Negro males represent 2.1 percent of all male technicians while Negro females represent roughly 10 percent of all female technicians. It would appear therefore that there are proportionately 4 times as many Negro females in significant white collar jobs than Negro males. . . .

The testimony to the effects of these patterns in Negro family structure is widespread, and hardly to be doubted.

Whitney Young:
Historically, in the matriarchal Negro society, mothers made sure that if one of their children had a chance for higher education the daughter was the one to pursue it.

The effect on family functioning and role performance of this historical experience [economic deprivation] is what you might predict. Both as a husband and as a father the Negro male is made to feel inadequate, not because he is unlovable or unaffectionate, lacks intelligence or even a grey flannel suit. But in a society that measures a man by the size of his pay check, he doesn't stand very tall in a comparison with his white counterpart. To this situation he may react with withdrawal, bitterness toward society, aggression both within the family and racial group, self-hatred, or crime. Or he may escape through a number of avenues that help him to lose himself in fantasy or to compensate for his low status through a variety of exploits.

Thomas Pettigrew:

The Negro wife in this situation can easily become disgusted with her financially dependent husband, and her rejection of him further alienates the male from family life. Embittered by their experiences with men, many Negro mothers often act to perpetuate the mother-centered pattern by taking a greater interest in their daughters than their sons. . . .

Robin M. Williams, Jr. in a study of Elmira, New York:

Only 57 percent of Negro adults reported themselves as married–spouse present, as compared with 78 percent of native white American gentiles, 91 percent of Italian-American, and 96 percent of Jewish informants. Of the 93 unmarried Negro youths interviewed, 22 percent did not have their mother living in the home with them, and 42 percent reported that their father was not living in their home. One-third of the youths did not know their father's present occupation, and two-thirds of a sample of 150 Negro adults did not know what the occupation of their father's father had been. Forty percent of the youths said that they had brothers and sisters living in other communities: another 40 percent reported relatives living in their home who were not parents, siblings, or grandparent. . . .

Williams' account of Negro youth growing up with little knowledge of their fathers, less of their fathers' occupations, still less of family occupational traditions, is in sharp contrast to the experience of the white child. The white family, despite many variants, remains a powerful agency not only for transmitting property from one generation to the next, but also for transmitting no less valuable contacts with the world of education and work. Children today still learn the patterns of work from their fathers even though they may no longer go into the same jobs.

White children without fathers at least perceive all about them the pattern of men working.

Negro children without fathers flounder—and fail. . . .

The combined impact of poverty, failure, and isolation among Negro youth has had the predictable outcome in a disastrous delinquency and crime rate. . . . Negroes represent a third of all youth in training schools for juvenile delinquents. . . .

A national effort towards the problems of Negro Americans must be directed towards the question of family structure. The object should be to strengthen the Negro family so as to enable it to raise and support its members as do other families. . . .

FIGURE 14.3
Throughout the late sixties and early seventies, Congress held hearings on various programs intended to reduce poverty and high levels of public assistance. The National Welfare Rights Organization, founded in June, 1966, was often called upon by Congressional liberals to testify about the conditions of women receiving Aid to Families with Dependent Children (AFDC). This hearing on a bill to provide a Guaranteed Annual Income was held by the Senate on June 11, 1969. (*Photograph by Marion S. Trikosko; courtesy of Library of Congress, Prints and Photographs Division, U.S. News and World Report Magazine Collection, LC-U9-21147, Frame 17.*)

GOING OUT AND CLEANING MRS. A'S KITCHEN

While the Moynihan Report recommended the creation of employment programs directed at African American *men,* members of Congress were calling for a change in public assistance policy that would affect large numbers of African American *women.* In an effort to shift policy from welfare to "workfare," legislators sought to require poor single mothers who were receiving public assistance to find employment. Many of the women to be targeted by this reform were African American.

Debates over the proposed policy revealed how feminist positions on employment were crosscut by race and class. On the one hand, white middle-class feminists argued that employment was the key to women's independence and self-fulfillment. Poor women and women of color, for whom jobs were not a choice but a necessity,

Source: U.S. Congress, Joint Economic Committee. Subcommittee on Fiscal Policy, *Income Maintenance Programs* (Washington, D.C.: GPO. 1968), pp. 77–79.

rejected this view; instead, they sought the right to stay at home and care for their children.

The clash between these views came to the fore in a 1968 Congressional hearing on welfare legislation. Representative Martha Griffiths (Democrat-Michigan), who saw herself as one of the few feminists in Congress, encountered Beulah Sanders and George Wiley, both officers of the newly formed National Welfare Rights Organization (NWRO). What does Griffiths mean when she calls herself a feminist? What group of women is she representing? Why does Sanders object to her position on employment? Are she and Wiley feminists?

Mr. WILEY: . . . Our feeling is that a good number, in fact the vast majority, of the welfare recipients and many of the other people who need income support legitimately should not be in the labor force because they have other important responsibilities at home, to take care of their families. . . .

It is an important question for many people, that they find jobs. But the important thing is that the men, that the people who are able to be heads of households or ought to be the legitimate heads of households, be the ones that get those jobs. . . .

Rep. GRIFFITHS: Now, I regret to say, Mr. Wiley, you are speaking to the most dedicated feminist we have in Congress. I want to point out to you what I think the welfare program does.

In the first place, we discovered in [the House Committee on] Ways and Means that the welfare department [Health, Education and Welfare] and the Labor Department are not really trying to find jobs for people on welfare at all, that if they had their choice between a person who was on welfare [most likely a woman] and a person who was just out of a job [most likely a man] and both were equally qualified, they would simply put on the people who were out of a job. If you are going to do it this way, you are going to have forever in this country a group of people who are on welfare. . . . These people have a right to participate in the economy of this country. They have just as much right to have a job as anyone else.

You say that this work incentive program will be used to force mothers to work. . . . But if you do not say anything about mothers working, then [the Labor Department is] going to see to it that none work. . . . And in my opinion, this is wrong. . . . If you give the welfare officials the chance, and the Labor Department, you are going to consign the women to welfare. I just do not think that is fair. I am a woman, Mr. Wiley, and I know the kinds of discriminations that have been used against women. . . .

Mrs. SANDERS: One of the things we are concerned about is being forced into these non-existing positions which might be going out and cleaning Mrs. A's kitchen. I am not going to do that because I feel I am more valuable and can do something else. This is one of the things people are worrying about, that they are going to be pushed into doing housework when they can be much more valuable doing something else. But they do not have the training, they do not have the experience, they do not have the college degree.

. . . We have children, small children that we have no day care facilities for. We have nobody to leave our kids with that we can feel that if we go to work, our kids are going to be taken care of properly. These are the things we are worried about.

MY CHILD DOESN'T KNOW ME
Barbara Wagner and Roberta Grant

Despite right-wing protest, from the 1960s on, American women were increasingly moving away from the full-time homemaker role. By 1980, over half of America's married couples were "dual-earner families," and over half of America's mothers were in the labor force. Despite the increase in female labor force participation, the United States continued to fall short of feminists' vision of gender equality. Instead of being "liberated" by employment, wage-earning mothers now found themselves shouldering the double burden of work and family—what sociologist Arlie Hochschild has called "the second shift."

Social arrangements had clearly not kept pace with changing employment patterns. Reliable, affordable child care was in short supply. Job conditions continued to be based on the male-breadwinner model—that is, on a worker with a full-time homemaker-wife assuming all domestic responsibilities. Few firms offered options such as flextime or job-sharing which would allow parents to reconcile work and family responsibilities more easily. Moreover, women who chose to go on the "mommy track" found their careers losing momentum. Given these realities, a number of wage-earning mothers decided it made more sense for them to leave their jobs and stay home with their children.

The following article describes how this process worked for one group of women. What factors went into their decisions? How did their options differ from those of mothers like Beulah Sanders? Can you think of social policies that might have offered different options to both groups of women?

What's the difference between a homemaker today and one in the past? Plenty!

When Sharon Schneider returned to work a few months after giving birth at twenty-seven to her daughter, Gretchen, she had a beautiful baby girl, a devoted husband and a new position as head nurse at a major California medical center, a definite promotion over her last job. "I felt as though I had achieved everything," she recalls. "But the honeymoon didn't last long. While I loved my new job, the twelve-hour days were exhausting. I saw Gretchen for about one hour each day, and it seemed as if she thought the baby-sitter was her mother. Soon I began to feel I wasn't achieving my goals at work, my child didn't know me, I wasn't a wife to Frank. I couldn't seem to have any of it, let alone "have it all." After careful thought, and at considerable financial sacrifice, Sharon, now thirty-three, decided to leave her career and return home to be a full-time wife and mother.

Nancy Kaplan, a thirty-one-year-old New York City interior designer, found that being a working mother just didn't pay. "When Brian was six months old," she remembers, "I went back to work. Before the baby, although my salary wasn't huge, the money I made had been ours to spend; suddenly, everything went to the baby-sitter." Nancy weighed the pros and cons of her work situation and decided to put her career on hold in order to take care of Brian full-time.

Source: Barbara Wagner and Roberta Grant, "The New One-Paycheck Family," *Ladies' Home Journal* 101, 9 (September 1984), pp. 87–89, 142, 144, 146, 150.

"I've had a successful career," says Maggie Scott (not her real name), at thirty-five the mother of two young children. Maggie once relished the power and prestige of her highly paid position as vice-president at a large Chicago advertising agency, but now she wants to experience the rewards of being home. "I've won the accounts, taken the trips, had the business lunches at elegant restaurants," she says. "Now I want to enjoy spending time with my children."

Maggie, Nancy and Sharon exemplify a new breed of American homemaker. Like millions of wives, during the past fifteen years they've experienced both the benefits and the stresses of the two-paycheck marriage. Now, however, they have young children and they've decided that home is the right place for them to be.

Although there are more working mothers with children under six than ever before, the past five years have seen a steady decline in the number of mothers with children this age who enter the work force each year. According to statistics from the U.S. Department of Labor, 55 percent of women who gave birth in 1982 did not reenter the labor force even after a full year of mothering. Dr. Amitai Etzioni, an eminent sociologist and professor at George Washington University in Washington, D.C., says, "There's definitely a trend toward women leaving their careers to be with their families. Nineteen-eighty-two was the first year in seventeen years that the divorce rate went down. We're now seeing a general return to the traditional values and family structure. The thrust of the seventies, where a woman placed her career ahead of her children, is definitely over."

Of course, millions of women never totally espoused the seventies career rhetoric in the first place. They may have been working wives but they always counted on being stay-at-home mothers at some point. Still, what's intriguing about this new generation of homemakers, and one factor that separates them from their fifties and sixties counterparts, is that being home today is a conscious decision, an actively chosen way of life. Two decades of feminist struggle for career opportunities and equal pay have also earned women the right to find individual solutions to the puzzle of combining personal goals with marriage and motherhood. And while it's true that many young mothers must continue to work due to financial necessity, when circumstances allow, some women have the courage and the conviction to choose the more traditional role of full-time homemaker, even if the choice defies today's most frequent media message: that women should be covering all the bases simultaneously.

Still, new stay-at-homes need every bit of confidence they can muster, for although their choice may seem, superficially, a return to tradition, it is freighted with emotional and financial complexities that their predecessors never had to face. A woman during the fifties and even in the sixties knew every nuance of the role she was supposed to play as a full-time homemaker. Every voice she listened to—her mother, her husband, her favorite magazines—articulated what to do and how to be, even how to think and feel. Yet today there are fewer rules and role models for the new stay-at-home mothers than for any other group of women in our society. For example, how does a woman accustomed to earning an income and wielding authority feel when she's suddenly dependent on her husband for grocery money? Can their "equal partnership" withstand this sudden imbalance? How does the two-paycheck family adjust to the sudden jolt of living on one salary? How does this new homemaker fill her days? How does she feel about herself? None of the answers come easily, but many women today are finding they're willing to tackle these problems in order to enjoy the privilege of coming home.

And coming home is a privilege to these new homemakers, because unlike the stay-at-home mothers of previous decades, they are not afraid to make time for selfish pleasures—indeed, they are accustomed to doing so. "A wife used to focus only on what was best for her husband and children," says Karen Greenwood, the twenty-five-year-old mother of a six-month-old girl. . . . "I'm trying to do things that are important for *me* as well as for my family." . . .

"It's a real pleasure to be home," says Maggie Scott, the former advertising executive. "I love calling my time my own. I read voraciously, I play the piano, and with help from a baby-sitter, I can get out to play tennis."

Women are finding this new relaxed pace can add greatly not only to their own satisfaction but also to their entire family's sense of well-being—even on a reduced income. . . .

"When you're busy getting up, making breakfast, going to work, making dinner and going to bed," observes Sharon, "there's not a lot of time to think about your marriage. But when I stopped working, I had the time, and I saw things I wanted to change between us. We discussed them, and now our relationship is much better."

Still, if being at home brings obvious benefits in terms of personal satisfaction and marital well-being, it is in their relationship with their children that the new stay-at-home mothers find the most significant dividends. Maggie Scott savors the hours she spends with her two preschoolers. "I love taking them to the library or to a movie, or reading them a story. The media tell you that quality time is fine if you can't give quantity. But I happen to know my kids prefer quantity."

Maggie admits that when she was a working mother, she felt tremendous guilt at being away from her children. According to Dr. Jerome Kagan, a developmental psychologist at Harvard University, going home for Maggie was doubly beneficial. "What makes the mother happy is good for the child," he says. "Ultimately, it's not a matter of whether the mother works or not, but how she feels about herself. Her children will sense whether she feels frustrated and guilty or confident and satisfied, and they will react accordingly."

"Many women have to work, or need to work in order to feel good about themselves," says Karen Greenwood. "And I'm sure their kids will turn out fine. But I would rather be home right now, enjoying this phase of my life." Karen worked in the art department of a magazine.

This idea of enjoying adult life in different phases is another of the strikingly new attitudes shared by today's full-time homemakers. In the past, being in the home was simply a fact of life: a mother's destiny, not to be questioned until she was suddenly confronted with an empty nest and time on her hands. Now, however, staying home with the kids can be one of many stages in the life of a modern woman. "A woman *can* have it all," says Maggie Scott, "but it's a lot more fun if it's done sequentially." . . .

Yet if having a career and motherhood in sequence is an option that provides multiple benefits to the new homemaker and her family, it is also one that can be exercised only after serious financial discussions. . . . Families today must decide whether they can afford the loss of that extra paycheck. Census Bureau figures show that the average two-paycheck family earned $28,073 in 1982, while the average single-salary household earned only $18,913.

"We had to cut back on absolutely everything by more than half," recalls Sharon Schneider, who had been earning several thousand dollars more than her husband before she quit to be with their daughter. "We eliminated going out to dinner, for example," says Sharon. "Even at fast-food places, you can drop ten dollars real easily. And our furniture is getting tattered. But whenever I think how nice it would be to have a new sofa, I think of all the benefits of not working and I realize I don't want those material possessions that badly."

The Schneiders' reward for giving up material luxuries is what many experts predict will become the number-one luxury during the rest of this century: leisure time. To Sharon, the trade-off seems well worth it. . . .

Sharon remains convinced she made the right decision in choosing to stay home, but making the choice was a nerve-racking experience. She was fortunate, however, that her husband gave her his full support. Other women are not always so lucky. Leslie Rush (not her real name), thirty-one-year-old mother of Emma, worked as a publicist at a major film company before giving birth. Her $30,000 salary, coupled with her husband Jim's $40,000 income as a salesman, allowed the Rushes a sophisticated and very comfortable New York City lifestyle. When Emma was born, the couple both assumed that Leslie would return to work after a three-month leave. But as the date of her return approached, Leslie was increasingly torn. "I found myself crying as I counted down the days I had left at home with Emma. I wanted to stay with her all the time."

When Leslie told Jim she was thinking of making her maternity leave permanent, he "exploded," Leslie recalls with a grimace. "He said it would be impossible for us to survive without my salary. We had just moved into a new apartment and our rent had doubled, and we saw how expensive it was to have a baby. We were both scared, and we fought a lot. But finally he agreed with me, and it hasn't turned out to be so bad. We're in a lower tax bracket now, and I think that helps."

Ironically, Jim's reaction was the complete opposite of his counterparts thirty years ago, when a man felt shame if his wife worked. "Men are afraid to be the sole breadwinners today and they're reluctant to admit it," says Marjorie Hansen Shaevitz, a counselor at the Institute for Family and Work Relationships in La Jolla, California. "They're often in conflict about whether their wives should work or stay home with their children. While they want their wives to work for the financial benefits, they still have the image of their own mothers staying at home with them. This contradiction can result in tension in the marriage."

Marital tensions and masculine fears can give way, however, in deference to that powerful image of the full-time mother. Most husbands realize that, although they may be the sole wage earners once again, there are tangible rewards to be gained from having their wives at home. "We have a happy baby," says Leslie, "and Ron is convinced it's because I'm with her most of the time. He also likes coming home to home-cooked meals and he enjoys the sense that we're a real family unit."

Karen Greenwood agrees. "My husband really respects my decision to stay home. He compliments me on what a good mother I am. He was proud of me when I was working and now he's proud of me as a mother."

Still, not all marital adjustments are so positive or smooth. Joan Klein, a thirty-year-old former employment manager, found decision-making power in her family subtly altered when she stopped working.

"I was no longer contributing, and I began to feel that he had more right to make the decisions because he was paying for everything. He tried to reassure me, telling me, "It's *our* money," but emotionally I think he sometimes feels it's really *his* money."

Joan's experience is fairly typical. According to Marjorie Hansen Shaevitz, the stay-at-home wife "moves into a supportive household role and places her family's needs before her own. She has to negotiate and ask her spouse for money. With a diminished feeling of self-worth, it's natural for her to feel she doesn't have as big a role in decision-making. While the difference is subtle and never acknowledged in direct terms, the wife's power erodes."

Maintaining self-esteem and a strong sense of identity can be the major challenge for today's stay-at-home mothers. "It makes me very uncomfortable," says Joan Klein, "when other women ask me, "You're not working?" in a tone that implies I'm some sort of feminist traitor. Even the men in my business find it difficult to believe I've given up my job." . . .

[Maggie Scott], like many other [wage-earning mothers], was fed up with the world of work. "I'd had it," she says. "As a new mother in the office, I found myself cutting corners and coasting on my past success. Then I'd dash home to be with the kids. I wasn't surprised when my boss passed me over for a promotion, and, frankly, I was tired of the juggling act."

"Any life choice has its opponents," says Dr. Weinberg. "But it does seem unfair that these women are condemned for abandoning their children if they're working, yet equally condemned for abandoning their careers and their roles as breadwinners if they choose to stay home. What we all must learn is to go ahead and do what seems best and most pleasurable. If you feel good about yourself, you'll be able to withstand some scorn from certain quarters."

For many [new full-time homemakers, their] goals include an eventual return to the workplace, for both financial and emotional reasons. . . .

Returning to the work force can be essential for a woman's own emotional health as well. . . . "It's not just a matter of keeping busy once the kids are in school," says Joan Klein, the former employment manager. "I don't want to wind up at fifty totally dependent on my husband or, worse, widowed and unable to support myself."

Yet how easy is it for a woman to return to the work force after many years at home? Women today seem more acutely aware than ever before of the risks they're taking in temporarily abandoning their jobs or professions. "For a doctor or lawyer, taking a few years off can be a death knell," says Maggie Scott. "Hospitals and law firms just don't make allowances for any kind of extended maternity leave, and your colleagues who continue to practice will leave you in the dust." . . .

"Having babies is the major issue for working wives today," says New York City psychotherapist Natalie Shainess, author of *Sweet Suffering*. . . . "If we valued women for having children, we would guarantee that new mothers could return to their jobs after a specified amount of time for a maternity leave. The change must come not from women but from business and social institutions. In my opinion, the whole thrust of the women's movement was to have this freedom of choice without being penalized by men or by society but so far, women are not getting their just desserts."

So it may seem that struggling to have it all, even sequentially, is a daunting task for today's new stay-at-home mothers. Yet these women are the true inheritors of the ongoing struggle for equal rights. Far from running away from today's choices and challenges, when they return home to their kitchens and their children they are entering a new arena of personal commitment and growth. How they fare, both at home and in their eventual return to the workplace, will depend as much on society's acknowledgment of their unique contributions as on their own courage and dedication to seeking the best way of life for themselves and their families.

RECOMMENDED READING

Bronski, Michael. *The Pleasure Principle: Sex, Backlash, and the Struggle for Gay Freedom.* New York, 1997.

Faludi, Susan. *Backlash: The Undeclared War Against American Women.* New York, 1991.

Gibson, James William. *Warrior Dreams: Violence and Manhood in Post-Vietnam America.* New York, 1994.

Ginsburg, Faye D. *Contested Lives: The Abortion Debate in an American Community.* Berkeley, CA, 1989.

Jacoby, Kerry N. *Souls, Bodies, Spirits: The Drive to Abolish Abortion since 1973.* Westport, CT, 1998.

Jeffords, Susan. *The Remasculinization of America: Gender and the Vietnam War.* Bloomington, IN, 1989.

Klatch, Rebecca. *Women of the New Right.* Philadelphia, 1987.

Luker, Kristin. *Abortion and the Politics of Motherhood.* Berkeley, 1984.

Mansbridge, Jane. *Why We Lost the ERA.* Chicago, 1986.

Mathews, Donald G., and Jane Sherron De Hart. *Sex, Gender, and the Politics of ERA: A State and a Nation.* New York, 1990.

Sommers, Christina Hoff. *Who Stole Feminism? How Women Have Betrayed Women.* New York, 1994.

Weaver, Mary Jo. *New Catholic Women: A Contemporary Challenge to Traditional Religious Authority.* San Francisco, 1965.

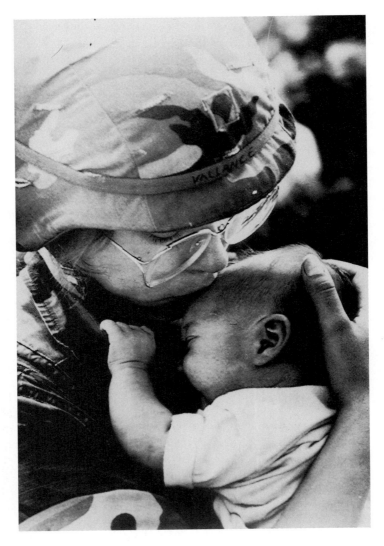

FIGURE 15.1

This soldier, Spec. 4 Hollee Vallance, saying goodbye to her seven-week-old daughter, Cheyenne, was one of 40,000 women sent to fight in the Gulf War in 1991. The presence of so many women—including mothers—in the military regendered the usual images of soldiers going off to war. It also heightened concerns about what it meant to have women in battle. *AP/World Wide Photos.*

CHAPTER 15

Through the Glass Ceiling?

American society at the end of the twentieth century is filled with paradoxes. The end of the Cold War seemed to eliminate the need for the United States to continue its military buildup, but recurring crises in regions such as Bosnia, Rwanda, and the Middle East have kept the nation on alert. Amidst rapidly changing political alignments, many believe the United States must retain its role as military superpower and "world policeman."

America's economy is another site of paradox. As Europe and then Asia underwent dramatic financial upheavals, the United States remained on an even keel, with productivity rising while inflation stayed level. Yet the "rising tide" failed to "lift all boats." Executive salaries increased and unemployment fell, but the gap between the richest and poorest Americans continued to yawn. With the elimination of the social "safety net" and a shrinking number of low-skilled jobs, the plight of the poor has only worsened.

Paradox also characterizes America's gender system. On the one hand, women and men increasingly enjoy many of the same rights and opportunities, and the range of gender and sexual expression is broader than ever before. On the other hand, oppression and discrimination based on gender and sexual orientation persist. Women continue to earn less than men on average and still encounter preferential hiring and sexual harassment. Gay men, lesbians, bisexuals, and transsexuals may find congenial communities, but they frequently meet with anger and violence when they venture into "mainstream" society.

A number of different factors have slowed the gender revolution. Since 1980, backlash has taken different, more subtle, forms. Efforts to "remasculinize" American society have given way to the men's movement, a loose coalition of groups committed to bringing men together for the purpose of renewing their commitment to family and community. Though purportedly responding to feminist critiques of male privilege and power, the movement rouses feminist concerns because of its gender exclusivity and links to Christian fundamentalism, which calls for opposition to homosexuality and abortion.

Gay men and lesbians continue to struggle for their civil rights, including same-sex marriage and participation in the military. Their demands for increased resources for medical research and treatment of AIDS have led to the development of complex pharmaceutical "cocktails," which can greatly extend life expectancy. However, because of expense and practical difficulties, these medications have remained beyond the reach of millions of people with AIDS, both in the United States and abroad.

Women entering fields once monopolized by men soon find themselves bumping up against a "glass ceiling." In 1996 women earned 75 percent of what men did (compared to 61 percent in 1978), but since more had become heads of households, their earnings had to stretch further. Thus, though women, lesbians, gay men, bisexuals, and transsexuals have made important gains since 1865, the gender revolution remains unfinished.

NO FUNDAMENTAL RIGHT TO ENGAGE IN SODOMY
Supreme Court of the United States

As gay men and lesbians became more active and more visible, states seeking to prosecute them frequently invoked sodomy statutes which had laid dormant on the law books for decades. By 1980, the gay rights movement had succeeded in eliminating these statutes in thirty-four states by means of either repeal or successful court contests. Georgia, however, was not among them. In 1982, a gay man named Michael Hardwick challenged the constitutionality of Georgia's sodomy statute. When a Federal District Court ruled in Hardwick's favor, Michael Bowers, the attorney general of Georgia, took the case to the Supreme Court. Signalling its conservative turn, the Court upheld Georgia's anti-sodomy statute. What was the Court's reasoning? Why did the justices refuse to recognize *Roe* v. *Wade* as a precedent in this case?

(a) The Constitution does not confer a fundamental right upon homosexuals to engage in sodomy. None of the fundamental rights announced in this Court's prior cases involving family relationships, marriage, or procreation bear any resemblance to the right asserted in this case. And any claim that those cases stand for the proposition that any kind of private sexual conduct between consenting adults is constitutionally insulated from state proscription is unsupportable. . . .

(b) Against a background in which many States have criminalized sodomy and still do, to claim that a right to engage in such conduct is "deeply rooted in this Nation's history and tradition" or "implicit in the concept of ordered liberty" is, at best, facetious. . . .

(c) There should be great resistance to expand the reach of the Due Process Clauses to cover new fundamental rights. Otherwise, the Judiciary necessarily would take upon itself further authority to govern the country without constitutional authority. The claimed right in this case falls far short of overcoming this resistance. . . .

Source: *Bowers* vs. *Hardwick*, No. 85-140, Supreme Court of the United States, decided June 30, 1986.

(d) The fact that homosexual conduct occurs in the privacy of the home does not affect the result. . . .

(e) Sodomy laws should not be invalidated on the asserted basis that majority belief that sodomy is immoral is an inadequate rationale to support the laws. . . .

In August 1982, respondent Hardwick (hereafter respondent) was charged with violating the Georgia statute criminalizing . . . sodomy by committing that act with another adult male in the bedroom of respondent's home. After a preliminary hearing, the District Attorney decided not to present the matter to the grand jury unless further evidence developed. . . .

Respondent then brought suit in the Federal District Court, challenging the constitutionality of the statute insofar as it criminalized consensual sodomy. . . . He asserted that he was a practicing homosexual, that the Georgia sodomy statute, as administered by the defendants, placed him in imminent danger of arrest, and that the statute for several reasons violates the Federal Constitution. . . .

A divided panel of the Court of Appeals for the Eleventh Circuit reversed. . . . Relying on [the Supreme Court's] decisions in *Griswold* v. *Connecticut* . . . (1965); *Eisenstadt* v. *Baird* . . . (1972); *Stanley* v. *Georgia* . . . (1969); and *Roe* v. *Wade* . . . (1973), the court [held] that the Georgia statute violated respondent's fundamental rights because his homosexual activity is a private and intimate association that is beyond the reach of state regulation by reason of the Ninth Amendment and the Due Process Clause of the Fourteenth Amendment. The case was remanded for trial, at which, to prevail, the State would have to prove that the statute is supported by a compelling interest and is the most narrowly drawn means of achieving that end.

Because other Courts of Appeals have arrived at judgments contrary to that of the Eleventh Circuit in this case, we granted the Attorney General's petition for certiorari questioning the holding that the sodomy statute violates the fundamental rights of homosexuals. We agree with petitioner that the Court of Appeals erred, and hence reverse its judgment. . . .

This case does not require a judgment on whether laws against sodomy between consenting adults in general, or between homosexuals in particular, are wise or desirable. It raises no question about the right or propriety of state legislative decisions to repeal their laws that criminalize homosexual sodomy, or of state-court decisions invalidating those laws on state constitutional grounds. The issue presented is whether the Federal Constitution confers a fundamental right upon homosexuals to engage in sodomy and hence invalidates the laws of the many States that still make such conduct illegal and have done so for a very long time. The case also calls for some judgment about the limits of the Court's role in carrying out its constitutional mandate.

We first register our disagreement with the Court of Appeals and with respondent that the Court's prior cases have construed the Constitution to confer a right of privacy that extends to homosexual sodomy and for all intents and purposes have decided this case. . . . *Pierce* v. *Society of Sisters* . . . (1925), . . . and *Meyer* v. *Nebraska* . . . (1923), were described as dealing with child rearing and education; *Prince* v. *Massachusetts* . . . (1944) with family relationships; *Skinner* v. *Oklahoma ex rel. Williamson* . . . (1942), with procreation; *Loving* v. *Virginia* . . . (1967), with marriage; *Griswold* v. *Connecticut* [1965] and *Eisenstadt* v. *Baird* [1972] with contraception; and *Roe* v. *Wade* . . . (1973), with abortion. The latter three cases were interpreted as construing the Due Process Clause of the Fourteenth Amendment to confer a fundamental individual right to decide whether or not to beget or bear a child. . . .

Accepting the decisions in these cases, . . . we think it evident that none of the rights announced in those cases bears any resemblance to the claimed constitutional right of homosexuals to engage in acts of sodomy that is asserted in this . . . case. No connection between family, marriage, or procreation on the one hand and homosexual activity on the other has been demonstrated, either by the Court of Appeals or by respondent. Moreover, any claim that these cases nevertheless stand for the proposition that any kind of private sexual conduct between consenting adults is constitutionally insulated from state proscription is unsupportable. . . .

Precedent aside, however, respondent would have us announce, as the Court of Appeals did, a fundamental right to engage in homosexual sodomy. This we are quite unwilling to do. It is true that despite the language of the Due Process Clauses of the Fifth and Fourteenth Amendments, which appears to focus only on the processes by which life, liberty, or property is taken, the cases are legion in which those Clauses have been interpreted to have substantive content, subsuming rights that to a great extent are immune from federal . . . or state regulation or proscription. Among such cases are those recognizing rights that have little or no textual support in the constitutional language. Meyer, Prince, and Pierce fall in this category, as do the privacy cases from Griswold to Carey.

Striving to assure itself and the public that announcing rights not readily identifiable in the Constitution's text involves much more than the imposition of the Justices' own choice of values on the States and the Federal Government, the Court has sought to identify the nature of the rights qualifying for heightened judicial protection. In *Palko* v. *Connecticut* . . . (1937), it was said that this category includes those fundamental liberties that are "implicit in the concept of ordered liberty," such that "neither . . . liberty nor justice would exist if [they] were sacrificed." A different description of fundamental liberties appeared in *Moore* v. *East Cleveland* . . . (1977) . . . , where they are characterized as those liberties that are "deeply rooted in this Nation's history and tradition." . . .

It is obvious to us that neither of these formulations would extend a fundamental right to homosexuals to engage in acts of consensual sodomy.

WE WERE IN FOR A RUDE AWAKENING
Debbie Emery

During his first campaign for the presidency, Bill Clinton reached out to gays and enjoyed considerable support in return. He vowed to support their struggles for civil rights and increased resources to fight AIDS, and promised to end discrimination against gays in Federal employment and in the military.

One of Clinton's first steps as president was to institute a new policy concerning gay men and lesbians in the armed services: "Don't Ask, Don't Tell." Presented as an improvement over the previous policy—an outright ban on homosexuals—this policy was intended to allow homosexuals to serve in the military, provided they kept their sexual orientation private.

Source: Debbie Emery, "The Mother of All Witch-Hunts," *Out*, June 1996, p. 176. Reprinted with permission of Debbie Emery, with special thanks to Servicemembers Legal Defense Network, and to her courageous daughter Shannon.

In practice, however, the policy has backfired. In 1997, nearly one thousand military personnel were discharged for homosexuality, an increase of 67 percent from 1994, the first year the policy was fully implemented. According to the Pentagon, the high rate of discharge for homosexuality is the result of misunderstanding on the part of commanding officers. To gay rights and feminist groups, however, it is a form of continuing harassment and a sign of ongoing homophobia.

To complicate matters, the Pentagon has been grappling with the implications of the growing presence of women in the military. Since passage of the ERA in 1971, the Defense Advisory Committee on Women in the Services (DACOWITS) has campaigned for greater integration of women into all aspects of military service, including combat. Women, however, have met with increasing hostility; incidents like the 1991 Navy Tailhook convention and repeated harassment of female trainees at the Aberdeen Proving Ground in Maryland reveal that one of the greatest obstacles to servicewomen is sexual harassment—and the military's unwillingess to confront the problem.

In some instances, women may find themselves in double jeopardy, victims of both a lax policy on sexual harassment and continuing persecution of homosexuals. Did it make any difference that Shannon Emery was not, in fact, a lesbian?

My name is Debbie Emery. My daughter, Shannon, is a specialist in the Army. Shannon, 24, has always been civic-minded and adventurous, so I was not surprised when she asked my husband and me for permission to join the Army two years ago. One of our family's proudest moments was when Shannon graduated at the top of her training class as a military police officer.

When Shannon was notified of her first assignment, to the 728th Military Police Battalion in Korea, she was elated to be performing a real mission, patrolling the roads every day. Within a short time of arriving in the unit in January 1994, Shannon was winning high praise from her non-commissioned officers and being selected for the toughest assignments.

Despite this success, however, I began to be concerned. Shannon was one of only a handful of women in her company. In our phone conversations, she began to mention that other women were "getting a hard time." She told me that some of her married male leaders were having affairs with the young female soldiers in the barracks and that she had been warned that if she did not succumb, she would be labeled a lesbian. Shannon assured me that she could withstand any pressure for sex.

In mid-September, however, I got a call from my daughter that made my heart stop. Shannon had been attacked and nearly raped by drunken male soldiers in her barracks. She had fought back, and her screams had gotten the attention of a corporal who lived on the hall. Shannon said to me, "Mom, they had me pinned against the wall. My feet couldn't touch the floor. If [the corporal] hadn't pulled them off of me, I would have been raped there, or even worse." My husband and I were beside ourselves with worry and anger and our inability to protect our daughter more than 2,000 miles away.

My husband and I encouraged Shannon to immediately report this attack to her chain of command. We were all still naive; it didn't occur to us that her officers would do anything but protect our daughter and punish the men who attacked her.

We were in for a rude awakening. Shannon's commander treated her report with a lack of interest, to say the least. Nothing was done to the men who attacked her. In the meantime, the men retaliated against Shannon. They told her supervisors that they would not back her up on the road patrols. They started false rumors that she was a lesbian and that she was having affairs in the unit. Within days, Shannon's commander launched an investigation against her as a suspected lesbian, which quickly turned into a witch-hunt against other women in the unit.

Shannon was told that if she wrote down a list of 10 to 15 other women who she thought might be lesbians, her commander would show her leniency and give her an honorable discharge instead of throwing her in prison for 10 years. She refused. I am proud to say that my daughter did not try to save her neck at the expense of other women.

When the battalion commander made good on the threat and sent Shannon to a court-martial in December 1994, a military judge threw out the trumped-up charges simply for lack of evidence. My family breathed a sigh of relief. Shannon's year-long tour of duty was up in January 1995. You can imagine our dismay when Shannon's commander put her transfer on hold and started administrative discharge proceedings based on the same false allegations that were thrown out of court.

Servicemembers Legal Defense Network, a legal advocacy group, found a volunteer attorney for me, and we prepared to sue. In July 1995, only after another commander took over, all charges were dropped and Shannon was released to her next assignment, in the United States. Unfortunately, another woman was discharged as a result of the witch-hunt.

No family should ever have to go through the hell that this has caused our family, emotionally and financially. This witch-hunt has taken something even more valuable than money from me and my family. It has taken away our idealism and trust in our government and military leaders to do the right thing. That is something we can never get back.

WE BELIEVED WE WOULDN'T HAVE TO WORRY ABOUT DISCRIMINATION
Laurie Ouellette

By the 1980s, the momentum of the women's movement seemed to be slowing. The ranks of feminist organizations thinned as the original members fell away and younger women appeared uninterested in taking their places. To some of the "daughter" generation, feminism sounded too rigid, too "politically correct." In *The Morning After: Sex, Fear and Feminism on Campus* (1993), Katie Roiphe, a Princeton graduate student, deplored the impact of ideology on relationships between women and men. But others, like Laurie Ouellette, felt that with new energy and new direction, the women's movement still had much to offer her and her contemporaries. For Ouellette, which issues have divided women? Which ones have the potential to unite them?

I am a member of the first generation of women to benefit from the gains of the 1970s women's movement without having participated in its struggles. I grew up on

Source: Laurie Ouellette, "Building the Third Wave: Reflections of a Young Feminist," *On the Issues,* Fall 1992, pp. 8–11, 60. Reprinted by permission of *On the Issues: The Progressive Woman's Quarterly.* © Choices Women's Medical Center, Inc., 1992.

the sidelines of feminism—too young to take part in the movements, debates, and events that would define the women's movement while at the same time experiencing firsthand the societal changes that feminism has demanded.

Ironically, it is due to the modest success of feminism that many young women like myself were raised with an illusion of equality. I never really thought much about feminism as I was growing up, but looking back, I believe I've always had feminist inclinations. Having divorced parents and a father who was ambivalent about his parental responsibilities probably has much to do with this. I was only five when my parents separated in 1971, and I couldn't possibly have imagined or understood the ERA marches, consciousness-raising groups, or triumphal passing of *Roe v. Wade* that shortly would make history. Certainly I couldn't have defined the word *feminism*. Still, watching my young mother struggle emotionally and financially as a single parent made the concept of gender injustice painfully clear, teaching me a lesson that would follow me always.

My first real introduction to feminism came secondhand. During the height of the seventies' women's movement, I watched my mother become "liberated" after the breakup of yet another marriage. It was she, not I, who sought some answers from the counterculture of the time. It was confusing, if not terrifying, to watch her dramatically change her life—and, by association, mine—during those years, transforming herself into a woman I barely recognized. She quit her job and returned to college and then graduate school, working odd jobs and devoting her time to books and meetings and new-age therapy and talking it all out with her never-ending supply of free-spirited divorced comrades. I was thirteen the year I found her copy of *The Women's Room*,[1] a book which so intrigued me that I read it cover to cover in the course of only a few nights. Like the heroine of the book, my mother was becoming "independent" and "hip," but I had never been so miserable.

Like most women my age, though, I never really considered feminism in terms of my own life until I reached college. It was during those years that I first took an interest in feminist classics such as *The Feminine Mystique, Sisterhood is Powerful,* and *Sexual Politics.* As powerful as these texts were, they seemed to express the anger of an earlier generation, simultaneously captivating and excluding me. Reading them so long after the excitement of their publication made my own consciousness-raising seem anticlimactic. These books and countless others that I encountered seemed to speak more to my mother's generation than mine. They explained a great deal about the limited choices awaiting such women and attempted to guide them in ways to overcome patriarchal oppression. But I, like many of my white, middle-class friends, saw women's liberation from quite a different perspective. Many of us really believed that we wouldn't have to worry about issues like discrimination, oppression, and getting stuck in the housewife role. Indeed, many of my friends considered my interest in feminism "radical" and irrelevant to the times.

Although I participated in feminist activities sporadically in college, including pro-choice demonstrations, it was really in my experiences outside of that environment where my feminist politics took root. Several events stand out as catalysts. First was an internship I held at a public television station while in college. Armed with an eager attitude and practical experience, I felt my enthusiasm wane when I was given mainly menial and secretarial tasks to perform while my male co-interns,

---

[1] *The Women's Room* is a novel by Marilyn French published in 1977.

who had less experience than I, were frequently asked to do editing assignments and were invited along on shoots. I had never before experienced sexual discrimination, and in fact honestly believed it was something I would never have to face. In retrospect, this experience marked my first realization that there was much work to be done in creating a world where women and men were treated with equal respect, on the job and off.

Living in an inner-city neighborhood and my involvement in community issues there were also important. I saw the dire need for drastic political change in the lives of the poor women, elderly women, and women of color who were my neighbors. Watching these women, many of them single parents, struggling daily to find shelter, child care, and food made me realize that they, unlike me, had not been touched at all by the gains of the seventies' women's movement. How could women's liberation possibly be perceived as won when these women had been so forgotten? I began to reconsider feminism in an attempt to find the answers.

Today I am among the minority of young women who have committed themselves to feminism in the hopes of achieving social and political goals for all women. While we are attempting to carve out a place for ourselves in a movement still dominated by another generation, the majority of young women have been reluctant to do the same. Confused about their roles in relation to the media stereotypes about feminists or intimidated by the legacy of the women's movement past, many have become "no, but" feminists. That is, they approve of—indeed, demand—equal pay, economic independence, sexual freedom, and reproductive choice but are still reluctant to define themselves with the label "feminist." . . .

Yet the evidence clearly shows that young women's situations are dismal: *Roe v. Wade* is under fire, and if overturned, my generation and those to come will be affected most profoundly; parental consent laws, which require parental notification or permission for abortion, have been mandated in many states; date rape and violence against women have become epidemics on college campuses and everywhere; eating disorders, linked to the unreasonable societal standards for women's body sizes, have claimed the lives of thousands of us; and we still can expect to earn 70 cents for every dollar earned by men. Sure, our chances of having professional careers are greater. However, more of us than in any previous generation have grown up in single-parent families—we have seen the myth of the "supermom" professional "bringing home that bacon and frying it up in a pan" and can call it for what it is. In these hard economic times, young women can look forward to mandatory full-time jobs and second shifts of house care and child care in their homes. Where are the parental-leave policies, the flexible schedules, the adequate health care, the subsidized day care, and the male cooperation that will ease these situations? As yet, nowhere to be found, and considering the present political climate, there doesn't seem to be much hope for the near future.

Given all this, what can explain why so many young women have shunned feminism? In her survey of young women, *Feminist Fatale: Voices from the Twentysomething Generation Explore the Future of the Women's Movement,* Paula Kamen found that media-fueled stereotypes of feminists as "man-bashers" and "radical extremists" were behind the fact that many young women don't identify with the women's movement.

But those are not the only reasons. Kamen also points to the lack of young feminist role models as an important factor. The failure of a major feminist organization such as NOW to reach out to a wider spectrum of women, including young women, must be acknowledged as a part of this problem. While individual chapters do have young feminist committees and sometimes officers, they and the national office are led and staffed primarily by older women, and consequently often fail to reflect the interests and needs of a complex generation of young women.

Yet another reason young women have turned away from feminism may lie within its history. If the young women who have gained the most from feminism— that is, white, middle-class women who took advantage of increased accessibility to higher education and professional employment—have been reluctant to associate themselves with feminism, it is hardly surprising that most economically disadvantaged women and women of color, who have seen fewer of those gains, have not been eager to embrace feminism either. The women's movement of the seventies has been called an upper-middle-class white women's movement, and to a large degree I believe that is true. More than a few young feminists—many influenced by feminists of color such as Flo Kennedy, Audre Lorde, and bell hooks— have realized that feminism must also acknowledge issues of race and class to reach out to those women whose concerns have been overlooked by the women's movement of the past. Indeed . . . young African-American women are more likely than white women to acknowledge many of the concerns conducive to a feminist agenda, including a need for job training and equal earning power outside the professional sector. But for them, feminism has not provided the only answer. Only by making issues of class and race a priority can feminism hope to influence the lives of the millions of women for whom the daily struggle to survive, not feminist activism, is a priority. Will ours be the first generation of feminists to give priority to fighting cuts in Aid to Families with Dependent Children (AFDC) establishing the right to national health care, day care, and parental leave, and bringing to the forefront other issues pertinent to the daily struggle of many women's lives? If there is to be a third wave of feminism, they must.

While the women's movement of the seventies focused primarily on the ERA, getting women into high-paying, powerful occupations, and combating sexual discrimination in the workplace, these issues—though still critical—must not be the only goals of feminism. My sister is an example. We have taken very different paths indeed. I have focused on attending graduate school and writing about women's issues; she has chosen to forfeit similar plans, for now, in favor of marrying young and raising a family. Does she signify a regression into the homemaker role of the 1950s? On the contrary. In fact, she is among the feminists I most respect, even though she herself believes that the feminist movement may not have a place for her because of the choices she has made. For her, issues such as getting midwifery legalized and covered by insurance plans, providing information about the importance of breast-feeding to rural mothers, countering the male-dominated medical establishment by using and recommending natural and alternative healing methods, protecting the environment, and raising her own daughter with positive gender esteem are central to what she defines as a feminist agenda. Who am I to say that she—and other young women like her who are attempting to reclaim the power and importance of motherhood—aren't correct? If there is to be a third wave of feminism, it must acknowledge and support a wide range of choices for all women.

Surely the greatest challenge facing all young women is the frightening assault on reproductive rights, and if any issue can unite women from all backgrounds, it is this. While we have never known the horrors of coat-hanger abortions, we have seen our reproductive rights drastically shrink. If the legacy of the women's movement has left young women confused about their roles in a structure still heavily dominated by older white women, this is one issue on which the torch must be shared. If feminism is to succeed in challenging this patriarchal assault on women's bodies, a coalition of women from all backgrounds will have to join forces to address the underlying assumptions of this attack. Young women have been among the first to organize on this fight, witnessed by the proliferation of pro-choice activity on college campuses around the United States. Still, if this movement is to progress beyond a single-issue campaign, uniting women inside and outside the academy in the name of feminism, it will mean expanding the agenda: insisting upon birth control options for all women and giving equal energy to addressing the lack of educational opportunities, child care, . . . and health care options that are fundamental to the campaign for reproductive choice.

Only by recognizing and helping provide choices for all women, and supporting all women in their struggles to obtain those choices, will the women of my generation, the first raised in the shadow of the second wave and witness to its triumphs and failures, be able to build a successful third wave of the feminist movement. The initial step must be to reclaim the word *feminism* as an appealing, empowering term in women's lives by building a movement that commits to all women while recognizing their multiple concerns.

IMAGINE THE WORST
Women's Committee of 100

The women's movement was once again roused to action when President Clinton, joined by both parties, began debating major changes to the Aid to Families with Dependent Children program in 1994. Though Republicans and Democrats differed on the details, they concurred that welfare policy had failed and that it was time for recipients to "take responsibility" for themselves and their families by finding employment. Feminists, however, argued that AFDC mothers were already working by taking care of their children. They believed that the proposed legislation, which would limit public assistance to five years, was unnecessarily harsh and would have dire effects on women and their children.

Seeking to block the legislation, in the spring of 1995 a group of women academics, public advocates, and social service professionals formed the Women's Committee of 100 (the name refers to Newt Gingrich's claim that Congress would enact significant parts of his "Contract with America" within the first 100 days of the 104th Congress). Via fax and e-mail, they tapped into feminist networks across the country and soon mobilized many hundreds of women to lobby Congress.

Despite these and other protests, in August, 1996, Congress passed the Personal Responsibility and Work Opportunity Act and President Clinton signed it into law. AFDC was replaced with Temporary Assistance to Needy Families (TANF). Though welfare rolls have dropped significantly—by as much as one-third in some cities and states—there is no reliable data on what has become of former recipients of public assistance. Anecdotal evidence suggests that many have been unable to

Source: Women's Committee of 100, "Why every woman in America should beware of welfare cuts," leaflet reprint of advertisement appearing in *The New York Times,* August 8, 1995.

find work while others have taken jobs but lost them because of breakdowns in transportation, child care arrangements, and other difficulties.

The Women's Committee of 100 believed that Congress was operating on a series of misconceptions or myths about the women who relied on AFDC. In August 1995 they ran the following advertisement in *The New York Times*. What strategies did the ad use to dispel negative images of welfare mothers?

WHY EVERY WOMAN IN AMERICA SHOULD BEWARE OF WELFARE CUTS

Welfare is the ultimate security policy for every woman in America. Like accident or life insurance, you hope you'll never need it. But for yourself and your family, sisters, daughters and friends, you need to know it's there. Without it, we have no real escape from brutal relationships or any protection in a job market hostile to women with children. Why is Congress trying to take it away?

Imagine the worst. You're laid off from your job. You lose your health insurance. Your marriage falls apart. Your young children need child care. And you have no family close enough to help.

This is the kind of thing that "happens to someone else." Someone we like to think is "different." And to underline the difference, we usually figure the woman is somehow at fault.

"Why did she have kids if she can't support them?" we ask. "What's the matter with her?"

But at heart, we know how uncomfortably close we are, ourselves, to being without support, without savings. All it takes is a few strokes of hard luck. Hard luck so common, it strikes millions of women with children every year. Women with no job security, in unstable or abusive relationships, with nowhere to turn but welfare. . . .

Would you let your employer take away your health insurance? Of course not. But the public program that benefits struggling women most—Aid to Families with Dependent Children (AFDC)—is now considered fair game in Washington. And women are supposed to be quiet about it.

What Myths Underlie the Attack on Welfare?

The welfare "reform" proposal in Congress is based on myths about women *and* about welfare.

Even the phrase describing the bill—the "Personal Responsibility Act," taken from Newt Gingrich's Contract with America—exploits these myths.

It implies that impoverished women with children, unlike people who get VA [Veterans' Administration] benefits or retirees on Social Security, are responsible for their own troubles and need a whack from a morality paddle to get back in line.

This is not only insulting but dangerous.

Those who want to cut welfare assume the American job market is hungry for untrained, unskilled workers. It's not. Mothers shoved off welfare will not find jobs waiting. And even if a mother finds a job available, chances are it won't pay a living wage that's enough to cover child care, let alone include health insurance.

Everybody agrees that the current welfare system is flawed. But these reckless and irresponsible cuts do nothing to fix anything. They only make it harder for a woman raising her children to recover from life's hard knocks—which today's system, even with all its flaws, actually manages to do.

That's why we say that welfare isn't supporting failure. In most cases, it's enabling success.

The fact that most women who must resort to welfare find a way off within two years by their own efforts, while keeping their children fed and clothed, says a great deal about them. It certainly demonstrates their "personal responsibility." And it should make the rest of us ask why they're being maligned, threatened, and lectured. . . .

THE REAL WAR IS BETWEEN FEMINISTS THEMSELVES
Ice T

Since the mid-1970s, feminists have been embroiled in debates over pornography. Women Against Violence Against Women, a group founded in 1976, argued that there was a direct link between pornography and violence against women. In 1984 author Andrea Dworkin and law professor Catherine MacKinnon succeeded in having an antipornography law passed in Indianapolis, but two years later the Supreme Court struck down the ordinance on the grounds that pornography did not, as Dworkin and MacKinnon contended, constitute a form of sexual discrimination. Antipornography feminists then turned their attention to rap music lyrics.

In the following excerpts, Ice T, one of America's most popular rap musicians, defends himself and his work against the accusations that his lyrics and the images associated with his albums are pornographic and demeaning and harmful to women. How persuasive do you find his arguments? Is he consistent? Are his personal attacks against certain feminists (concerning, for example, their appearance) fair?

> Since the beginning of my career, I have been accused of sexism because I am honest and vocal about the way men perceive women. The accusers' perception of me is so far from the truth. I believe the only reason we're on this planet is for men and women to trip off each other. In my work, I deal in sexuality, not sexism. I am sexual. I deal with sex in its most blatant and raw form—real. I've talked to more feminists on this topic than feminists have, because I travel around the country and deal with them regularly.
>
> If women want to be treated equally, earn equal wages, and attain equal status in the workplace, then I'm a feminist. A sexist views women just as pieces of meat. The fact is, men look at women's butts and women look at men's butts. Is that sexist? At times, people will make fun and treat each other like sexual objects, but do they really feel that way in their hearts?
>
> I don't believe the conflict with feminists is between feminists and men. I think the real controversy is between feminists and other feminists. All women want their rights and respect, and that should be dealt with. There are plenty of people who feel this is a man's world, and therefore, men have an advantage over females. I agree that's wrong.

A lot of feminists have very different expectations. They have no consistent definition of feminism. Do women want to get into a foxhole? Do they want to go to war? Does a woman want her door opened for her? Does a woman want to be treated like a woman? Is that a sexist statement? If you want equality, are you looking to lose those niceties? The real war is between the feminists themselves, between the woman who wants to wear a miniskirt and the woman who finds that demeaning.

A woman will say, "My sexuality is something I have, and I don't mind using it to my advantage. I enjoy it. I enjoy wearing makeup and looking nice. This is who I am." If I were a woman, I would enjoy what a woman is. I would enjoy being treated as a woman, and I don't know if I'd want to give up my femininity. Equal rights and being treated as feminine should be two totally different things.

A real live conflict exists with women who can't deal with blatant sexuality. My girlfriend and I went through all this drama when she wore her bathing suit on the cover of the *Power* album. I explained to her in advance what message the image of the album cover was supposed to get across. We were going to show the power of sex, the power of weapons, and the power of deception. I told her to be on the cover she'd need to wear something sexy, and she came out with her bathing suit. She's proud of her body. She had been in a gym night and day, and this was a chance for her to show herself off. . . .

Feminists came up to me and asked, "Why did you make her do that? Why did you exploit her?" It wasn't exploitation. She knew what she was doing. She was down with it. All artists or models exploit themselves. I know I can rap, so when I get onstage, I show it. I scream, I roll on my back, I fall down, I pull my pants down. Whatever it takes. And I get paid for it. Now, if I feel comfortable with what I'm doing, there's no exploitation.

If a girl makes a living getting paid to do bikini contests, somebody will tell her she's allowing herself to be exploited. But she may point out she's making $1,000 a night, and she likes the attention. She just might dig it.

If, on the other hand, somebody is forced or tricked into doing something they do not want to do, then that is exploitation. When you accuse somebody of being exploited, you better ask them first if they were taken advantage of, because maybe, just maybe, they dig it.

Within the core group of feminists, there is little or no acceptance of women who like to flaunt what they got. The truth is, most hardcore feminists I've seen are ugly, and that's just the bottom line. They can get as angry as they want, but most of them have leaned toward the masculine side of life. They want to wear the pants.

Feminists who enjoy dressing sexy are on a whole different level. They just want to get their respect, and in that sense, I think everyone should be a feminist. There's a point, though, where certain feminists begin infringing on other women's rights. They'll look at Madonna and accuse Madonna of denigrating women. That's the equivalent of me saying I don't like gay people because gay men are making men look bad, and I say that, you'll call me homophobic.

As a straight male, I can say I don't completely understand homosexuality because a man cannot turn me on sexually. I don't know where they get that feeling. It's just like I can't expect somebody from a rich white neighborhood to understand gang membership. It's something so distant and foreign to them. Don't even ask them to reach for it—and don't condemn it, either. . . .

A lot of people try to suppress the sexual channel in their brain, but rappers get off on exposing it. They talk about it in a blunt form—with just words and bass, no melody. In music, that's as close as you're going to get to reading a sexy novel. And people get off on it.

2 Live Crew made a living off sex, because people like sex. They like hearing about it. It's entertainment. There is no limit to the way you can talk about it. Every issue of *Playboy* could show the same girls year-round in different poses, and it wouldn't matter. People would still buy it. Sex is something we are instinctively attracted to. The best 2 Live Crew record ever made was "We Want Some Pussy." When you're on the dance floor, and you're moving in a sexual way and Luke's yelling, "Hey, we want some pussy," what he's really doing is describing the moment. Dancing is like mating. Why not have music that goes along with what you're actually doing?

It takes more than a record to make people want to fuck. If there were a record you could put on that was guaranteed to make people have sex, then I don't think there would be another record ever made. That would be *the* record. . . .

The people who are most offended by blatant sexuality are the Christian right. They have a certain moral standard that defines right and wrong. To be honest, they have a total hang-up with sex from the ground up.

They feel they should only have it after marriage. They feel it should only be done in the missionary position, and they don't believe in oral sex. I think they're just missing out on the whole reason we're here and what human beings are about. How can they look at an animal enjoying sex and then turn around and say, "Well we shouldn't do it like that, because we're evolved."

Other religions have a totally different angle on sex. If you read the *Kama Sutra,* they teach you to fuck down the house. If you try to keep up with that book, you'll be with your girl the rest of your life. . . .

The Christian right is quick to call anything they don't want to see in public "pornographic." Life is pornographic. There is violence in the streets, there is violence on the news. To me, that's more pornographic than anything sexual. The injustices and suffering that go on in the streets are pornographic. Life is X rated; it's not rated R. . . .

There is no proof 2 Live Crew caused teen pregnancies. These are just smokescreens the opponents to the information exchange throw up. . . .

TREAT THE LADY GENTLY . . . BUT LEAD
Jeff Wagenheim

The roots of the men's movement may be traced to the publication of *Iron Man: A Book About Men,* by poet Robert Bly, in 1991. Calling upon American males to abandon their stoical stance and share their feelings, Bly spread the word at men's meetings around the country. Several years later Bill McCartney, a former football coach at the University of Colorado, linked Bly's message of emotional liberation to Christian fundamentalism, filling stadiums with men eager to confess publicly their failures as husbands and fathers. In 1996 Louis Farrakhan, leader of the Nation of Islam, summoned African American men to Washington, D.C. for a "Million Man March." The format of all of these meetings is similar: men are encouraged to

Source: Jeff Wagenheim, "Among the Promise Keepers," *New Age Journal* (March/April 1995), pp. 78–81, 126–30; reprinted by permission of *New Age: The Journal for Holistic Living.*

renounce their former ways and commit themselves to family and community, whether through New Age ritual, Christianity or Islam.

Though the men's movement blames male behavior for the rise of teen pregnancy, drug abuse, and a range of other social ills, feminists have reserved judgment. In an article entitled "Queen for a Day," Debra Dickerson, an African American woman, conceded that she enjoyed being called "sister" or "daughter," rather than "baby," "bitch," or "ho," but was skeptical that such practices would continue once the Million Man March was over. Feminist columnist Ellen Goodman has referred to both the march and the Promise Keepers as expressions of "benevolent patriarchy, . . . better than business as usual, but short of what real equality can be." NOW president Patricia Ireland goes even further, calling men's ministries "stealth political cells." And feminists are unanimous in denouncing the Promise Keepers' opposition to abortion and homosexuality.

The following document is a report by Jeff Wagenheim, a contributing editor of *New Age Journal,* who attended a Promise Keepers convention in Dallas in October 1994.* What, according to Wagenheim, is the Promise Keepers' definition of manhood? Do you think feminists and gays are right to distrust this organization?

The jam-packed stadium is a stunning spectacle of men, smiling and back-slapping men, cheering and foot-stomping men, good-old boys alongside bad-looking hombres alongside exemplary family men alongside failed husbands. There are father-and-son pairs everywhere—some with Dad in his thirties, others in which Junior looks to be about that age. There are bearded, scraggly bikers in black leather, their Harleys parked out in the lot—probably right next to the Chrysler minivans that brought in the groups of clean-scrubbed athletic types dressed in caps and T-shirts bearing football team insignias, looking like they've come to Texas Stadium to root for its home team, the Dallas Cowboys.

But this crowd's Sunday hero doesn't wear shoulder pads and a helmet. That point is being made cloud and clear by a chant arising from one section of sideline seats and rocking the place all the way to the upper deck: "We love Jesus, yes we do," a thousand men are proclaiming in one voice. "We love Jesus, how 'bout *you?*" Cheers of spirited affirmation explode from the other sideline, followed by an answer: "*We* love Jesus, yes we do. . . ."

My God, what have I gotten myself into? I've danced to the drumbeat and been moved by the mentoring muse of Robert Bly at a mythopoetic men's gathering. I've sat in a weekly circle of support and bounced my forever-buried fears and desires off the guys in the group. Hell, I've even unleashed my weekend wild man, roaring alongside my buddies at the brute force of our beloved Giants, in a football stadium much like this one. But nothing I have ever experienced has prepared me for Texas II, a stadium-sized men's conference run by an evangelical Christian organization known as Promise Keepers.

Ever since I first heard of the group, Promise Keepers has been something of a puzzle. What was I to make of an organization that seemed to combine the men's movement of Robert Bly with the conservative Christianity of Pat Robertson? Perhaps this Bible-based work filled a void for men who felt safer in the sanctity of

*We attempted to reprint an excerpt from the Promise Keepers' book, *Seven Promises of a Promise Keeper,* but were denied permission from Focus on the Family, a Colorado organization which controls the rights.

their inner holy man than in the company of that threatening wild man. But could the group also be a shrewdly disguised vehicle for furthering the political agenda of the religious right?

Promise Keepers was founded in 1990 by Bill McCartney, who until recently served as head coach of the University of Colorado's football team. With the same fiery faithfulness he had used to elevate the Buffaloes into college football's elite, McCartney has transformed his weekly prayer and fellowship group of seventy-two men into an organization that today has twice that many *employees.* After holding men's conferences in Boulder in each of its first three summers and achieving its goal of filling 50,000-seat Folsom Field in 1993, Promise Keepers took the show on the road in 1994, reaching nearly 300,000 men in seven stadiums scattered around the country. The 1995 schedule includes thirteen stadium-sized events, with the goal of attracting 600,000 comers. And the organization is also trying to ride its runaway momentum to draw a million men to a gathering in Washington in 1996.

How to explain this group's burgeoning growth? Looking for answers, I bought a copy of *Seven Promises of a Promise Keeper,* a collection of essays that has become the Promise Keepers' second bible. The book lays out the seven promises that form a foundation for this group's work, promises that essentially establish a man's spiritual commitment in his relationships with God, other men, his wife, his family, his church, and his community. Though most of what the book's numerous contributors write is loving, commitment-affirming guidance, there are passages here and there that you definitely won't find excerpted in *Ms.* magazine.

In instructing husbands how to reclaim their manhood . . . pastor Tony Evans writes: "The first thing you do is sit down with your wife and say something like this: 'Honey, I've made a terrible mistake. I've given you my role. I gave up leading this family, and I forced you to take my place. Now I must reclaim that role.' Don't misunderstand what I'm saying here. I'm not suggesting that you *ask* for your role back, I'm urging you to *take it back.* If you simply ask for it, your wife is likely to say, 'Look, for the last ten years, I've had to raise these kids, look after the house, and pay the bills. I've had to get a job and still keep up my duties in the home. I've had to do my job *and* yours. You think I'm just going to turn everything back over to you?' Your wife's concerns may be justified. Unfortunately, however, there can be no compromise here. If you're going to lead, you must lead. Be sensitive. Listen. Treat the lady gently and lovingly. But *lead!*'

After reading this, it probably will come as no surprise to hear that, around its home base of Boulder, Promise Keepers has been assailed as the second coming of the Spanish Inquisition. The organization's stance that men must reclaim the leadership in their families spooks feminists. And gays are nervous about the ramifications of the group's position statement that "homosexuality violates God's creative design for a husband and a wife and . . . is a sin." Protests have dogged each summer's Promise Keepers gathering in Boulder, the acrimony coming to a head in 1993 when the group filled Folsom Field for the first time. As men filed into the stadium, they had to pass by a gauntlet of heckling protesters chanting slogans such as "Get a Name Tag, Kill a Fag." In a bizarre twist on a Bible story that's particularly salient for men, two protesters, dressed as Jesus and Judas, flamboyantly embraced and kissed, not so much for the sexiness of such a display, one surmises, as for its shocking symbolism. . . .

What brought out that kind of opposition, I suspect, was not the essays in *Seven Promises* or even what was being said at the gatherings so much as the controversial politics of the group's founder, Bill McCartney. The charismatic CU coach first made headlines back in the mid-'80s when he battled the American Civil Liberties Union over his practice of leading the team in pregame prayer. His notoriety reached something of a peak in 1992 during the debate over Amendment 2, a state ballot question aimed at blocking civil rights for gays and lesbians. After McCartney authorized the amendment's sponsor, Colorado for Family Values, to use his name and affiliation on its fundraising letters, the university received complaints about this apparent violation of policy. The coach agreed to ask the anti-gay rights crusaders to drop his name from their printed materials and called a news conference to make the announcement. There . . . McCartney proceeded to urge Coloradans to support Amendment 2 and termed homosexuality "an abomination of almighty God." This prompted campus protests and a reprimand from the university president. US Rep. Patricia Schroeder (D-Colo.) called McCartney a "self-anointed ayatollah."

But McCartney seems to be more enigma than ayatollah. At the same time that he was taking his civil rights-denying stance regarding gays, he was a vocal and demonstrative supporter of racial equality—the only head coach in Division I-A, in fact, to have on his staff as many black coaches as white. And when he resigned in January, and his long-time assistant, Bob Simmons, was passed over for a less-experienced white replacement, McCartney sided with an unlikely ally, Rev. Jesse Jackson, in charging racism. . . .

In the parking lots nearest the main stadium gates are a few large tents—one for registration (a surprisingly reasonable $55, including two meals), one for dispensing literature about related organizations (Christian Men's Network, Focus on the Family, etc.), one for selling Promise Keepers books and merchandise. . . . These tents and other projects of the day—such as setting up 45,000 box lunches—are being run almost exclusively by women. "We're all here as volunteers supporting this ministry and the men in our lives," says the middle-aged woman behind the cash register. "I'm here with my husband. This is his second event, and after the last one he was a changed person. Attentive. Positive attitude. Closer to God. So I'm happy to help an organization that has had such a positive effect on our marriage."

As I finally enter the stadium, Christian Men's Network president Edwin Cole . . . launches into a fire-and-brimstone sermon preaching celibacy until marriage. . . . For a while Cole sounds—dare I say it?—positively feminist as he talks about how respect for women is lost when a man is pursuing sex without love. Then, suddenly, per Cole's request, dozens of young men all around the stadium are standing to take a vow of chastity. . . . Cole is winding up with an impassioned message for fornicators everywhere: "We're trying to take society to a place where *we* want to go, and you're trying to take us back to Sodom and Gomorra!"

Bible-thumping conservatism is by no means unexpected at a gathering like Texas II. But, at least for the present, the Promise Keepers organization insists it's less concerned with winning political votes than with winning hearts and souls. In fact, the only overtly political statement of the weekend came in the conference's very first speech, by pastor Greg Laurie. "When a man makes a promise to his wife—a marriage vow—and doesn't keep it, he is teaching her not to trust him," he said. "And isn't it true that we have a problem like this with some of our leaders today?" Wild applause. "I see some of you are ahead of me," said Laurie with a smile.

That shared humor at the President's expense reveals something about these men that I have trouble overlooking: When push comes to shove, these and the thousands of other Promise Keepers will likely pull whatever voting-booth levers will abolish abortion or curtail gay rights. Ultimately, these men are a voting block—an Evangelical Christian voting block. . . .

But all is not serious at Texas II. In the midst of some resolute speeches about men's relationship to mentors, to worship, to God's word, to integrity, to other men, Gary Smalley—the president of Today's Family, whom you may have seen on late-night cable TV hawking his better-relationships videotape series through info-mercials featuring couples such as Kathie Lee and Frank Gifford—jokes about some possible titles for his talk, the best being "Why a Vacuum Cleaner is Not an Appropriate Christmas Gift."

Smalley. . . is also responsible for one of the most moving moments of the weekend. At the time I am standing in the press box, high above the playing field. Smalley. . . asks the men to break into groups of four and five to discuss pet peeves and possibilities. In small groups, the men come alive—even in the press box, where a couple of small groups form to discuss marital issues. . . . I can't help but think, This doesn't look like a bunch of guys working toward becoming tyrants in their households.

Throughout the weekend, as conference speakers delve deeper and deeper into issues that tear couples and families apart—a husband or father being emo-tionally distant or neglecting his responsibilities being among the common ones—it becomes apparent that these things can tear apart a man as well. And as the various speakers' condemnations of various male actions—though, pointedly, never of males themselves—hit home for more and more in the crowd, I notice that some of the men seem to be fighting back tears, while a few have no fight left: They're crying freely as the men around them offer the comfort of a touch, an em-brace, or a quiet word. . . .

There's so much camaraderie among the whites, blacks, and Hispanics who are filling the place, so much of a web of fraternal connection being spun in this sta-dium, that I can't help but feel alone. Just then the man to my right, who is joined to a long row of hand-holding men, reaches out his hand to me. I hesitate. Should I take it? Will I be "a man of integrity" if I hold a hand in Christian brotherhood while not truly sharing the evangelical beliefs being espoused?

This is no time to think. The music is starting. I take the man's hand and reach out my free hand to the man on my other side. It's time to sing, time to participate. . . .

As surprised and touched as I was by the proceedings . . . I know full well what it was that was bothering me. . . . I could never be a Promise Keeper. Promise Keepers, by and large, are certain they have found The Truth. I am not. . . . While no one at Texas II tried to demonize me, whenever a Promise Keeper drew me into a discussion—on anything from culture to theology—I would get the feeling I was talking to a brick wall. A friendly and talkative brick wall, but an unmovable object nonetheless. It was either his Scripture-based worldview or . . . *splat*. And that's troubling, because, ultimately, and despite the group's assertions to the contrary, Promise Keepers is an organization with vast political influence. . . .

Even if the Promise Keepers don't join lock step with the religious right—as they claim and as the diversity of their members at Texas II suggests—some of the group's views are, at the very least, disturbingly divisive. Take [their] position that homosexuality is a sin. Sure, they take the "inclusive" stance of inviting gay men to come receive "God's mercy, grace, and forgiveness." But what kind of invitation is that? . . .

"That's a subtle form of homophobia, a low-level victimization," counters Cheryl Schwartz, executive director of the Denver-based Gay, Lesbian and Bisexual Community Services Center of Colorado. "It's not blatant verbal or physical attack on the gay community, but a more moderate form of hate crime. The implication is that we're right and you're not, and I think it's oppressive to tell people that they have to conform if they want to be invited. It's like telling an African-American person that they have to change their skin color."

Or like telling a woman that she must change genders? To be sure, Promise Keepers does not condone spousal abuse; in fact, the organization's written materials and conference speakers encourage men to treat a wife like the most important being on this Earth. But not like the head of the household. At a Promise Keepers event, a man is taught how to become the spiritual leader of his family—in essence, benevolent king of his castle. A woman may be better off with him than she would be living under the thumb of a domineering, abusive king, but a king is a king. And in the Promise Keepers' kingdom, a woman is nothing but a peasant.

[Promise Keepers President] Randy Phillips puts a less chauvinistic spin on the matter. "It comes down to whether you understand what it is to be a spiritual leader, which we define in the person of Jesus Christ," he says. . . . From a biblical perspective, a spiritual leader is not one who lords authority over others; spiritual leadership is the absolute commitment to serve and to honor. It means involving yourself in the life of your wife, hearing her needs and responding to those needs, just like Jesus responded to our needs. . . .

With rhetoric like that, notes Rev. Priscilla Inkpen, a United Church of Christ minister from Boulder who has been one of the group's more prominent opponents, "It's difficult to be 100 percent critical of the Promise Keepers. . . . But I just don't like [their] angle: encouraging men to reclaim their place at the head of the family. That is definitely unsettling to anyone who has a feminist perspective."

. . . And so the question remains: Will the Promise Keepers be able to blend moral values and personal change to truly bring integrity into the lives of American men? Or, in the end, will the group descent into the demagoguery and extremist politics that have come to characterize the religious right?

IT JUST DIDN'T FIT
David Harrison

One sign of America's new freedom of gender and sexual expression is the growing transsexual community. The most recent *Diagnostic and Statistical Manual of Mental Disorders (DSM-IV),* issued by the American Psychiatric Association, defines "persistent cross-gender identification" as a sign of "gender identity disorder" requiring treatment which would, presumably, eliminate the condition. But advances in medical technology, in conjunction with a loosening of sexual and social mores in at least some quarters, have made it possible for individuals who feel uncomfortable with their bodies to change sex rather than eliminate the desire to be other than the way they were born. (Those who change from female to male are designated "F2M," from male to female, "M2F.") As David Harrison's account indicates, undergoing such a transformation is a complex process both for the individuals themselves and for those they encounter. What were some of the difficulties he faced?

Source: "David Harrison," *Body Alchemy: Transsexual Portraits,* photographs by Loren Cameron (Pittsburgh and San Francisco: Cleis Press, 1996), p. 73.

FIGURE 15.2
Photographer Loren Cameron (himself a transsexual) took pictures of David Harrison before
and after his sexual transformation. (Source: Body Alchemy: Transsexual Portraits,
photographs by Loren Cameron [Pittsburgh and San Francisco, Cleis Press, 1996], pp. 74–75.)

On some level, I was always attracted to men, but I just couldn't relate to them when
I was a woman. It just didn't fit. When I was female, I was a lesbian. As a man, I find
that I still like that same-sex relationship dynamic. There's something more sexually
exciting about it. I don't have to be so aware of what gender I am. The culture constantly reinforces gender stereotypes in male/female relationships, which makes them
very complicated. I know some people enjoy that contrast, but it's not what I prefer.

My attraction to men is very visceral. I enjoy them aesthetically, in terms of
muscles, genitals and legs. I look at male bodies a lot, and maybe I look at myself
in relation to them because of my own physical evolution as a transsexual man.
When I placed a personals ad for male sex partners, I was completely pre-operative
(I had breasts and a vagina), but I looked male by all outward appearances. In the
ad, I explained that I was female-to-male, and elaborated more completely to any
phone respondents.

I got a lot of responses from men who were primarily straight but said that they
were bisexual. In actuality, they may have had only one or two experiences with
men. When they came over, I wasn't what they expected, although I had told them
on the phone that I looked male and that they might not be attracted to me if they
were heterosexual. I think it really flipped them out to be dealing with my genitals
in the context of such a masculine presence and appearance.

There were a few men who handled it. One of them said that, after being with
me, he realized that being sexual wasn't so much about bodies as about erotic energy between two people, and that to him, I was a man.

RECOMMENDED READING

Abraham, Ken. *Who Are the Promise Keepers? Understanding the Christian Men's Movement.* New York, 1997.

Bronski, Michael. *The Pleasure Principle: Sex, Backlash, and the Struggle for Gay Freedom.* New York, 1997.

Duggan, Lisa, and Nan D. Hunter. *Sex Wars: Sexual Dissent and Political Culture.* New York, 1995.

Heywood, Leslie, ed. *Third-Wave Agenda: Being Feminist, Doing Feminism.* Minneapolis, 1997.

Jeffords, Susan. *Hard Bodies: Hollywood Masculinity in the Reagan Era.* New Brunswick, NJ, 1994.

Kaminer, Wendy. *True Love Waits: Essays and Criticism.* Reading, MA, 1996.

Messner, Michael. *Politics of Masculinities: Men in Movements.* Thousand Oaks, CA, 1997.

Rimmerman, Craig, ed. *Gay Rights, Military Wrongs: Political Perspectives on Lesbians and Gays in the Military.* New York, 1996.

Roiphe, Katie. *Last Night in Paradise: Sex and Morals at the Century's End.* Boston, 1997.

Shilts, Randy. *Conduct Unbecoming: Lesbians and Gays in the United States Military.* New York, 1993.

Signorile, Michelangelo. *Life Outside: The Signorile Report on Gay Men: Sex, Drugs, Muscles and the Passages of Life,* New York, 1997.

Stacey, Judith. *Brave New Families: Stories of Domestic Upheaval in Late Twentieth-Century America.* New York, 1990.

Wolf, Naomi. *Fire with Fire: The New Female Power and How It Will Change the 21st Century.* New York, 1993.